THE ALLEMANDE, THE BALLETTO, AND THE TANZ

VOLUME I
THE HISTORY

RICHARD HUDSON
PROFESSOR OF MUSIC
UNIVERSITY OF CALIFORNIA, LOS ANGELES

CAMBRIDGE UNIVERSITY PRESS

CAMBRIDGE
LONDON   NEW YORK   NEW ROCHELLE
MELBOURNE   SYDNEY

Published by the Press Syndicate of the University of Cambridge
The Pitt Building, Trumpington Street, Cambridge CB2 1RP
32 East 57th Street, New York, NY 10022, USA
10 Stamford Road, Oakleigh, Melbourne 3166, Australia

© Cambridge University Press 1986

First published 1986

Printed in Great Britain at
the University Press, Cambridge

Library of Congress catalogue card number: 85-4163

British Library Cataloguing in Publication Data
Hudson, Richard
The Allemande, the Balletto and the Tanz.
1. Dance music – Europe – History and criticism
I. Title
785.4'1'094   ML3403

ISBN 0 521 33108 0 (set of two volumes)
ISBN 0 521 24852 3 (Vol. I)
ISBN 0 521 30167 X (Vol. II)

SE

CONTENTS

VOLUME I

List of Plates	*page* vii
List of Tables	viii
Preface	ix
List of Abbreviations	xiii

Part I: The Renaissance

1 THE DEUTSCHER TANZ FOR LUTE, CITTERN, AND KEYBOARD IN GERMANY 1540–1603   3
The Melodies and Their Structure 4   The Melodic Cadence 7   The Harmony 10   The Phrases 14   The Nachtanz 15   The Instruments 20   Coloration 21   Melodies from Lieder 22   The Influence of Lied Transcriptions 24   The Influence of Chanson Arrangements 27   The Influence of Italian Dances 33   The Individual Titles 34   The Social Situation 39

2 THE ALMANDE FOR LUTE, GUITAR, CITTERN, AND INSTRUMENTAL ENSEMBLE IN FRANCE AND THE LOW COUNTRIES 1546–1603   43
Concordances with the Deutscher Tanz 43   Melodies without Tanz Concordances 46   The Musical Traits 49   The Social Background 52   The Choreography 55

3 THE BALLETTO TEDESCO FOR LUTE, KEYBOARD, AND ENSEMBLE IN ITALY 1561–1615   62
Concordances with the Tanz and the Almande 62   The Musical Characteristics 66   The Social Setting 68   The Choreography 68

Part II: The Transition

4 VECCHI, GASTOLDI, AND THE VOCAL BALLETTO IN ITALY DURING THE 1590s   81
Vecchi and the *Villotta* 82   Gastoldi and the Balletto *a 5* 86   Gastoldi and the Balletto *a 3* 90

Contents

5 **THE VOCAL BALLETT AND THE INSTRUMENTAL ALMAIN FOR KEYBOARD, PLUCKED STRINGS, AND ENSEMBLE IN ENGLAND 1550–1650** 97
The Almain for Keyboard and Plucked Strings 97 The Ballett for Voices 102 The Almain for Viols and Other Instrumental Ensembles 108 Social Function and Choreography 112

6 **THE VOCAL AND INSTRUMENTAL BALLET FOR LUTE IN FRANCE 1603–1619** 119

7 **THE VOCAL AND INSTRUMENTAL TANZ, BALLETT, AND ALLMAND IN GERMANY 1598–1628** 124
The Tanz and the Ballett in Southern Germany 124 The Allmand and the Ballett in the North of Germany 129 Influence between the North and the South 132

8 **THE VOCAL AND INSTRUMENTAL BALLETTO IN ITALY 1615–1640** 137
Brunelli and the Vocal Balletto 137 The Instrumental Balletto 141

Part III: The Baroque Period

9 **THE ALLEMANDE FOR LUTE, CLAVECIN, GUITAR, VIOL, AND ENSEMBLE IN FRANCE 1630–1731** 147
Musical and Social Function 147 The French Baroque Style 149 General Traits of the French Allemande 151 The Cadences 154 Types, Titles, and Tempo 158

10 **THE BALLETTO AND ALEMANDA FOR GUITAR, KEYBOARD, AND ENSEMBLE IN ITALY 1640–1730** 162
The Alemanda and Balletto for Guitar 162 The Chamber Forms 167 The Cadences 174

11 **THE ALLEMANDE AND BALLETT FOR ENSEMBLE AND KEYBOARD IN GERMANY AND ENGLAND 1636–1750** 178
The German Allemanda and Ballett for Instrumental Ensemble 178 The German Allemande and Ballett for Keyboard 192 The Ensemble Almain and the Keyboard Almand in England 205

THE CADENCE 211

Notes 219
Bibliography 253
Index 257

PLATES

I	Heckel: *Des Printzen Tantz* and beginning of the *Proportz auff den Tantz* for lute (1562)	*page* 17
II	Ammerbach: *Wer das Töchterlein haben wil* and *Proportio* for keyboard (1571)	18
III	Map of central Europe in 1606	40
IV	Arbeau: choreography of the Allemande (1589)	56
V	Arbeau: execution of the *grève*	58
VI	Negri: two couples preparing to dance the *Balletto detto l'Alemana d'Amore* (1602)	69
VII	Negri: first page of instructions for the *Balletto detto l'Alemana d'Amore*	70
VIII	Negri: second page of instructions for the *Balletto detto l'Alemana d'Amore*	71
IX	Negri: music for the *Balletto detto l'Alemana d'Amore*	72
X	Gastoldi & Vecchi: top voice of a *Balletto a 5* and a *Canzonetta a 4*, with Italian and Dutch texts (1657)	85
XI	Gastoldi: *Balletto a 3, Il Tedesco*, top voice and lute tablature, from the first publication in Venice (1594)	92
XII	Gastoldi: *Il Tedesco*, top voice, from the publication in Antwerp (1606)	94

(Plates XIII–XXIV are in Volume II)

vii

TABLES

1 Location of the Forms in Europe between 1540 and 1750   *page* x
2 Incidence of the Alemanda and Balletto in Italian Guitar
   Sources 1640–1692   165
3 Incidence of the Balletto and Alemanda in Selective
   Italian Chamber Sources 1650–1700   169

PREFACE

This is the first of two volumes devoted to the evolution of the Allemande, the Balletto, and the Tanz from 1540 to 1750. This volume presents a prose history of the forms; Volume II is an anthology of musical compositions.

A new Tanz appeared in Nuremberg around 1540. It soon spread to other lands, where it was known by names that indicated its country of origin. It was called *Almande* in France and the Low Countries, *Almain* in England, and *Balletto tedesco* in Italy, and in Germany itself it was finally known as the *Deutscher Tanz*. Its evolution spans two centuries and two of the stylistic periods in music history. It involves the principal countries of western Europe and their national musical styles, the interaction of popular social music and serious art music, the traditions of instrumental and vocal performance, and the social milieu in which the dance served a functional role.

The history falls into three periods. During the Renaissance (1540 to 1590) the forms, performed by plucked strings, keyboard, or instrumental ensemble, developed a fairly uniform musical structure that differed only in details from country to country. In a transition period (1590 to 1640) the vocal and theatrical trends of the time produced a lute Ballet in France and a vocal Balletto in Italy. The latter traveled to England, where the Almain had previously been imported from France and the Low Countries. The Italian, French, and English forms then all moved back to Germany, where the Deutscher Tanz was still in existence. This is the central moment in the story, for it is the only time in the entire history when all the forms, and in both vocal and instrumental versions, coexisted in the same country. During the Baroque period (1640 to 1750) the Allemande and the Balletto again evolved more consistent types of structure, especially in Italian chamber music and in keyboard examples from England, France, and Germany. Thus the Renaissance and the Baroque period are characterized by the steady evolution of

Preface

Table 1. *Location of the Forms in Europe between 1540 and 1750*

(A roman numeral indicates the chapter in which the form is discussed)

	Germany	France	Italy	England
Renaissance	I **Deutscher Tanz** 1540–1603	II **Almande** 1546–1603 (also in the Low Countries)	III **Balletto** **Tedesco** 1561–1615	V **Almain** 1550–1650
Transition	VII **Tanz, Ballett,** **& Allmand** 1598–1628	VI **Ballet** 1603–1619	IV & VIII Vocal **Balletto** 1590–1621 Ensemble **Balletto** 1615–1640	V Vocal **Ballett** 1595–1627
Baroque	XI **Allemanda,** **Ballett,** **& Allemande** 1636–1750	IX **Allemande** 1630–1731	X **Balletto** **& Alemanda** 1640–1730	XI **Almain** **& Almand** 1650–1750

definite instrumental forms, whereas the transition period produced dramatic changes and experimentation with diverse types.

Table 1 shows how the forms generally distributed themselves geographically within the three periods of time. The years sometimes represent the exact dates of publications or manuscripts, at other times only an approximation. The Roman numerals indicate the chapter in which a form is discussed. The Tanz and all the vocal forms disappeared during the 1620's. The Thirty Years War in Germany from 1618 to 1648 interrupted developments in that country, although a few sources survive from those years. The titles are spelled in different ways in almost every country and period. For this study, however, I have in general selected in each case one of the most frequent versions, especially one that is different from those in other countries and other periods. I have formed plurals according to the rule of the native language: thus, *Balletti* in Italy, *Balletts* in England; *Allemanden* in Germany, *Alemande* in Italy, and *Allemandes* in France.

My interest in these forms began in 1972, when I wrote an article on the instrumental Balletto for *The New Grove Dictionary of Music and Musicians*. In 1976 I resumed research on the Italian chamber Balletto of the 17th century, which led me to the 16th century, to the German Tanz, and eventually to the Allemande. Late in 1976 I completely rewrote the *New Grove* article to incorporate new discoveries.[1] Since that time I have been pursuing various facets of this history and finally felt that there was a need for a book in which the history of the three dances – each treated as an equal, since they are in fact the *same* dance – could be broadly outlined. I would like to express my indebtedness to Ernst Mohr's *Die Allemande*, published in 1932. This, in my opinion, is an excellent study – concise, well organized, full of many facts and important ideas, and accompanied by a carefully selected anthology of musical examples. It is my hope, however, to expand the scope of Mohr's subject in two dimensions: by giving as much attention to the Tanz and the Balletto as to the Allemande, and by considering sources for additional media, especially the plucked-string instruments of Italy and England.

It is not my intention to list every example, nor even mention every source. I am concerned primarily with the broad events in the lives of these forms as they move back and forth across the face of Europe. It is my aim to trace the main outlines of the evolution clearly and accurately enough that other scholars can later study smaller portions of the history with greater insight. The history of these forms unfolds in a unified musical evolution that extends from 1540 until around 1750. I will not be concerned, in general, with the appearance of the terms *Allemande* or *Balletto* in the basse danse before 1540,[2] nor in the Allemande dance that becomes popular in Europe after 1750.

The most persistent and conspicuous musical element that unifies the development from 1540 to 1750 is a special cadence. I have identified it first in Exx. 3, 5, and 6, and summarized its history, finally, in Ex. 83. In Part I, the reader will frequently encounter the *Printzentantz* or *Almande Prince*, one of the most popular of the recurring Renaissance melodies. It is shown in Ex. 1 and, since it has an appealing melody as well as the briefest possible duration (four bars in each of two sections), I have used it to illustrate various notational or choreographic points.

Since geography is a matter of special significance in this history, I have included a map of part of western Europe in 1606 as Plate III. A numbered citation in Volume I, such as "No. 4," refers to a composition in Volume II. The brief musical examples (marked "Ex. 1" etc.), as well as the three Tables, are all in the first volume. The plates are divided between the two volumes, with I–XII in the first volume, XIII–XXIV in the second.

Pitches are designated in the following manner: $c'-b'$ for the ascending octave beginning on middle C, $c''-b''$ for the next higher octave, $c-b$ for the octave below middle C, $C-B$ for the octave below that.

I want to thank Prof. David Fuller, at the State University of New York at Buffalo, for an exchange of ideas concerning the French forms. He is now preparing a book on French harpsichord music for publication by Cambridge University Press. I thank Victor Coelho, a graduate student in musicology at

xii *Preface*

UCLA, for helping me locate literary references, Carolann Busch from the Dance Department for valuable help with choreography, Francesca Savoia for aid with the Italian language, Darwin Scott for Latin, Evelyne Berman for French, Kim Lessing for Spanish, and Ann York for German history. I want to express my appreciation to the personnel of the UCLA Music Library, especially for their generous support during the spring and summer of 1983. I am grateful to the University of California, Los Angeles, for providing research grants, and to the libraries in the list of RISM sigla for making printed and manuscript sources available to me.

RICHARD HUDSON

University of California, Los Angeles (UCLA)

ABBREVIATIONS

A list of *RISM* library sigla appears at the end of Volume II. Other abbreviations, occurring mainly in the notes, are as follows:

Brown	Howard Mayer Brown, *Instrumental Music Printed Before 1600* (1965).
CEKM	*Corpus of Early Keyboard Music.*
CNRS	Centre National de la Recherche Scientifique
Dieckmann	Jenny Dieckmann, *Die in deutscher Lautentabulatur überleiferten Tänze des 16. Jahrhunderts* (1931).
DDT	*Denkmäler deutscher Tonkunst.*
DTB	*Denkmäler der Tonkunst in Bayern.*
DTÖ	*Denkmäler der Tonkunst in Österreich.*
EDM	*Das Erbe deutscher Musik.*
HAM	*Historical Anthology of Music*, revised edition, ed. Archibald T. Davison and Willi Apel (1949).
Land	J. P. N. Land, "Het Luitboek van Thysius," in *Tijdschrift der Vereeniging voor Noord-Nederlands Muziekgeschiedenis*, Vols. I–III (1884–1888).
LP	*Le pupitre.*
Merian	Wilhelm Merian, *Der Tanz in den deutschen Tabulaturbüchern* (1927).
Moe	Lawrence H. Moe, "Dance Music in Printed Italian Lute Tablatures from 1507 to 1611," Ph.D. dissertation, Harvard University, 1956.
Mohr	Ernst Mohr, *Die Allemande* (1932).
MB	*Musica Britannica.*
MGG	*Die Musik in Geschichte und Gegenwart.*
MMN	*Monumenta musica neerlandica.*
New Grove	*The New Grove Dictionary of Music and Musicians* (1980).

PART I
The Renaissance

1 THE DEUTSCHER TANZ FOR LUTE, CITTERN, AND KEYBOARD IN GERMANY 1540–1603

THE DANCE that finally became known as the *Deutscher Tanz* originated in the south of Germany around 1540. Its music is relatively homophonic, with the melody in the top voice usually harmonized by three other voices below it. The main dance is in duple meter, with four substantial beats in each measure. This is followed by a *Nachtanz*, in which the melody and harmonies of the duple dance are transformed into triple meter. Both Tanz and Nachtanz are in several sections, each usually to be immediately repeated, either exactly or with variations added.

The Deutscher Tanz replaced the older *Hoftanz*, which appeared earlier in the same century and had some essentially different musical characteristics. The *Hoftanz* belonged to the basse danse tradition. It was in a broad triple meter, and its melody could sometimes be in an inner voice. The titles *Schwarzknab*, *Benzenhauer*, and *Der ander Tanz* referred to the three most commonly occurring melodies. The opening dance was coupled with another in a diminished triple meter. Until 1577 the *Hoftanz* appeared from time to time in the same lute and keyboard sources that included the Deutscher Tanz and sometimes took over from the newer dance some of its traits.[1]

The earliest examples of the Deutscher Tanz seem to occur in Hans Neusidler's *Ein newes Lautenbüchlein*, published at Nuremberg in 1540. Pieces called *Der Bethler Tantz*, *Der Nunnen Tantz*, and *Der Zeuner Tantz*, as well as others with titles from German Lieder, begin to display the characteristics of the new dance. In the lute book of Wolff Heckel (Strassburg, 1556) other titles also appear: *Des Printzen Tantz*, *Der Maruscat Tantz*, *Ein Bocks Tantz*, *Graff Johan von Nassaw Dantz*, *Ein schöner schwäbischer Tantz*, *Der Künigin Tantz*, *Ein schöner Burger Tantz*, as well as *Wider ein guter Tantz, mit vier Stymmen*. The latter title indicates a change from the three voices used by Neusidler to four, which becomes the standard texture for the Deutscher Tanz. Elias Nikolaus Ammerbach has examples for keyboard in 1571 called *Bruder Cunrads Tanzmaass*, *Der Allmeyer Dantz*, *Hertzog Moritz Dantz*, *Pastorum Dantz*, and many just entitled *Ein sehr guter Dantz* or *Ein kurtzer Dantz*. In 1573 Bernhard

Jobin published in Strassburg many lute examples entitled *Dantz* or *Deutscher Dantz*, and in 1575 Sixt Kargel and Johan Dominico Lais, also from Strassburg, entitled individual pieces for cittern *Almanda Teutscher Tanz*.

With Neusidler in 1540, the expression *Teütsch Tentz* appears only in the title of the book to distinguish from *Welsche Tentz*, the Italian dances. In his 1549 version of *Das ander Buch* there is a separate subtitle preceding the German dances: "Nun volgen die Teutschen Tentz." Some *Hoftänze* are included along with the newer type, but in one case the title *Der Bentzenawer, Tantz weyss* suggests that the old *Hoftanz* of that name has been modified to conform to the new dance. In Benedikt de Drusina's lute book of 1556 a subtitle reads "Sequuntur Choreae Germanicae" (that is, "Deutscher Tanz" in Latin), and individual pieces are called simply *Tantz*. It is around 1573, finally, that the expression *Deutscher Dantz* or *Teutscher Tantz* begins to occur as the title of an individual piece, and thus seems to become the official name for the dance. Alliteration seems to be preferred, so that both of the words usually begin with either *d* or *t*. When making general reference in this book, however, I will conform to modern spelling. The expression was no doubt the translation into German of *Almande* or *Balletto tedesco*, the names given to this new German dance in France and Italy.

The Melodies and Their Structure

Nos. 1 through 11 in Volume II present eighteen examples from 1540 to 1591 for lute, cittern, or keyboard. As suggested by the numerous titles already cited, many different melodies are involved. Quite a number, however, recur in different settings and in more than one source. Some become so popular that they appear in many versions spanning sometimes a considerable number of years. Some of them, as we will see later, also occur in sources outside Germany. The most popular melodies have been included, among others, in Volume II, and nine of them are shown in Exx. 1 and 2.

The idea of a basic melody is something of an abstraction, however, since a composer could employ variation technique even in the opening statement of a section. The first four lines of Ex. 1 show four different German versions of the *Printzentantz*, one of the most popular of the melodies. The simplest is the first one. In (b), by comparison, we see that ornamentation has been added, especially in measures 3 and 6. Here smaller note values have simply filled in or revolved around notes of the simpler framework. In (c), however, the same bars display more substantial alteration. In (d), an anacrusis has been added at the beginning and other modifications made. Still further changes occur, as we will see later, in (f), when the same tune moves to France.

The melody thus may change through variation every time a composer creates his own version. Sometimes such a change results in a permanent alteration of the basic framework as perceived by a later composer. The

Ex. 1: The evolving melody of the *Printzentantz*.

(a) DK-Kk, MS *Thott 4° 841*, Lute book of Petrus Fabricius, fol. 76^v: *Heckerling und Haberstro*.

(b) Heckel, 1556: *Des Printzen Tantz* for lute (No. 3 in Volume II).

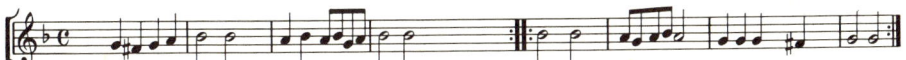

(c) Ammerbach, 1571: *Wer das Töchterlein haben wil* for keyboard (No. 4).

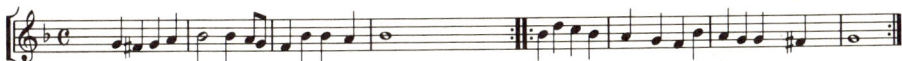

(d) Waissel, 1591: 35th *Tantz* for lute.

(e) Gorzanis, 1563: *Bal todesco* for lute (No. 73).

(f) Phalèse & Bellère, 1571, fol. 9^r: *Almande Prince* for ensemble (see also Nos. 39c & 41, and Plate XVI).

changes in bar 3 of (b), for example, are quite incidental and may be considered a form of variation. The cadence structure at the end of the opening section in (c) and (d), however, is far more significant and lasting, for it creates a parallelism with the cadence at the end of the second section. This change occurs so often in later examples that it seems to become itself part of the basic melody. Each melody therefore has its own history. For our purposes, however, it is enough to note that the *Printzentantz* constitutes the melodic idea represented collectively by the first four lines of Ex. 1. This example also shows the variety of titles that become associated with a melody.

Ex. 2 shows a simple version of eight other popular melodies. The number of sections varies from one to the other and sometimes between different versions of the same melody. The *Proficiat* occurs in Ex. 2h with two sections, but in No. 10d of Volume II with no repeated sections at all in the opening duple part. The melodies in Exx. 1, 2b, 2c, and 2g each have two sections. Ex. 2e also displays two sections, but another version, in No. 7b of Volume II, divides the

6   *The Renaissance*

Ex. 2: Some of the most popular melodies of the Deutscher Tanz.

(a) D-Mbs, MS 1512, fol. 49[v]: *Ein gueter Danntz Der Petler* for lute (cf. No. 1a).

(b) Kargel, 1578: *Almande. Ich ging ainmal spaciren* [*Nonette*] for cittern (see also Exx. 21 & 28, and Nos. 5a, 42, 75, 97, & 129).

(c) Waissel, 1591: *Tantz* [*Bruynsmedelijn*] for lute (see Exx. 20 & 39, No. 5b, and Plates XVI & XX).

(d) D-W, Hainhofer MS, 1603: *Deutscher Dantz* [*Don Frederico*] for lute (cf. No. 7a and Plate XVIII).

(e) Ammerbach, 1583: *Ein Schlesier Dantz* [*Der alten Weiber Tantz*] for keyboard (cf. No. 7b).

(f) Ammerbach, 1583: *Gut Gesell du musst wandern* for keyboard (No. 10b; see also No. 76).

(g) Ammerbach, 1583: *Der Magister Dantz* [*Almande Poussinghe*] for keyboard (No. 10c; see also No. 46 and Plate XXI).

(h) M. Neusidler, 1574: *Proficiat ir lieben Herren* (transposed) for lute (cf. No. 10d).

same melody into three sections. In the pieces of Volume II, I have marked each varied repeat, as well as the beginning of a new section following such a repetition. In Ex. 2a only the first of two sections is repeated; another version of the same tune in No. 1a shows the same melody divided into three sections, with only the outer two repeated. Ex. 2f has three repeated sections, Ex. 2d four. These examples therefore show that the Tanz may have one to four sections, with some of them repeated. Most often, however, there are two or three sections, with each immediately repeated.

The Melodic Cadence

Each section may contain one or more musical phrases, each of which often concludes with the typical cadence shown in Ex. 3. We have already seen this melodic cadence at the end of the first section of Exx. 1c and 1d. In this case the emergence of the cadence created not only a parallelism with the final cadence, but a sense of unity between this melody and most of the others associated with this dance. The cadence therefore becomes one of the chief musical traits of the Deutscher Tanz. It does not occur in every example, and it sometimes appears in other forms as well.[2] But it recurs with sufficient frequency, I believe, to be perceived as belonging especially to the Deutscher

8   *The Renaissance*

Ex. 3: The typical cadence.

( ) = a quarter-note on any pitch except 4.

Ex. 4: Vocal cadence of the 16th century.

(a) As sung.

(b) As sometimes transcribed for instruments.

Ex. 5: Various ways of approaching the typical cadence (the *a'* may be flatted).

Tanz. Contained within this cadence are melodic and rhythmic properties vital to the essence of the dance.

The cadence no doubt derives from contemporary vocal cadences such as the one in Ex. 4a. In vocal music the flow of counterpoint is smoothly slowed down and finally terminated by the use of suspensions. Ex. 4a ordinarily involves two suspensions in succession. The dance choreography, on the other hand, required vigorously accentuated beats. Thus, the suspensions were replaced by repeated notes, resulting in the pattern of Ex. 3. This cadential formula could be approached in the different ways shown in Ex. 5. The most natural approach, I suppose, is by scale degree 2, since it appeared also in the vocal model in Ex. 4a. Ex. 5a depicts this situation, with the stemless notes representing other tones that may precede scale degree 2 in various rhythms. Thus 2 itself is often preceded by 3, and 3 sometimes by 4, and 4 by 5. This succession creates a downward motion that contrasts with the final upward motion of 7 to 1. The sense of circling 1 from both directions was no doubt a significant feature in the vocal cadence of Ex. 4a. Ex. 5a also shows a less frequent method of approaching 2 through 1, which itself might be preceded by 7.

Also frequent, however, is the approach to the cadence through 6, 5, or 3. Ex. 5b shows scale degree 6 before the cadence, as well as the 5 that often precedes it. To the right is a common variant that contains a passing-tone. In Ex. 5c, 5 precedes the cadence, with 5 often approached by 6. In Exx. 5b and 5c the roles of 5 and 6 are thus reversed. Scale degree 3 introduces the cadence in Ex. 5d; it, in turn, can be approached from above through 4, or 5 and 4, or from below by 2. Less common is the approach to the cadence by 7 (Ex. 5e), and very rare the approach by 1 (Ex. 5f).

Examples of these various types occur abundantly in the melodies of Exx. 1 and 2. The approach to the cadence by 2 (Ex. 5a) appears at the end of Exx. 1c, d, and f, at the end of the first section of Ex. 2c, and at the end of the final section of Exx. 2d, f, g, and h. The approach by 6 (Ex. 5b) concludes the melody in Ex. 2b; that by 5 (Ex. 5c) ends the first half of Ex. 1c. Scale degree 3 (Ex. 5d) precedes the cadence at the end of the first section of Ex. 2e and the end of the final section of Ex. 2c. Ex. 1 illustrates, finally, 7 and 1 before the cadence, the first at the end of the opening section of (d), the other concluding the second section of (a) and (b). Numerous other examples fill the pages of Volume II, not only in the German sources, but in those from other countries as well. A similar half-cadence occasionally occurs, as at the end of the opening section of Nos. 7a and 10a. In addition, the final tone of a cadence may be repeated again on the third beat, as at the end of each section in Exx. 1a and b. The repeated notes may also follow other cadential structures, as at the end of the opening phrases in Nos. 1a, 3, 5b, and 11 of Volume II.

The method of composing the usual four-measure phrase was therefore a matter of setting a typical cadence on the pitch desired. The cadence occupied almost the entire second half of the phrase. The opening half was then a way of approaching the cadence via some of the pitches suggested in Ex. 5. The typical cadence thus constituted a familiar method of punctuation. The ear could often anticipate its arrival; its completion meant that some pitch center had been clearly established and articulated. Some melodies present a series of tone centers, each identified by the typical cadence. In Ex. 2g, for example, the three phrases end on g', d', and g', respectively, and each of these pitches is confirmed by the melodic and rhythmic effect of the typical cadence.

10   *The Renaissance*

Ex. 6: Chords to harmonize the typical cadence.

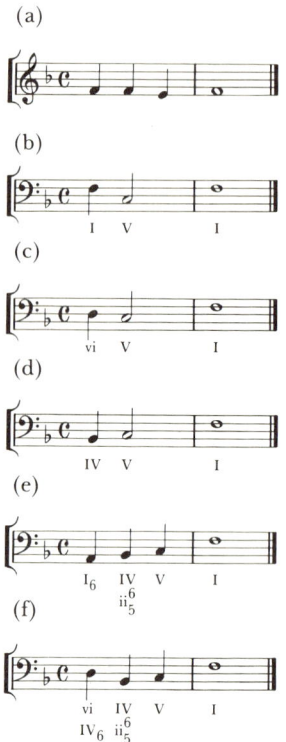

The Harmony

Ex. 6 gives some harmonizations for the cadence when it moves to a major tonic triad. Similar progressions occur when the central tonic is a minor triad. Below the melody in Ex. 6 are five bass lines with chord symbols (upper-case Roman numerals indicate major triads; lower-case, minor). In the first three harmonizations, the second of the two repeated notes in the melody becomes an appoggiatura above a V chord. In the last two, each pitch of the melody receives its own chord. The number of chords in the penultimate measure has an impact upon the rhythm. Ex. 7 shows the effect of changing the number of chords: (a) is a very rare example from Ammerbach's 1571 book in which the measure is filled with only a single chord. Ex. 7b shows two chords in this bar. More common would be three, as in (c), or four, as in (d). The four beats of the measure are made even more substantial when some passing-tones are included, as in Ex. 7e.[3] Thus the harmony can support, to one degree or another, the rhythmic energy inherent in the four beats of the penultimate measure.

Harmony on a broader scale seems often related to a particular technique that had originated in the preceding century. Around 1480 Guilelmus Monachus explains how to construct a *fauxbourdon* in four voices.[4] The method

Ex. 7: Harmonization of the concluding two measures of a phrase (examples transposed, where necessary, to F major).

(a) One chord in penultimate bar (Ammerbach, 1571: *5. Ein kurtzer Dantz*, end of first section).

(b) Two chords (No. 7b, end of first section).

(c) Three chords (No. 5a, end).

(d) Four chords (Ammerbach, 1571: *8. Ein ander Dantz*, end of first section).

(e) Four chords and passing-tones (No. 10b, end of first section).

is useful, however, in creating a four-voice harmonization of any melody. In Ex. 8 I have set the melody of the *Printzentantz* from Ex. 1a in the upper voice. The first voice to add is the tenor (Ex. 8a), which moves in parallel sixths with the upper voice, except for an octave on the opening and closing chords. I have considered some of the melodic notes in the penultimate measure of each half to be ornamental tones that do not require harmonization. This establishes a duet between soprano and tenor that is complete by itself and becomes the

12 The Renaissance

Ex. 8: The *Printzentantz* (from Ex. 1a) harmonized by the rules of Guilelmus Monachus.

basic inner structure of the harmonization. The bass is then added (Ex. 8b) in such a way that it forms a unison or octave with the tenor on the first and last chords and elsewhere alternates a third and a fifth below the tenor, but with the fifth occurring on the penultimate chord. Thus one can place a *d* below the tenor *a* in the penultimate bar and then work backwards, alternating a third and then a fifth below each tenor note. Similarly, the alto alternates a third and a fourth above the tenor, with a fourth appearing above the penultimate tenor note. So, above the tenor *a* in the next-to-last bar the alto will sound a *d'* a fourth above. Again, working backwards, the alto is formed by alternating these two intervals above each successive tenor note. If this method were applied independently to each half of the *Printzentantz*, then each four-measure phrase would begin and end with soprano and tenor at the octave (using the notes in parentheses in Ex. 8a), and the two inner measures would appear as shown in Ex. 8c. Comparison of Ex. 8 with No. 3 in Volume II will show how closely actual settings of the *Printzentantz* follow this theoretical construction of Guilelmus Monachus.

If one considers the VII chord in the third measure as a variation chord that prolongs the III chord on either side, then the chordal progression that emerges is the familiar scheme which occurs in the later folia and which I have labeled "Scheme V" in various articles.[5] The chordal schemes of the Renaissance dance style thus seem closely related to the method of harmonization described by Guilelmus Monachus. Psalm tones could utilize it to produce *falsobordoni*. Some of the more chordal of the secular vocal forms, such as the chanson and the German Lied, also show signs, from time to time, of this type of construction. Cadences in the Burgundian chanson often involve parallel sixths between soprano and tenor that resolve finally to an octave.[6] Many later Parisian chansons display even more extensively the inner structure of soprano and tenor in sixths.[7]

In addition to parallel sixths, this method produces also the particular cadential configuration in which scale degree 7 in the soprano and 2 in the tenor move by contrary motion to an octave. This means that when a melody is in the top voice, as it is in the Deutscher Tanz, it will cadence ordinarily from 7 to 1. On the other hand, a melody placed in the tenor, as in most German polyphonic Lieder before 1550, will cadence most often from 2 to 1. Therefore, as a glance at the cadences in Exx. 1, 2, 3, and 5 will show, the overwhelming preference in the Deutscher Tanz is the final movement of a phrase of melody from 7 to 1.

Some examples are clearly built on the Renaissance chordal schemes. The opening section of No. 9 in Volume II, for example, presents essentially the succession of chords used by the *romanesca*, and the last section uses Scheme V. Since the piece is for cittern, some of the actual bass notes are missing, and the cadence at the end of the opening section, like others in the same source, does not change the tonic chord to V in the penultimate bar. In No. 8 of Volume II, the scheme of the *romanesca* spans the entire composition. No. 11 illustrates a broader application of the schemes: the first section simply circles around a C-minor triad, but the second section moves on up to the VII and III chords, and the last section moves back down through VII to i, V, and finally i. Comparing this example with the harmonization of the *Printzentantz* in Ex. 8 will, I think, reveal an approach similar to all of the Renaissance chordal schemes in the mode *per B molle*: the setting up of two chordal centers on i and III, and then prolonging them or moving between them through the dominant chord of each (V and VII). The melody shown in Ex. 2b is also usually harmonized in this manner, with the opening section concerned with a G-minor chord center; in the second half, the opening three bars are devoted to III or a B-flat center, with VII in the fourth bar and thereafter a return to a final cadence on the opening G-minor level.

Not all examples of the Deutscher Tanz, however, are related to these fixed successions of chords. Most often pieces end in the same center in which they begin. Ex. 2e, on the other hand, commences on a B-flat-major center, but concludes on F (see the setting in No. 7b). The succession of cadences outlines the overall harmonic plan of a piece most clearly. The melody in Ex. 2d, for example, ends its opening section on a half-cadence in G minor; succeeding levels on D minor, B-flat major, and a return to G minor are marked by the cadences at the end of each four-bar phrase. No. 7a presents a harmonization of this melody. Most often the typical cadences of Ex. 5 catch the ear's attention first, and as they move from one pitch level to another, they create within the piece as a whole a sense of harmonic design. The first phrase usually comes to a cadence on the same level as the opening and closing chords of the piece, either with a full cadence (No. 7b) or a half (7a). Sometimes, however, the opening phrase moves to another level, most often V (No. 1a), IV, or III (No. 3).

The Phrases

The length of the phrase can vary. There seems to be an expectancy for phrases of four bars and many occupy exactly this length. Others, however, may span six or eight measures. Some of those with six bars seem to be constructed of a regular four-bar phrase followed by a two-bar extension: see the opening section of No. 11, which reaches a cadence on G at the end of four bars, but then adds another cadence on C to extend the phrase another two bars. In the second section of No. 5b, the similarity of the third and fourth measures to the first and second creates a design of 2 + 4. Again, it seems as though a four-bar phrase has been extended, this time at its beginning. Similarly, phrases of eight bars also seem to contain some recurring rhythmic or melodic units. In the opening section of No. 10b, the rhythm of the first two measures recurs three times before the two measures of cadence; furthermore, bars 2 and 4, as well as 3 and 5, correspond exactly, but on different pitch levels. In the second section of Ex. 2b, repetition in measures 4, 5, and 6 serves to sustain the phrase over a length of eight measures. Disposition of the phrases within sections can also vary. Most often the opening section contains a single phrase, but in the melody of Ex. 2h there are two. The second section may also contain a single phrase (Ex. 2c), but often has two (Exx. 2a and e).

We have already noted some of the repetition that can occur to give a sense of organization to a melody. The typical cadence provides the most distinctive motivic element that recurs within a melody. Other repetitions, described above, operate to extend the usual four-measure phrase to six or eight measures. In addition, there is a tendency to utilize repeated notes, not only in the typical cadence, but also elsewhere (see Ex. 2b, measures 2 and 3, for example, or the opening of Ex. 2g). This adds to the energy of the melody, and also helps to emphasize the four beats in a measure. Some melodies are content with these rather modest types of repetition (Ex. 2d, for example). Others, however, create more extensive organization through repetition. In the melody of Ex. 2g, the second phrase is somewhat parallel to the first (compare especially measures 2 and 6), and the last three measures of the piece are identical to measures 2-4 in the opening phrase. In Ex. 2h the entire last phrase is identical to the second. A similar feeling of return occurs in the final section of Ex. 2f, when the first three beats of the opening two bars echo the motive that had recurred earlier in bars 2 and 4 of the first section.

The Nachtanz

In almost all cases the initial presentation of the Tanz in duple meter is followed by a Nachtanz in which the musical substance is somehow transformed into triple meter. A glance at the Table of Contents for Nos. 1–11 in Volume II will show the variety of names used for the triple dance: *Nachtantz, Hupff auff, Sprung, Proportz, Proportio, Proportio tripla.* The second and third refer, no doubt, to hopping or jumping movements involved in the choreography, the last three to the tempo relationship between the duple and triple parts. Nos. 3 and 4, both settings of the music of the *Printzentantz*, show the two techniques of transforming the musical material of the duple dance into triple. In No. 3 each measure of the duple dance has been changed into two measures of triple meter. No. 4, on the other hand, shows a measure of duple transformed into a single triple measure. The first two lines of Ex. 9a show the usual notation for these two methods. In almost all examples for lute, cittern, and keyboard from 1540 to the end of the century, the Tanz is notated with four minims (half-notes) in a measure, the Nachtanz with three. The symbol in the tablature for the minim is a vertical line with a single flag to the right. I have transcribed this music in Volume II and in Exx. 1–23 by reducing the values by half. Thus, instead of the original four minims in a measure of 4/2 followed by three minims in a measure of 3/2, we have the more familiar situation of four quarter-notes in 4/4 and three quarter-notes in 3/4.[8] This will facilitate comparison of the earlier examples with those after about 1590 in which the minim is replaced as the basic pulse by the semiminim or quarter-note.

Plates I and II show the original notation for Nos. 3 and 4. In the top photograph of Plate I, the duple *Printzentantz* commences at the end of the third line of the tablature (half of the first measure appears on this line, the other half on the next). The symbols 5, *t*, 5, *k*, *p* stand for the opening pitches of the melody: g', f'-sharp, g', a', b'-flat. Comparing, then, the opening of the *Proportz* on the lower photograph, one can note that each measure now contains three minims or vertical lines with single flags at the top instead of four. The same succession of symbols can be seen, but here it outlines the pitches of the melody in triple meter and in accordance with the method of transformation illustrated on the first line of Ex. 9a. The other method is used in Plate II. The title for the second piece occurs in the middle of the plate, and the duple dance begins on the second line of the right-hand page. The symbols used in organ tablature are more familiar: *g*, *f* (the curl at the right means "sharp"), *g*, *a*, *b* (the German letter-name for B-flat). Again, one can see how the melody reshapes itself into triple meter and note that there are four minims in each bar of the duple dance and three in each bar of the *Proportio*.

The remaining rhythmic problem, then, is the tempo relationship between the duple and triple dances. The names *Proportz, Tripla,* and *Proportio tripla,* as well as the sign ¢3 on Plate II, all refer to the proportion that relates the two

16   *The Renaissance*

Ex. 9: Transformation of the duple Tanz into the triple Nachtanz (applied to part of the *Printzentantz* of Ex. 1a).

(a) Usual notation

(b) Less common notation

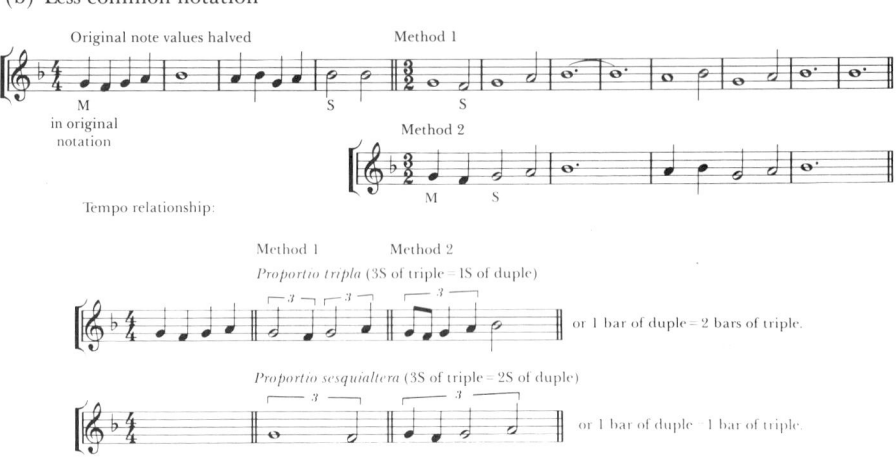

meters. One encounters two difficulties, however, in connection with directly applying *proportio tripla*: (1) the designation 3/1 can at this time in history mean either *proportio tripla* or *proportio sesquialtera* (ordinarily denoted by 3/2), and (2) the proportional equivalency, although theoretically involving the semibreve, seems sometimes to deal instead with the minim.[9] Accordingly, I show in Ex. 9a, under the heading "Tempo relationship", the two possible proportions applied to each of the two methods of transformation. In both cases the proportions seem to yield reasonable results only in reference to the minim: for *proportio tripla*, three minims of triple meter take the time of one in duple; in *proportio sesquialtera*, three minims of triple occupy the time of two in duple. The third and fourth lines of Ex. 9a show a single measure of duple followed by a

Plate I: *Des Printzen Tantz* and beginning of the *Proportz auff den Tantz* for lute (transcribed as No. 3 in Volume II).

Wolff Heckel, *Tenor, Lautten Buch* (Strassburg, 1562), pp. 132–133 (reproduced by permission of the Music Department, Österreichische Nationalbibliothek, Vienna; call number S.A.76.C.27).

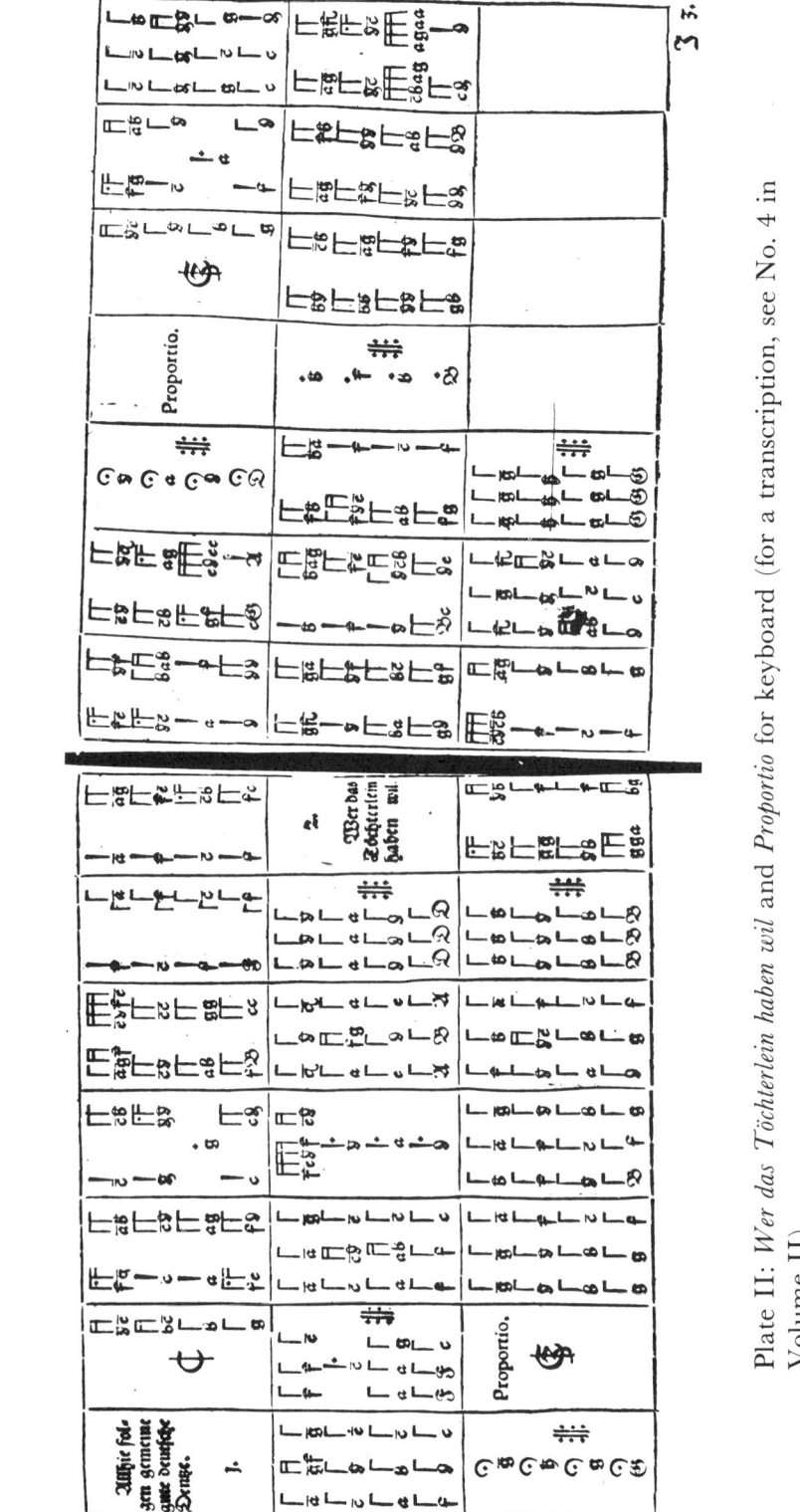

Plate II: *Wer das Töchterlein haben wil* and *Proportio* for keyboard (for a transcription, see No. 4 in Volume II).

Elias Nikolaus Ammerbach, *Orgel oder Instrument Tabulatur* (Leipzig, 1571), fols. I_2^v-I_3^r (reproduced by permission of the Syndics of Cambridge University Library).

single measure, still in 4/4, for each method of transformation reckoned in each of the two proportions. The results from *proportio tripla* seem rather hurried, especially for Method 2; this would require four bars of triple, as depicted on the second line of Ex. 9a, to occupy the time of one bar of duple. This could conceivably be the case for Method 1. *Proportio sesquialtera*, however, produces a more moderate tempo, so that two triple bars of the original notation correspond to one duple. In the case of Method 1, then, the melodic substance continues to move at the same pace in the triple section, whereas in Method 2 it is twice as fast.

It is perhaps instructive to consider the less common type of notation depicted in Ex. 9b. Here the tablature sets 4/2 meter together with 3/1 (or, in my transcriptions, 4/4 and 3/2). Three examples in Ammerbach's book of 1571 utilize this notation for transformation by Method 2.[10] The third and fourth lines of music in Ex. 9b show the tempo relationships for each method, again for the two possible proportions. This time *proportio sesquialtera* results in a triple dance in which one bar of duple replaces in time one bar of triple. This slows down the movement considerably, especially for Method 1, and can scarcely be appropriate for the increase of animation suggested by the terms *Hupff auff* and *Sprung*. Applying *proportio tripla*, however, and using the semibreve as the unit of reference (three semibreves in triple fitting the time of one in duple), we get the same results we obtained in Ex. 9a by using *proportio sesquialtera*. In this case, two bars of triple (referring to the first two lines of Ex. 9b) occupy the time of one bar of duple. Occasionally a diminished version of Ex. 9b occurs, in which a semiminim is the basic beat in the Tanz and a minim in the Nachtanz. This occurs in one of Ammerbach's pieces that uses Method 2.[11] It is also in three examples from Jobin's lute book of 1573, two of them associated with Method 2, one with Method 1.[12] Kargel's cittern book of 1578 also contains one example using Method 2.[13] Presumably this notation was meant to convey the same relationship as that in Ex. 9b.

The melody of one of Jobin's examples that uses the diminished version of Ex. 9b recurs in a setting by Melchior Neusidler in 1574 with the usual notation of Ex. 9a.[14] One of Ammerbach's pieces notated as in Ex. 9b recurs in his later book of 1583 notated according to Ex. 9a.[15] All of these facts suggest that a certain amount of experimentation was going on in connection with notation. I suspect that Ex. 9b represents the actual tempo relationship desired, notated correctly according to the Renaissance theory of *proportio tripla*. Ex. 9a may then simply signify the same relationship, but notated in a manner that had become traditional, perhaps because it was easier to read. The diminished version of Ex. 9b may be still another notation that produces the same results as Ex. 9b. At work here may be the process that associated progressively smaller note values with the basic beat in music. In 1540, when the Deutscher Tanz begins its history, the beat was notated as a minim. By the next century, however, the same basic beat was often notated as a semiminim or quarter-note.

Thus, the relationship shown on the fourth line of Ex. 9a and the third line of Ex. 9b seems to be the most logical solution. That on the third line of Ex. 9a seems too fast, that on the fourth line of Ex. 9b too slow. Perhaps they should all be considered possibilities. Perhaps the changing notation reflects changes in the tempo relationship. Finally, of course, one should keep in mind the possibility that the relationship was flexible and that the tempo of a triple dance might depend to some degree on the acoustics, the dancers, the time of day, or the general spirit prevailing at a given moment in a social setting. In any case, the general tempo for the Deutscher Tanz was slow and solemn, if we can judge from descriptions of the dance in other countries.

The Instruments

The surviving sources are for keyboard, lute, and cittern. The keyboard instrument used was presumably the harpsichord. The cittern, unlike the lute, had wire strings and was played with a plectrum. Although considered of lower social status, it became exceedingly popular during the second half of the 16th century, particularly in France and England. The four-course cittern utilized reentrant tuning (that is, the pitches of the open courses did not sound in order) and, as a special curiosity, a whole tone existed between the third and fourth frets. In the resulting music, some of the chords seem to be lacking their proper bass note, producing what appear to be second-inversion triads (in No. 9, for example, see the chords at the beginning of bars 1, 3, 4, and 5). This is an unusual trait that reappears in the 17th century with the Spanish guitar. Citterns could also have six courses, in which case the music became more lute-like, as shown by No. 8.

It is not known whether the music in these sources for keyboard and plucked-stringed instruments actually accompanied the dance or whether it was independent instrumental music. There are, curiously, no German sources for ensemble. Hans Gerle included no dances among the ensemble works in his book of 1546, although there is a *Saltarello* among the pieces for solo lute. The book, however, was published in Nuremberg, the city where he lived as a lute maker and where Hans Neusidler had just six years previously published the first lute examples of the new Deutscher Tanz. In 1555 Paul and Batholomeus Hessen's *Etlicher gutter Teutscher und Polnischer Tentz* appeared in Breslau for four and five instruments of any sort. All of the 155 dances have five voices, although the fifth seems optional, and all have a second part in which the material of the duple first part is transformed into triple. Unfortunately, there are no titles to distinguish the German dances from the Polish and, worse yet, the *cantus* partbook is missing. Several features, however, suggest that these dances belong to an older tradition and not to the Deutscher Tanz that concerns us here. The title page and introduction appear only in the tenor book, and rests are sometimes placed in the tenor part to separate phrases of melody. This suggests that the main melody occurs in this voice. In addition, the same brothers also published in the same year another book, which contained numerous works from other countries, many of which concord with *pavanes* and *gaillardes* published in 1530 by Attaingnant. Thus, both books seem to be retrospective in nature and to belong to older traditions.[16]

Coloration

At the time the Deutscher Tanz first appeared, the technique of varying a melodic line had been well established for a very long time. It was applied most frequently to the intabulation of vocal pieces, with the most elaborate ornamentation occurring often in the upper voices. This sort of ornamentation was referred to as "diminution," "division," or, by the German composers, as "*Coloratur*" or "coloration." In the case of the Deutscher Tanz, coloration is applied in various ways and to differing degrees. Most of the examples of Ammerbach (1571 and 1583) and those in Waissel's 1591 book utilize a minimum of coloration and give the music for each section of a piece a single time, with signs to indicate that it should be repeated. Nos. 4, 10c, and 10d are keyboard examples in which all four voices move in my transcriptions mostly in quarter-notes, with only occasionally dotted notes, longer notes, or eighth-notes that provide a passing-tone in one of the voices. No. 11 is a similarly simple example for lute, No. 9 one for cittern. These relatively unornamented pieces allow the four beats of each measure to be heard very clearly and hence would no doubt have been easier for dancers to follow.

More often, however, the repetition of a section of melody is written out. In this case very slight changes might occur between the two statements, as in the opening phrase of No. 1a, or, on the other hand, many ornaments may be added the second time, as in the first section of No. 8. In the latter, the first four bars present the opening section in a very simple manner; the next four bars restate the same material, but with many ornamental notes added. Less extensive ornamentation occurs in No. 3, and here the repeats, which are written out completely in the original tablature, are almost identical to the opening statements. The technique of coloration is thus usually applied with relative moderation.[17] For the most part it consists of turn-like figures (see No. 3) or short scale passages (No. 5a, measures 6 and 9, or the opening bars of the second section of the Nachtanz). Although some ornamentation may occur briefly in the lower voices (No. 3, for example), it is more extensively applied ordinarily to the upper voice (No. 5a). Since this is the voice that carries the melody, coloration thus usually acts to intensify the central position of the upper voice.

Melodies from Lieder

Since texts are not provided for the Deutscher Tanz in any 16th-century sources, the dance was apparently not sung. Some of the melodies, however, are adapted from German Lieder. Ex. 10 shows the melody of *Ich weiss ein' stolze Müllerin* as it appears in the tenor voice of Ludwig Senfl's setting for four voices.[18] In No. 1b it has been adapted by Hans Neusidler for a Tanz by adding a triple Nachtanz, by repeating the second section, at least partially, in the Nachtanz, by omitting the rests between the lines, and by changing the final cadence from 2-1 to 7-1. This Lied, like many others, was in Bar form, so it was already designed in two sections, with the first repeated.

Ex. 11 shows another Lied changed into a Tanz by the same composer. On the top line is the tenor of *Ein Ziegler in der Hütten* from Georg Forster's setting for four voices in *Der ander Theil, kurtzweiliger guter frischer teutscher Liedlein, zu singen vast lustig* (Nuremberg, 1540).[19] Ex. 11b shows the top voice of Neusidler's Tanz *Der Ziegler in der Hecken*, published in the same city in the same year.[20] This time, the tenor melody itself is not in Bar form and has no repetition. To transform it into a Tanz, Neusidler thus divided it into two sections, wrote out the repeat of each, and added a Nachtanz to correspond. The tenor melody has three cadences, the middle one exactly like the typical cadence we have noted in the Deutscher Tanz. Neusidler therefore changed only the two outer cadences from 2-1 to 7-1. Exx. 11c and d show the opening measures for comparison. The tenor of Forster's Lied can be seen in the soprano of the Tanz. Ex. 11c displays fairly clearly the type of construction, already described, in which soprano and tenor start and end a phrase in octaves, with parallel sixths between. The sixths are broken for a few beats, but they are made unusually conspicuous at the beginning of the phrase. One can also see the typical Tanz cadence in the soprano of the third measure, appearing as a counterpoint to the tenor's movement from 2 to 1.

Neusidler treats a number of other Lieder in this manner, and for those in his 1549 book he adds to the title the expression *Tanz weyss*, as in *Ich stund an einem Morgen/Tantz weyss*. Thus *Wie möcht ich frölich werden/Tantz weyss* (No. 2) becomes a Deutscher Tanz that recurs in a number of later settings. In 1574 his son Melchior published a version (No. 7c) in which a number of changes occur. Comparing Nos. 2 and 7c, one can note that the opening phrases of five plus seven bars in the earlier setting have changed to regular phrases of four measures each in the later. In addition, the suspension cadence that Hans associates with the 7-1 movement has been changed by Melchior, at the end of each of these two phrases, to the typical cadence of Exx. 3 and 5. The regularity of phrase length and the four solid beats provided by the typical cadence were both features important in the Deutscher Tanz. Other titles, such as *Wer das Töchterlein haben wil* (No. 4), *Gut Gsell du must wandern* (10b), and *Proficiat ir lieben Herren* (10d), suggest texts and therefore may also represent borrowed melodies.

Ex. 10: *Ich weiss ein' stolze Müllerin* from the tenor of the four-voice setting of Senfl (transposed from C).

Ex. 11: *Der (Ein) Ziegler in der Hecken (Hütten)*.

(a) Tenor from Georg Forster's setting (transposed up an octave), 1540.

(b) Melody in the top voice of H. Neusidler's setting, 1540.

+ Der Hupff auff

(c) Opening phrase of Forster's Lied.

(d) Opening phrase of Neusidler's Tanz.

The involvement of the Deutscher Tanz with the Deutsches Lied may be even more extensive, however, for the same books that contain the Tanz also include three other important categories of composition: transcriptions of Lieder, arrangements of French chansons, and Italian dances. As a background for the origin of the Deutscher Tanz, it will be useful to consider these three types of music and their possible influence.

The Influence of Lied Transcriptions

From around 1500 until 1550 a type of German polyphonic Lied developed, mainly in the southern German cities, in which the principal melody appeared in the tenor part of a four-voice composition. The first printed collections come from Augsburg (Erhard Oeglin in 1512) and Mainz (Peter Schoeffer, 1513). At the same time, transcriptions of works by Paul Hofhaimer, Wolfgang Grefinger, and Heinrich Finck begin to appear in tablatures for lute (Hans Judenkünig) and keyboard (Hans Kotter). In the 1530's the tablatures of Gerle and Neusidler contain arrangements of Lieder by composers such as Thomas Stoltzer and, above all, Ludwig Senfl. The number of Lied transcriptions increases gradually until it reaches a high point of about fifty in Hans Neusidler's *Ein newgeordent künstlich Lautenbuch* of 1536. Such intabulations continue in lute and keyboard books throughout the rest of the century and after 1570 often involve the new type of Lieder written by Regnart and Lassus.

The manner in which the composers of lute and keyboard music treat the Lied reveals interest in some features later found in the Deutscher Tanz.[21] Above all, they seem to emphasize, in various ways, the significance of the upper voice and the importance of four substantial beats per measure. Ex. 12a shows the opening phrase of *Nach willen dein* by Paul Hofhaimer (in the original all voices are texted).[22] The melody is in the tenor, and the soprano makes with the tenor an independent duet which begins and ends at the octave, with sixths and sometimes thirds in between. The tenor cadences 2 to 1, the soprano accompanying it with 7-1. Neusidler arranges this Lied in several ways. In Ex. 12b he makes a piece intended for the instruction of beginners; it uses only the two lower voices from the Lied.[23] Now the main melody is in fact in the upper voice. Also, some notes of the original have been replaced in the first three measures with repeated notes of smaller value. Perhaps this acts to compensate (as on the opening note) for the rapid decay of the tone on the lute. In the second and third bars, however, such repetitions emphasize the rhythmic pace of the quarter-note. Ex. 12c shows another arrangement of the same Lied, this time for three voices.[24] Here the alto is omitted; the original soprano has been ornamented and the second half of the third measure altered in both tenor and bass. The coloration attracts the main attention to the upper voice. The tenor, which in the Lied was the main melody, is now not only relatively inconspicuous, but is regarded so little that one of its original tones is altered. In Ex. 12d even more elaborate coloration occurs.[25] At the same time the tenor has been simplified, so that, along with the original bass, it seems like an inconspicuous accompaniment to the dazzling figuration in the upper voice. In this case coloration has been applied in a far more elaborate manner than in the usual Deutscher Tanz.

The opening phrase of *Ich schrei und rief* appears in Ex. 13a in its four-voice vocal setting from Arnt von Aich's *LXXV hubscher Lieder myt Discant, Alt, Bas,*

Ex. 12: *Nach willen dein*, opening phrase.

(a) Paul Hofhaimer, Lied.

(b) Hans Neusidler, transcription (transposed down a fourth) for two voices, 1536.

(c) H. Neusidler, transcription omitting the alto, 1540.

(d) H. Neusidler, transcription with highly colored soprano, 1536.

Ex. 13: *Ich schrei und rief*, opening phrase.

(a) Arnt von Aich, Lied from *LXXV hubscher Lieder*.

(b) Arnolt Schlick, transcription for voice and lute, 1512.

26 *The Renaissance*

und Tenor (Cologne, c. 1512–20).[26] As in most examples before 1536, the text appears only in the tenor. This may indicate that only the tenor was sung, with the other voices played on instruments. Ex. 13b presents, for comparison, the arrangement of this music for a single voice and lute from Arnolt Schlick's *Tabulaturen etlicher Lobgesang und Lidlein uff die Orgeln und Lauten* (Mainz, 1512).[27] Schlick's voice part, which he notates in mensural notation but without text, sings the soprano line from Ex. 13a without alteration. The intabulated lute part then includes the bass from the Lied, with a little coloration in the opening measure, and its tenor, also slightly altered in measures 2 and 4. The alto from the Lied, as in Ex. 12c, is omitted. The center of attention in this unusual arrangement is therefore on the voice, which is singing a part which was not the main melody in the Lied. The lute part by itself, however, has the original Lied melody as its upper voice.

As a final example of Lied transcription, Ex. 14 shows two cadences from *Ach edler Hort*, first from the original vocal piece by Hofhaimer,[28] then in a keyboard transcription by Ammerbach.[29] In both cases the suspensions have been replaced with repeated notes. The first cadence in Ex. 14b is shown also in Ex. 4b to demonstrate its relationship to the vocal cadence. This cadence, with its 1-1-7-1, constitutes a transition to the second cadence in Ex. 14b, which is the typical Tanz cadence in Ex. 3.[30] Ammerbach rearranges the notes on the first two beats of the penultimate measure and adds a third in the final chord and a passing-note in the alto to precede it. The texture becomes, in general, more chordal, with attention on the top voice as the bearer of melody and the bottom as the support for the harmony. In other words, the flowing polyphony of the Lied, with its emphasis on suspensions and the avoidance of accents, tends to be transformed into a kind of homophony in which four beats are accentuated in each measure.

It is clear that the early composers of the Deutscher Tanz were at least

Ex. 14: *Ach edler Hort*, cadences of the first and last phrases.

(a) Hofhaimer, Lied, before 1537.

(b) Ammerbach, transcription, 1571.

equally concerned with the Lied. Neusidler's book of 1540 contained both the Lied arrangement in Ex. 12c and the Tänze in No. 1b and Ex. 11 that borrow the main melody from a Lied, as we have seen, and place it in the soprano. By the time the Tanz first appeared in 1540, however, a number of the basic musical ideas utilized in it had already previously existed, as Exx. 12 and 13 demonstrate, in the Lied transcriptions from earlier in the century. Of the six Lieder from which Neusidler borrows the melodies in 1540 and 1549, only one actually occurs earlier in a Lied arrangement. This is *Ich stund an einem Morgen*, which Neusidler sets in 1536 in two parts (with the Lied tenor on top and the Lied bass below it, as in Ex. 12b), and in 1549 as *Ich stund an einem Morgen/Tantz weyss*. In the latter, only the melody is borrowed, as in No. 1b; it is then altered to fit the Tanz situation and new lower voices are added.[31] Only one of the six Lied titles, *Ich weiss mir ein schöne Müllerin* (No. 1b), occurs as a Tanz in sources after mid-century.

The Lied obviously played some role in the origin and development of the Deutscher Tanz. The exact extent of this role is difficult to determine, especially since the same sources also contain other types of composition, such as chansons from France and dances from Italy, which may also have exerted an influence.

The Influence of Chanson Arrangements

Chanson intabulations began to appear in German sources with Gerle's lute book of 1533. Here, as well as in Neusidler's tablatures of 1536, the chansons were by Flemish composers, chiefly Josquin Desprez. Commencing in 1540, however, Neusidler's books are increasingly concerned with the chansons of Sermisy, which had been published by Attaingnant in 1528 and the years immediately following. Sermisy is the main composer associated with the so-called "Parisian chanson," a type that has some striking similarities to the Deutscher Tanz, which, as we have seen, emerged around 1540. The Parisian chanson is a setting for four voices, with the melody in the top voice. Other voices are accompanimental and often very chordal. The minim beat is emphasized, either through repetition of notes or chords, or through the dactylic rhythm that had often characterized the beginning of a chanson even before this time. Phrases are often four bars in length and are clearly marked off by rests or by repetition. A feeling of flowing counterpoint still persists, however, especially in the succession of suspensions that almost always accompanies the cadence (usually the one in Ex. 4a). In addition, many examples display the construction, depicted in Ex. 8, in which the soprano and tenor, moving mostly in sixths, provide the inner framework of the piece.

Ex. 15 gives the beginning of Sermisy's *Dont vient cela*.[32] The opening phrase displays essentially chordal movement in its first three measures, moving to a twofold suspension cadence (Ex. 4a). Repeated notes, as well as emphasis of

28   *The Renaissance*

Ex. 15: *Dont vient cela*, opening phrases.

(a) Sermisy, chanson (transposed up a fourth; *musica ficta* omitted), 1528.

(b) Hans Neusidler, *Du Fiensela*, 1544.

(c) Hans Neusidler, *Du wentzela. Ein welscher Tantz*, 1540.

(a) Sermisy (continued).

(b) Neusidler 1544 (continued).

(c) Neusidler 1540 (continued).

the quarter-note beat (referring to the halved note values in my transcription), occur at the beginning of the second phrase. This excerpt also illustrates very clearly the construction of the soprano and tenor in sixths and octaves. In fact, these two phrases together have the same basic framework as the *Printzentantz* harmonized in Ex. 8, with cadences on B-flat and G, respectively. I have omitted the text again in Ex. 15a and have added no *musica ficta*. Set below Ex. 15a are two transcriptions by Neusidler: a simple one from his 1544 book[33] and a colored version from 1540.[34] He calls the latter, curiously, *Ein welscher Tantz*, but the later version is in a section of the book headed "Hie nach volgen etliche frantzösische Stück." He may have used the term *Tantz* because he was familiar with the ensemble *gaillarde* published by Attaingnant in 1530 in which Sermisy's *Dont vient cela* is transformed into triple meter.[35]

In both lute arrangements of Ex. 15, the alto part of the chanson is omitted. According to the method of construction illustrated in Ex. 8, this is the last voice added and hence the least important structurally. Ex. 15b is, for the most part, a simplification of the original chanson. It emphasizes the quarter-note in various ways: by omitting the sixteenths in the bass of measure 3, by restriking the suspension in the following measure, by breaking half-notes into repeated quarters in the soprano and tenor of measure 6 (and hence emphasizing the sixths between them in this and the succeeding measure), by omitting the eighth-note in the bass of measure 7, and by eliminating the suspension at the beginning of measure 9. Both cadences have been substantially altered. In the other intabulation (Ex. 15c), moderate coloration is added to the upper voice, while the two lower voices remain almost the same as in Ex. 15b. Coloration is most elaborate at the beginning of a phrase or in the approach to the cadence. The final chord is not ornamented, and the rests in all voices remain to set one phrase off from another. The line that is being ornamented in this case is, of course, the main melody of the chanson.

The beginning of another chanson by Sermisy appears in Ex. 16a[36] and, below it, the corresponding measures from settings by Neusidler in 1540[37] and 1549.[38] In the first, the upper voice is ornamented moderately, whereas in the second it is somewhat more florid. Both add repeated notes that accentuate the quarter beat in measures 1, 3, 5, and 6. The alto is lacking from the first, but the other adds it in measures 2–5. The voices overlap in the fourth and fifth bars of the chanson, but not in the arrangement in Ex. 16c. Measures 3 and 4 in Ex. 16c achieve a texture much like the later Deutscher Tanz, with the melody in the top voice and the three lower voices accompanying in chords. Neusidler himself, however, uses only three voices for his Tänze. Although the coloration in Exx. 15 and 16 occurs exclusively in the soprano, other chansons can include bits of ornamentation in any of the voices, as shown by Ex. 17.[39]

Other chansons of Sermisy, such as *Amy souffrez, Le content est riche, Le vray amy, Languir me fais,* and *Vous perdez temps,* also appear in the lute books of Neusidler and succeeding lute composers. It is perhaps significant to note that

30 *The Renaissance*

Ex. 16: *C'est a grant tort*, opening phrases.

(a) Sermisy, chanson (transposed down a whole step; *musica ficta* omitted), 1528.

(b) Hans Neusidler, *Cesta grand. Ein welscher Tantz,* 1540.

(c) Hans Neusidler, *Cest a grant*, 1549.

(a) Sermisy (continued).

(b) Neusidler 1540 (continued).

(c) Neusidler 1549 (continued).

Ex. 17: *En espérant*, first phrase.

(a) Sermisy, chanson (transposed down a whole step), 1536.

(b) Hans Neusidler, arrangement, 1544.

Ex. 18: The two phrases used in the monophonic chanson *Héllas, madame, que je désire tant*, c. 1500.

French intabulations for lute and keyboard of the same pieces produce somewhat different results. French lute intabulations published by Attaingnant in 1529 and 1530 also omit the alto voice. However, they add eighth-note movement (and occasionally sixteenth-notes) in any voice and even between the phrases. Thus, attention is not concentrated as firmly on the upper voice and the phrases are not as clearly articulated.[40] Attaingnant also published keyboard versions in three books appearing in 1531. These generally utilize all four voices and apply profuse ornamentation, first in one voice, then in another. Again, the line is kept moving between the phrases, resulting in an almost endless flow of figuration.[41]

The German composers thus tended to emphasize the top voice of a chanson through coloration, and the accentuation of four beats in a measure through note repetition. Most chansons, and most German intabulations as well, employ the twofold suspension formula (Ex. 4a) at the cadence, as was customary in vocal music of the time. Very few Sermisy chansons display the typical Tanz cadence of Exx. 3 and 5.[42] There were, however, a number of monophonic chansons, popular in the secular theater around 1500, that did include the Tanz cadence, as well as others that seem to represent a transition between the vocal and Tanz cadences.[43] In the Bayeaux manuscript (Paris, Bibliothèque Nationale, MS fonds fr. 9346), almost all of the chansons cadence from 2 to 1, like the tenor voice of a polyphonic composition. One, however, differs from the others in its use of the Tanz cadence that resolves from 7 to 1. Ex. 18 shows the two phrases which alternate in various ways to constitute the melody, which begins and ends with phrase (a).[44] The two cadences match Exx. 5a and c. The piece, with its cadences on G and B-flat and its regular four-bar phrases, reminds us once again of the *Printzentantz* (compare Ex. 18b with the first half of Ex. 1c, and Ex. 18a with the second half of Ex. 1c).

The other main source of monophonic chansons is MS fonds fr. 12744 in the Bibliothèque Nationale. Of its 143 melodies, twenty-five include one or more cadences that resolve from 7 to 1, thus being the sort of lines that could serve as the top voice of a polyphonic setting. Ex. 19 shows the different cadence structures that occur. Many exhibit the form of Ex. 19a, which appears related to the vocal cadence shown in Ex. 4a. The progression of pitches is the same, as well as the opening suspension. The anticipatory eighth-note on the second half of the first beat of the opening measure of Ex. 4a is missing in Ex. 19a, and the succeeding note has been replaced by two quarter-notes. Other melodies have cadences like Ex. 19b, in which two quarter-notes substitute also for the opening suspension. When the second degree of the scale appears on the opening beat of the penultimate measure in the Deutscher Tanz, it is not ordinarily (in the examples I have seen) preceded by 2 (see Ex. 5a). Ex. 19c, in which 3 or 7-1 precedes 2 on the first beat, does, however, occur in the Tanz (see Ex. 5a) and also in a few of the chansons. In addition, the chanson cadences include several examples of 5 and 7 on the first beat of the penulti-

Ex. 19: Cadences in monophonic chansons c. 1500.

(a)

(b)

(c)

(d)

(e)

mate measure (Exx. 19d and e), and these also occur in the Tanz (Exx. 5c and e).[45] Some of the monophonic chansons appear also in polyphonic settings, usually as a tenor, but occasionally after 1500 in the soprano. Some of the cadences of Ex. 19 therefore occur also in a few of these polyphonic pieces.[46]

It is thus tempting to perceive in the cadences of Ex. 19 a transition between the vocal cadence of Ex. 4a and the Tanz cadences in Ex. 5. Although I can find no direct link between these monophonic melodies and the composers of the Deutscher Tanz, it does seem remarkable to find the Tanz cadence in the chanson literature only a few decades before the Parisian chanson emerged. Although Sermisy seldom used this cadence himself, he did incorporate, as we have seen, some of the other important features that were found also in the Deutscher Tanz.

The Influence of Italian Dances

In addition to transcriptions of German Lieder and French chansons, the Tanz sources also include Italian dances. Spanish sources from the end of the 15th century provide the first evidence of certain chordal schemes that eventually become the main frameworks of composition in the Renaissance dance style of Italy and Spain. Although the principal schemes crystallize and become widespread only around the middle of the 16th century, some examples occur earlier. Neusidler's lute books of 1536, 1540, and 1544 include most of the main types. The scheme which becomes associated with the *romanesca* and which appeared first in some Attaingnant *gaillardes* from 1530, occurs in *Ein gütter Venecianer Tantz* from Neusidler's 1540 book.[47] Curiously, the earliest examples of the chordal schemes of the *passamezzo antico* and *moderno* occur in his books of 1536 and 1540, respectively.[48] The fourth chordal scheme, the one we have already encountered in Ex. 8 as the progression that matches the *Printzentantz*, appears in Neusidler's book of 1544 in a setting of the Italian piece *La cara cosa*.[49]

We have already seen how Tanz melodies, such as the *Printzentantz*, can be generated by a chordal scheme. In pieces based on the progressions, any of the voices of the chords can be activated melodically. The result is often much the same as the coloration we have already observed in the intabulations of vocal models. Neusidler's pieces on the schemes of the *romanesca* and *passamezzo* are in three voices, the two lower providing harmony while the upper one moves in rapid figuration with smaller note values.

The *passamezzo*, like the *pavana* which occurs even earlier, is usually paired with a *saltarello* on the same scheme. The idea of pairing a duple and triple dance extends far back in history. In the basse danse, such a pair would share the same succession of tenor notes. Early in the 16th century, however, the relationship between the dances of a pair becomes somewhat closer, so that gradually more of the melodic and harmonic substance of the duple dance recurs in the other. In Casteliono's lute book, published at Milan in 1536, the *pavana–saltarello* pairs correspond fairly closely, both in harmony and in the melody of the top voice.[50] Examples of the *Hoftanz* in Neusidler's book of the same year display some similarity in both melody and harmony between the main dance and its *Hupff auff* in some cases, but less in others.[51] However, the relationship between the paired dances becomes far closer in the Deutscher Tanz, which, in a sense, represents the final stage of a general trend that gradually brought the duple and triple dances closer together.

It is difficult, of course, to determine precisely the influence of the Italian dances, since early in the century composers in both countries were concurrently developing musical features that later appeared in the Deutscher Tanz. In any event, dances from Italy appeared, along with intabulations of vocal pieces from France and Germany, immediately before, as well as in the same sources that contained the earliest Tänze. Musical construction in the German Lied was based on the tenor part, in the French chanson on the upper voice, and in the Italian popular pieces on a chordal scheme, which involved, therefore, a special concern with the bass. Although quite different in approach, each of these three categories seems to display certain musical characteristics that became important, finally, in the Deutscher Tanz. The concept of an after-dance, as we have seen, developed earlier. The idea of repeated sections had occurred previously in Italian, French, and German dances, as well as in the French chanson and those German Lieder that were in Bar form. The technique of instrumental coloration, utilized often to produce a varied repetition of a section, had also existed before, especially in Italian dances. For new ideas, however, the German composers seemed to be attracted to the French chanson, with its melody on the top and its four accentuated beats per measure. Perhaps, at the same time, they felt a desire to derive the new dance from their own Germanic traditions, and hence manipulated the Lied in various ways, as we have seen, in order to emphasize the qualities of the chanson.

In any event, the Deutscher Tanz emerges around 1540 with its main constructive element a newly composed or borrowed melody in the upper voice – a melody that recurs in a Nachtanz and is itself divided into repeated sections, and a melody that through its cadences and repeated notes emphasizes four beats in a measure. At first the pieces were in three voices, the usual texture in earlier Italian, French, and German lute music, as well as in most of the arrangements of chansons and Lieder. Ex. 16c shows, however, an interest in the four-voice sound of the chanson, and by 1556 this new texture had become a standard feature of the Deutscher Tanz.

The Individual Titles

There were many different melodies associated with the Deutscher Tanz. The largest printed collection, in Waissel's book of 1591, includes forty. Heckel's book of 1556 and Ammerbach's of 1583 each contain twenty-three. Most of the printed sources have from six to sixteen examples. Many others exist in manuscripts. Some of the tunes, as we have already noted, become popular and recur in a number of different sources. I will describe the most important of these melodies in the following list, along with their sources. Since they also begin to appear around 1546 in France and the Low Countries, and around 1561 in Italy, it is not always possible to determine the country of origin. Some of the following titles, although occurring in German sources, may therefore actually appear earlier in some other country.[52]

Der Allmeyer Dantz
This title occurs in Ammerbach's book of 1571. The melody also appears as *Teutscher Dantz* in the book published by Jobin in 1573 (fol. F_3^r); as *Der Almoier Tantz* in D-KA, the manuscript bound with A678, fol. 7^r; as *Almoyer Tantz* in DK-Kk, Ms Thott 4°. 841 (lute book of Petrus Fabricius), fol. 97^r; and, according to Dieckmann (p. 86), as Der Almöier Tantz in a German lute manuscript at NL-Avnm. This melody, as far as I know, occurs only in German sources.

Der alten Weiber Tantz (Ex. 2e)
The melody first occurs as the second *Tantz* in Benedikt de Drusina's *Tabulatura* (Frankfurt/O., 1556) and is printed by Adalbert Quadt in *Lautenmusik aus der Renaissance*, Vol. II, p. 50. The title first appears in M. Neusidler's book of 1574 (see No. 7b). The melody is called *Almanda Imperiala* in Kargel's cittern book of 1575; *Der Imperial. Ein fürstlicher Hofdantz* in the *Zwey Bücher* of Bernhard Schmid (i) (Strassburg, 1577), printed in Merian, p. 107; *Ein Schlesier Dantz* in Ammerbach's 1583 tablature; and simply the 17th *Tantz* in Waissel's 1591 book. It appears as *Geissler Tanz* in the Berlin manuscript dated 1593 and printed in Merian, p. 205; and as *Des Hertzog Augusti Dantz* in A-Wn, MS 19259, fol. 4^r, which is printed in *DTÖ*, Jahrgang XVIII/2, Vol. 37, p. 119. The melody occurs later in both Flemish and Italian sources.

Der Betler Tantz (Ex. 2a)
This is one of the earliest melodies, appearing in H. Neusidler's book of 1540 (see No. 1a), as well as *Das erst Buch* of 1544. Heckel includes it in his 1562 *Lautten Buch* (first published in 1556). It is called *Ein gueter Danntz Der Petler* in D-Mbs, MS 1512, fol. 49^v, transcribed by Heinz Bischoff and Heinz Zirnbauer in *Lieder und Tänze auf die Lauten*, p. 18. The melody seems confined to German sources.

Gut Gesell du musst wandern (Ex. 2f)
This melody occurs only in Ammerbach's 1583 work (see No. 10b) and on fol. 19^r in the *Vierter Thail* of the Hainhofer MS at D-W cited for No. 12 in Volume II. Although not in many German sources, it does reappear later, as we will see, in Italy and The Netherlands.

Ich ging einmal spazieren (Ex. 2b)
The melody seems to originate as a traveller's song, given in the Dresdener Codex, M. 53 from around 1560 with two texts: the first a *geistliches Wegelied* beginning *Ich gieng einmal spazieren/ein Weglein, das war klein*, apparently a parody of an earlier secular hunting song; the second the chorale *Von Gott will ich nicht lassen*. See Ludwig Erk and Franz Böhme, *Deutscher Liederhort*, Vol. III (Leipzig, 1894), pp. 307 and 703–706; Moe, pp. 267–269; and

John Wendland, "'Madre non mi far Monaca', the Biography of a Renaissance Folksong," *Acta musicologica*, Vol. XLVIII (1976), pp. 185–204. The melody is entitled *Teutscher Dantz* in the book published by Jobin in 1573 (see No. 5a); *Tantz* in Waissel's 1573 tablature (fol. M$_2^r$); *Ich gieng ein mal spacieren* in M. Neusidler's 1574 book; and *Almande Ich ging ainmal spaciren* in Kargel's cittern tablature of 1578. Dieckmann mentions on p. 87 *Ein ander gütter Tantz Matth. Wais.*, which is a copy of Waissel's 1573 piece, in the manuscript at NL-Avnm; and on p. 91 *Ich gieng ein mal spatzieren* from the manuscript pages at the end of Wyssenbach's *Tabulaturbüch uff die Lutten* (Zurich, 1550). The text *Von Gott will ich nicht lassen* appears with the melody in Joachim Magdeburg, *Christliche und tröstliche Tischgesäng* (Erfurt, 1572) (printed by Wendland on p. 200 of the article cited above), and a *Tantz, Von Gott wil ich nicht lassen* and *Der Sprunngkh drauff* occur in August Nörmiger's manuscript *Tabulaturbuch* of 1598 (printed in Merian, p. 243). The melody recurs numerous times in French, Flemish, English, and Italian sources with the title *Almande Nonette, Almande Une jeune fillette, Alemana,* or *The Queenes Almain.*

Ich weiss mir ein schöne (stoltze) Müllerin

H. Neusidler transforms this melody, which originates apparently as the tenor voice of a Lied by Senfl (see Ex. 10), into a Tanz in 1540 (see No. 1b) and in *Das erst Buch* of 1544 and 1547. It recurs in Heckel's book of 1562 (1556) as *Wider ein schöner Tantz, Ich weysz mir ein schöne Müllerin*, and in Jobin's book of 1573 (fol. H$_1^v$) as *Dantz*. It is called *Die Milnerin* in A-Wn, MS 18688 (the lute book of Stephan Craus), printed in *DTÖ*, Jahrgang XVIII/2, Vol. 37, p. 98. Dieckmann (p. 86) also lists it in the manuscript at NL-Avnm. The melody is, as far as I know, the only well-known Tanz that derives from an identified Lied. However, I can find it only in German sources.

Der Magister Dantz (Ex. 2g)

This title is used only by Ammerbach in 1583 (see No. 10c). The melody occurs in Waissel's work of 1591 as the second *Tantz*. It is far more popular, however, in Flemish sources, where it appears as early as 1569, usually with the name *Almande Poussinghe*. It recurs also in Italy.

Man ledt uns zu der Hochzeit freud (Ex. 2d)

This melody is called simply *Dantz* or *Tantz* in Jobin's work of 1573 (fol. G$_1^v$) and in Waissel's book of the same year (fol. M$_1^v$). M. Neusidler in 1574 entitles it *Ein lieblicher und sehr güter Tantz* (see No. 7a), whereas Bernhard Schmid (i) uses the title in the heading above preceded by *Ein guter Dantz* (printed in Merian, p. 108). It is a *Tantz* in DK-Kk, MS Thott 4° 841 (fol. 77^v) and a *Deutscher Dantz* in the Hainhofer manuscript at D-W (*Vierter Thail*, fols. 20^v and 33^r). The melody becomes well known after 1574 in French and Flemish sources, where it is sometimes entitled *Almande de Don Frederico*.

Mein Hertz ist frisch, mein Gmüt ist frey

M. Neusidler employs this title in 1574, whereas Jobin calls the same melody merely *Dantz* in 1573 (fol. G$_3^v$). In DK-Kk, MS Thott 4° 841, *Main Hertz ist frisch* is on fol. 79^v. The same melody appears somewhat later in France as an Almande.

Der Printzen Tantz (Ex. 1)

The earliest German source of this melody seems to be Heckel's book of 1556 (see No. 3). According to Dieckmann, the title *Des* or *Der Printzen Tantz* or *Dantz* appears in CH-Bu, MS F.X.11, and in the manuscript pages at the end of Wyssenbach's *Tabulaturbüch uff die*

Lutten (Zurich, 1550), the latter version printed in Carl Parrish and John F. Ohl, *Masterpieces of Music Before 1750* (1951), pp. 76–77. Ammerbach calls the melody *Wer das Töchterlein haben wil* in 1571 (see No. 4). It is entitled *Heckerling und* (or *unnd*) *Haberstro* by Ammerbach in 1583; in DK-Kk, MS Thott 4° 841, fol. 76ᵛ; and in the manuscript listed by Dieckmann on p. 86 at NL-Avnm. In 1591 Waissel calls it simply *Tantz* (fol. D₂ᵛ). Kargel in 1578 has an *Almande du Prince*, the title that was most common in Flemish sources. The earliest source of the melody is Susato's collection of 1551. The tune spread all over Europe eventually, appearing also in England, France, and Italy.

Proficiat ir lieben Herren (Ex. 2h)

Jobin in 1573 entitles this melody *Dantz Proficiat*. Both M. Neusidler in 1574 and Ammerbach in 1583 (see No. 10d) use the full title. On p. 91 Dieckmann also lists *Proficiat* in a Berlin manuscript. The melody appears later, as we will see, in an Italian source.

Die schena Somer zeytt

This title appears only in the manuscript of Christoph Loeffelholz von Colberg (Merian, p. 184). Waissel calls the melody *Tantz* as well as *Almande damour* in 1573 (see No. 6). The latter title occurs in DK-Kk, MS Thott 4° 841, fol. 97ᵛ, and in the Dresden manuscript in Dieckmann, p. 95. The title *Almande d'amours* occurs in many Flemish sources, commencing in 1564. The melody thus may have been of Flemish origin.

Tantz (Ex. 2c)

There is a melody that occurs as *Tantz* in Jobin's book of 1573 (see No. 5b) and Waissel's work of 1591 (fol. D₃ᵛ), and as *Ein ander Teuttscher Tanntz* in August Nörmiger's manuscript of 1598 (Merian, p. 248). It had appeared in 1551, however, in Flemish sources, where it became popular under the name *Almande Bruynsmedelijn* (see Ex. 20a). J. P. N. Land, in *Tijdschrift der Vereeniging voor Noord-Nederlands Muziekgeschiedenis*, Vol. I (1884), p. 163, suggests that this title comes from the German words *braun's* (that is, *braunes*) *Mädelein*. He mentions the text *Mir ist ein fein brauns Medelein*, which, however, uses a different melody that was set as a dance by M. Neusidler in 1574 and Paix in 1583. A melody close to Ex. 20a does occur, however, with the title *Das Meidlein das ist hübsch und fein* in a German lute manuscript in the library of the Vereeniging (now at NL-At).

Ex. 20 shows some possible influences from vocal music. The top line gives the simple

Ex. 20: Possible influence of previous vocal pieces on the Tanz called *Almande Bruynsmedelijn* in Flemish sources.

(a) *Allemaigne* of Susato, 1551 (see plate XVI in Volume II).

(b) Tenor from Stephan Zirler's Lied *Ach Gretlein*, 1540 (transposed up a fifth).

(c) Middle section of Sermisy's chanson *Au joly boys*, 1529.

version of the melody printed by Susato in 1551. The striking similarity of the opening phrase to the middle section of Sermisy's *Au joly boys* (Ex. 20c) has been previously mentioned by John Ward.[53] I would like to suggest an even closer relationship to Stephan Zirler's German Lied in Ex. 20b.[54] First of all, the Lied, unlike most others, has two repeated sections like the Tanz. The first section is almost the same, ending with the typical Tanz cadence. In this case, the Lied opens with a dialogue, so that the opening section is first sung only by tenor and bass, then repeated by soprano and alto. Each time, the cadence appears in the highest sounding voice, and thus can move from 7 to 1. The second section opens with the repetition of a two-bar motive, and this is matched almost exactly in the Tanz. The final cadence of Ex. 20b ends, as in most Lied tenors, with 2 moving to 1. When the melody appears in the soprano of the Tanz, however, the cadence is changed to 7-1 and the last note of the eighth measure changed to 3 in order to approach the cadence in a manner parallel to the end of the first section. No titles link the Tanz with either a chanson or a Lied, but the similarities suggest some sort of influence. The Tanz melody appears also in Italy and England.

Wie möcht ich frölich werden

This title occurs with H. Neusidler in 1549 (see No. 2) and his son in 1574 (see No. 7c). Heckel in 1562 (1556) calls it *Graff Johan von Nassaw Dantz: Wie kan ich frölich werden*, Jobin in 1573 (fol. H_1^r) simply *Dantz*. It appears also in the Loeffelholtz manuscript (Merian, p. 180) and, according to Dieckmann (pp. 85 and 91), in the manuscripts at NL-Avnm and D-Bds. H. Neusidler's expression *Tantz weyss* suggests that the melody originally belonged to a song that required some adjustment before becoming a Tanz. It occurs later in Flemish sources as an Almande.

Der Zeuner Tantz

H. Neusidler includes this title in *Ein newes Lautenbüchlein*, 1540 (printed in *DTÖ*, Jahrgang XVIII/2, Vol. 37, p. 39), as well as in *Das erst Buch* of 1544 and 1547. It is in Heckel's book of 1562 (1556), in D-Mbs, MS 1512, fol. 45^v, and in the Lublin Tablature (MS 1716) at PL-Kp (*Czayner Thancz*), printed by John Reeves White in *CEKM* 6/V, p. 35. The melody seems to exist only in the earlier sources from Germany and Poland.

These, then, are the melodies that recur most often in the Deutscher Tanz. As one can see, some have complex histories and invite endless speculation concerning their origin. An entire book could (and, in some cases, no doubt will) be written on some of them. New ones joined the repertoire in the later keyboard sources. In 1577 Schmid has an *Alemando novelle. Ein guter neuer Dantz* and *Ein guter neuer Dantz. Du hast mich wöllen nemmen*, the latter hinting again at vocal origin. Jakob Paix, in *Ein schön nutz unnd gebreüchlich Orgel Tabulaturbuch* (Lauingen, 1583) includes eight dances called *Ein güter newer Teutscher Tantz* or, to make the novelty even clearer, *Ein güter gar newer Teutscher Tantz*. There were, however, enough recurring melodies, as well (as we have seen) as recurring musical traits, to give a strong sense of continuity to the development of the Deutscher Tanz from 1540 to the end of the century.

The Social Situation

Plate III shows the geography of central Europe as it existed, for the most part, during the 16th century. Gerardus Mercator (1512–1594) was the great cartographer of the century, and his world atlas, which was published posthumously in 1595, was revised and translated in many later editions. The national boundaries in Plate III are taken from the map of Europe by Jodocus Hondius in his edition of Mercator's *Atlas* published at Amsterdam in 1606.[55] France and Italy have approximately the same borders they do today. The Low Countries, however, constituted a single unit often called "the Netherlands", a name that referred then to most of the region we now call Belgium, Luxembourg, and the Netherlands. Occupying the large central portion of the map is Germany, known at the time as the Holy Roman Empire of the German Nation and labeled *Germania* on the Mercator maps. Its boundaries, however, were so vaguely defined that each map might display them differently. Hungary and Bohemia, for example, are not included in some maps, but sometimes the Netherlands are.[56] In addition, some modern maps also include within the Empire the conquered parts of northern Italy. For our purposes, however, the boundaries depicted in Plate III are more useful, for they match more nearly the distribution of languages, with the Italian-speaking areas in Italy and, with only a few exceptions, the German-speaking in Germany.

The Holy Roman emperor in 1540 was Charles V, who was also king of Spain and ruler of the Netherlands, Franche-Comté, Milan, Naples, Sicily, Sardinia, and Spanish America. He was continually in conflict with France to the west and with invading Turkish forces to the east. Since he himself lived mostly in Spain, he delegated authority in Germany to his brother Ferdinand, who was elected king of the Romans in 1531 and who succeeded Charles in 1558, finally, as emperor. It was Ferdinand who in 1536 issued from Vienna the privilege to Hans Neusidler to publish his first book of lute music.

The Holy Roman Empire, however, was a very loose confederation of a great number of diverse political units ruled by secular princes, religious authorities, or city councils. These various units contended with each other or with the imperial authority in matters of power and influence. In addition, the Reformation, begun with Luther's theses of 1517, left many parts of Germany in opposition to the Catholic emperor. Of all the political divisions, however, the sixty-five or so free imperial cities seem to have thrived most successfully, in terms of industry, the arts, and general quality of life.

Three of the largest of these relatively independent cities – Nuremberg, Strassburg, and Augsburg – seem to be the main location for the Deutscher Tanz. These southern cities were all important in commerce and trade. They had all become strong centers of Protestantism. Each was ruled by a council of patricians (that is, citizens from old and respected families).

Melchior Neusidler became a citizen of Augsburg and served a member of

Plate III: Central Europe in 1606.

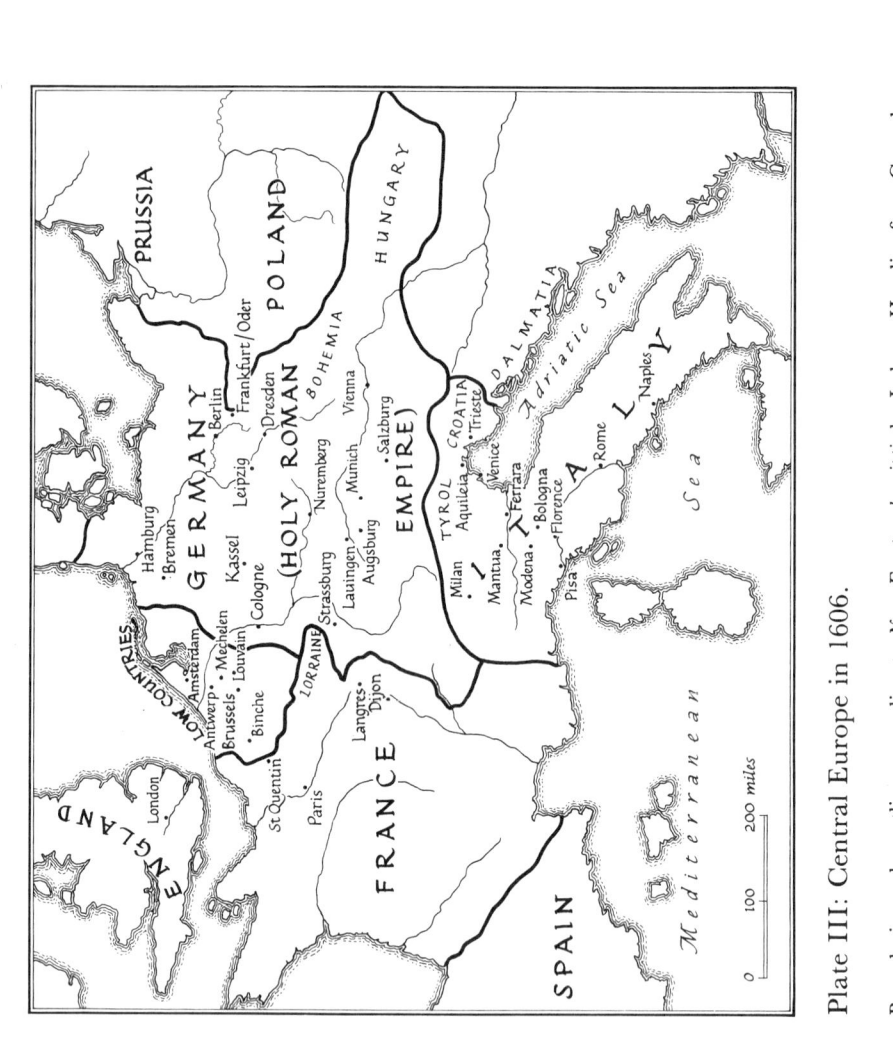

Boundaries and coastlines according to *Nova Europae descriptio* by Jodocus Hondius from Gerardus Mercator's *Atlas* (Amsterdam, 1606).

the wealthy Fugger family. Heckel was a citizen of Strassburg, the city where Jobin published the lute book of 1573 as well as later works of Schmid, Kargel, and Lais. Paix lived in the nearby city of Lauingen (halfway between Strassburg and Augsburg) and published there his keyboard tablature of 1583. For the early history of the Tanz, however, Nuremberg seems the most important city of them all. Hans Neusidler arrived in 1530, became a citizen, and published his tablatures here from 1536 to 1549. It was here also that Forster's collections of Lieder were published from 1539 to 1556. Nuremberg was a leading center, then, not only of music publishing, but also of instrument making and musical performance.

Next to the chambers where the city council met was a large and elegant hall, eighty feet in length, where receptions, dances, and weddings took place. This is where the patricians held their formal dances, and this, it seems to me, is where the Deutscher Tanz must have been introduced around 1540 and cultivated as the main social dance. There is a painting from the 16th century that depicts the patricians dancing in the Great Hall: couples seem to be making walking-steps, while music is provided by five wind players on a raised platform in the back.[57] Since there is no date on the painting, however, we cannot determine whether this is the Deutscher Tanz or the earlier *Hoftanz*. Unfortunately, I have been unable to find much accurate verbal or iconographic information on the choreography, instrumental accompaniment, or social circumstances of the Deutscher Tanz in Nuremberg. Considering that the City Council prescribed detailed regulations concerning every aspect of life, there is every probability that surviving city records do indeed contain information on these matters.[58]

Michel de Montaigne, the French essayist, visited a private home in Augsburg in 1580 and wrote that "we also saw the dance of these people: it was only *Alemandes*: they stop at the end of the room and [the men] take the ladies back to sit down on the benches which are on each side of the room . . . After having paused, they go and ask them to dance again."[59] This at least confirms the presence of the Deutscher Tanz and the fact that it occurred in the homes of prominent citizens. Many other questions, however, remain unanswered, for he makes no mention of choreographic movements, the number of people dancing at one time, or what instrument or group of instruments was playing. Surviving sources of the music, as we have seen, are only for a solo plucked-string instrument or for keyboard, and not for ensemble. One wonders if a single lute or harpsichord could provide a sound loud and percussive enough to guide a large group of dancers in a large ballroom. There is always the possibility that the dance itself was accompanied by ensemble, and that the tablatures represent purely instrumental pieces based on the same music. It would seem strange, under such circumstances, however, that no printed sources for ensemble exist, especially considering the thriving publishing business in Nuremberg and Strassburg.

A few sources come from cities further north. Ammerbach was organist at the Thomaskirche in Leipzig and published his 1571 book there. Drusina's lute book of 1556 and Waissel's tablature of 1573 appeared in Frankfurt an der Oder, not far from Leipzig. Nörmiger, who compiled the keyboard collection in 1598, lived in Dresden. In addition to Deutsche Tänze, his manuscript contains also pieces called *Erster, Ander, Dritter,* or *Vierder Mummerey* (masked) *Tantz*, and others entitled *Intrada* or *Aufftzugkh* (*Aufzug*, procession or parade). We will see these titles more frequently in sources from the next century, when there seems to be a closer relationship between the masked dance and the development we are tracing.

Fortunately, there is much more information about the dance when it moves to other countries. The Deutscher Tanz thus travels first to the north and west as the Almande, and then to the south as the Balletto Tedesco. We will turn our attention first to the Franco-Flemish Almande, whose history commences shortly after 1540.

2 THE ALMANDE FOR LUTE, GUITAR, CITTERN, AND INSTRUMENTAL ENSEMBLE IN FRANCE AND THE LOW COUNTRIES 1546–1603

THE NAME *Almande*, of course, reveals a link with something German. A number of German titles that we have already noted in passing suggest the equivalence of the two dances: the *Tantz. Almande damour* (No. 6) by Waissel in 1573; the *Almanda, Teutscher Tantz* (No. 8) of Kargel and Lais, 1575; and *Alemando novelle. Ein guter neuer Dantz* by Schmid in 1577. The latter two sources come from Strassburg, a city near the French border, where both names were no doubt well known. The Almande occurs, like the Tanz, for keyboard and for solo plucked-string instruments, although now the guitar joins the lute and the cittern. Unlike the Tanz, however, the Almande also appears frequently for instrumental ensemble. Many of the musical traits of the Tanz continue in the Almande, as we will see, and the melodies can be either new or borrowed from the Tanz. Nos. 34–49 in Volume II illustrate the evolution of the Almande in France and the Low Countries from 1546 to 1603. Sources come chiefly either from Paris, or from Antwerp and Louvain in the area we now call Belgium.

Concordances with the Deutscher Tanz

Seven of the individual melodies described in the last chapter recur now as Almandes, sometimes, as in the case of the *Almande Prince*, with the same title, more often with a new one. The first appearance of the melody of the *Printzentantz* occurs in an ensemble *Allemaigne* of Susato in 1551. The title *Almande Prince* or *Almande du Prince* becomes attached to the melody from 1564 on. Susato's eighth *Allemaigne* (Plate XVI),[1] as well as the ensemble example published by Phalèse and Bellère in 1571, uses the melody in the form shown in Ex. 1f. Comparing this version with the German ones above it, one can note important differences in two areas: in Ex. 1f the pitch rises in the second measure to a *d‴*, which allows the same approach to the typical cadence that occurs at the end of the second section (see c and d); and the opening two bars of the second section are now based on chords VII and i instead of III and VII and use the same melodic figure in sequence. The modifications thus all act to increase internal symmetry, and the anacrusis in the middle of the first section and in most of the measures of the second enhances the sense of forward momentum. Viaera's example for cittern in 1564 (No. 41), on the other hand, has an opening section more like Ex. 1a, but Vredeman in 1569 has an *Almande du Prince* that is more like Ex. 1f. Since Ex. 1f actually occurs historically before any of the other versions, one wonders if there might have been two different melodies that originated independently, but were sufficiently similar that they were finally united under a single title. The *Allemande* in the Thysius lute book from 1595–1601[2] has an opening section that does not move to d'', and the *Almande Prynce* in the Suzanne van Soldt keyboard manuscript from around 1570 follows Ex. 1f.[3] Earlier examples for cittern are reprinted by the firm of Phalèse and Bellère in 1570 and 1582. There is also an *Almande Prince* in Adriaenssen's *Pratum musicum* of 1584 that is based not on this melody but on the *Wilhelmus van Nassouwe*, the present-day national anthem of the Netherlands.[4]

The melody of *Ich ging einmal spazieren* (Ex. 2b) appears in Franco-Flemish sources as *Almande Nonette* or *Une jeune fillette*. Ex. 21 shows some of the variants that occur in the opening phrase. German sources seem to follow (a), with its ending on scale degree 5. Although usually harmonized by a i-chord, the 5 is

Ex. 21: The evolving opening phrase of *Almande Nonette*.

(a) Waissel, 1573: *Tantz* for lute.

(b) Kargel, 1578: *Almande. Ich ging ain mal spaciren* for cittern (Ex. 2b).

(c) Phalèse, 1568: *Almande Nonette* for lute (No. 42).

(d) Gorzanis, 1579: *Balo todesco* for lute (No. 75).

(e) *The Queenes Almayne*, c. 1583 for lute (No. 129, transposed).

(f) Besard, 1603: *Allemande Une jeune fillette* for lute (transposed).

replaced in (b) by 7, which would require V. Although some Flemish examples, such as the *Almande de la Nonette* in the van Soldt manuscript,[5] continue using (a), others modify the phrase by ending it on 1. Ex. 21c occurs in a lute example published by Phalèse in 1568 (No. 42). Further alteration then produces, as in Ex. 21f, the typical cadence, preceded on the last beat of the second bar by scale degree 5. This produces an almost exact parallelism with the end of the second section, as it occurs in Jobin's *Teutscher Dantz* (No. 5a) or Kargel's piece (Ex. 2b). Again, as in the *Almande Prince*, the changes that occur tend to emphasize the internal organization of the melody. The title *Almande (de) (la) Nonette* appears in Phalèse's lute book of 1568, in Phalèse (ii) and Bellère's books for lute (1574) and cittern (1582), in Adriaenssen's *Pratum musicum* (Antwerp, 1584) for lute, and in the Thysius lute book.[6] *Une jeune fillette* appears with the melody as the title of a song as early as 1576,[7] but not until Besard's *Thesaurus harmonicus* of 1603 is it linked with the Almande (see Ex. 21f). In Adriaen Valerius' *Neder-landtsche gedenck-clanck* of 1626, the melody is labeled *Almande Nonette, of: Une jeusne fillette*.[8] Curiously, there seems to be no setting of this melody for ensemble. After about 1603 the melody occurs only rarely in Franco-Flemish sources as a dance, although it continues to live until the 18th century as a song, a theme for variations, and an organ *noël*.[9]

Another popular Almande is *Bruynsmedelijn*, whose melody is in the *Tantz* of Ex. 2c and in the seventh ensemble *Allemaigne* from Susato's book of 1551 (see Ex. 20a and Plate XVI).[10] The latter is the earliest appearance of the melody, whereas the title starts to occur in 1565 as *Frisch Meechdelyng* in Jan Fruytiers' translation of *Ecclesiasticus*.[11] The title *Almande smeechdelijn* appears in Phalèse's book of 1568 for lute, and *Almande Smedelijn* in his ensemble book of 1571. The complete word *Bruynsmedelijn*, finally, is in Vredeman's book of 1569 and Phalèse and Bellère's book of 1570 for cittern, Phalèse (ii) and Bellère's ensemble collection of 1583, and the Thysius lute manuscript.[12] Suzanne van Soldt's keyboard manuscript contains *Almande Brun Smeedelyn*.[13]

The title *Almande damour* occurs, as we have seen, in a German source from 1573 (No. 6) for the melody elsewhere called *Die schena Somer zeytt*. Plate XVII shows a simpler version of the melody from Phalèse and Bellère's ensemble collection of 1571 (see Ex. 37a).[14] The spelling of the title varies only slightly: *Almande (de) amour*, *Almande damours*, or *Almande d'amour(s)*. It appears first in Viaera's cittern tablature of 1564, then in the cittern books of Vredeman (1568) and Phalèse (ii) and Bellère (1582), the ensemble collection of the same publishers from 1583, the lute books of Denss (1594) and Thysius,[15] and the keyboard manuscript of Suzanne van Soldt.[16]

The melody listed in the last chapter as *Man ledt uns zu der Hochzeit freud* (see Ex. 2d) recurs now as simply *Almande* or as *Almande de Don Frederico*. The former title is in the lute book of Phalèse in 1574, the Philidor collection for ensemble, with the date 1582,[17] the Thysius lute manuscript,[18] and Besard's 1603 book.[19]

The title *Almande de Don Frederico* seems to appear first in the cittern collection of Phalèse (ii) and Bellère in 1582. It occurs in their ensemble book the following year (Plate XVIII),[20] and in Adriaenssen's *Pratum musicum* (1584)[21] and Joachim van de Hove's *Florida* (Utrecht, 1601)[22] for lute.

The melody in Ex. 2g appears in sources from the Low Countries as *Almande* or *Almande Poussinghe*. In Vredeman's cittern book of 1569 and Adriaenssen's lute book of 1584 it is merely *Almande*. The title *Almande Poussinghe*, however, appears in Phalèse and Bellère's cittern collection of 1570, and in Phalèse (ii) and Bellère's lute book of 1574 (transcribed as No. 46), cittern book of 1582, and ensemble collection of 1583.[23] The melody called *Wie möcht ich frölich werden* in German sources (Nos. 2 and 7c) appears in Adriaenssen's *Pratum musicum* of 1584[24] and his book of 1592 (see No. 47) as *Almande*. The tune of *Gut Gesell du musst wandern* (Ex. 2f and No. 10b) occurs as *Almande Regine Sweden* in the Thysius lute book.[25] *Mein Hertz ist frisch* reappears in the Philidor collection as *Allemande faite l'an 1583*.[26] *Der alten Weiber Tantz* (Ex. 2e) recurs in the lute book of Denss in 1594 as *Allemande Imperial*, a title we have noted also in German sources.[27]

Thus, many melodies exist as both a Deutscher Tanz and an Almande. It is difficult to determine in each case the country of origin. No doubt melodies were borrowed in both directions. In addition to these, however, there are other melodies with French titles that do not appear in German Tanz sources and thus seem to be more clearly of French or Flemish origin.

Melodies without Tanz Concordances

By far the most important of these melodies is the one eventually called *Almande Loraine*, named, no doubt, after the region in France. Examples occur in at least sixteen sources from France and the Low Countries between 1551 and 1583. Sources from both Italy (Mainerio, 1578) and Germany (Paix in 1583)[28] call it *Ballo francese*. Ex. 22 shows the melody from the earliest ensemble example of Gervaise[29] and a later version from 1571 (Plate XVII).[30] Again, as in the case of *Nonette* and *Prince*, adjustments are made to enhance melodic symmetry. In the later one, the ninth and tenth measures match the first two, thus creating a sort of rounded binary form. In addition, the middle section of the earlier dance, along with its repetition, has been incorporated into the second (and last) section of the later one. The earliest example, the *Almande* in Adrian Le Roy's lute book of 1551,[31] however, also has the sections disposed as in Ex. 22b. In Le Roy's guitar collection of the following year, the same melody is called *Almande tournée* (see No. 37b). It is entitled simply *Allemande* in Morlaye's *Second livre* for guitar in 1553, and *Almande* in Phalèse's lute tablature of 1563[32] and Le Roy's *Second livre* for cittern of 1564.[33] The first source to use the title *Almande Loreyne* is Vredeman's cittern book of 1569. This title then

Ex. 22: Evolution of the *Almande Loraine*.

(a) Gervaise, 1557: *Almande* for ensemble.

(b) Phalèse & Bellère, 1571: *Almande Lorayne* for ensemble (Plate XVII).

(a) Gervaise (continued).

(b) Phalèse & Bellère (continued).

occurs in all subsequent examples: publications of the Phalèse firm for guitar (1570), cittern (1570 and 1582), and ensemble (1571 and 1583), the Thysius lute book,[34] and the Suzanne van Soldt keyboard manuscript.[35] We will also meet the melody later in Italy and England.

Although the *Almande Loraine* far exceeds all others in frequency, a number of other titles also recur in different sources. The melody of the *Almande Guerre, guerre gay* is given in Ex. 23a.[36] It first appears in Vredeman's cittern book of 1569 (see No. 43a). The melody occurs as *Almande Guerre, guerre* in cittern books from the Phalèse press in 1570[37] and 1582. It also exists, as we will see later, in an English source.

Ex. 23b shows the melody of *Almande Spiers*. Vredeman has the earliest example for cittern in 1569. The same piece, according to Brown, occurs as *Almande de Philippine* in Phalèse and Bellère's cittern book of 1570. The *Almande de Spiers* in Phalèse's lute books of 1568 and 1574, however, share a different melody, and the *Almande Spiers* in the Thysius manuscript[38] is different from both of them. The *Almande (de) Bisarde*, which has the melody in Ex. 23c, appears first in Vredeman's cittern book of 1569 (see No. 43b). It is also in the Phalèse cittern collections of 1570 and 1582 and Adriaenssen's lute book of 1584. *Almande (de) Court* has the melody in Ex. 23d in Adriaenssen's lute books of 1584 and 1592, as well as in the Thysius lute book.[39] Viaera's *Almande du Court* of 1564, however, has a different melody. *Allemande* or *Almande Monsieur* appears in the Thysius manuscript (Ex. 40a), in Van den Hove's *Florida* (Utrecht, 1601),[40] and in Valerius' *Neder-landtsche gedenck-clanck*.[41] The *Almande Fortune hélas pourquoy* is in Phalèse (ii) and Bellère's ensemble book of

48   *The Renaissance*

Ex. 23: Other Almande melodies without Tanz concordances (varied repeats omitted).

(a) Valerius, 1626: *Almande Guerre, guerre gay* (see No. 43a).

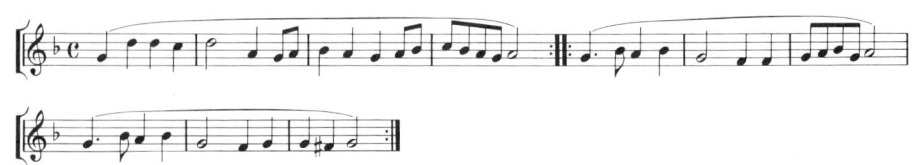

(b) Phalèse (ii) & Bellère, 1583: *Almande Spiers* for ensemble.

(c) Phalèse (ii) & Bellère, 1583: *Almande Bisarde* for ensemble (see No. 43b).

(d) Adriaenssen, 1592: *Almande de Court* for lute.

(e) Phalèse (ii) & Bellère, 1583: *Almande Fortune hélas pourquoy* for ensemble.

1583 (see Ex. 23e),[42] with lute settings in Adriaenssen's *Pratum musicum* of 1584, Nicolas Vallet's *Secretum musarum* (Amsterdam, 1615),[43] and the Thysius lute book.[44]

Other titles occur less often or only a single time. Some sound like the opening words of a French text: the Almandes *La mon amy la* (No. 36), *Le pied de cheval* (No. 37a), and *Noseroit on dire*. A few, such as *Almande Slaepan gaen*, suggest a Flemish text. One, the *Allemande Ich dancke Gott*, is unusual both for being German and for being religious. Many refer to geographical locations, such as Almandes *d'Anvers, de Spaigne, de Liège, de Worms, Brusselles, Coloigne*, and *France*.

Still other titles are *Les Bouffons, Brunette, De deux dames, Deux trois aes*, and *Jolie*. Many of the titles accompanied new melodies, and these joined the more popular tunes, described above, to constitute the rather sizeable musical repertoire of the Renaissance Almande.

The Musical Traits

Most of the characteristic features of the Deutscher Tanz continue in the Franco-Flemish Almande. The melody is almost always the top voice in a simple homophonic texture. There are usually four voices, except in the guitar settings, which alternate mostly between two, three, and occasionally four voices (see Nos. 36–38 and 44), and an occasional lute piece *a 3* (No. 34b). Most Almandes have two sections, although some have three (see Nos. 37a and 45) and even four. On rare occasions, a melody may, as we saw in Ex. 22 with the *Almande Loraine*, have two sections in one source, three in another. *Wie möcht ich frölich werden*, which had two sections in the German sources (Nos. 2 and 7c), changes to four sections in Adriaenssen's *Almande* in No. 47. Phrases are usually four bars in length, but may sometimes be shortened to three (the first section of No. 38b) or extended to six, usually by repeating measures (see the final sections of Nos. 38a, 38b, 45, and 48). Most often the opening section contains one or two four-measure phrases.

Repetition of a section is sometimes marked simply with a repeat sign (No. 43); at other times it is written out almost exactly or with coloration added (No. 35). In Le Roy's guitar setting of the melody of *Almande Loraine* in No. 37b, only the opening section is repeated with diminution, but then the entire piece recurs *plus diminuée*, with more elaborate coloration. Adriaenssen does much the same thing in No. 47. The technique of coloration is ordinarily applied rather moderately in the Almande, amounting at most to an occasional stream of eighth-notes (see Nos. 35 and 42). The typical cadence is sometimes present, as at the end of Ex. 23c, although it sometimes appears shifted a half-measure (see the end of Exx. 23a and b) so that the final note falls in the middle of a measure. In No. 46 it appears in the third measure, when the melody seems to disappear into the tenor voice, and again at the end of the first statement of the second section. Cadences also often end with repeated notes in one or more voices (see Exx. 22 and 23c, and No. 39a).[45]

In all these matters the Almande follows fairly closely, for the most part, the style of the typical Deutscher Tanz. It differs, however, in three ways: in the instruments used to perform it, in the frequent lack of a triple after-dance, and in a special concern with melodic organization. Printed keyboard sources, such as those in Germany, are lacking for the Almande. The manuscript of Suzanne van Soldt is, as far as I know, the only source for keyboard. Ensemble examples, on the other hand, which were not present in Tanz sources, are now, as we have seen, fairly numerous. They appear in collections from both the

Low Countries and France: Susato (1551) in Antwerp, the publishing house of Phalèse (1571 and 1583) in Louvain and Antwerp, Gervaise (1557) and d'Estrée (1559) in Paris. In addition, ensemble Almandes also appear, as we have noted, in the Philidor collection. Susato indicates on the title page that the pieces are to be played "op alle musicale Instrumenten." The works of Phalèse and Bellère in 1571 are "convenable sur tous Instrumens Musicalz." Jean d'Estrée states that his works are "appropriés tant à la voix humaine, que pour jouer sur tous instruments musicalz." Likewise, the music of the 1583 Phalèse collection is "accommodées aussi bien à la Voix, comme à tous Instrumens Musicaux." No specific instruments are named, however, and I presume that instrumental performance was preferred to accompany dancing.

Since many of the ensemble Almandes are already available in modern editions,[46] I have transcribed only two in Volume II. The first (No. 45) shows how simple and chordal the ensemble versions usually were – much like the Ammerbach keyboard Tänze in No. 4, 10c, or 10d. The other is a similar work from d'Estrée's collection (No. 39a). Although the partbooks for only the outer two voices are still in existence, one can easily imagine, I think, the complete sound of such a setting. These simple Almandes, in which all four voices move in essentially the same rhythm, tend to emphasize some of the rhythmic qualities of the dance: the accentuation of four beats in a measure (note especially measures 1 and 5 of No. 39a), and the percussive quality of the repeated chords at the ends of phrases (the conclusion of each section in No. 39a).

I have included also in Volume II three plates that show the top voice of a number of ensemble Almandes. Plate XVI shows Susato's versions of Almandes *Bruynsmedelijn* and *Prince*: the first (*VII. Allemaigne*) appears on the top line with signs to indicate sectional repetition; in the other (*VIII. Allemaigne*), on the second and third lines, the repeats are written out, but without any alterations.[47] Repetition in the Almandes *Lorayne* and *d'amours* in Plate XVII is indicated by sign, except for the middle section of the first, which again is written with no changes. Plate XVIII, however, shows that coloration can, on occasion, be applied to ensemble music in the same way we have observed it in the works for solo plucked strings. Here the *Almande Don Frederico*,[48] as in the Tanz of No. 7a, has four sections, each immediately repeated with ornamentation. The repetition of the opening section starts in the middle of the first line on Plate XVIII. The coloration consists mostly of eighth-note movement, as it did in the lute examples such as No. 42, but occasionally sixteenth-notes appear in a trill-like figure that replaces the typical cadence at the ends of the second and third sections.

Throughout its entire history, the Deutscher Tanz was almost invariably coupled with a Nachtanz in which the musical material, as we have seen, was transformed into triple meter. It is significant that the only example of a Tanz in Volume II that does not possess a Nachtanz has a French title: the *Tantz. Almande damour* of Waissel in 1573 (No. 6). Some Almandes have an afterdance, usually called *reprinse* or sometimes *recoupe*, while others, often in the same collection, do not. In addition, d'Estrée, in his third book of 1559 and fourth book of 1564 (and from the latter source reprinted by Phalèse and Bellère in 1571), has several separate pieces in triple meter entitled *Allemande courante*. The two earliest Almandes (Nos. 34a and 34b), however, have untitled *reprinses*.[49] Examples with and without a *reprinse* coexist in most sources throughout the century, but the triple dances gradually diminish in number and have completely disappeared by the time of Besard's anthology in 1603.

The titles that almost always have a *reprinse* are the most popular of those that have concordances with the Tanz: the Almandes *Prince*, *Bruynsmedelijn*, and *Poussinghe*. Plate XVI shows a *recoupe* to the melody of the *Prince* and, following this, another version in which the discant of the first *recoupe* appears in the tenor. The *reprinse* in Viaera's *Almande du Prince* (No. 41), however, follows the melody of the duple dance more exactly. In Suzanne van Soldt's keyboard manuscript a similarity of words is recognized in the spelling of the titles *Almande prynce* and *Reprynse de prynse*.[50] Phalèse and Bellère's ensemble book of 1571 is one of the few sources in which the Almandes *Prince* and *Bruynsmedelijn* do not have *reprinses*. The latter is also without a *reprinse* on the top line of Plate XVI. *Almande Nonette* sometimes has a *reprinse* (as in No. 42), sometimes does not. Most of the other well-known titles usually do not. Only in Phalèse (ii) and Bellère's ensemble collection of 1583 do I find a triple dance for the *Almande Loraine*, and in this case it is called *Saltarello*, since it has been reprinted (as we will note later) from an Italian source. Similarly, *Almande Bisarde* seems to possess a *reprinse* only in Adriaenssen's book of 1584.

In the *reprinse*, as in the Nachtanz, the melody of the duple dance is transformed by the two methods shown in Ex. 9. Method 1 appears in Nos. 41 and 42, Method 2 in Nos. 34a and b. The notation of Susato's example in Plate XVI follows Ex. 9a, where there are four minims in a duple measure and three in triple (the note values are halved in Ex. 9, so that here each quarter-note represents a transcribed minim). More common in Almandes, however, is the plan of Ex. 9b, with the minim as the basic beat in the duple dance and the semibreve in the triple, or, increasingly in later sources, a diminished version of Ex. 9b in which the duple and triple beats are semiminim and minim respectively (exactly the values used in Ex. 9b). We have already noted this diminished version occasionally in German sources. In my transcriptions in Volume II, I have left the original values for the duple dances, but halved them in the triple. About half the ensemble examples in Phalèse and Bellère's 1583 book use the notation in Ex. 9b; the other half, the diminished values. Rather than indicating any distinction of tempo, this may represent only the transition of the basic pulse from the minim to the semiminim which occurred in the notation in general during the late 16th and early 17th centuries. For the *Almande du Prince* in No. 41, Viaera uses a rare type of notation in which there are four minims in a duple measure followed by three semiminims in a triple – just the reverse of the diminished version of Ex. 9b described above.

The third way in which the Almande seems to differ conspicuously from the Deutscher Tanz is its greater interest in repeating brief portions of melody to create an internal design of parallel phrases or other patterns of symmetry. We have already seen this attitude at work in connection with the Almandes *Prince* (Ex. 1f), *Nonette* (Ex. 21), and *Loraine* (Ex. 22). A good example of this constructive method is the Almande of d'Estrée in No. 39a, where each section consists of two parallel phrases that begin alike and where, in addition, corresponding phrases in each section end the same. Thus, measures 1-2 = 5-6, 9-10 = 13-14; the melody of 3-4 = 11-12; and measures 7 (last half) and 8 = 15-16. Other examples display a similar figure at the beginning of each section (No. 34a), melodic sequence (second section of Ex. 23c), or the repetition of entire phrases (see No. 37a, where the second phrase reappears in the second section, and No. 40, in which measures 5-8 recur twice at the end of section 2).

When the Deutscher Tanz moved to France and the Low Countries, then, it retained a sufficient number of the melodies and enough of the musical characteristics to maintain its identity. At the same time, however, some new traits appear that often give the Almande a special flavor. Interest in melodic organization may have simply been a manifestation of the same constructive approach seen also in the Parisian chanson. The numerous examples for ensemble and the frequent lack of a *reprinse* may, on the other hand, have been a response to social conditions or dance choreography.

The Social Background

The musical development of the Almande reflects the cultural unity between France and the Low Countries. Flemish sources for plucked strings utilize French tablature. As we have seen, many of the titles of pieces are in French. Eventually, the titles of books also include this language. The title page of Susato's book of 1551, published in Antwerp, is in Flemish. The instrumental books from the publishing firm of Phalèse before 1571 use Latin, the ensemble books of 1571 and 1583 both Latin and French.

Before 1477, the Netherlands (that is, the Low Countries) and a portion of France around Dijon were both a part of Burgundy. In that year, however, the Burgundian Netherlands came under the rule of the Habsburgs, and the southern portion became part of France. Charles V inherited the Netherlands in 1506 and was raised in Mechelen (southeast of Antwerp) at the court of his aunt, Margaret of Austria, who was regent from 1506 to 1530. When he came of age in 1515, Charles moved his court to Brussels. In 1516 he became king of

Spain and in 1519 emperor of the Holy Roman Empire. He had moved to Spain in 1517, where his son Philip was born and raised. Mary of Hungary, sister of Charles, succeeded Margaret as regent of the Netherlands, with her court mainly at Brussels.

Thus in the 1540's, when our story begins, the Netherlands, with strong historic connections with France, its arts, and its language, was politically under the rule of Mary of Hungary, regent for the Holy Roman emperor and the king of Spain. By this time Charles had moved to Spain and was preparing his son Philip to take over the Netherlands. For this purpose he planned a trip for the prince to Italy, Germany, and the Netherlands during the years 1548 to 1550, so that he and his future subjects could become acquainted. He also sent along Juan Calvete de Estrella, who recorded everything that happened in *El felicisimo viaje del muy alto y muy poderoso Príncipe Don Felipe*, published in Antwerp in 1552.[51] Three references to the Almande appear in this account, because Philip, fortunately for us, was fond of dancing. In August of 1549 Mary of Hungary arranged elaborate festivities to celebrate the visit of Charles and his son to the city of Binche, near Mons. Calvete describes a scene in which six couples, wearing masks of old persons, enter "all in good order and dancing a *dança alemana* with so much precision and rhythm that it was a beautiful thing to see."[52] On Mardi Gras in the following year, Prince Philip gave a masked entertainment at Brussels, in which "gods and nymphs entered with the instrumentalists, dancing an *alemana*."[53] At another occasion, twenty masked men "entered with the instrumentalists, dancing an *alemana*, with white wax torches lit in their hands. In this way they made a turn through the room dancing; then, leaving the torches behind, they all danced with the ladies."[54] At the time of Philip's visit to the Netherlands, the Almande, as we have seen, had already appeared in several lute publications from Louvain (Nos. 34 and 35 from 1546 and 1549).

In 1555 Philip became ruler of the Netherlands, and in the following year king of Spain. In the meantime Almandes by Le Roy and Susato for guitar and ensemble came from Paris and Antwerp (Nos. 36 and 38 from 1551 and 1552), and Rabelais (d. 1553) had included *L'alemande* in a list of chansons and dances performed after a royal banquet in the fifth book of his series on Gargantua and Pantagruel.[55] Philip, who continued his father's struggle against the French, won a great victory in 1557 at St. Quentin (north and a little east of Paris). This was the year Gervaise's Almandes appeared in Paris. In 1559, the year of d'Estrée's ensemble Almandes from Paris (No. 39a), Philip returned to Spain and married Elizabeth of Valois, daughter of the French king Henry II, thus winning a period of peace with that country. The following year, the wedding was celebrated in Guadalajara (near Madrid) and, again, the *alemana* is mentioned in the accounts: "Don Diego de Córdoba began the dancing and took Doña Ana Fajardo; they danced a *pavana* and an *alta*, and after this the duke appeared and danced an *alemana* with Doña Isabel

Manrique; afterwards the Duke of Infantazgo appeared and danced another [*alemana*] with Madame de Monpensier, and behind them all the Spanish and French ladies came to dance an *alemana* [four couples are named]."[56]

Philip remained in Spain for the rest of his life. Enrique de Cock, in his *Viaje de Felipe II á Zaragoza, Barcelona y Valencia* of 1585, describes the Duke of Savoia and the Prince of Spain (presumably the future Philip III, the son of Philip II) dancing an *alemana*, the prince with his sister and the duke with his wife.[57] In the meantime, the Netherlands was ruled by a Spanish governor in Brussels. Feeling gradually grew in the Netherlands against the Spanish rule, and around 1562 the struggle began that ended only in 1648 with complete independence of the northern Protestant provinces (the area we call the Netherlands today). In 1563, the year of the lute Almande in No. 40, a cardinal who wanted to introduce the Spanish inquisition to the Netherlands was expelled. The harsh tactics of the Duke of Alba, who became the Spanish governor in 1576, finally crystallized the opposition of the northern provinces under the leadership of William the Silent (William of Orange). He expelled the Spanish from the north in 1572–74, and united all of the Netherlands in 1576. Alessandro Farnese, Prince of Parma, became Spanish governor in 1578 and recaptured the southern provinces. The following year the northern provinces formed the Union of Utrecht and in 1581 declared their independence. The map from Amsterdam on which Plate III is based made a silent protest in 1606 by omitting the large city of Brussels, which was the seat of Spanish power in the Netherlands. In 1609 a twelve-year truce occurred, although fighting resumed later. The Peace of Westphalia in 1648, at the conclusion of the Thirty Years War in Germany, recognized finally the independence of the north, while the southern provinces remained in Spanish hands and were reconverted to Catholicism.

During all these turbulent years from around 1563 to the end of the century, however, Almandes continued to appear and social life apparently managed somehow to endure. All of the Almandes in Volume II from No. 40 in 1563 through No. 47 in 1592, as well as those on Plates XVII and XVIII from 1571 and 1583, come from the publishing house of Phalèse. The earlier works of Pierre Phalèse (i) come from Louvain (just east of Brussels). After Jean Bellère joined him in 1570, title pages include both Louvain and Antwerp. Later works, after Pierre Phalèse (ii) replaced his father in the partnership sometime between 1574 and 1576, come from Antwerp. Yet in 1576 Antwerp was sacked and six thousand people killed by the Spanish troops, and in 1584–85, after a siege of fourteen months, it was captured by the Spanish forces under Farnese. Although the Phalèse firm survived until 1592, the terrible violence in the Netherlands at this time may explain why the later works of Denss (No. 48) and Besard (No. 49) were published in Cologne.

The strange coexistence of violent struggle and continuing social and artistic life is illustrated by Valerius' *Neder-landtsche gedenck-clanck*, mentioned already in passing. This work is a prose history of events in the Netherlands up to 1625, interspersed with the texts of songs, each to be sung to a popular tune. The melodies are given in mensural notation, as well as in settings for lute and cittern. There are seven Almandes, including *Kits, Pekelharing, Mary Hofmans*, and *Monsieur*. The *Almande Guerre, guerre gay*, which we have encountered above (Ex. 23a), accompanies a text that describes the lifting of the siege of Leiden in 1574. The *Almande Prins de Parma*, which is also in the Thysius manuscript,[58] occurs with a song that deals with events in 1579, shortly after Alessandro Farnese, the Prince of Parma, became Spanish governor. Similarly, events in 1600 are involved in a text sung to the *Almande Nonette* or *Une jeusne fillette*.[59]

Thus the very period that produced the flowering of the Renaissance Almande in France and the Low Countries was, at the same time, filled with great upheavals in human affairs.

The Choreography

Although most of the music for the Almande comes, after 1563, from the southern provinces of the Netherlands, information on its choreography comes to us from France. In Langres (north of Dijon on the map in Plate III), Thoinot Arbeau published in 1588 his dance manual called *Orchésographie*. He describes the Almande as follows:

The *Allemande* is a dance filled with a certain gravity, familiar to the Germans, and I believe that it is one of our most ancient ones, because we descend from the Germans. You will be able to dance it in company: for having a young lady in hand, several others will be able to stand behind you, each holding his partner. You will dance all together, walking forward and, when one wishes, backwards, in duple meter, three steps and one *grève* or *pied en l'air* without leap, and in some places by one step and one *grève* or *pied en l'air*. And when you have gone to the end of the room, you will be able to dance while turning, without letting your lady go. The other dancers, who will follow you, will do the same when they reach the end of the room. And when the instrumentalists finish this first part, each man will stop and engage in light conversation with the lady, and everyone will start again as before for the second part. And when the third part comes, you will dance it in the same duple meter, but lighter and more lively and with the same steps, adding some little springs as in the *courante*. This you will understand easily by the notation, which is almost unnecessary, because there is very little variety of movement. Nevertheless, so that you can see the whole idea more clearly, I will not spare myself the effort of giving it to you in writing.[60]

On the two pages shown in Plate IV, Arbeau explains how the steps match the music. I give the melody again in Ex. 24, with each of its three parts on a single line and with dance steps below the proper notes. The abbreviations are as follows: *s* is a walking step, usually forward, but sometimes, as Arbeau says above, backwards; *G* is a *grève*; *l* refers to the left and *r* to the right for either movement. The *grève* or *coup de pied*, which is also used in the *gaillarde*, occurs when the dancer raises one foot in the air in front of him "as though he wanted

ORCHESOGRAPHIE

Air de l'Allemande pour Mouvements qu'il fault
la premiere & seconde faire pour dancer l'Al-
partie. lemande.

Pas du gaulche.
Pas du droit.
Pas du gaulche.
Greue droicte.

Pas du droit.
Pas du gaulche.

Pas du droit.
Greue gaulche.
Pas du gaulche.
Pas du droit.
Pas du gaulche.
Greue droicte.
Pas du droit.

Pas du gaulche.
Pas du droit.
Greue gaulche.
Pas du gaulche.
Greue droicte.

Pas du droit.

Greue gaulche.
Voyez en ces deux dernieres mesures, qu'il n'y
a qu'vn pas & vne greue en chacune, parceque
l'air le requiert ainsi.

DE THOINOT ARBEAV.

Continuation de l'air.   Continuation des mouvements
de l'Allemande.

Pas du gaulche.
Pas du droit.
Pas du gaulche.
greue droicte.
Pas du droit.

Pas du gaulche.
Pas du droit.
Greue gaulche.

Tabulature de la troisieme partie de l'Allemande, qui se dance par mesure
binaire, comme la courante, avec les mouvements.

Pas du gaulche.

Pas du droit.

Pas du gaulche.

Greue droicte.
Reuers.
Pas du droit.

Pas du gaulche.

Pas du droit.

Greue gaulche.
Et ainsi continuant, s'en repetant le commencement.

Plate IV: Choreography of the Allemande.

Thoinot Arbeau, *Orchésographie* (Langres, 1589), fols. 67ᵛ and 68ʳ (reproduced by permission of the Huntington Library, San Marino, California)

Ex. 24: Arbeau's choreography and melody for the Almande (s = a walking step, G = *grève* or foot in the air, * = a little spring, *l* = left, and *r* = right).

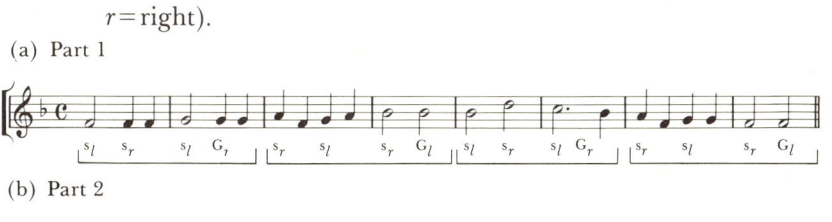

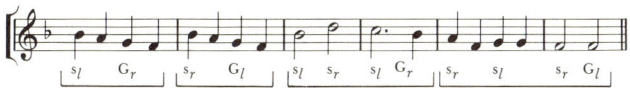

(a) Part 1

[musical notation with annotations: s_l s_r s_l G_r | s_r s_l s_r G_l | s_l s_r s_l G_r | s_r s_l s_r G_l]

(b) Part 2

[musical notation with annotations: s_l G_r | s_r G_l | s_l s_r s_l G_r | s_r s_l s_r G_l]

(c) Part 3

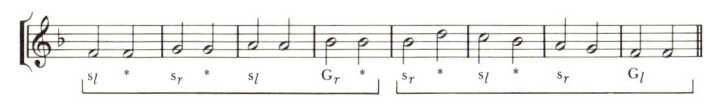

[musical notation with annotations: s_l * s_r * s_l * G_r * | s_r * s_l * s_r * G_l]

to kick someone."[61] A *pied en l'air* is made when the foot is raised only slightly off the ground, but in the *grève* the foot should be lifted boldly and very high.[62] Arbeau gives an illustration (Plate V) of a man executing a *grève* with the right foot and one with the left. The basic sequence of steps, which I have bracketed in Ex. 24a, thus includes three walking steps followed, without any further forward movement, by raising the foot as in Plate V. This unit occupies two measures of music, with two dance movements per measure.

In the first two bars of the second part (Ex. 24b), the pattern is changed to a one-measure unit consisting of one walking step and a *grève*. Arbeau explains that this is done because the melody, which also repeats a one-bar unit, requires it (see the bottom of fol. 67ᵛ in Plate IV). The last four bars of the second part have the same choreography as the last four in the first part. Part 3, with a simplified version of the melody of the opening part, is "lighter and livelier" because "the white minims which are empty here take the place of rests and pauses or of little springs as described for the *courante*."[63] I have placed an asterisk in Ex. 24c below those minims in the first, second, and fourth bars on which one could make a lilt, or a spring, or even a hop on the way to the next walking step. It does not seem graceful to me, however, to include such a spring in the third bar, which leads to the *grève* in the fourth. The measures preceding the *grèves* are perhaps the places where the "rests and pauses" are appropriate. The bracketed sequence of movements is otherwise the same as in Ex. 24a, but augmented in time to fill eight bars instead of four.

The basic Almande pattern thus seems to be the two-bar unit of Ex. 24a, which can be abbreviated (as in Ex. 24b) when a shorter melodic phrase recurs, or augmented (as in Ex. 24c) to accommodate the springing motion.[64] Of the few Almandes in Volume II that have three sections, the *Almande le Pied*

ORCHESOGRAPHIE

elles monstrent à nud les genoulx, si elles ne mettent la main à leurs habits pour y obuier.

Capriol.

Ceste mode ne me semble belle ny honneste, si ce n'est pour dancer auec quelque bonne galoise de chambeliere.

Arbeau.

Ie ne laisseray de vous donner cy aprez la tabulature pour la dancer : Ce pendant voiez cy les figures des mouuements de greue & de pied en l'air.

Greue droicte,   Greue gaulche,
     OV   OV
Pied en l'air droict. Pied en l'air gaulche.

Ledit mouuement de greue est faict & causé aulcunesfois, quand le danceur gette & met l'vn de ses pieds en la place de l'aultre pied, & cependant ledit autre pied est esleué en l'air deuant : Et tel mouuement s'appelle entretaille, & en est aussi de deux sortes, comme il y a deux sortes de greue : Sçauoir entretaille du gaulche, causant greue droicte, & entretaille du droict, causant greue gaulche.

Capriol..

Plate V: Execution of the *grève*.

Fol. 45^v of the source for Plate IV.

Ex. 25: Arbeau's choreography applied to the *Almande Prince*.

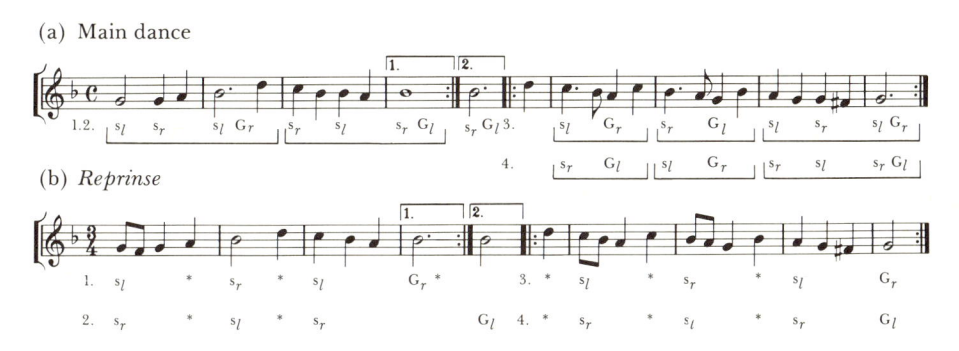

(a) Main dance

(b) *Reprinse*

de cheval in No. 37a seems best suited for Arbeau's choreography. I have tried to apply this choreography, however, to the more typical melody of the *Almande Prince* in Ex. 25. I have started with the basic four-bar pattern for the opening section, and this can be repeated upon repetition of the music. For the melodic sequence in the first two bars of the second section, I use the abbreviated pattern that Arbeau used at the beginning of his second part. Since the section then ends with the right foot raised in a *grève*, the repeat must begin with the right foot. Arbeau's third part, curiously, is also notated in duple meter, as is his example of the *courante* earlier in the book. Although a triple *reprinse*, as we have seen, only occasionally accompanied the Almande, it might have included Arbeau's springing motions as I show in Ex. 25b. The effect of hearing a tune in triple meter that one had just heard in duple would, it seems to me, enhance the "lighter and livelier" feeling produced by the springing steps.

All of these movements occur, then, within a slow processional dance in which couples are lined up one behind another. The couples are some distance from each other, I presume, not only because of space required for costume, but also in case some gentleman with long legs executes a particularly vigorous *grève*, or the lead couple suddenly decides to take a walking step backwards instead of forwards. The conventional place for the man is at the left side of the lady, and the man's right hand is holding the lady's left. As Arbeau says above, the entire column can make a turn at the end of the room and start back the other way. He also implies that the music stops after the first part, when the dancers talk together. This seems strange from a musical point of view, since the opening sections of other Almandes, such as the *Prince* in Ex. 25, do not end on the tonic chord of the piece. Arbeau ends his description of the Almande by saying that "while dancing the *Allemande*, the young men sometimes steal the ladies, taking them away from the hand of those that are leading them, and the one who is robbed tries to get another. But I do not approve of this way of doing things, because it can cause quarrels and discontent."[65]

60   *The Renaissance*

Ex. 26: Arbeau's *pavane* choreography and melody (+ = bring other foot up, with heels together).

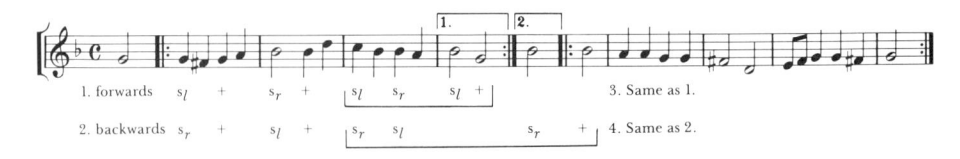

[musical notation]

1. forwards s_l + s_r + s_l s_r s_l +   3. Same as 1.
2. backwards s_r + s_l + s_r s_l   s_r +   4. Same as 2.

The Almande seems to be one of a series of solemn dances that became popular for processions. Earlier, and also concurrent with it, was the *pavane*, which was also in duple meter, but slower than the Almande. Since the two dances are, I believe, similar in function, some of Arbeau's comments on the *pavane* may cast some light on the Almande. Ex. 26 shows his *pavane* melody, which is very much like the *Almande Prince* and which he harmonizes in four voices and supplies with a text and a drum part.[66] The quarter-notes in Ex. 26 are actually notated as minims, with two in a bar; in Ex. 24, however, the note values are given exactly as Arbeau wrote them (Plate IV). The difference in notation may reflect the somewhat faster tempo of the Almande. The choreography of the *pavane* is also shown in Ex. 26, where the plus sign means that after taking a step with one foot, the dancer brings the other foot up beside it. Thus, in the opening bar, one takes a step with the left foot, then brings the right up beside it; the second bar is the same with the feet reversed. The third and fourth bars, however, consist of three walking steps followed by bringing the right foot up beside the left. The four measures in a bracket therefore constitute a pattern comparable to that in the Almande (Ex. 24a). In each, three walking steps are followed by some other movement that does not continue the forward motion: in the Almande the *grève*, in the *pavane* just bringing one foot up even with the other.

Arbeau says that instrumentalists play the *pavane* at weddings and to lead a procession of a notable confraternity.[67] It is used on solemn feast days when kings, princes, and great noblemen want to display their fine clothes. It announces a grand ball and lasts until the dancers have circled the hall two or three times. It also accompanies the entrances of gods, goddesses, emperors, and kings in masked entertainments.[68] We have already noted the Almande used as such a processional dance during the course of Philip's journey: as an entrance for nymphs and gods, as a procession of men with torches, and as a column of many couples at a grand ball.

Arbeau mentions *pavanes* played on oboes and sackbuts at a ball.[69] Both the *pavane* and the basse danse may be played not only with flute and drum, but also with viols, spinets, transverse flutes, flutes with nine holes, oboes, and all sorts of instruments.[70] The same variety of instruments may have been used when the Almande became the chief processional dance, but probably, in accord with the general trend toward homogeneous sound, with a group of like instruments playing together: a group of viols, or a group of wind instruments. Noticeably absent from Arbeau's list are the plucked instruments, whose tablatures we have encountered so often in the history of both the Almande and the Deutscher Tanz.

Although we have little information so far concerning the social function and choreography of the Tanz, it seems likely to me that both Tanz and Almande were the popular processional dances of the time. They would occur, thus, in social dances, in masked entertainments, and in the many types of parade or procession that occur in the civic and religious life of a court or city. Being slow and solemn, such a dance would involve, for the most part, very simple walking or marching movements. We can only speculate whether the Tanz had a choreography like Arbeau's Almande or whether it was even simpler, like his *pavane*. In any event, Arbeau's very carefully presented choreography adds a significant new dimension to our understanding of the Franco-Flemish Almande, and, in a sense, completes our history of this form. We will turn now to the Italian development, for the Deutscher Tanz spread not only to the north and west but also to the south.

3 THE BALLETTO TEDESCO FOR LUTE, KEYBOARD, AND ENSEMBLE IN ITALY 1561–1615

All of the instrumental sources of the Balletto Tedesco come from the northernmost cities of Italy, and all, with the exception of one book for ensemble and one for keyboard, are for lute. A glance at the Table of Contents of Volume II, beginning with No. 72, reveals the changes in terminology that took place during the course of the century in the lute books of Gorzanis, Barbetta, and Terzi. The first word of *Deutscher Tanz* occurs initially as *todescho, todesco,* or *tedesco,* but changes with Terzi in 1599 to *alemano. Tanz* was translated at first as *bal,* and then, with No. 75, as *balo; baletto* finally appears in No. 76, although Terzi in 1593 uses *ballo* and in 1599 both *ballo* and *balletto.*

The equivalency of these titles is confirmed by a few recurring melodies: the *Baletto todesco* of Barbetta in 1585 is a setting of the same melody used by Gorzanis in his second *Bal todescho* of 1564, and the *Balletto alemano* of Terzi in 1599 has the same melody as Barbetta's *Baletto todesco ditto il Terzo* (No. 76). Barbetta's book commences with some Italian dances such as the *padoana,* then, under the general title *Baletti de diverse nationi secondo il costume loro,* includes the *Baletto de Rusia, Baletto d'Inghilterra, Baletto francese, Baletto polaco,* and others, in addition to the *Baletto todesco.* The term *baletto* refers here, then, to various foreign dances, although, as we will see, the words *ballo* and *balletto* may also sometimes mean simply "dance" in general. The names for the Nachtanz are drawn from contemporary Italian dances that are in triple meter: the *saltarello, padoana,* and *gagliarda.*

Concordances with the Tanz and the Almande

Specific titles, such as *Prince* or *Nonette,* seldom occur in Italy. Furthermore, the Italians preferred, in general, to write new melodies in the style of the Tanz rather than borrowing those already well known. Titles such as the *Ballo tedesco novo de l'autore* in No. 79 indicate this tendency. There are, however, a few precious concordances that confirm the identity of the form as it moves to Italy.

The melody of the *Printzentantz* or *Almande Prince* occurs in Gorzanis' book of 1563 (see No. 73), where it closely resembles the version used by Waissel in 1591 (compare Exx. 1d and 1e). Although the duple dance in No. 73 seems to follow the German form of the melody, its *padoana* rises to d''', like the Flemish Almande in Ex. 1f. Another arrangement occurs as the first *Balo todesco* in Gorzanis' 1579 collection. The melody also occurs, in a form much like Ex. 1f, as a *Danza* and as an *Allemanda* in the lute manuscript of Chilesotti.[1] It is also, according to Moe, in *Di bello Amante Allamanna* and *Alamanna C'amor e fatto* in a manuscript from Lucca.[2] It occurs with the title *Madama mi domanda* in Antonio di Becchi's *Libro primo d'intabulatura da leuto* (Venice, 1568),[3] and as *Balletto di Madama* in the guitar book of Pietro Millioni in 1627.[4] There are a number of pieces called *Balletto, Balletto tedesco, Balletto alemano*, or just *Alemana* in the tablatures for the five-course Spanish guitar published in Italy beginning in 1606. Until around 1630 guitar music was almost exclusively *rasgueado*, referring to the strumming of chords. Some of the chord progressions seem to fit melodies we have encountered. In Ex. 27 I have set the tune of the *Almande Prince* from Phalèse and Bellère's 1571 ensemble book above a *rasgueado* guitar piece by Colonna entitled simply *Balletto*.[5] The notation on the lower staff indicates the roots of the triads that are played, with the stems showing the direction in which the hand strums the chords. The Spanish guitar, which almost completely replaced the lute in Italy around 1600, thus extends the life of some of our melodies on into the 17th century.

The melody of the *Almande Nonette* or *Ich ging einmal spazieren* appears in 1579 as a *Balo todesco* in Gorzanis' book (No. 75). In Ex. 21 its opening phrase is compared with those from other countries. In measure 4 it ends at first on the fifth degree of the scale, like the Waissel example in (a), but then moves up to 1 to match Phalèse's Almande in (c). Barbetta in 1585 has a setting called *Baleto francese detto Alemande*, and Terzi another in 1593 entitled *Ballo tedesco, & francese*. Both titles suggest that the Italian composers knew the melody from French sources.[6] Caroso includes it in his dance manual *Il ballarino* (Venice, 1581) as *Alta Morona, Balletto*[7] and in *Nobiltà di dame* (Venice, 1600) as *Celeste*

Ex. 27: *Almande Prince* melody from Ex. 1f with the *rasgueado* guitar accompaniment of Colonna's *Baletto*, 1620.

Ex. 28: Melody from Pario's song *Madre non mi far monaca*, 1610 (transposed down a fourth), with guitar accompaniment from the *Alemana* of Sanseverino, 1620.

giglio, Balletto.[8] It occurs in the Bentivoglio lute book of 1615 with the title *Alemana in soprano baletto*,[9] and is the subject of a set of variations for chitarrone in the *Partite variate sopra aria francese detta l'Alemana* of Piccinini in 1623.[10] The guitar books sometimes include a chord progression that seems to fit; in Ex. 28 I have set an *Alemana* by Sanseverino in 1620 on the lower staff,[11] with the melody from Pario's collection of 1610 above it. Even more interesting harmonically is Corbetta's *Alemana* of 1639 in No. 97; here some dissonant chords are used and the upper notes of the chords sometimes suggest the melody, especially the typical cadential figure. An *Alemana* in Calvi's guitar book of 1646 includes the melody in a setting in the lute-like *punteado* style that had developed by this time in guitar music.[12] This melody thus lived far longer as a dance than any of the others, and far longer in Italy than anywhere else. It continued even longer in all countries as a song, a chorale, or an instrumental piece.

Other concordances occur in Mainerio's *Il primo libro de balli* (1578) for ensemble. Here the word *balli* refers to any dance, since the book contains the native Italian *passamezzo* as well as dances from other countries. Mainerio includes three pieces entitled *Tedescha* or *Todescha*, which recur, exact in all four voices, in Phalèse (ii) and Bellère's ensemble book of 1583 as *Almande Bruynsmedelijn, Almande Poussinghe*, and *Almande*.[13] The top voice of the first is shown in Plate XX, which can be compared with versions by Waissel in Ex. 2c and Susato in Ex. 20a. Other settings of the melody occur in the Bottegari lute manuscript of 1574 as *Ballo alla Tedesca*,[14] in Caroso's *Il ballarino* of 1581 as *Balletto Bassa Ducale*,[15] and in his *Nobiltà di dame* of 1600 as *Balletto Bassa Savella*.[16] Caroso uses the term *balletto* rather broadly, however, and perhaps with some choreographic significance, since most of his dances are called either *balletto* or *cascarda*.

The melody of *Almande Poussinghe* and *Der Magister Dantz* appears also in Facoli's keyboard collection of 1588, with the title *Tedesca dita l'Austria* (Plate XXI).[17] Comparison with Ammerbach's melody in Ex. 2g shows the greatest difference in the final section, where Facoli has apparently omitted, probably by error, the fourth measure from the end. Facoli also has a *Tedesca dita la Proficia*, a setting of the *Proficiat ir lieben Herren* in Ex. 2h and the only Italian example I know that has the same descriptive title as the corresponding Tanz.[18] In addition, Mainerio's work contains a *Ballo francese*, which is a setting of the melody of *Almande Loraine*, and *La Billiarda*, the equivalent of an *Almande* of Phalèse (ii) and Bellère in 1583.[19]

The tune of *Gut Gesell du musst wandern* (Ex. 2f), which we have already encountered in the *Almande Regine Sweden* in the Thysius lute book, wanders now to Italy in the lute tablature of Barbetta (see No. 76). Here the title is *Baletto todesco ditto il Terzo* – referring perhaps to Terzi, who includes another setting, entitled *Balletto alemano*, in his book of 1599. The melody of *Der alten Weiber Tantz* (Ex. 2e) appears as *Un pezzo tedesco*, followed by *Nachtanz*, in Chilesotti's lute manuscript.[20] In addition, the *Bal todescho* of Gorzanis in No. 74 seems to be another setting of Ammerbach's *Ein ander kurtz Dentzlein* in No. 10a.

New melodies were written in the style of the older ones, sometimes borrowing phrases or portions of phrases from them, as well as the typical cadence. Terzi's *Ballo tedesco novo de l'autore* in No. 79 starts with a phrase like the beginning of the *Almande Fortune hélas pourquoy* in Ex. 23e. Its third section is like the second half of the *Almande Prince* in Ex. 1f. The melodic figure in the opening two bars of this last phrase provides the basis for the sequence in measures 2, 3, and 4 of the second section. The *Balletto dell'auttore detto l'Alemana d'Amore* of Negri (No. 82), although not like the *Tantz. Almande damour* in No. 6, has a familiar sound to it. The first three measures are the same as *Bruynsmedelijn* in Ex. 2c, and it contains no less than five typical Tanz cadences. The first six bars of this piece constitute the opening section of a *Pezzo tedesco* in the Chilesotti manuscript.[21] Terzi's *Ballo alemano* in No. 81 begins with two measures like *Bruynsmedelijn* (Ex. 20a) and reaches a typical cadence in the seventh and eighth bars. The repeated two-bar phrase at the beginning of the second section, with its descending motion, reminds one of a similar construction at this point in *Bruynsmedelijn*.

As late as 1620 Giovanni Picchi has a *Todescha* that is probably newly composed, but that sounds, with its Tanz cadences and repeated notes, almost as familiar as the well-known melodies. Curiously, the following triple version is labeled Balletto.[22] Although terminology seemed to change continually, the Italian form of the dance seems to clearly crystallize, with melodies either borrowed from German or Franco-Flemish sources or closely imitating them. Influence, as we have noted from time to time, comes sometimes from the Tanz, at other times from the Almande.

The Musical Characteristics

The essential traits of the Deutscher Tanz and the Almande continue also in the Balletto Tedesco. We have already noted examples of the cadences in Ex. 5. I have found only a few of these cadences in the *passamezzo* and other duple Italian forms of the period.[23] As in the Tanz and the Almande, the final note or chord of resolution is sometimes repeated again on the third beat (see Plate XX and the ends of the duple dances in Nos. 73 and 75). The melody, as expected, is in the top voice. The number of voices is usually four, with the exception of some five-note chords in the earliest lute example (No. 72), in the 17th-century guitar pieces, and in the keyboard work on Plate XXI, and some three-voice passages for lute in No. 82. There are most often two sections, with repeats either indicated by sign or written out exactly or with variation. Sometimes, as in No. 79, there are three sections, and the *Tedesca* on Plate XXI divides into three sections the melody that occurs in Ex. 2g with only two. Usually each section is immediately followed by a varied repeat, often with somewhat more elaborate coloration the second time (No. 73 or 76). The phrases are ordinarily four bars in length, but may be six (middle section of No. 79, for example) or eight (the two sections of No. 81, each disposed as 2+2+4).

These are the characteristics that are also shared, for the most part, by both the Tanz and the Almande. The latter, as we noted in the last chapter, differed to some extent from the Tanz in regard to the media, the after-dance, and the melodic organization. The Balletto Tedesco, like the other two, is often for a plucked-string instrument. Italian 16th-century examples, however, are exclusively for lute, with examples for guitar and chitarrone (No. 83) only after 1600. Like the Almande and unlike the Tanz, there is only a single source for keyboard. There is also only one book for instrumental ensemble, but *Il primo libro de balli* of Mainerio was no doubt influenced by the more numerous French publications for ensemble that preceded. Like d'Estrée's book of 1559, Mainerio's *balli* are "accommodati per cantar et sonar d'ogni sorte de istromenti."

Except for the keyboard examples by Facoli, almost all the duple dances before 1599 are faithfully followed, exactly like the Tanz, by a triple version based on the same musical material (Nos. 72–76 and 79). The melodic transformation, again, may use Method 1 in Ex. 9 (Nos. 72 and 73) or Method 2 (Nos. 74 and 76). The notation varies from source to source, as it did for the Tanz and the Almande. Gorzanis (in No. 72 from 1561 and No. 74 from 1564) and Terzi (in No. 79 from 1593) use Ex. 9a, the plan preferred in the Tanz, but with semiminims replacing minims in both duple and triple dances. Ex. 9b, the notation favored in the Almande, occurs with diminished values in No. 76 by Barbetta in 1585 and in Mainerio's *Todescha* on Plate XX. Here there are four semiminims in a measure of duple, three minims in a triple bar (exactly the same values used in Ex. 9b). In addition, the reverse of this notation, which we previously observed in the *Almande du Prince* of Viaera, appears in Gorzanis' pieces in Nos. 73 and 75 from 1563 and 1579; here four minims in the duple dance are followed by three semiminims in the triple.

In 1599, however, Terzi omits the triple dance in No. 81, as well as in the other nine examples in his book. Negri includes a triple section in No. 82 that utilizes the material from only the first six bars of the duple dance. Kapsberger's piece in No. 83a has no triple dance, and No. 83b includes a triple section that is not related melodically, harmonically, or structurally to the duple parts. Throughout its entire history the Almande seems to appear sometimes with and sometimes without an after-dance, but with the latter preferred. The Italian form seems to follow the Tanz until 1599, with its strict inclusion of a triple dance. It was, at the same time, continuing the earlier Italian tradition established in the *pavana–saltarello* pairs. After this date, however, the Balletto Tedesco seems to abandon the practice and henceforth appears, as we will see later, either without an after-dance or with one based less obviously, or not at all, on the musical substance of the duple dance.

Melodic organization in the Balletto is seldom achieved, as it is in the Almande, by obvious repetition of entire measures of music. The repetition of two bars at the beginning of the second section of No. 81 is the most extensive example I can find. Phrases are seldom parallel, either in beginnings or endings. More typical is the subtle sort of organization we have already noticed in No. 79. In this regard, the Italian dance is much closer in style to the Tanz.

We have already seen how the Italian composers treated well-known melodies such as the *Prince* and *Nonette* and how they were influenced sometimes by the Franco-Flemish version, at other times by the German. It was this dual set of influences, then, that acted upon the Italian Balletto Tedesco in determining the many detailed aspects of its musical style. Essentially the same as the Almande and Tanz in its basic elements, it could follow one or the other in less important matters. Perhaps the most conspicuous way the Balletto was different was the almost complete lack of descriptive titles to identify specific melodies. As we noted, there were only two or three such titles and of these only one matched the corresponding Tanz title. Actually, the latest sources for the Tanz and Almande also omit titles, for each of the forty examples in Waissel's book of 1591 is entitled simply *Tantz*, and in 1603 Besard has thirty-four dances called *Allemande*.

The Social Setting

During this period Italy consisted of a group of diverse and separate cities, unified only by language and the arts and by geographical location. There was no central government, not even the loose sort of imperial system employed in the Holy Roman Empire. From 1494 until 1559 Spain, joined under Charles V by the Empire, was fighting the French on Italian territory. Consequently, during the period of the Balletto Tedesco, some cities, such as Milan and Naples, as well as the island of Sicily, belonged to Spain. Some of the northern cities, such as Trieste and Aquileia, were under Austrian domination. Bologna was ruled by the Vatican, and other cities, such as Florence and Venice, were completely independent.

All of the examples of the Balletto Tedesco come from the cities of northern Italy. Almost all of the printed sources were published in Venice. Negri's dance manual, from which No. 82 comes, was published in Milan. Gorzanis, who is so important in the early history of the form (Nos. 72–75), became a citizen of the Croatian city of Trieste (across the Adriatic Sea from Venice) in 1557. The copyright declaration in Neusidler's 1536 lute book, mentioned already in Chapter 1, begins by listing the titles and possessions of Charles V's brother Ferdinand: "expander of the Empire in Germany, Hungary, Bohemia, Dalmatia, Croatia . . . Archduke of Austria, Duke of Burgundy and Wirtemberg and Count of Tyrol."[24]

Mainerio, whose ensemble example is on Plate XX, was *maestro di cappella* at the cathedral in Aquileia. Some of the 17th-century guitar books, such as those which include the pieces in Exx. 27 and 28, come from Milan or further south in Bologna.

The Choreography

Cesare Negri, an Italian dancing master, lived in Milan and published there in 1602 *Le gratie d'amore*, dedicated to Philip III, son of Philip II and ruler of Spain and Milan.[25] In this book Negri explains the dance steps and gives instructions for producing forty-three dances, including the *Balletto detto l'Alemana d'Amore* in No. 82. Preceding the instructions is an illustration (see Plate VI) showing two couples, garbed apparently in the appropriate costume for dancing, with each man about to commence the dance with his left foot. Verbal instructions for the dance appear on the next two pages (Plates VII and VIII). At the bottom of Plate VIII the melody begins, and the next page (Plate IX) includes the tablature for lute.

There are a number of problems, however, in actually reconstructing the

Plate VI: Two couples preparing to dance the *Balletto detto l'Alemana d'Amore*.

Cesare Negri, *Le gratie d'amore* (Milan, 1602), p. 184 (reproduced by permission of the Boston Public Library).

dance. First of all, Negri does not match the dance steps measure by measure as Arbeau did. He does specify in the heading above the melody the number of times each section is to be played, but since he has omitted the *quinta parte* of his instructions, this number is useful only in the *gagliarda* that begins with the *settima parte*. When one begins to set the dance steps to the music, it becomes apparent that in order for the choreography to fit there must be an irregular pattern to the repetition of sections. In addition, the notation of the triple part, if the note values are followed literally, produces strange melodic phrases of

Trattato Terzo. 185

BALLETTO DELL'AVTTORE DETTO L'ALEMANA
d'Amore si balla in quattro, due caualieri, & due dame.

In gratia dell Illustriss. Signora la Signora Contessa Delia Spinola, & Angosciuola.

PRIMA PARTE.

TVTTI quattro si fermano in mezo del ballo in quadrangolo, come si vede nel presente dissegno; faranno insieme la .R. & due .C. alla sinistra, & alla destra; i caualieri piglieranno'l braccio destro della sua dama, faranno due .SP. & vno .S. attorno alla destra tornando al suo luogo; poi pigliano'l braccio sinistro, e fanno li .SP. è il .S. attorno alla detta mano, tornando al suo luogo, & le cadenze di questo ballo si faranno con vn poco d'vn saltino.

SECONDA PARTE.

TVtti insieme faranno tre .S. in giro andando alla sinistra, e volgendosi à faccia à faccia. fanno vn .S. indietro col piè destro; due .SP. è vn .S. in torno alla sinistra. fanno poi altretanto attorno alla destra, tornando al suo luogo.

TERZA PARTE.

LE dame sole l'vna al dirimpetto dell'altra fanno due .P. & vn .S. innanzi col sinistro, & due .P. & vn .S. intorno alla destra; pigliano'l braccio destro, e fanno passando l'vno al luogo dell'altro due .SP. & vn .S. attorno alla sinistra; poi pigliano esso braccio è fanno altretanto, tornando al suo luogo, i caualieri soli faranno'l medesimo c'hanno fatto le dame tornando al suo luogo.

QVARTA PARTE.

LE dame solo fanno due .P. per fianco alla sinistra volgédo'l fianco destro. due .T. alla sinistra, & alla destra, vn. S. volgendosi à faccia à faccia. si fà altretanto alla destra; volgendo'l fianco sinistro; i caualieri pigliano'l braccio destro della lor dama è fanno due .SP. & vn .S. intorno alla destra tornando al suo luogo: poi pigliano'l braccio sinistro dell'altra dama, è fanno

Q 3 altre-

Plate VII: First page of instructions for the *Balletto detto l'Alemana d'Amore*.

P. 185 of the source for Plate VI.

a tretanto attorno ad essa mano tornando al suo luogo i caualieri soli fanno'l medesimo .P. è li .T. è il .S. per fianco c'hanno fatto le dame. poi esse da me pigliano'l braccio destro dell'vn caualiero, & il sinistro dell'altro, & tutti insieme fanno l'attioni di sopra.

SESTA PARTE.

Vtti insieme faranno due .P. & vn .S. andando alla sinistra con esso piede, è poi altretanto tornando alla destra. si fanno due .SP. & vn .S. intorno alla sinistra, il medesimo si fa attorno alla destra ritornando al suo luogo.

SETTIMA PARTE.
Mutatione della sonata in gagliarda.

Vtti insieme faranno andando alla sinistra quattro .SP. è due .S. col detto piè volgendosi à faccia à faccia. si fanno due .SP. & vn .S. intorno alla sinistra, e poi li .SP. è il .S. attorno alla destra.

OTTAVA PARTE.

LE dame sole fanno due .S. all'incontro vno innanzi, e l'altro indietro. due fioretti di gagliarda innanzi, è due .T. alla sinistra, & alla destra vn .S. intorno alla sinistra. si pigliano per lo braccio destro, e fanno due .SP. si lasciano è fanno vn .S. attorno alla sinistra. poi pigliano'l braccio sinistro, è si fa altretanto; tornando al suo luogo; i caualieri faranno li medesimi .S. è li fioretti, & l'attioni delle dame.

NONA PARTE.

Vtti insieme faráno otto .SP. in treccia passando prima i caualieri nel mezo, è poi di fuori, è nel mezo, è di fuora. che sono quattro volte tornando ogn'uno al suo luogo; pigliano'l braccio della lor dama, è fanno due .SP. è vn. S. attorno alla destra tornando al suo luogo, poi pigliano'l braccio sinistro è fanno'l medesimo tornando al suo luogo, e volgendosi tutti à faccia à faccia faranno la .R. con finir'il ballo gratiosamente.

La Musica della sonata con l'Intauolatura di liuto dell'Alemana d'Amore. Le prime due parti si fanno sei volte, è due volte per parte, la gagliarda si fa tre volte, è due volte per parte, sin'al fin del ballo.

Plate VIII: Second page of instructions for the *Balletto detto l'Alemana d'Amore*.

P. 186 of the source for Plate VI.

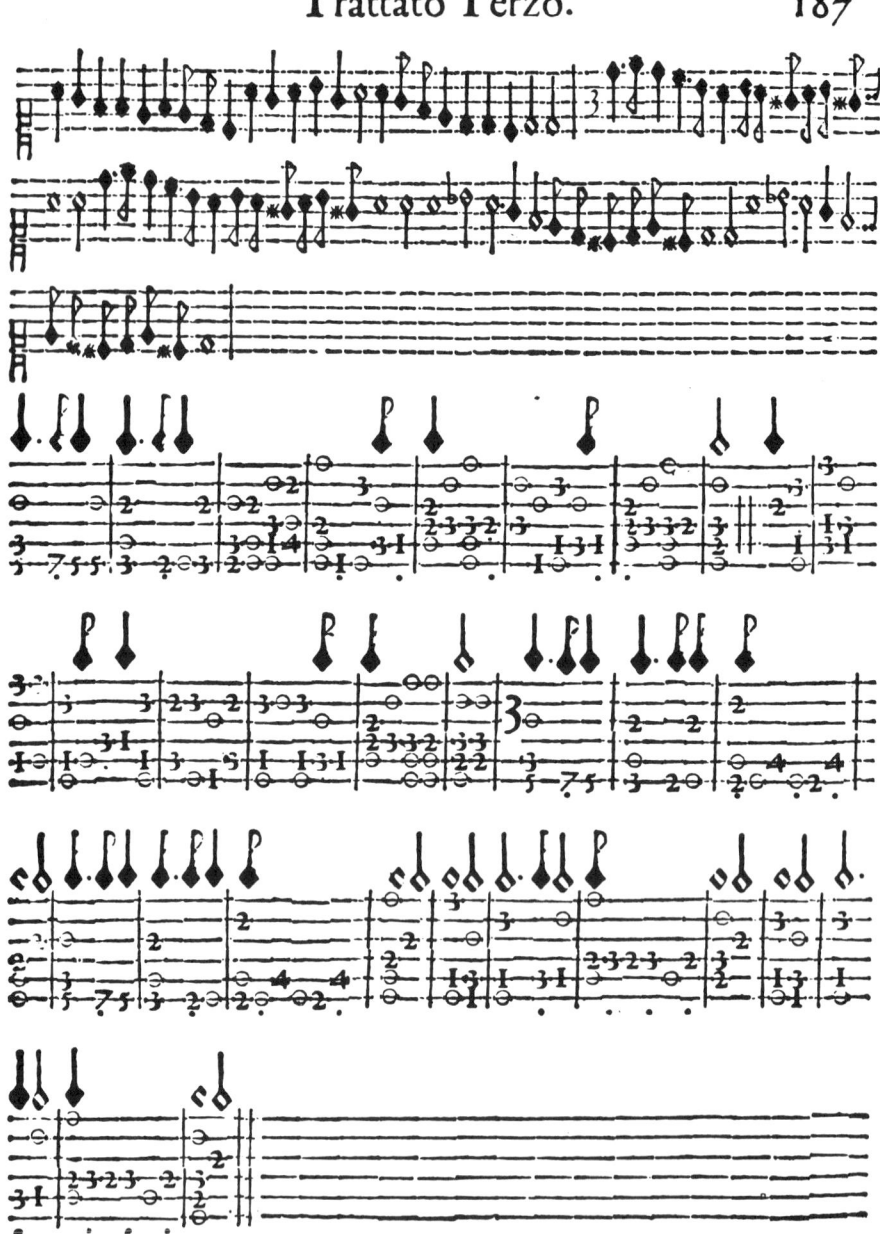

Plate IX: Music for the *Balletto detto l'Alemana d'Amore* (see No. 82 in Volume II).

P. 187 of the source for Plate VI.

five and seven bars, and the repeats, unlike those in the duple part, are written out. One possible solution is given in Ex. 29, where the capital letters are the abbreviations used by Negri on Plates VII and VIII for the dance movements, and each number in parentheses corresponds to a numbered *parte* of his instructions. I have further subdivided each *parte*, with lower-case letters indicating units that fit a section of music.[26]

The dance movements are as follows:[27]

R = *riverenza* (four measures). The man, facing the lady, moves his left foot forward in the opening measure. At bar 2, he draws the left foot back until the toe is even with the right heel, while keeping the body straight. At bar 3, he inclines his body and spreads the knees apart gracefully, and at the last bar he straightens up again and moves the left foot even with the other.

C = *continenza* (two measures). When made to the left, the man makes a small step to the left, brings the heel of the right foot to the middle of the left, lowers himself, then rises gracefully to his toes, while raising the left hip, and then lowers his heels to the ground. For the *continenza* to the right, the directions are reversed.

SP = *seguito spezzato* (one measure). On the first beat one takes a step forward with the left foot. In the middle of the measure, the right toe moves up and touches the left heel, and both heels are raised and then lowered again. Thus the entire body makes a bounce up and down. Perhaps the left foot may, on occasion, even leave the ground slightly. The bounce or lilt that takes place during the second half of the measure seems to me to be one of the most characteristic movements in the dance.[28] When a second SP follows the first, it commences with the right foot and the directions above are reversed.

Ex. 29a: Negri's choreography for the *Balletto detto l'Alemana d'Amore*, first section of duple part (see No. 82 for the lute part).

(1a) All	R	. . .	. . .	. . .	C and SP,	C left, SP, and	C and S	C right. left, Cad.
(1b) All	SP,	SP, and	S	right;				
(3a) Ladies	P,	P,	S	left;	P,	P,	S	right.
(3b) Ladies exchange positions	SP,	SP,	S	left;	SP,	SP,	S	right.
(3c) Men	P,	P,	S	left;	P,	P,	S	right.
(3d) Men exchange positions	SP,	SP,	S	left;	SP,	SP,	S	right.
(4c) All	SP,	SP,	S	right;	SP,	SP,	S	left.
(6a) All	P,	P,	S	left;	P,	P,	S	right.
(6b) All	SP,	SP,	S	left;	SP,	SP,	S	right.

Ex. 29b: Negri's choreography, second section of duple part.

(2a) All	S,		S,		and	S to the	left.
(2b) All	S	back;	SP,	SP,	and	S to the	left.
(2c) All	S,		S,		and	S to the	right.
(2d) All	S	back;	SP,	SP,	and	S to the	right.
(4a) Ladies	P,	P left,	T&T left,	T&T right,	S . . .	. . .
(4b) Ladies	P,	P right,	T&T left,	T&T right,	S . . .	. . .
(4d) Men	P,	P left,	T&T left,	T&T right,	S . . .	. . .
(4e) Men	P,	P right,	T&T left,	T&T right,	S . . .	. . .
(4f) All	P,	P left,	T&T left,	T&T right,	S . . .	. . .
(4g) All	P,	P right,	T&T left,	T&T right,	S . . .	. . .

Ex. 29c: Negri's choreography, triple part.

(7a) All	SP,	SP,	SP,	SP, (7c) SP,	SP, and	S	left.
(7b)	S,	and	S	left. (7d) SP,	SP, and	S	right.
(8a) Ladies	S	forward,	S	back. (8c) SP and	SP;	S	left.
(8b)	F, F,	T&T left,	S right	. . (8d) SP and	SP;	S	right.
Men alone repeat (8)							
(9a) All	SP,	SP,	SP,	SP, (9c) SP,	SP, and	S	right;
(9b)	SP,	SP,	SP, and	SP. (9d) SP,	SP, and	S	left. ‖R

S = *seguito ordinario* (two measures). In the opening measure, the left foot moves forward, then the right. During the second measure, one makes a *seguito spezzato*. Since the latter itself begins with a step, the entire S includes three walking steps and then the bouncing or lilting movement.

P = *passi gravi* (one measure). The left foot moves forward, then the right.

T = *trabucchetto grave* or *minimo* (one or two in a measure). One jumps to the left side, brings the right foot to within an inch or so of the left, while raising the hip, then moves the right foot back. One can do the same to the right.

F = *fioretto* (two in a measure). With the left foot extended, one jumps forward, putting both feet on the ground. Then one hops forward with the left foot and raises the right foot.

If another F follows, it begins on the right foot. The *cadenze* at the end of line (1b) in Ex. 29a is a forward jump somewhat like the first half of the *fioretto*; it occurs, presumably, on the last quarter-note beat of the measure, after the preceding S has been completed.

An R and four C's occur at the beginning of most dances, with the R like a stylized bow, the C's like introductory gestures. P, as well as the beginning of SP and most of S, consists simply of walking steps. The end of SP includes a little bounce, whereas T and F involve more animated jumps. C, T, F, and SP can begin with either foot. When there are two F's or SP's in succession, the first begins on the left foot, the other on the right. The P and S, however, commence with the left foot, but their steps can lead the dancers to the left, right, forward, or back. These directions are indicated in Ex. 29 along with the abbreviations for the movements. Negri's instructions for the first part are then as follows (see Plate VII). The movements are set to the melody of the opening duple music in Ex. 29a.

All four start in the quadrangle shown in the illustration [Plate VI]. They will do together the R and two C's to the left and to the right. Each man will take the right arm of his lady and they will make two SP's and one S around to the right, and return to their original position. Then each man will take the left arm of the lady and make the SP's and the S around at the left and return to the original position, and the *cadenze* of this dance will be made with a little jump.

The movements described in the second part seem to require four statements of the second duple section of music, as shown in Ex. 29b:

All together they will make three S's around to the left. Turning face to face, they make an S back with the right foot and two SP's and one S around at the left. They then do the same thing around at the right, going back to their original positions.

The third part, in turn, then requires four statements of the first part of the duple music (Ex. 29a):

The ladies alone, one in front of the other, make two P's and one S forward with the left foot and two P's and one S around at the right. Taking right arms and exchanging positions, they make two SP's and one S around at the left. Then they take the right arm and do the same thing, returning to their position. The two men alone will do the same thing that the ladies have done and return to their places.

The fourth part includes more animated T's and seems to utilize both duple sections, with six statements of the second half, only one of the first. Part 6 is considerably simpler, with only walking steps and bounces. Parts 7, 8, and 9 belong to the triple *mutatione* of the music. I have assumed in Ex. 29c (as well as in No. 82) that some of the note values are twice as long as they should be. Instead of phrases of five and seven measures, then, we have two four-bar phrases.[29] The choreography seems to fit this plan better, although the number of times the triple dance must be played, if one counts the repetition of the *ottava parte* by the men, exceeds the specified three times. Negri concludes his choreography of the *Balletto detto l'Alemana d'Amore* by describing the *nona parte* in this way:

76   *The Renaissance*

All together they will do eight SP's crossing by each other, the men passing in the middle first and then coming out, then back in the middle – that makes four times, after which each goes back to his place. Each man takes the arm of his lady and they make two SP's and one S around to the right and return to their places. Then they take the left arm and do the same thing and return to their places. All of them, turning face to face, will do the R̄, thus ending the dance graciously.

Taken as a whole, Negri's choreography seems so complex and varied that one tends to assume it was a stage dance for professional performers. At that time, however, the cultivated gentleman and lady knew how to dance and could execute complex sequences of steps. Simpler choreographies might have been appropriate to less elaborate social situations. Most of the movements in the dance are those involving only walking steps and the special bouncing motion in the SP. Each of Negri's movements is actually a compound series of smaller steps. I show in Ex. 30 a phrase similar to the first four measures of the melody, along with a sequence of movements, SP, SP, and S, which occurs frequently in Ex. 29 (at the beginning of lines 1b, 4c, and 6b, for example). Below Negri's abbreviations in Ex. 30, I have placed letters that show the component parts of each movement. Each SP involves a walking step and a bounce, each S three steps and a bounce. If each step is represented by a small s and the bounce by a capital B, then the units on the bottom line of Ex. 30 emerge. The two-bar typical cadence thus accompanies a two-bar choreographic unit in which the quarter-notes correspond to the forward steps, the notes of resolution to the lilting bounce.

Comparing Ex. 30 with Arbeau's choreography in Ex. 24b, one sees similar one- and two-bar units, with two motions in each bar. In both Arbeau and Negri, one or three walking steps lead to a movement that is executed in place without further forward motion: with Arbeau this is the *grève*, with Negri it is the bounce-like conclusion of the *seguito spezzato*, in which the dancer's body rises and then falls. Like the *grève*, the *seguito spezzato* occurs in other dance forms as well. However, the main impression of an observer of an Almande, it seems to me, would be the foot extended in a *grève*. For Negri's Balletto, one of the principal effects must be the lilting rise and fall of the dancers' heads as they lightly rise to their toes, then fall back on their heels in the execution of the *seguito spezzato*.

Ex. 30:   Basic unit of Negri's choreography, broken into component steps
          (s = walking step, *l* = left, *r* = right, B = bounce).

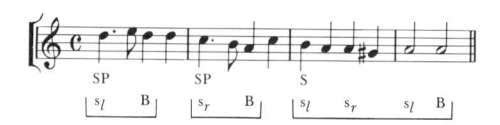

The Balletto Tedesco and the Almande thus have both similarities and differences in choreography as well as in music. They both share with the Tanz, as we have seen above, a basic musical style. The Balletto, like the Tanz and the Almande, sometimes includes well-known melodies common to them all. The titles of the Balletto almost never identify such melodies by name, and composers seem to prefer melodies that are new but in the same style. Concerning certain details of construction, the Balletto, as we have seen, follows sometimes the Tanz, at other times the Almande. Although usually bearing the full title, the Balletto Tedesco, like the Almande, can sometimes be called merely *Tedesco* (Plate XX). Like the Tanz, it can at other times be entitled simply *Balletto* (Ex. 27). In spite of small differences in choreography, music, titles, media, notation, and geographical location, however, the instrumental Deutscher Tanz, Almande, and Balletto Tedesco trace, it seems to me, a remarkably unified development as they evolve between 1540 and the early years of the next century. It is thus somewhat unexpected when a new type of *vocal* Balletto suddenly appears in Italy during the 1590's and plays a dramatic role in the future evolution of the forms in Italy, England, and Germany. This development is so significant that it will be treated in a separate chapter. Furthermore, it inaugurates a period from around 1590 to 1640 that is characterized by experimentation and change, and hence will be treated here as a transition between the Renaissance and the Baroque.

PART II

The Transition

4 VECCHI, GASTOLDI, AND THE VOCAL BALLETTO IN ITALY DURING THE 1590's

WE HAVE NOTED in passing, in the last three chapters, various ways in which vocal music was involved with the instrumental Tanz, Almande, and Balletto Tedesco. The Tanz sources contain innumerable intabulations of vocal pieces, which, to one extent or another, may have exerted an influence. Early examples of the Tanz actually borrow and adapt melodies from vocal works. A number of other Almandes and Tänze bear titles that suggest vocal origin. The *Nonette* melody seems to have been a song before, during, and after the life-span of the Tanz, the Almande, and the Balletto. In addition, several ensemble sources, including Mainerio's collection, declare on the title page that the dances can be sung, as well as played on all sorts of instruments. Texts are not provided in any of these sources, however, and we can only speculate concerning the social situation in which ensemble dances might have been sung.

As the 1590's approach, a number of sung dances appear. We have already noted Arbeau's *pavane* with text. Other examples occur in connection with dramatic presentations, especially for festivities celebrating an important social event. The most elaborate productions of this sort were the *intermedi* for the wedding of Ferdinando de' Medici and Christine of Lorraine at Florence in 1589. Emilio de' Cavalieri composed and choreographed the dance that concludes the final *intermedio*, and this vocal *ballo*, beginning with the text "O che nuovo miracolo," became famous during the 17th century as the *Ballo del Gran Duca* or the *Aria di Fiorenza*. Two of the internal phrases of the five-voice musical setting conclude with a typical Tanz cadence.[1] Such choreographed vocal music was part of the experimentation with various ways of combining drama and music which became increasingly important at the end of the century and led, finally, to the invention of opera. Both large and smaller dramatic forms emerged, some transitory, others enduring long enough to establish a new type. The vocal Balletto often appears from 1591 to around 1620 in choreographed or semi-dramatic works of a small, chamber size.

Ex. 31: Frottola *Fortuna d'un gran tempo*, cadence.

(a) Odhecaton, 1501, for voices.

(b) Spinacino, 1507, for lute.

Vecchi in Modena and Gastoldi in Mantua are both involved in the early stages of this development.

Vecchi and the *Villotta*

The earliest vocal examples that seem to belong to our history are those of Orazio Vecchi in 1590 (see the two pieces in No. 77). Three characteristics of his works, however, occur in earlier Italian sources: the typical cadence, *fa-la* syllables, and an interest in *Tedesco*. The *frottole* of the late 15th and early 16th centuries are usually, like the Tanz, the Almande, and the Balletto, *a 4*, with the melody in the top voice. Cadences, however, almost always involve a simple suspension.[2] Only occasionally is such a cadence transformed into the typical Tanz cadence when intabulated for lute, as in Ex. 31.[3] There is a lighter vocal form, however, called the *villotta*, which seems to emerge during the 1520's and which reaches a high point around mid-century. The *villotta* not only has four voices with the melody in the soprano, but also sometimes has *fa-la* passages, references to *Tedesco*, and numerous examples of the typical cadence. Some are strophic, and many are based on the Renaissance chordal schemes.

Un cavalier di Spagna, for example, is a *villotta* from *Canzoni, Frottole e Capitoli, Libro primo. De la Croce* (Rome, 1526). At the end it changes to triple meter and becomes very chordal, as though a popular dance were being quoted. The concluding phrase, which is repeated, ends with the typical cadence.[4] This same work appears also in I-Vnm, MS It. IV, 1795–1798, among a series of twelve *villotte*.[5] This manuscript dates presumably from early in the century, and six of its other *villotte* display one, two, or three typical cadences.[6] Aluvise Castellino's *E d'una viduella* from *Il primo libro delle Villotte* (Venice, 1541) has three Tanz cadences.[7] Still other examples come from Filippo Azzaiolo's three books of *villotte* around mid-century. *Al dì, dolce ben mio* from *Il primo libro de Villotte alla padoana . . . intitolate Villotte del fiore* (Venice, 1557) contains five Tanz cadences, two of them in the opening two phrases.[8] In *Il secondo libro de Villotte del fiore alla padovana* (Venice, 1559), such cadences occur frequently in three pieces labeled *Villotta* and in one *Napolitana*.[9]

The typical Tanz cadence thus seems to occur rather regularly throughout the history of the *villotta* as a frequent characteristic of style. Since its presence in this form predates the birth of the Deutscher Tanz around 1540, one wonders about possible influence. I can find no link, however, between the Tanz and the *villotta* at this time. The latter was not one of the vocal types transcribed in the earliest Tanz sources. The situation seems to be similar to that of the monophonic theatrical chansons, the only other vocal form in which numerous Tanz cadences occur. As we have already seen, there also seems to be no direct connection between these chansons and the Tanz. Of course, the cadence itself is such a natural transformation of the usual vocal cadence that it could easily have emerged independently in a number of popular song and dance forms. Although we cannot establish an influence of the *villotta* at this early period, it does, I believe, have a rather direct impact on the Italian Balletto of the 1590's.

Nonsense syllables also occur sometimes in the *villotta*. The use of the syllables *fa-la* goes back at least to Azzaiolo's first book of 1557. *Al dì, dolce ben mio*, mentioned above, changes to triple meter after the fourth Tanz cadence and apparently quotes the music of *La cara cosa*, a popular dance song, with the text "Fa la la, fa la la."[10] *Poi che volse de la mia stella*, another *villotta* from the same book, combines "fa" and "la" with other nonsense syllables.[11] A later example, from *Villotte mantovane* (Venice, 1583), concludes with the line "falala lalala la."[12]

There are also references in the *villotta* to *Tedesco*, the German mercenary (*Landsknecht*). As we have already noted, Spain and the Holy Roman Empire were almost continually at war with France from 1494 until 1559 over the control of various cities in Italy. Thus the German soldier became a familiar sight, and Italian literature often included him as a comic character who had difficulty speaking Italian and who was frequently drunk. Such a German character or *Tedesco* appears in the *canti carnascialeschi* at Florence, as well as in the later *villotte* from the second half of the century.[13] *Villotte* with texts dealing with the character are often labeled *Todesco* or *Todesca*. *Trince got è malvasia*, for example, appears in *Villotte alla napolitana a tre voci, con una Todescha* (Venice, 1566). Azzaiolo includes the todesca *Patrone, belle patrone* by Girardo da Panico in his 1557 book of *villotte*. In his second book of 1559 appears the todesco *Bernarde non può stare*, each strophe of which ends with the refrain "Deridon deridon deridon da ra ra ra da, deridon deridon deridon ra ra ra don da."[14]

84 *The Transition*

The *villotte*, with their Tanz cadences, *fa-la* syllables, and *Tedeschi*, were thus well known to Vecchi when he published in 1590 his *Selva di varia ricreatione*. Included in this work is an extraordinary madrigal for nine voices, five originally composed by Marenzio and four added by Vecchi. Most of the characters in this "miniature madrigal comedy"[15] come from the *commedia dell'arte*. One, however, is *Tedesco*, a drunken German soldier, whose text begins, with incorrect Italian, "Mi star bon compagnon." The *Tedesca a 5* (see No. 77a) also appears in the same book, although its text makes no reference to the *Landsknecht* or his comic character. Perhaps the title in this case refers, as in Mainerio's *Tedesche* of 1578, to the *Balletto tedesco*. The piece is in five voices rather than the usual four; a lute part is provided, and a second stanza of text. A typical Tanz cadence occurs in the lute part at the end of the first section, where it is followed by two repeated chords in all parts, and in both soprano voice and lute at the conclusion of the second section.

The *Aria a 4* (No. 77b) from the same book includes *fa-la* syllables at the end of each of its two sections. It has the more usual four voices, as well as a lute part and nine additional stanzas of text. Although there is no indication from the title that this *Aria* is involved with a dance, Negri in 1602 gives the melody and lute part in his *Balletto So ben mi chi ha buon tempo, corretto dall'Auttore si balla in due*.[16] Negri adds a triple Nachtanz, and also makes some alterations in Vecchi's melody. He changes the end of both sections to a typical Tanz cadence and includes two more at the beginning of the second section. Ex. 32 compares the second section of Vecchi's top voice (a) to Negri's melody (b) and lute part (c).[17] This piece apparently became popular, for it also appears in the Bottegari manuscript for solo voice and lute with a melody like Vecchi's[18] and in a lute setting almost identical to Negri's in *Balletti moderni facili* (Venice, 1611).[19]

Another work by Vecchi appears on Plate X, which comes from a book of

Ex. 32: Second section of the Aria and Balletto *So ben mi chi ha bon tempo*.

(a) Vecchi's melody, 1590 (see No. 77b).

(b) Negri's melody, 1602.

(c) Negri's lute part, 1602.

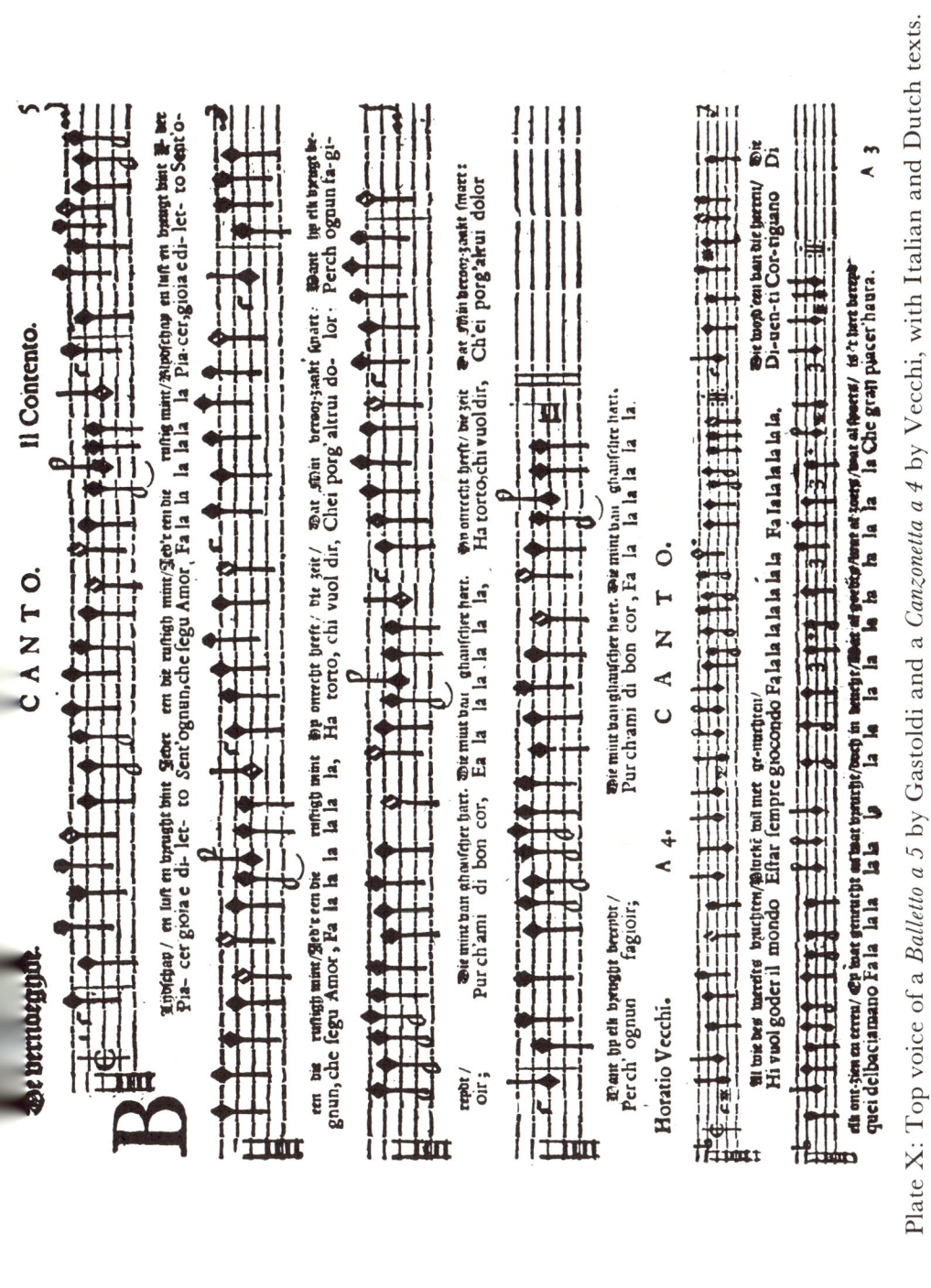

Plate X: Top voice of a *Balletto a 5* by Gastoldi and a *Canzonetta a 4* by Vecchi, with Italian and Dutch texts. *Italiaansche Balletten* (Amsterdam: Paulus Matthysz, 1657), canto partbook, p. 5 (reproduced by permission of the British Library, London).

86 The Transition

Italiaansche Balletten published by Paulus Matthysz at Amsterdam in 1657. The original Italian version, first printed in 1597, has a *fa-la* passage in each section, as well as a typical cadence at the close of the opening phrase.[20] This work illustrates how long Vecchi's works were popular and how far they traveled. It also shows a relationship with the Balletto by Gastoldi on the same page, for the two men were concurrently working on the development of this type of form. Vecchi's examples show a strong tie with the past in the cadences, the *fa-las*, and the *Tedeschi*. He also was involved in relatively small-scale dramatic works, such as the madrigal with nine characters mentioned above, or his famous madrigal comedy *L'Amfiparnaso* from 1597. All of these ideas also influence future developments, and it is Gastoldi, finally, whose name becomes identified with the Balletto and whose works become most popular.

Gastoldi and the Balletto *a* 5

In 1591 Gastoldi published in Venice his *Balletti a cinque voci con li suoi versi per cantare, sonare, & ballare; con una Mascherata de Cacciatori a sei voci, & un concerto de Pastori a otto*.[21] The work was so enormously popular that it reappeared in at least twenty-seven later editions – eight in Venice up to 1613, as well as eleven in Antwerp (1596 to 1640), one in Rotterdam (1628), four in Amsterdam (1641 to 1658), two in Nuremberg (1600 and 1606), and one in Paris (1614). The book begins with an *Introduttione a i Balletti*, followed by fifteen Balletti, each with a descriptive title, and ends finally with a *Mascherata*, a *Canzonetta*, and a *Concerto*. The titles of the Balletti refer to "The Jolly Fellow," "The Contented One," "The Scoffer," "The Prize Winner," and other persons, as well as to "The Glory of Love" and "Victorious Love." The format suggests some sort of theatrical performance, involving perhaps costumes, mime, or a unified choreography.[22]

The *Balletti a 5* are so well known that I have not transcribed any of them in Volume II in their original form. No. 12, however, is a German lute arrangement of the ninth Balletto, *Amor vittorioso*, and Plate XXII shows the top voice of the eleventh Balletto. Sharing Plate X in this volume with the Vecchi piece is the *cantus* part of Gastoldi's third Balletto, *Il Contento*. Negri provides a choreography for the first one, *L'innamorato*, in the *Balletto a due detto Alta Mendozza di M. Stefano*,[23] and its music was used for the chorale *In Dir ist Freude* (see Ex. 43 for the melody). Ex. 33 shows the melodies from four other Balletti.[24] All of them are strophic, and all five voices are supplied with text. All have the melody in the *canto* part, but the *quinto* often overlaps with it. They are usually chordal, with many repeated notes or repeated chords. There are four strong beats in a bar (or three for those in triple meter), each notated, as in my transcriptions, by the quarter-note (see Plate XXII and Ex. 33c). Phrases are often constructed of two-bar units, either separated by rests (Ex. 33b) or not (Exx. 33a, c, and d). Eleven are in duple meter, two are triple, and two alternate both meters. There is no pairing of duple and triple dances. Eight are

The Vocal Balletto in Italy 87

Ex. 33: Melodies from Gastoldi's *Balletti a 5*, 1591 (in the *fa-las*, only the first and last "la" of a group are shown; however, every note is to be sung to a separate syllable).

(a) IV: *Speme amorosa*.

(b) V: *Lo Schernito*.

(c) XI: *La Sirena* (for the original notation, see Plate XXII).

(d) XV: *L'acceso*.

88 *The Transition*

in the mode *per B quadro* and usually sound exactly like the later major mode (see No. 12 in Volume II, for example). The others utilize the mode *per B molle* and often clearly outline the chord-rows of the popular dance style. In Ex. 33c, for example, Scheme III (the one used in the *romanesca*) harmonizes the *fa-las* at the end of the opening section; the preceding four bars simply sustain (through the variation chords that relate as IV and V) the opening chord of the scheme.[25]

Two traits of the Balletti are shared also by the *villotta* and the works of Vecchi: the Tanz cadence and the *fa-las*. The typical cadence occurs frequently, as in Ex. 33a (the end of each section), Ex. 33b (end of the first section and just before the *fa-las* of the second), Ex. 33c (three in the opening section and another at the end of the second), and Ex. 33d (end of the first section and just before the *fa-las* of the third). Although the sixth Balletto has "lirum" for its nonsense syllables and the second "la-la-la," all the rest employ the usual "fa-la-la." I have shown where each "fa-la-la" commences in Ex. 33 and indicated the first and last "la" for each.

There are usually two sections in a Balletto, with the "fa-la" text at the end of each (Exx. 33a, b, and c). Two Balletti have three sections; the one in Ex. 33d includes *fa-las* at the end of the first and third sections, the other one (*La Bellezza*, the twelfth Balletto) at the end of only the third. The two *fa-la* settings at the ends of the usual two sections may be totally different musically (Ex. 33a or d), or they may be almost (Ex. 33c) or exactly identical (see *Il Contento* in Plate X). They may be united by a common motive (as in the sixth, *Gloria d'Amore*), or by inverting a motive from the first in the second (Ex. 34). The *fa-la* music tends to be more animated, with shorter note values, and often to be more organized, with sequences (Ex. 33a, end of second section) and contrapuntal imitation between voices (Ex. 34). These devices often cause the

Ex. 34: *La-la* music from Gastoldi's second *Balletto a 5, Il bell'humore*.

(a) End of first section.

(b) End of second section.

phrases to span an irregular number of bars and to be longer than the four-bar phrases that usually precede. The tiny sequence during the *fa-las* at the end of the first section of Ex. 33b, for example, extends the phrase to five measures, contrasting to the preceding two-bar phrases. Ex. 34 shows the tiny motives that sometimes recur in dialogue or echo as the voices assume more contrapuntal independence during the *fa-las*.

Melodic organization also occurs elsewhere and sometimes on a broader scale. Adjacent phrases can be identical, as at the beginning of Exx. 33c and d, or share the same rhythm. The first three phrases of Ex. 33a are, in addition, partially sequential. The two opening two-bar phrases in the second section of Ex. 33c are even more exactly in sequence. In the same example, the two halves of each *fa-la* portion sound parallel by including the same descending pitches. In Ex. 33b, the last three notes of the opening phrase (indicated by a bracket) become a motive that recurs in sequence during the second section. The downward third at the end of this motive occurs at the end of the first phrase of a number of the Balletti. In the second full measure of Ex. 33b, it moves from 7 to 5 within a dominant chord. In other cases it moves from 3 down to 1 during a tonic chord, as in Exx. 33a and d. These are early examples of a device we will notice later, especially in Italian chamber works. The downward third occurs at the same position at the end of a two- or four-bar phrase where we have often previously seen repeated notes or chords. The Balletto in No. 12 illustrates both situations, with the downward third in measure 2 and the repeated chords in measure 4.

Gastoldi's five-voice Balletti thus display a number of the traits we have noted in the instrumental Tanz, Almande, and Balletto Tedesco. The melody is generally on the top, with many repeated notes and usually two- or four-bar phrases. The texture is mostly chordal, which adds to the vigorous rhythmic quality and the insistent quarter-note pulse. Each Balletto has two or, less often, three sections, usually with each immediately repeated. None of the melodies seems to concord with previous pieces, and, as in the later instrumental Balletti, there is no pairing of a dance with an after-dance. More striking than the similarities, however, are the ways in which Gastoldi's works differ from the earlier instrumental forms. First of all, they are vocal, and the phrase "con li suoi versi per cantare" on the title page makes clear that these pieces, unlike earlier ensemble works of Mainerio and others, are actually provided with texts. Second, they are in five voices rather than four. In addition, they are apparently arranged in the collection with some sort of unified dramatic purpose in mind. The mood, and hence probably also the tempo, varies from one Balletto to another, although the *fa-la* passages create a generally cheerful and lively spirit that must have contrasted with the slow processional dance for instruments alone. They also, as we have seen, sometimes include brief passages of a more contrapuntal nature. Finally, the full name of *Balletto tedesco* or *Balletto alemano* is now reduced to simply *Balletto*.

Gastoldi and the Balletto *a 3*

In the year following the appearance of the five-voice Balletti, Gastoldi published his *Canzonette a tre voci, con un Balletto nel fine* (Venice, 1592). The single Balletto in this book is entitled *Intermedio de pescatori*, again suggesting that dancing, mime, and costume, as well as singing, are to be combined in this tiny theatrical piece to be inserted between acts of a play. The music (see No. 78) has three texted voices, alternating triple and duple meter, and two sections, each to be repeated and each concluding with *fa-la-las*. There are also briefer *fa-las* in the middle of the second section. The longer two *fa-la* parts are identical, except for exchanging the two upper voices. The typical cadence appears at the end of the brief *fa-las* and at the end of the duple part. The work is not strophic and hence the music, as in a madrigal, fits the text more exactly. The piece opens with a group of fishermen saying that heaven does not want to see happy men, so put down the nets and sing about the love of nymphs and shepherds. When the music changes to duple meter, the text contains an exhortation to plunge the boat into the waves, because Venus is hiding there. During the last five bars of duple meter, the concluding couplet states "here you will find her naked; keep plunging and you will find her." The phrase "spingi pur" (keep plunging) recurs several times to a brief repeated musical motive.

This work constitutes a transition, in a sense, between Gastoldi's *Balletti a 5* and the main source of his three-voice examples, the *Balletti a tre voci, con la intavolatura del liuto, per cantare, sonare, & ballare* published at Venice in 1594.[26] It reappeared between 1598 and 1664 in some fourteen later editions from Venice, Nuremberg, Antwerp, Amsterdam, and Rotterdam. The title again declares that the Balletti are sung, played, and danced. This time, however, the number of voices is three and a lute part has been included. The titles of the sixteen Balletti refer to various people, such as "The Happy One," "The Curious One," "The Offended One," and "The Tormented One." The first Balletto, *Il Ballerino* (The Dancer), acts as an introduction to the collection and begins: "Play me a Balletto; I want to dance with my love."[27] Since these Balletti are not as well known as those in five voices, I have included three of them in Volume II (Nos. 80a, b, and c).

All of them, like those *a 5*, are strophic. The melody is in the *canto*, but the *tenore* part frequently overlaps. The two upper voices often exchange positions, as in the opening two bars of No. 80a, or move in thirds, as in the last five bars. Two-measure phrases are again frequent (Nos. 80b and 80c). Ten are duple, five triple; one combines both meters. Eight of them sound like the later major mode; seven are minor. Many exhibit the standard chordal schemes of the Italian popular style. There are many examples of the typical Tanz cadence, many repeated notes, and the same strong sense of the quarter-note beat seen in the *Balletti a 5*.

Although the *Balletti a 3* have the same general style and spirit as those *a 5*, there are a number of important differences. First of all, there are no *fa-las*, although in the sixteenth Balletto the syllable "na" from the text recurs many times. Secondly, there is a lute part, which we saw also in Vecchi's pieces in No. 77. The three vocal lines are complete in themselves, and the lute for the most part merely doubles their notes. It is somewhat free, though, for notes are sometimes in a different octave level or omitted altogether. The lute, presumably, could play with the three singers. Plate XI shows, however, that the *canto* part and the lute tablature were carefully placed on adjacent left and right pages so that both could be seen simultaneously.[28] Since the lute part is only in the *canto* partbook, this suggests the possibility of a performance with a solo singer on the *canto* part accompanied by lute, perhaps played by the singer.

The piece on Plate XI, which is transcribed in No. 80b, is entitled *Il Tedesco*, and its text portrays the traditional drunken German soldier who sings "Long live Bacchus, always with his sweet and good beverage; let's everybody drink." This was the image of *Il Tedesco* that we saw also in the *villotta*. I wonder, however, if Gastoldi might also have intended this title to provide a link with the instrumental Balletto Tedesco, for its melody, it seems to me, bears a striking resemblance to the well-known *Printzentantz*. In Ex. 35 I have pieced together a melody by alternating between the two upper voices of Gastoldi's piece, which is completely transcribed in No. 80b. A comparison with Gorzanis' version of the *Printzentantz* in Ex. 1e shows, I think, remarkable similarity. The top voice of Gastoldi's lute part does, in fact, alternate between the upper two vocal lines and matches Gorzanis' melody fairly closely in the opening section (compare No. 80b with No. 73 or Ex. 1e).

Il Tedesco also illustrates another unique feature connected with ten of the Balletti in this book. Plate XI and No. 80b show that the lute tablature, unlike any of the vocal parts, has a double bar (but no repeat signs) in the middle of the second section. In addition, each vocal part has two endings, but the lute does not. It seems to me that Gastoldi is thus indicating that the last four bars of the piece are to be used by the lute for a *ritornello* between the strophes, and perhaps also at the beginning and end of the performance. In this case, the *canto* alone or all the voices would sing the first stanza accompanied by the lute

Ex. 35: Melody formed by alternating upper voices from Gastoldi's *Il Tedesco* (see No. 80b, and compare with the melodies of the *Printzentantz* in Exx. 1e and f).

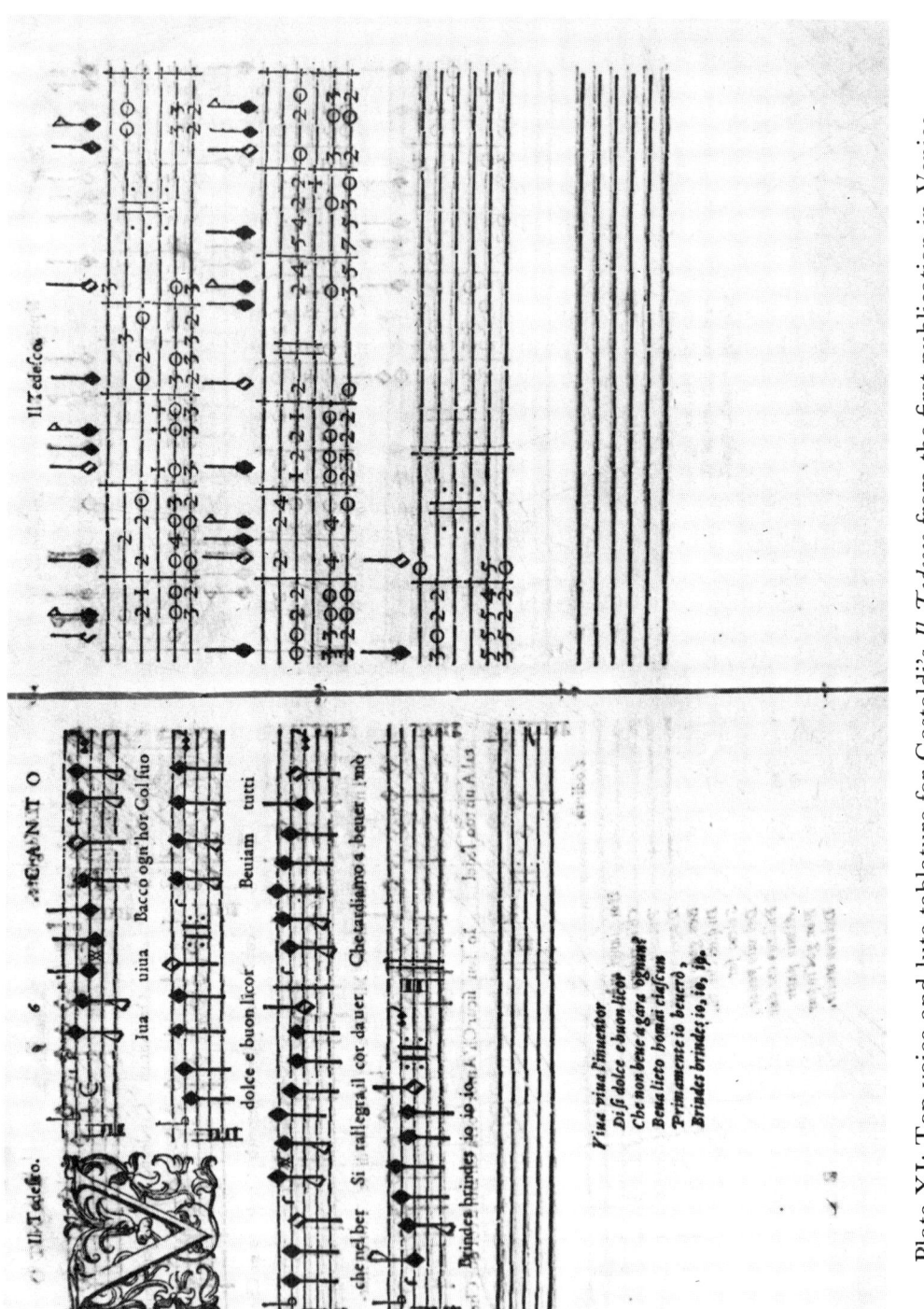

Plate XI: Top voice and lute tablature for Gastoldi's *Il Tedesco* from the first publication in Venice (see No. 80b in Volume II).

Giovanni Giacomo Gastoldi, *Balletti a tre voci, con la intavolatura del liuto, per cantare, sonare, & ballare* (Venice, 1594), *canto* partbook, the piece numbered 6 (reproduced by permission of the Staats- und Universitätsbibliothek Hamburg Carl von Ossietzky).

and with text and music of each section immediately repeated. At the end of the second statement of the second section the voices require a second ending so that they can hold the final note longer. At the same time, however, the lute goes on playing alone, starting at the double bar in the middle of the second section. Since this phrase begins with two eighth-notes of anacrusis, the lute part does not require a different ending. The tradition of a *ritornello* or *ripresa* goes back to the early years of the century and was an integral part of the Italian Renaissance popular style. There is also evidence of solo singing to instrumental accompaniment in some lute and keyboard *arie per cantare* from the second half of the century, which display simple music during a main scheme and then change to shorter note values during the *ripresa*.[29] Ordinarily the instrumental interlude between strophes would consist of two *ritornelli*, each four bars in length. Therefore, in *Il Tedesco* the lute may play the concluding four measures of Ex. 80b twice as the customary pair of *ritornelli* between the strophes.

Plate XII shows the *canto* part of the same Balletto published in Antwerp in 1606. Editions from outside Italy lack the lute part and often replace mention of it in the title by the phrase "con li suoi versi," which comes from the title of the *Balletti a 5*. In addition, the notation in Plate XII shows the repeats written out in full. Here, however, after the usual two statements of the opening section, the first four bars of the second section (up to the double bar in the original lute tablature) are sung only once, whereas the last four bars are done twice.[30] This reveals, I believe, a misunderstanding of the original notation by someone who was not familiar with a method of performance that involved instruments and *ritornelli*. Although the edition from which Plate XII comes includes "per cantare, sonare, & ballare" on the title page, others sometimes omit the word "ballare." Paulus Matthysz published in Amsterdam an edition called *Balletten lustigh om te zingen, en speelen* (that is, only to sing and play). He provides Dutch religious texts and adds "een nieuwe Alt, ofte vierde Parthye" (a new alto or fourth part, actually labeled "tenor" in the partbook), presumably so that the Balletti could be performed by the same four-member ensemble groups that played Almandes. Ex. 36 gives the music of the opening phrase of *Nieusgierigh eyt baest zonde* or *Ruste des gemoedts*,[31] which can be compared to *Il Tedesco* in No. 80b. Matthysz writes out the musical repetition exactly as in the Antwerp edition shown in Plate XII.

Both the *Balletto a 5* and the *Balletto a 3* were born during a period, spanning the late 16th and early 17th centuries, when the attitudes and ideas of one great epoch in music history were declining and those of another were just emerging. Some of the traits of the Balletti seem more conservative, belonging to the Renaissance tradition, others more progressive and pointing ahead to the Baroque. Vocal music in five voices was a conservative idea at that time, for

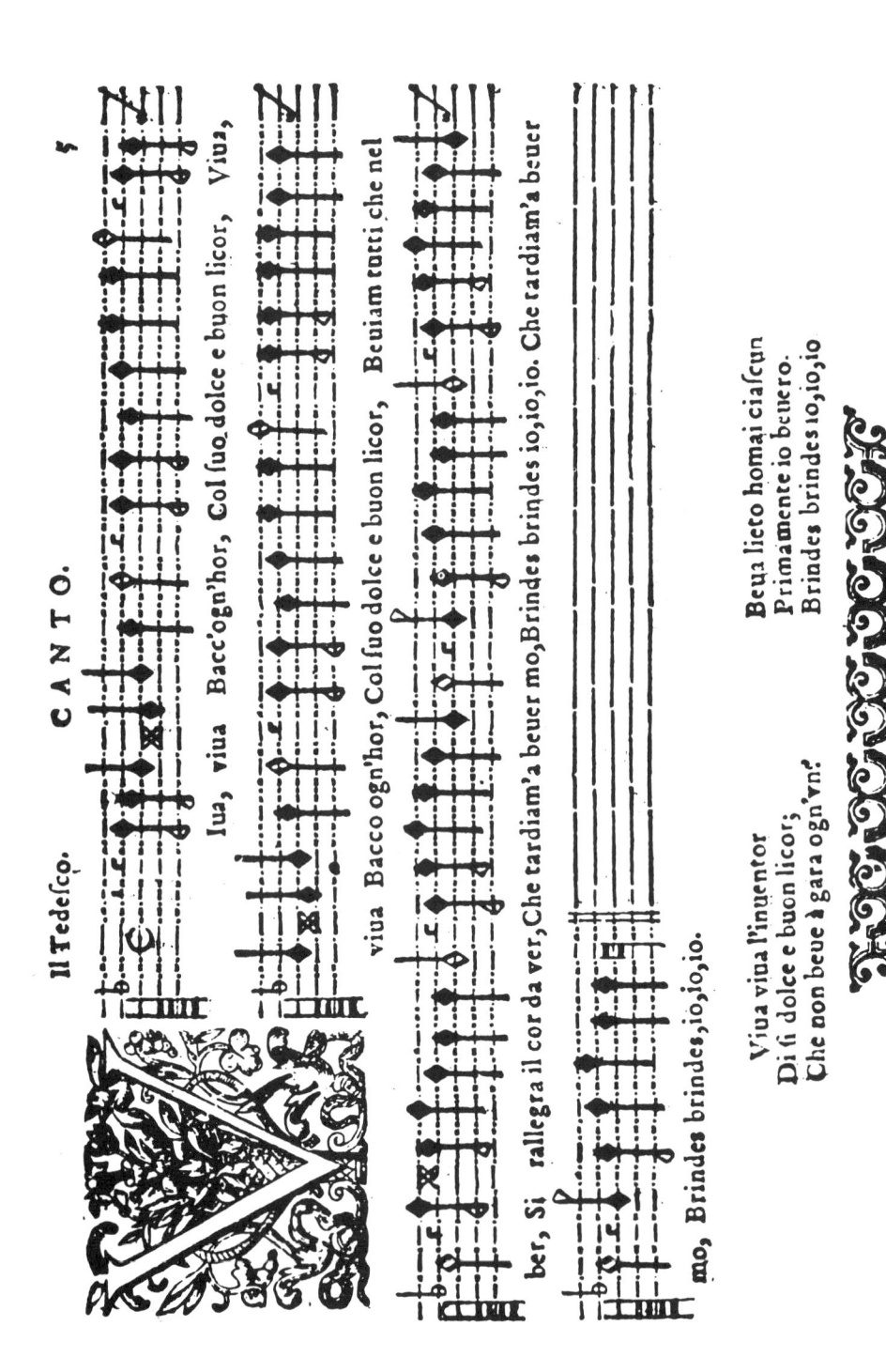

Plate XII: Top voice of Gastoldi's *Il Tedesco* from the publication in Antwerp.

Giovanni Giacomo Gastoldi, *Balletti a tre voci con li suoi versi per cantare, sonare & ballare* (Antwerp: Pierre Phalèse [ii], 1606), canto partbook, p. 5 (reproduced by permission of the Centrale Bibliotheek, Rijksuniversiteit, Ghent).

Ex. 36: Amsterdam version of the opening section of the music of Gastoldi's *Il Tedesco* with added fourth voice.

this was the predominant texture after around 1520 for vocal art forms like the mass, motet, and madrigal. Music in three voices, although it was inspired no doubt by lighter forms such as the *villanella*, points forward to the Baroque trio style, with its two overlapping voices in a high range supported by a bass. Instrumental doubling or substituting on a vocal line was a conservative element in the *Balletti a 5*. Providing a relatively independent (or at least independently printed) lute part for the *Balletti a 3* was progressive, for it made possible a performance by only one (or perhaps only two) singers along with the lute. It was only a few years later that monody emerged and played a leading role in the formation of opera.

The Renaissance had a special interest in what voices did together, and hence in making them similar to one another through imitation, rhythm, and instrumentation. The Baroque ideal, on the other hand, involved a concern with the organization of individual lines and their differentiation from each other. The note-against-note texture in most of the Balletti, in which all the voices have the same rhythm, is part of Renaissance chordal construction, as manifested also in the chordal schemes of popular music and the familiar style of art music. The contrapuntal activity we have noted occasionally in the *fa-la* parts of the *Balletti a 5*, however, is mainly a part of the Baroque development, for, although it is sometimes imitative, it also involves tiny patterned motives that act, often through sequence, to organize individual lines and enliven them with a new type of rhythmic energy.

On the whole, the *Balletti a 5* seem to be generally more conservative in nature and the *Balletti a 3* more progressive. This plays a role, as we will see, when Gastoldi's music travels to other countries. The use of the lute in the *Balletti a 3* establishes a sense of continuity with the lute *Balletti tedeschi* of Gorzanis, Barbetta, and Terzi. Many details of musical construction form a link between the vocal Balletti and their instrumental predecessors. The relatively sudden appearance of vocal examples, with five or three voices instead of four and with a different spirit and no doubt a different tempo, was indeed a dramatic event. Both coexisted for a while in both Italy and other countries. One of the first places to which Gastoldi's Balletti traveled was England, so we will turn our attention next to this country, where we will find both the vocal Ballett and the instrumental Almain.

5 THE VOCAL BALLETT AND THE INSTRUMENTAL ALMAIN FOR KEYBOARD, PLUCKED STRINGS, AND ENSEMBLE IN ENGLAND 1550–1650

SOON AFTER the instrumental Almande established itself in France and the Low Countries, its name begins to appear in English sources. Robert Wedderburn, in *The Complaynt of Scotland* from around 1550, includes it in a list of dances performed by shepherds and their women in a pastoral setting: 'thai dancit al cristyn mennis dance, the northt of scotland, huntis up . . . Robene hude, . . . the gosseps dance, . . . the alman haye . . ."[1] The word "haye," meaning "in a file,"[2] probably refers to the procession of couples described by Arbeau. At the end of the century, following the publication of Gastoldi's Balletti, a series of English Balletts appears, commencing with those of Morley in 1595. The Ballett, however, seems to be a purely vocal form in this country. Therefore the English probably suspected no historical connection at all between their instrumental Almain and their vocal Ballett or *Fa la*.

The Almain for Keyboard and Plucked Strings

The English name *Alman* or *Almain*, spelled in various ways, reveals its derivation from the Franco-Flemish Almande. In addition, there are a few concordances with some of the well-known Almande melodies, both those that correspond with a Deutscher Tanz and those that seem to originate in France and the Low Countries. Ex. 37b shows the upper voice of an *Allemana d'Amor* for ensemble that appears in a manuscript dated around 1548.[3] For comparison, Ex. 37a is the Flemish version, which differs in many details, yet follows the basic melodic shape (see also the *Tantz*, No. 6 in Volume II). Typical cadences occur in the English version at the end of the first and last sections.

The Dublin Virginal Manuscript, an early keyboard source from around 1570, contains four untitled pieces that concord with Almandes. One has the melody of the *Almande Prince* in the alto voice, as shown in the opening phrase in Ex. 38. This is followed, as was customary in this particular Almande, by a *reprinse* in triple meter. The others have a melody in the upper voice and possess no *reprinse*. They include settings of the *Almande Bruynsmedelijn* (Ex. 39 shows

98   *The Transition*

Ex. 37: Flemish and English versions of the *Almande d'amour*.

(a) Phalèse and Bellère, 1571: *Almande damours* for ensemble (see Plate XVII).

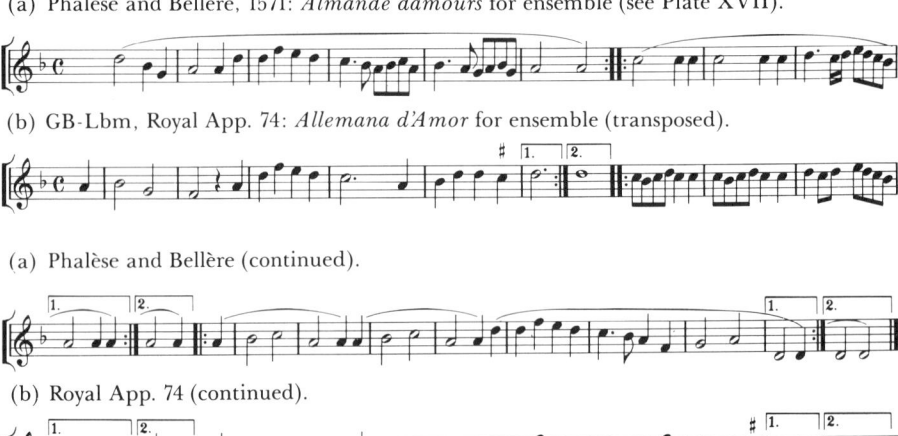

(b) GB-Lbm, Royal App. 74: *Allemana d'Amor* for ensemble (transposed).

(a) Phalèse and Bellère (continued).

(b) Royal App. 74 (continued).

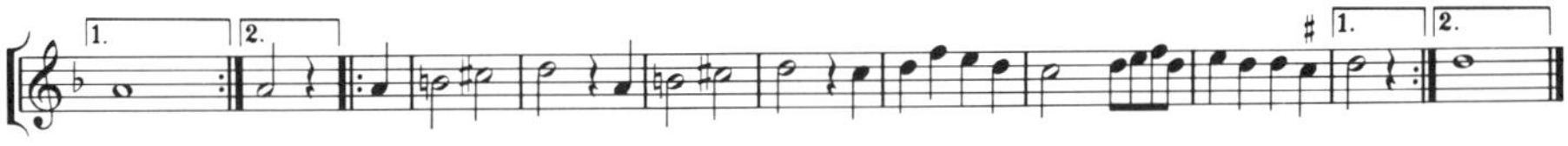

Ex. 38: Opening section of the untitled *Almande Prince* from the Dublin Virginal Manuscript (c. 1570), with the melody in the alto.

Ex. 39: First section of the untitled *Almande Bruynsmedelijn* from the Dublin Virginal Manuscript (c. 1570), with the melody on top.

the opening section), *Almande Guerre, guerre gay* (see Ex. 23a), and *Almande Le pied de cheval* (No. 37a).[4] Exx. 38 and 39 reveal the simple style of these Almains and their percussive insistence on the quarter-note beat.

The *Almande Nonette* occurs in England with different titles. It is *The Queenes Almayne* in the Dallis Lute Book from around 1583 (see No. 129). This is a very simple setting with no varied repeats and with the opening phrase ending on

Ex. 40: Flemish and English versions of the *Almande Monsieur*.

(a) Thysius MS: *Allemande Monsieur* for lute (transposed from Land II, p. 200).

(b) Holborne, 1597: *Mounsiers Almayne* for cittern.

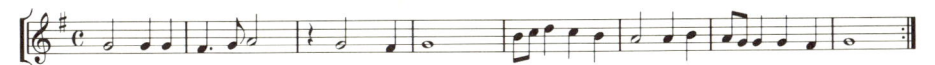

(a) Thysius (continued).

(b) Holborne (continued).

(c) Byrd, variation on the opening phrase of *Monsieurs Alman* for keyboard.

scale degree 2 (see Ex. 21e for comparison with other versions). *The Queenes Alman* by William Byrd appears in the Fitzwilliam Virginal Book (copied 1609–19).[5] Its opening phrase ends on 5, following Ex. 21a. A varied repeat follows each section and this entire structure is then varied two more times, resulting in a set of three variations. The same melody is called *The Oulde Almaine* in *The Cithran Schoole* (London, 1597) of Anthony Holborne.[6] Here each section has a varied repeat, and the opening phrase is based on Ex. 21f and ends with the typical cadence and scale degree 1.

The *Almande Monsieur* appears in England in *Mounsiers Almayne* for cittern by Holborne[7] and William Byrd's *Monsieurs Alman* for keyboard.[8] Ex. 40 shows a continental version of the melody (a) compared to Holborne's (b). The latter includes a typical cadence at the end of each section and in the middle of the second. In Byrd's setting, each section is followed immediately by a varied repeat and this entire structure recurs in a second variation. This piece is followed in the Fitzwilliam Book by a *Variatio*, which contains three more variations.[9] *Monsieurs Alman* is the only example that I can discover of a continental melody that retains its descriptive title in England. In addition, the melody of the *Almande Loraine* occurs in *An Almane* for two lutes (see No. 135

and compare with the melodies in Ex. 22), and *The Duke of Brunswick's Alman* by John Bull[10] seems to bear some resemblance to the *Almande Bruynswijck* that appears in the cittern books of Vredeman (1569) and the firm of Phalèse and Bellère (1570).

There are still other melodies, of course, that do not seem to have continental concordances. A few of these bear titles, such as *Meridian Alman* and *Dalling Alman* in the Fitzwilliam Book, *Almaine Hartes Ease* or *Honi-suckle*, *The Choyce*, and *The Nightwatch* from the works of Holborne, *The King's Jewel* and *Nann's Mask* or *French Alman* by Gibbons,[11] *Almane Delorne* and *Ane Alman Moreiss* in the Skene manuscript from Scotland (c. 1615–20).[12] Some recur in more than one source, such as the *Almaine* by Francis Cuttinge in the Pickeringe lute book of 1616, which appeared earlier in William Barley's *New Booke of Tabliture* (London, 1596).[13] In addition, *The Princes Almayne* of Robert Johnson (No. 136 in Volume II), which is not based on the melody of the *Almande Prince*, occurs as an *Alman* in the Fitzwilliam Book.[14] Neither has varied repeats, but the latter includes some dotted notes and written-out trills not found in No. 136.

The Fitzwilliam Virginal Book contains twenty-three Almains. About one-third have three sections, most of the rest have two. Some are very simple, with no varied repeats. Others include a repeat written out following each section. Still others take the latter as a structure for a set of variations. Thus, in *Monsieurs Alman* and *The Queenes Alman* of Byrd, as we have noted above, a set of variations is built upon a framework which itself contains varied repeats labeled "Rep." It is in these works of Byrd also that we can see the fully developed technique of variation that dominates the style. Ex. 40c shows, for example, one of Byrd's variations for the opening phrase of *Monsieurs Alman*,[15] which can be compared to the simpler melody in Ex. 40b. There is contrapuntal vitality; interest in brief, animated motives, often separated by rests; and detailed melodic organization through repetition or sequence.[16] We have already seen motivic structure and counterpoint on a more modest scale in the *fa-la* portions of Gastoldi's Balletti. Melodic organization on a broader scale we have noted in the French Almandes.

Unity on a formal level can be seen in the lute *Allman* No. 130, where the opening two sections each consist of two parallel two-bar phrases. In No. 133a, measure 4 of the second section repeats measure 6 of the first, and the last halves of each section are almost identical. Organization on a more detailed level is evident in No. 130 in the playful rhythmic motive of a quarter-note, two eighths, and a quarter. Another common patterned motive occurs with dotted rhythm, as in No. 131. Here the melodic pattern in the top voice of the fifth measure moves in the following measure to the bass and in the next measure back to the soprano. In No. 132, patterned rhythms, preceded by rests, occur in measures 5 and 6 of the second section. Motives are used in sequence in measures 1, 5, and 6 of the first section of No. 136, as well as measures 1-4 of the second. A motive consisting of two eighth-notes and a quarter opens the first section with ascending motion and starts the second by descending. Contrapuntal devices also appear sometimes, as in the canonic sequence in the tenor and bass in bars 3 and 4 of the second section of No. 136, or the imitation at the beginning of the varied repeat of the second section in No. 133b.

Elaborate variation technique occurs mainly in the keyboard examples, as part of the general style. Almains for plucked strings tend to be simpler, with more modest application of some of the same stylistic features. Holborne's examples, except for *Mounsiers Almaine* and *The Oulde Almaine*, have no varied repeats at all. They have many typical cadences, however, as well as the modified version seen at the end of each section of Ex. 40b. Here the usual quarter-note on the opening beat of the penultimate measure is replaced by two eighth-notes moving from 2 to 1, in the manner of the vocal cadence in Ex. 4a. Once before, in Ex. 21f, we encountered eighth-notes on this opening beat (compare also the end of No. 129, which is a setting of the same melody). The English expand the idea of flowing eighth-notes in this measure by including them sometimes on the second and third beats in the figure shown in Ex. 41a. The cadence resembles the tenor part (see Ex. 42) that often accompanies the usual vocal cadence. This tenor occurs, as a matter of fact, at the end of the duple portion of Ammerbach's setting of the *Printzentantz* in No. 4, in counter-

Ex. 41: 2-1 cadences that form a counterpoint to the Tanz cadence.

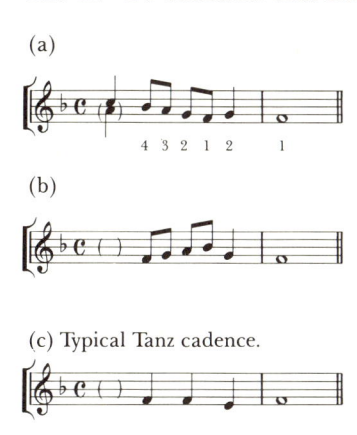

(a)

(b)

(c) Typical Tanz cadence.

Ex. 42: A counterpoint to the vocal cadence in Ex. 4a.

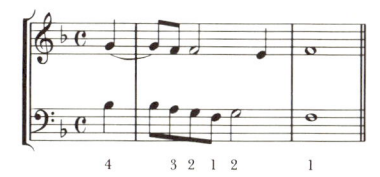

point with the typical cadence in the soprano. In the tenor of the penultimate measure of Exx. 38 and 39, the fourth degree of the scale is held, so that the eighth-note flow is on the second and third beats. Here again, the typical cadence is in counterpoint with it. Moving this tenor up to the soprano, then, and shifting scale degree 4 over to the second beat, we get the cadence of Ex. 41a. It concludes Nos. 130 and 133b, the end of the first statement of the third section of No. 134, and the end of the first section of No. 136. Although this new cadence fits contrapuntally with the typical cadence in Ex. 41c, they seldom occur together. The cadence in Ex. 41a not only adds flowing eighth-note motion, but also makes its final resolution from 2 to 1 instead of the 7-1 of the typical cadence.

The English Almain for lute and keyboard continues many of the traits seen in the Deutscher Tanz, the Almande, and the Balletto Tedesco. As we have seen, however, the chordal texture is sometimes replaced, especially in the keyboard examples, by counterpoint, sequence, motivic structure, and patterned rhythms – the features, in short, characteristic of a new style that exhibited special concern for the organization of individual voices. A glance at the examples in Volume II from No. 129 through No. 136 will show that the usual texture involves two or three voices, with four only in an occasional chord. The typical cadence still occurs, but, as we have noted, there is also a new one derived from it. The Almains are all in duple meter. Except for the *reprinse* attached to the setting of *Almande Prince* in the Dublin Virginal Manuscript, there are, as far as I know, no after-dances associated with English Almains. The examples for lute continue the tradition established in the other countries for this instrument. Those for keyboard are involved, as we have seen, in the dramatic variation style developed by the Elizabethan virginal composers, who thus sometimes bring the keyboard Almain to a level of inner animation and linear complexity not known in its continental counterpart.[17]

The Ballett for Voices

During the last decade of the 16th century, Italian vocal forms were imported and English composers, influenced by the style, began to write similar music of their own. In 1588 Nicholas Yonge published in London *Musica transalpina: Madrigales Translated*, followed in 1590 by Thomas Watson's *Italian Madrigalls Englished*. Thomas Morley was the leading figure to adopt the Italian forms, publishing in 1593 his *Canzonets, or Little Short Songs to Three Voyces*, and in 1595 *The First Booke of Balletts to Five Voyces*.[18] The climax of the English development occurred during the last three years of the century with the madrigals of such composers as Weelkes and Wilbye.

In 1597 Morley wrote in his *Plaine and Easie Introduction to Practicall Musicke* that "there be also an other kind of Ballets, commonlie called *fa las*. The first set of that kind which I have seene was made by Gastoldi. If others have laboured in the same field, I know not, but a slight kind of musick it is, & as I take it devised to be daunced to voices."[19] Neither Morley's own book of Balletts, however, nor any of the later English sources, makes any mention of dancing. There was, nevertheless, strong influence from Gastoldi, particularly from his *Balletti a 5*.

Morley also published his book of Balletts simultaneously in an Italian edition, *Il primo libro delle Ballette*, in which the same music has texts and titles in Italian. He borrowed eight texts from Gastoldi's *Balletti a 5*, but not the descriptive titles or the theatrical intent.[20] He entitles each individual piece with the opening words of its text. Therefore, Gastoldi's *La Sirena* (see Plate XXII) appears as *Questa dolce Sirena* or *My bonny lasse shee smyleth* (see Plate XXIV, which shows the upper voice from both the English and Italian editions).

At the same time Morley also borrowed musical ideas from Gastoldi. The closest correspondence comes in Morley's *Sing wee and chaunt it*, which follows its model (see Ex. 43) both melodically and, except for a slight extension of the final *fa-la* section, structurally. Ex. 44 shows the top voice and part of the *quintus* for the opening section of *My bonny lasse*, which can be compared to Gastoldi's melody in Ex. 33c. Morley's piece begins, like the model, with two two-bar phrases, but the melody is more like the beginning of Gastoldi's *Amor vittorioso* (see No. 12). Morley's version differs most in the length and complexity of the *fa-las*. I have included a lower voice also in Ex. 44 to show the imitative beginning. Other *fa-las* of Morley contain tiny motives in dialogue (as in the excerpt from Gastoldi in Ex. 34), or change to triple meter.

Ex. 43: Comparison of Gastoldi and Morley settings of the text *A lieta vita*.

(a) Gastoldi, 1591: *L'innamorato*.

(b) Morley, 1595: *Sing wee and chaunt it*.

(a) Gastoldi (continued).

(b) Morley (continued).

Ex. 44: Top voice of the first half of Morley's Ballett *My bonny lasse,* 1595 (see Plate XXIV for the original notation), with the *quintus* part added on the *fa-las.*

Morley also borrowed texts from other sources. The music of the well-known *Now is the month of maying* appears in the Italian edition with the text *So ben mi c'ha bon tempo* from Vecchi's *Aria* in No. 77b. Morley's piece has the same phrase structure, but a different melody and more animated *fa-las* at the end.[21] Fifteen of the twenty-one pieces in Morley's book have *fa-las* and hence, according to his own definition, are actually Balletts. Some are very simple and chordal, and others more complex and contrapuntal. In some, the verses (referring to the portions of text that precede the *fa-las*) are also more contrapuntal, with successive voice entries and imitation. Although no edition of Gastoldi's Balletti was published in London, his musical ideas were transmitted to England through this work of Morley. Morley follows Gastoldi by using five voices, by utilizing the same music for more than one strophe, by emphasizing a chordal texture, by using the typical cadence, and by including some pieces in triple meter. He expands on his predecessor, however, in the contrapuntal independence of the voices, especially in the *fa-la* passages.

Thomas Weelkes' *Balletts and Madrigals to Five Voyces* appeared in 1598.[22] He extends even further the length and complexity of the *fa-las.* Ex. 45a shows the outer two voices in the *fa-las* at the end of the opening section of his Ballett *On the plaines, fairie traines.* The upper two voices form a dialogue of two-note motives with the lower three. The outer voices of the first *fa-la* section of his Ballett *Ladie, your eye* are given in Ex. 45b, showing the remarkable ostinato figure repeated nine times in the *cantus.* A final example of Weelkes' *fa-la* complexity occurs in Ex. 45c (*Farewell my joy*), which shows first the *quintus* and *altus* and then the *cantus* and *altus* in a canonic sequence. This same sequence recurs later between other voices, so that the entire *fa-la* section spans eighteen bars. The same two-voice sequence appears at the end of Morley's Ballett *My lovely wanton jewell,* but here the section is only ten bars long. A few of Weelkes' Balletts are not strophic; hence they give more attention to expressing the meaning of the text and tend to commence with imitation.

There are a number of later vocal pieces with *fa-la* syllables, although they do not bear the name "Ballett." Since Morley equates the Ballett with *fa-las,*

Ex. 45: *Fa-la* music in the Balletts of Weelkes, 1598.

(a) *On the plaines fairie traines*, outer voices at the end of the first section.

(b) *Ladie, your eye*, outer voices at the end of the opening section.

(c) *Farewell my joy*, portions from the upper three voices at the beginning of the last *fa-las*.

Ex. 46: Greaves, 1604: *Come away sweet love*, outer voices in the *fa-las* at the end of the first section.

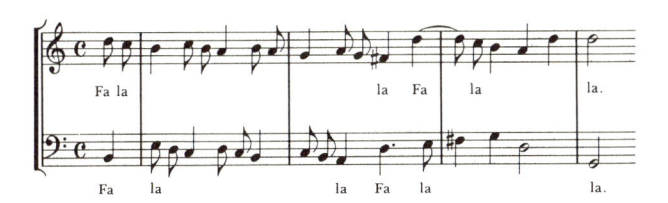

they should no doubt be included as part of this English development. Among the madrigals in Thomas Greaves' *Songes of Sundrie Kindes* (London, 1604) is one (*Come away sweet love*) with the canonic sequence shown in Ex. 46.[23] This is based on the same three-note motive seen in Gastoldi's Balletto in Ex. 34. Although the piece is not strophic, the verse parts are very chordal. The first three pieces in Thomas Vautor's *Songs of Divers Ayres and Natures* (London,

Ex. 47: Vautor, 1619: *Sing on sister,* cantus for the opening statement of each half of the piece, with excerpts from the *altus* and *quintus* (for the repetition of each half, the *cantus* and *quintus* exchange parts).

[Musical notation]

1619) have *fa-las*.²⁴ Two are strophic, but all of them begin each section chordally, then burst into counterpoint on the *fa-las*. Ex. 47 shows the upper voice for *Sing on sister*. I have included phrases from other voices to show the activity during the *fa-las*. The first *fa-la* section begins with a three-note motive, as in Exx. 34 and 46, then expands this to a seven-note figure, which then recurs at closer intervals as the climax is reached on the high e''. This example illustrates the contrapuntal activity between voices as they imitate each other, and, at the same time, the organization within a single voice, such as the *cantus*, as motives recur in sequence. The same approach is seen in the other *fa-la* portion of this piece, which is in sequence within a single voice, and in dialogue between voices. Each verse, as well as each of the main sections in this piece, ends with a typical Tanz cadence.

Eight of Thomas Tomkins' *Songs of 3, 4, 5, and 6 Parts* (London, 1622) have *fa-las*, and one other has similar passages on the word "no."²⁵ *O let me live for true love* and its second part, *O let me dye for true love*, are both *a 4* and are unified by sharing a common motive in the *fa-la* sections. The other *fa-la* pieces are in five voices. None is strophic, and therefore most begin with imitation that matches the meaning of the text. The *fa-la* sections, in contrast, have shorter note values and are even more animated. Following the tradition that Morley had established with his first English Balletts, Tomkins makes the *fa-la* passages the most brilliant and virtuosic parts of his songs.

Gastoldi's *Balletti a 3* seem to have had no influence in England, probably because those in the 1594 collection had no *fa-las* and his single work of 1592 (see No. 78), which did have *fa-las*, was unknown. There were, however, a few examples of English *Fa las* for three voices. At the end of Anthony Holborne's *The Cittharn Schoole* (London, 1597) appear "six short aers Neapolitan like to three voyces, without the Instrument: done by his brother William Holborne." Three of them have *fa-las*, and one of these also has the word "fa-la-ing" in the text.[26] One song, *Change then for lo she changeth*, is strophic, and so brief, chordal, and simple, even on the *fa-las*, that it seems to be modeled more on Azzaiolo's *villotte* from mid-century than on Gastoldi's Balletti. Another song, *Sit still and sturre not*, however, has a single stanza of text, begins imitatively like the five-voice examples, and has more active *fa-las*. In Henry Youll's *Canzonets to Three Voyces* of 1608, the last six pieces have *fa-las*.[27] None is strophic, but most are chordal, except on the *fa-las*. *Come mery lads let us away* begins with a two-bar phrase exactly like Morley's *My bonny lasse* in Ex. 44, then has *fa-las* on the three-note motive in Ex. 34 and ends the first section with the typical cadence. The work concludes, like one of Gastoldi's *Balletti a 5*, with the syllables "lirum" sung to the highly constructive music shown in Ex. 48. John Hilton (ii) published in 1627 his *Ayres or Fa la's for Three Voyces*.[28] According to Morley, the word "ayre" includes all vocal forms lighter than the madrigal. Hilton includes both simple and complex examples, although none is strophic, and seems to summarize all the possibilities that had developed since Morley. Ex. 49 from *To sport our merrie meeting* shows the motivic unity within a *fa-la* section; each voice is in canon, and each has the same motive in sequence.

The Balletts or *Fal las* from Morley in 1595 to Hilton in 1627 thus show a fairly consistent construction. Most are *a 5* and strophic, with chords at the beginning of each section followed by a dazzling motivic display on the *fa-las*. Others have a single text and, like the contemporary serious madrigal, portray its changing moods and images in points of imitation, phrases in the familiar style, or dance-like sections in triple meter. Renaissance counterpoint, as it had developed in the Flemish motet and the Italian madrigal, usually created through the imitation of indefinite melodic fragments a homogeneity of sound

Ex. 48: Youll, 1608: *Come mery lads let us away*, "lirum" music at end of piece.

Ex. 49: Hilton, 1627: *To sport our merrie meeting, fa-la* music at end of piece.

within an endless flow of time. In this context, individual voices became like one another and attention was centered not on individual voices, but on the effect they created together. Baroque counterpoint, on the other hand, is based on rhythmic and melodic motives that have a finite and usually brief length and, unlike the fragments in Renaissance imitation, have definite duration that marks off tiny units of time. These motives then act, through sequential or ostinato recurrence, to organize each individual line and attract attention to it. The result is a new kind of counterpoint in which the voices sound differentiated from each other and create a time sense that is more measured and finite in nature. We saw this new counterpoint emerging within the variation technique of the Elizabethan virginal composers, and now we meet it once again in the *fa-la* sections of the English Balletts. In the Ballett, moreover, there is a syllable on every note of the *fa-la* portion, so the finite musical motives, which represent the heart of the new style of the Baroque period, are articulated with unusual clarity. Stock motives seem to recur sometimes from composer to composer. Many of the motives, however, as well as the technique of joining them together, later become a significant part of the language of fully mature Baroque music.

The Almain for Viols and Other Instrumental Ensembles

Starting late in the 16th century, books of vocal music sometimes include in the title the phrase "apt for viols and voyces." This is found, for example, in the four books of madrigals published by Michael East from 1604 to 1618. It also occurs in the book from 1619 that contains Vautor's three *Fa las* discussed above. The full title of his book is *The First Set: beeing Songs of Divers Ayres and Natures, of Five and Six Parts: apt for Vyols and Voyces*. Thus, the English Balletts or *Fa las* could sometimes be played by a consort of viols instead of being sung. This practice is confirmed by Charles Butler in *The Principles of Musik in Singing and Setting* (1636), when he describes the aeolian mode: "The *Aeolik* moode is that which, with its soft, pleasing sounds, pacifyeth the Passions of the minde, and with instruments or dittiles [textless] *fa-la's*, in continued discant, delighting the sens, and not intending the minde of the hearer, like Mercuri's *Caduceus*, charmest affections and cares, and so lullest him sweetly a sleepe."[29] The beginning of the 17th century saw an upsurge of interest in the viol and in ensembles of viols, not only in "dittiles" *Fa-las*, but also in Almains.

We have already noted an isolated *Allemana d'Amor* from around 1548. During the second half of the 16th century a highly contrapuntal style developed in the *fancy* and the *In nomine* for viol consort. The early years of the 17th century brought an increased importance to this instrument, for in addition to its continued use in ensembles, it developed a solo literature and also played a role in accompanying vocal music. The Renaissance preference for like sounds and a homogeneous texture was being replaced by interest in unlike sounds and a differentiation of lines through instrumentation. The greatest contrast was achieved by setting instruments, with independent parts, against the voice.

Books of vocal music with instrumental accompaniment sometimes also contained independent pieces for the instruments alone. In 1607 appeared Thomas Ford's *Musicke of Sundrie Kindes Set forth in two Bookes. The First whereof are Aries for 4 Voices to the Lute, Orphorion* [orpharion, a wire-strung plucked instrument tuned like a lute], *or Basse-Viol . . . The Second are Pavens, Galiards, Almaines, Toies, Jigges, Thumpes, and such like, for two Basse-Viols, the Liera way* [lyra viols].[30] William Corkine published in 1610 *Ayres, to Sing and Play to the Lute and Basse Violl, with Pavins, Galliards, Almaines, and Corantos for the Lyra Violl*.[31] At the end of the book appear the *Lessons for the Lyra Violl*, which include two Almains. In 1612 appeared *The Second Booke of Ayres, Some to Sing and Play to the Base-Violl Alone, Others to be Sung to the Lute and Basse Violl, with new Corantoes, Pavins, Almaines . . . set to the Lyra-Violl*.[32] The *Lessons for the Lyra Violl* again include two Almains, one of which is *Mounsiers Almaine* on the same melody set by Byrd and Holborne. Other books similarly combine instrumentally accompanied vocal music with independent pieces for instruments alone. John Maynard, for example, in the *XII Wonders of the World* (1611), includes among the lute lessons *A Pavin, A Galliard to the Pavin*, and *An Almond to Both*.[33]

Still other books are devoted almost exclusively to instrumental music. Tobias Hume's *The First Part of Ayres* (1605) contains eight Almains for the "viole de gambo alone," including *Maister Crasse his Almayne, The Lord Beccus Almayne, Captaine Humes Almayne, My Mistresse Almaine*, and *Loves Almayne*.[34] Hume also presents *The Princes Almayne: A lesson for two to play upon one viole*, a

110 *The Transition*

technique described on the title page as his own invention. The music appears to be different from both the *Almande Prince* and *The Princes Almayne* of Johnson in No. 136. In 1607 appeared *Captaine Humes Poeticall Musicke*, which contains music with a bass part in mensural notation and two parts in tablature.[35] The title page lists eight different combinations of instruments that can play, including three bass viols, two tenor viols and a bass viol, and other combinations involving lute, orphorion, virginals, and a wind instrument. Among the pieces are four Almains, including *The Dukes Almaine* and *French Almaine*.

There are also printed books devoted entirely to instruments. A few are for solo lyra viol; others are for ensembles. The latter include Anthony Holborne's *Pavans, Galliards, Almains, and Other Short Aeirs both Grave, and Light, in Five Parts, for Viols, Violins, or other Musicall Winde Instruments* (London, 1599).[36] The word *aeir* or *ayre* refers in this case, and in some other sources of the 17th century, to purely instrumental pieces of a light nature. The same year, Morley published *The First Booke of Consort Lessons, made by Divers Exquisite Authors, for six Instruments to Play together, the Treble Lute, the Pandora* [or bandora, a plucked-string bass instrument with metal strings], *the Cittern, the Base-Violl, the Flute & Treble Violl*. This particular combination was known as a "mixed consort," and one of the pieces is a setting of the same *Mounsiers Almaine* that we have met before in English and Flemish sources.[37] There are also Almains for mixed consort by Richard Alison and Daniel Bacheler in the Walsingham Consort Books of 1588.[38] Still another combination of instruments appears in John Dowland's *Lachrimae, or Seaven Teares Figured in Seaven Passionate Pavans, with divers other Pavans, Galiards, and Almands, set forth for the Lute, Viols, or Violons in five Parts* (c. 1604); included are *Mistresse Nichol's Almand* and *M. George Whitehead his Almand*.[39]

Many of the ensemble Almains, however, are in manuscripts, and Nos. 137 through 141 in Volume II come from two of them. GB-Lbm Add. 10444 from around 1617 is the main source of masque dances from the time of James I (1603–25). The manuscript contains fourteen Almains, some with the name of a composer, such as Robert Bateman, Stephen Thomas, Gibbons, Maynard, and Dowland. Only treble and bass parts are given (see Nos. 137 and 138). The second Almain of Stephen Thomas recurs later in a German source, as we will see, as an *All'mand* of Robert Bateman, but now with five voices for viols or other instruments (see No. 19). Presumably, then, the entire collection was originally performed by five instruments. GB-Lbm Add. 17792–17795 from around 1624, however, has fifteen Almains for two viols (see No. 139) and eight for three viols (Nos. 140 and 141). A third manuscript, Add. 36993 from around mid-century, preserves only the bass part of seventeen Almains for four viols by composers such as John Jenkins, Morris Webster, and Charles Coleman.[40]

About half of the Almains in these three manuscripts have two sections, the others three. In the earliest source, all the sections are in duple meter except in one Almain, which is entirely triple. In the second manuscript, those in two sections are completely duple, whereas those with three sections may be all duple or may have the third section or the last part of the second or third section in triple meter. The Almains with three sections in the third manuscript favor a third section in triple, and those in two sections sometimes have the second section all or partly in triple. Phrases often end with repeated chords, as in Nos. 137, 138, and 19. The typical cadence is also present at the end of No. 137 and the middle of No. 138. The opening section of a binary Almain may end in the same key as the second (see No. 139) or in a different key, usually the dominant (No. 140). In ternary Almains, the outer two sections usually cadence in the main key, the middle one in the dominant (Nos. 137 and 138).

Most striking, however, are the sections that end like *fa-las* in a Ballett. The last six bars of No. 137 present a canonic sequence, reminding one of the descending figures used in the *fa-las* of Exx. 45c, 48, and 49. In No. 139, the opening four measures are relatively slow, solemn, and more or less note-against-note, like the verse of a Ballett; then the section becomes animated with two-note motives, as in Ex. 45a, and sounds more like *fa-las*. The second section of the same Almain does the same thing, with the opening six bars like a verse, the last four like *fa-las*. The three-note motive used for *fa-las* in Exx. 34 and 46 appears in the last half of the opening section of No. 19 and, with the opening note dotted, in the last five bars of No. 140. The final section of No. 19 concludes with five measures of canonic sequence using the motive again from the end of No. 137. The Almain in No. 141 begins with a phrase like Morley's *My bonny lasse* (Ex. 44), then turns for the remainder of the piece to precisely the sort of counterpoint we have seen in many of the *fa-la* sections of the Balletts.

This is the new Baroque type of counterpoint, not only with canon and imitation between the voices, but also with individual voices highly organized, mainly through sequence. We have seen this texture already in some of the keyboard Almains, but it is in later Balletts and ensemble Almains that it seems to attain full flower. It is tempting to speculate that the style was first performed by a viol consort when it played *Fa las* without a "ditty" or text, as Butler describes, and then penetrated into the Almain. In pieces such as Nos. 140 and 141, as well as in many *fa-la* sections of Balletts, it is difficult to say that the "main melody" is in any particular voice for the entire piece. During the highly motivic portions, often with many rests, the impression of a continuous melody comes from the collective action of several or perhaps all the voices.

At the same time, however, there continued to be simpler Almains that did have a clear melody in the upper voice. Ex. 50 shows two melodies from MSS 24.E.13-17 at the Fitzwilliam Museum in Cambridge. Both have a merry sound, produced in the first by repeated notes, dotted notes, and dactylic rhythm, in the second by eighth-notes, especially the motive of two eighth-

Ex. 50: Upper voice of Almains for wind ensemble, c. 1603-25.

(a) *Almande 8.*

(b) *Almande 7.*

notes and a quarter. Ex. 50b has sequential organization in the second section. They come from Almains for six wind instruments (the tenor is lost), probably part of the repertoire of the royal wind players from 1603 to 1665.[41] The manuscripts contain twenty *Almandes* from the time of James I, with composers indicated sometimes only by initials; there are also seven and parts of two other *Almandes* from a later period by Matthew Locke, Charles Coleman, and Nicholas Lanier. The pieces, according to Dart, are for cornetts or oboes and sackbuts,[42] and were no doubt used in the Jacobean masque. In addition, John Coprario has simple homophonic Almains for one or two violins, bass viol, and organ in suites that consist of *Fantasia, Alman,* and *Galliard.*[43]

Social Function and Choreography

The English Almain was one of the most popular social dances of the time. One of the most important moments when social dancing took place was during the masque, which flourished especially during the time of James I and Charles I. Fortunately, we have much musical and choreographic information concerning the masques and dances presented at the four Inns of Court in London. Lincoln's Inn, Gray's Inn, the Inner Temple, and the Middle Temple (originally the buildings that housed schools of law) were the societies of lawyers who controlled admission to the bar. A lawyer at the Inns of Court was expected to know how to dance, and elaborate instructions are given for the social dances, especially those involved with a masque.

The English masque had these parts:[44]

The Ballett and the Almain in England 113

1. Antimasquers' dances and songs
2. Loud music and discovery of the scene of the masque
3. First song
4. Masquers' entry dance
5. Second song
6. Masquers' main dance
7. Third song
8. THE MEASURES AND REVELS
9. Fourth song
10. Masquers' exit dance

The center of the masque consisted of the three dances of the masked performers. The music for these dances in GB-Lbm Add. 10444 bears titles such as *The Goat's Masque, The Fool's Masque, The First [Second, or Third] of the Prince, The First of the Temple Masques, Lincoln's Inn Masque,* and *Gray's Inn Masque, the Third*. The grotesque or fantastic antimasque dances contrast to the serious masque dances and act as a sort of prelude. Loud sounds then announce the discovery of the masquers, a stylized way of portraying their unexpected visit. The songs and occasional spoken dialogue weave themselves incidentally around the three dances of the masquers. Following the third song, the masquers invite the spectators to dance with them and thus participate in the fictional situation. There was a prescribed order for the dances with the spectators, which began with slow dances called the *measures*, and continued with the light triple ones or *revels*. In the six manuscripts, ranging from around 1570 to 1675, that describe these dances in detail, the *measures* include the following seven dances and in this order:[45]

1. *Quadran pavin*
2. *Turky Lony*
3. *The Earl of Essex*
4. *Tinternell*
5. *The Old Almain*
6. *The Queen's Almain*
7. *Sicilia Almain*

Others that appear in some but not all of these sources are *Lorayne Allmayne, The Newe Allmayne, The Blacke Almaine,* and *Brounswycke*.

The choreography for each dance appears in the manuscripts in prose. *The Queens Almain* from GB-Ob Douce 280 is described as follows:

Honour
A double forward & a.d. backe. 2 singles syde & a.d. rounde on your lefte hande. a.d. forwarde & a.d. backe. 2 s. syde & a.d. round on your right hande. 4 d. forward a.d. forward & a d. backe 2.s. syde as afore.

I have matched this choreography in Ex. 51 with the melody from *The Queenes Almayne* in No. 129.[46] A "double" consists of three walking steps with alternate

Ex. 51: Choreography from GB-Ob, Douce 280 for *The Queens Almain*, with the melody from No. 129 (s = walking step, l = left, r = right, $+$ = bring other foot up).

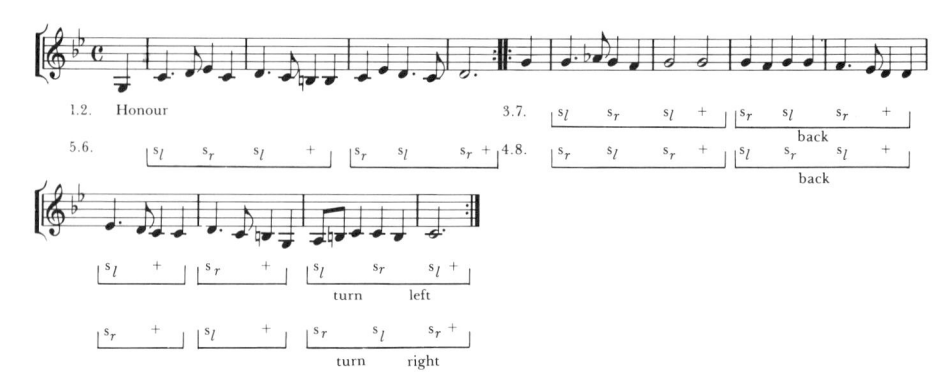

feet, followed by bringing the foot in back up even with the other; it can go forward or back and may commence on either foot. In Ex. 51 I show the component parts enclosed in a bracket, so that a double beginning with the left foot would be written $s_l\, s_r\, s_l\, +$, where s is a step, l is left, r is right, and $+$ means to bring one foot up even with the other. In a "single," the dancer takes one step forward and then brings the other foot up, thus: $s_l\, +$ or $s_r\, +$. It may go forwards, backwards, or to either side.

According to GB-Ob MS Rawl. D.864, one begins dancing this Almain "at the second strayne." The dancers therefore wait for the instruments to complete the opening section or use it for the "honour," that is, the *riverenza* or ℞ seen in Negri's choreography (Ex. 29a). They are presumably, as in Arbeau's description, in a column of couples, with the man's right hand holding the lady's left. The procession then proceeds with a "double forward," which, with two steps per bar, occupies the opening two bars of the second section of the music. Then a "double backe" follows, and each couple takes three steps backwards, commencing this time on the right foot. "2 singles syde" take the dancers first to the left, then back to their original positions. To perform "a double rounde on your lefte hande," one begins on the left foot and turns, while making the three steps, full circle to the left. Similar steps accompany the repetition of the second section of music, except that the concluding double makes a turn to the right. The two statements of the first section of music match "4 doubles forward." Then the instructions hint (and some of the other manuscripts confirm) that the opening steps are to be repeated to the two statements of the second section.

Some of the other sources also explain that the backwards doubles end with the partners face to face. In addition, GB-Ob Rawl.Poet.108 describes the steps for the first section as "a duble forward hoppe 4 tymes." "A double forward hop" means, presumably, that after one takes the three walking steps,

Ex. 52: Choreography from GB-Ob, Rawl. Poet. 108 for the *Lorayne Allemayne* set to the melody abstracted from No. 135 (H=hop).

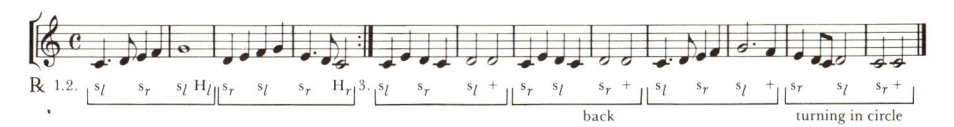

Ex. 53: English choreography applied to the alto voice of the *Almande Prince* in the Dublin Virginal Manuscript (first half in Ex. 38), omitting slight coloration in the repeat of the second half.

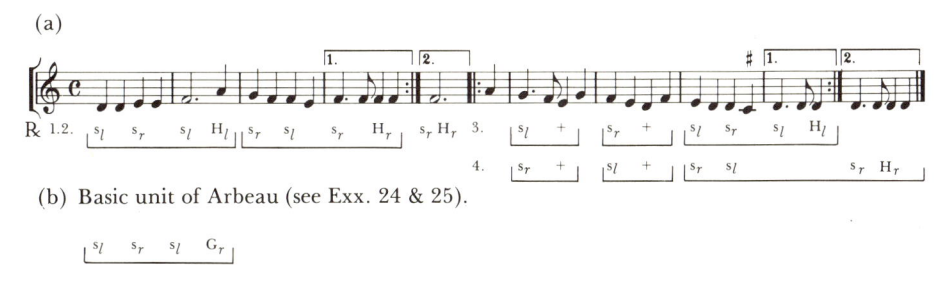

(a)

(b) Basic unit of Arbeau (see Exx. 24 & 25).

(c) Basic unit of Negri (see Ex. 30).

(d) Basic unit from Ex. 51 and Arbeau's pavan in Ex. 26.

one makes a hop on the foot that made the third step. If H_l signifies a hop on the left foot and H_r a hop on the right, the "double forward hop" would be either s_l s_r s_l H_l or s_r s_l s_r H_r.

In Ex. 52 I have extracted the basic melody from *An Almane* in No. 135, which is based on the tune of the *Almande Loraine*, and set to it the choreography of the *Lorayne Allemayne* from GB-Ob Rawl.Poet.108:

A Duble forward hoppe 4 tymes// a Duble forwarde repryme backe a Duble forward cast off a Duble round twyse//[47]

The expression "repryme backe" seems to correspond to "double backe" in the other manuscripts. "Cast off a Duble round twyse" apparently means that each partner turns away from the other in a full circle, with the man going to the left and the lady to the right. There is enough choreography to fit two statements of the first section and one of the second, and the entire instructions are repeated a second time.

I have applied the basic steps from these two relatively simple English Almains to the melody of the *Almande Prince* in Ex. 53.[48] Using the melody from

116   *The Transition*

the alto part of the setting in the Dublin Virginal Manuscript, I have used mostly the double forward hop, the basic two-bar unit. As Arbeau did in Part 2 of his Almande (see Ex. 24b and my version of the *Almande Prince* in Ex. 25b), I have matched the musical repetition or sequence with a corresponding one-bar unit, the "single side." The verbal description to match my imagined choreography would then read:

A double forward hoppe 4 tymes// 2 singles syde & a double forward hoppe// 2 singles syde & a double forward hoppe.

Ex. 53b gives the basic two-bar unit of Arbeau from Ex. 24, and Ex. 53c that of Negri from Ex. 30. Comparing these with the "double forward hoppe" in Ex. 53a above, one can see the similarity. All of them involve three traveling steps plus another motion in place. The only difference is the final motion, which in France is the *grève* or kick, in Italy the bounce that concludes the *seguito spezzato*, in England the hop.

Literary sources seem to use the word "leap" instead of "hop," in reference perhaps to the *petits saults* which Arbeau includes in the third part of his choreography (see Ex. 24c, where the little springs or leaps are indicated by asterisks). Randle Cotgrave, in *A Dictionarie of the French and English Tongues* (London, 1611), defines the word *saut* by quoting the expression "*Trois pas, & un saut*. The Almond leape."[49] The two-bar units in the opening half of Ex. 52 are thus described here as three steps and an Almain leap. The word "leap" seems to imply a rather active and vigorous movement. In Ben Jonson's play *The Devil is an Ass* (1616), the devil says:

> He may perchance, in tail of a sheriff's dinner,
> Skip with a rhyme on the table . . .
> and take his Almain leap into a custard.[50]

As late as 1687 a character in Charles Sedley's *Bellamira* boasts: "Why, I am the same man I was twenty years ago; as vigorous, as amorous . . . I will leap the half Almond with you."[51]

The expression "Alman haye" from *The Complaynt of Scotland* (c. 1550) seems to suggest, as we noted above, that couples danced one behind the other in a file or column. The same procedure may be suggested by George Chapman in the play *Alphonsus, Emperor of Germany* (1634). One character says, "Please it your Highness to dance with your Bride?" and another answers facetiously, "Alas I cannot dance your *German* dances." Still another says, "I do beseech your Highness mock us not, We *Germans* have no changes in our dances, an Almain and an upspring that is all, so dance the Princes, Burgers, and the Bowrs." Then two characters "have the fore dance with each of them . . . then Edward and Hedewick, Palsgrave and Empress, and two other couples after."[52]

The Almain is sometimes described as solemn, sometimes as lively. Morley says in 1597 that "the *Alman* is a more heavie daunce then this [the Italian galliard], fitlie representing the nature of the people, whose name it carieth, so that no extraordinarie motions are used in dauncing of it. It is made of strains, sometimes two, sometimes three, and everie straine is made by foure."[53] Mace in 1676, however, writes that "Allmaines are lessons very ayrey, and lively; and generally of two strains, of the common or plaintime."[54] In a play from the same year, Thomas Shadwell describes this droll scene: "I study insects; and I have observ'd the *tarantula* does infinitely delight in musick . . . I . . . caus'd a musician to play, first, a grave Pavin, or Almain, at which the black *tarantula* only mov'd; it danc'd to it with a kind of grave motion, much like the Benchers at the Revels."[55] These divergent descriptions suggest that the Almain could be solemn when it had a choreography like *The Queens Almain* in Ex. 51, but that when the hop or leap was added, as in Ex. 52, the dance became more lively, perhaps even boisterous.

As a social dance, the Almain thus displays considerable variety. The manuscripts from the Inns of Court make clear that each melody, although utilizing certain common choreographic units, had its own unique design. Justinian Pagitt, who was admitted to the Middle Temple in 1628, gives advice for dancing in GB-Lbm MS Harley 1026: "Write the marks for the stepps in every daunce under the notes of the tune, as the words are in songs."[56] This is what I have done in Exx. 51 and 52. On the other hand, the Germans, according to the quotation we have already noted from George Chapman, have "no changes" in their dances. Perhaps this means that in Germany the choreography of the Deutscher Tanz involved merely the repetition, for every melody, of the same two-measure unit. In addition, Morley's description above implies that the Germans themselves danced in a slow, heavy manner, and with "no extraordinarie motions." If this is true, then the unit in Ex. 53d, being the simplest and without a kick, a bounce, or a hop, was probably the one repeated over and over for every Deutscher Tanz.

Although the Almain occurred most often at the Christmas dances and at the entertainments and masques performed for royal visitors at such places as the Inns of Court, it also appeared in other settings. Anthony Munday describes its use in 1585 as music between acts of his play *Fedele and Fortunio*. Following the first act "the consorte of musique soundeth a pleasant Galliard," and after the third act "the consort sounds a sollemne Dump." Later, "the fourth Act being ended, the consort soundeth a pleasant Allemaigne," and "the fift act being done, let the consort sound a cheerefull Galliard, and every one taking handes together, departe singing."[57]

Several sources connect the Almain to a military situation. Perhaps the idea of a procession of couples in file one behind the other led to its application to marching soldiers. In *The Arraignment of Paris* by George Peele (1584) a character says:

> that thou mayst see
> What famous knights Dame Pallas' warriors be,

> Behold in Pallas' honour here they come,
> Marching along with sound of thundering drum.

This is followed by the stage direction "Hereupon did enter nine Knights in armour, treading a warlike Almain, by drum and fife."[58] Charles Butler, on the same page of *The Principles of Musik in Singing and Setting* (1636) in which he mentions the "dittiles *fa-la's*," explains the "Phrygian moode" as "a manly and cooragious kinde of Musik, which, with his stately, or loud and violent tones, rouseth the spirit, and inciteth to arms and activiti: such ar[e] Marches, Almains, and the warlike sounds of Trumpet, Fife, and Drum."[59]

William Bariffe, in *Mars, his Triumph* (1639), describes a military ceremony in 1638 at the Artillery Garden in London. First of all, the melody of a *Posture Almayne* or *Posture tune* appears, to be played with a drum and fife for a sort of manual of arms: "Turn the butt end of your Musketts to the right . . . Lay your Muskets properly on your shoulders." Then, another melody is given as *The Tune for the Motions*, a marching exercise: "Begin the *Almaine* tune for the *motions*: and the second time the Tune is played over, they begun [*sic*] their motions as followeth. Face all to the right, and march 6 paces. With the end of the first streyne, all face to the Front againe, and order Armes. Face all to the left and march 4 paces. This is to bring you into the midst of the Hall: then face to the Front, and order as before with the close of the second streyne." A note says that "the figures . . . in the margent declare how many times the whole tune is played over throughout the exercise."[60]

Both the Almain and the Ballett found a congenial home in England. As one of the popular social dances of the day, the Almain was so well known that authors and playwrights could make reference to it for more than a century. Its music appears in sources for every instrument and instrumental combination of the time, and it was no doubt often played as purely independent chamber music. The Ballett, no longer danced as it was in Italy, becomes a charming vocal piece with texts to celebrate the coming of spring, the singing of birds, the blooming of flowers, and the awakening of love. Although conservative in regard to its five-voice texture, which links it with Renaissance vocal polyphony, new progressive ideas emerge, as we have seen, in the differentiated vocal lines of the *fa-la* sections. Although the English turned to accompanied solo singing in their lute songs of the 17th century, the Ballett could not really adapt this format, for the charm of the *fa-las* depended upon a contrapuntal exchange between the voices.

Around the turn of the century, then, each country develops in turn its own vocal version. We have seen Gastoldi's Balletto in Italy, and now the Ballett in England. Before revisiting Germany, we will investigate first the *Ballet* in France, a dance form that was for lute alone or for a solo singer accompanied by the lute.

6 THE VOCAL AND INSTRUMENTAL BALLET FOR LUTE IN FRANCE 1603–1619

Jean d'Estrée included three *Ballets du Canat* in his *Tiers livre de danseries* of 1559. One of them, *Le petit Ballet* (No. 39c), has exactly the same melody as the *Almande Prince* (compare No. 39c with Ex. 1f). The other two, however, are longer and have a greater number of sections that contrast in texture (see No. 39b). It is difficult to determine what this isolated use of the word *ballet* means in France at this time. It was only in the early 1570's that the *ballet de cour* began to develop, with the first unified example in 1581: *Circé ou le Balet comique de la Royne*. The word *ballet* then referred not only to the complete work, but also to component parts, such as the *premier balet* or *entrée* and the *grand balet* at the end. The name, derived from the Italian verb *ballare*, suggests influence from Italian festivities such as the Florentine *intermedi*. The Philidor collection of ballet music from 1575 to 1620 contains, as we have already seen, a number of Almandes. Each danced or pantomimed *entrée* was accompanied by instrumental music, vocal ensemble, or solo songs accompanied by lute.

Besard's *Thesaurus harmonicus* of 1603 includes seventeen lute pieces entitled *Ballet* (Nos. 49b and 49c), in addition to the numerous Almandes we noted in Chapter 2 (see No. 49a). On the title page to *Liber octavus*, Besard mentions some branles "to which are attached afterwards some very choice *entrées* or Ballets, as they who are delighted by dancing songs call them."[1] Besard's Ballets are purely instrumental pieces for lute, yet his description implies that they are also somehow songs, presumably with texts, used for dancing. Similar pieces occur later also in Robert Ballard's two books of diverse pieces for the lute (Paris, 1611 and 1614), in Praetorius' *Terpsichore* (Wolfenbüttel, 1612), Fuhrmann's *Testudo gallo-germanica* ([Nuremberg], 1615), and both books of Nicolas Vallet's *Secretum musarum* (Amsterdam, 1615 and 1616), as well as in several manuscript sources. In addition, there are a number of pieces called *Ballet* in collections of *airs* for solo voice and lute.

A number of concordances exist between these sources, and the different titles cast some light on the meaning of the form. The melody of Besard's Ballet in No. 49b appears, together with a bass line, in the Philidor collection of

Anciens Ballete, where it is the *1.ʳᵉ Entrée* in the *Ballet fait à St. Germain-en-Laye au Mariage de Madame Soeur du Roy Henry 4.ᵉ avec M.ʳ le Duc de Lorraine l'An 1607*.[2] In Ballard's 1614 book, the same melody appears in a lute arrangement, where it is divided into two sections (following the fourth measure in No. 49b), with a varied repeat following each. Here it is called *Premier chant* (or song) of the *Grand Ballet de S. Germain*.[3] Praetorius includes it in *Terpsichore* as *Ballet a 4, Incerti* for instrumental ensemble,[4] and Fuhrmann has another lute arrangement entitled *Ballet 3*.[5] Similarly, the melody from the *2ᵉ Entrée* of the ballet of 1607 reappears in all these same sources.

A number of other lute pieces that Ballard entitles *chant* appear earlier in the Philidor collection as *Entrée* or *Air*. In his book of 1611, Ballard gives lute music from the *Ballet de la Reyne*. Under the category *Entrée de Luths* appears the *Troisiesme* [*chant*],[6] whose melody is in the Philidor collection as an untitled piece following *Le grand Ballet* of the *Ballet de la Reine, dansé l'an 1606*.[7] In 1609 the same melody, for solo voice and lute, is in Gabriel Bataille's *Airs de différents autheurs, mis en tablature de luth*, with the title *Pour la chaisne du mesme ballet* (referring to the *Ballet de la Royne*) and the text "Nos esprits libres & contents."[8] The melody is in mensural notation, with the lute tablature below it. Following the music are seven additional stanzas. The same melody and its complete text (but without the lute tablature) occur with the title *Ballet* in *Le recueil des plus belles chansons de dances de ce temps*, published in 1615 at Caen by Jacques Mangeant. It is among a group of *Airs de plusieurs ballets qui ont esté faits de nouveau à la Cour*.[9]

Another group of concordances concerns two untitled pieces from the *Ballet à cheval, dansé l'an 1610* in the Philidor collection.[10] They both occur next in Bataille's fourth book of *Airs*, under the heading *Airs de l'entrée du Ballet à cheval, de Monseigneur le Duc de Vandosme, fait par le sieur de Baïf*. The melodies appear now with the titles *Second Ballet* and *Troisiesme Ballet*. The first has a single stanza of text beginning "Comme à l'assaut marcher il faut"; the second has two stanzas commencing "Astre qui luisés au François Empire."[11] Finally, Ballard arranges the same melodies for solo lute in his book of 1614, where they appear as the *Second* and *Troisiesme* [*chant*] of the *Ballet des chevaux*.[12] This time he does not divide the pieces into sections, although he presents two statements of the second one, probably to match its two stanzas of text.

These examples show clearly that the melodies were both sung and danced, possibly in the original ballet productions. The versions for solo voice and lute, which may or may not originate in the ballet itself, become part of the growing repertoire of the *air de cour*. The arrangements for solo lute, however, often seem very much like the instrumental Tänze, Almandes, and Balletti that had appeared in lute books, as we have seen, for many years. Some of the vocal Ballets, such as the example mentioned above from the *Ballet de la Reine* and the *Second Ballet* from the *Ballet à cheval*, are in triple meter. Ballard, whose titles show a very close relationship to the original ballets, includes a number of these. Lute composers from other countries, however, simply entitle the pieces *Ballet* and tend, moreover, to favor almost exclusively those in duple meter.

I have therefore included in Volume II, for comparison, two duple Ballets for solo voice and lute (Nos. 50 and 51). Each has two repeated sections and four substantial beats per measure, and at the end of the opening section of No. 51 is a typical Tanz cadence. These can be compared to the solo lute examples by Besard (Nos. 49b and c) and Fuhrmann (Nos. 52b and c). The melody of No. 52b, the *Ballet de Madame Soeur de Roy* appears with the title *Ballet* also in Vallet's *Secretum musarum* of 1616,[13] Besard's *Novus partus* of 1617,[14] the Thysius lute book,[15] and MS 2350 for keyboard in the Bibliothèque Sainte Geneviève.[16] There is also a lute version in the Italian Bentivoglio manuscript from 1615, where it is entitled *Balletto fran^{se}*.[17] This is the only Ballet, as far as I know, that had such widespread popularity. Like a number of others in the major mode, it has a simple, tuneful quality.

Many lute Ballets, like the vocal examples in Nos. 50 and 51, exhibit Tanz and Almande traits. In fact, a setting of the melody in Fuhrmann's tenth Ballet (No. 52c) is entitled *Allemande* in 1603 by Besard.[18] The lute Ballets are in four voices, with the melody on top. They are usually in two sections, with one or both occasionally repeated with variations (No. 52c). Sometimes, as in No. 52c, sections end with the typical cadence moving from 7 to 1, in this case with one of the notes dotted.[19] In addition, other cadences resolve now from 2 to 1. Some of these take the shape of Ex. 41a, which we have encountered in English sources. It occurs at the end of Nos. 49b and 52b. Ex. 41b shows another 2-1 cadence that concludes No. 50, as well as three of the sections in No. 53. The latter piece, as well as No. 55b, comes from a somewhat later period, and No. 55d shows influence from the newly emerging French Baroque Allemande which we will investigate in a later chapter.

A number of lute Ballets come, curiously, from German sources. Besard, although Flemish himself, published his *Thesaurus harmonicus* in Cologne. Fuhrmann lived in Nuremberg and published there his *Testudo gallo-germanica*, which was international in scope and which includes the two Ballets in No. 52. A lute manuscript from the early 17th century at the Germanisches National-Museum in Nuremberg contains twelve Ballets, two called *Ballet du Roy*, one entitled *Balletto*.[20] The largest manuscript source, however, is the lute book of Albert Dlugorai dated 1619 (MS II.6.15) at the Musikbibliothek der Stadt Leipzig. This, like Fuhrmann's collection, contains dances from all over Europe, including the *passamezzo*, *pavana*, *galliarda*, *courrent*, and *volte*, as well as the *Chorea*, the *Tantz*, and the *Almande*.[21] Thirty-seven of them are entitled *Ballet*; two are called *Balletto Mertelij* or *Eliae Mertelij*, two others *Ballet del Mercurs*. Elias Mertel had become a citizen of Strassburg in 1596 and published his *Hortus musicalis* there in 1615. There are also four other known Ballets by Mercure d'Orléans, one of which sets the same melody as the *Premier chant* of Ballard's *Ballet de M. le Daufin* of 1611.[22]

The idea of a solo voice singing to the accompaniment of a lute goes back many years in French history. Attaingnant's *Très brève et familière introduction* of 1529 includes chansons for solo voice and lute, as does Phalèse's *Horti musarum* of 1553. In 1571, Adrian Le Roy published the *Livre d'airs de cour miz sur le luth*, and it was no doubt around this time, as the *ballet de cour* emerged, that the *air de cour* became associated with the dance. The same lutenists who accompanied the *air de cour* presumably also played the purely instrumental Almandes that we have already observed in the French and Flemish lute books. Perhaps it was the presence of the contemporary Almande that suggested the idea of arranging the sung dances from the ballet as lute pieces. In any event, the lute Ballets seem to emerge at the very moment when the Renaissance Almande is disappearing and seems for a brief time to replace it.

Thus at about the same time in both France and Italy, sung dances appeared that bore curiously similar names. In Italy Gastoldi used the term *Balletto*, which surely linked his dance songs, at least in the minds of the lutenists, with the instrumental Balletto Tedesco with which they were already familiar. In the *Balletti a 3* Gastoldi provided a tablature for lute – not, like the French, a purely accompanimental part (see Nos. 50 and 51), but essentially a reduction of the voice parts. Thus there were many performance possibilities: all voices could be sung, of course, but perhaps sometimes only the *superius* was sung and accompanied by the lute, as in the Ballet of No. 50 or 51; or perhaps the lute part was played alone, resulting in an instrumental dance like Nos. 49b and c and 52b and c. There is no direct evidence of influence between the French Ballet and Gastoldi. However, the trend in all countries at the end of the 16th century and the beginning of the next was away from unaccompanied polyphonic vocal music, in which voices strove to be like one another, and toward a new ideal of solo singing accompanied by instruments with independent and differentiated lines.

It is somewhat difficult to weave the French lute Ballet into the total history of our forms. It is perhaps an isolated development mirroring events elsewhere to some extent, but not really influencing future developments even in France itself. Perhaps all that we can safely do is to note in passing that one of the earliest Ballets in 1559 has the *Almande Prince* melody, and that later examples are often so much like Almandes that a melody from one could, as we have seen, bear the title of the other in a different source. And yet the form was apparently known in England, for Morley, in his *Plaine and Easie Introduction to Practicall Musicke* in 1597, seems to be defining this meaning of the word *ballet* before he describes the Italian type: "There is also another kind more light then this [the *villanella*], which they tearme *Ballete* or daunces, and are songs, which being song to a dittie may likewise be daunced. There be also another kind of *Ballets*, commonlie called *fa las* . . ."[23]

In addition, the unusually frequent appearance of the lute Ballet in German sources was apparently part of a general interest at the turn of the century in musical events in other countries. Although the French Ballet makes little impact, finally, on German developments, imported ideas from both Italy and England have a crucial effect. The forms, which originally represented the Deutscher Tanz as it traveled to France and the Low Countries in one direction and to Italy in the other, return now to Germany via England and Italy, coexist for a while with the Tanz, and then participate in the creation of new Baroque forms.

7 THE VOCAL AND INSTRUMENTAL TANZ, BALLETT, AND ALLMAND IN GERMANY 1598–1628

A<small>LMOST</small> fifty years after the Deutscher Tanz spread to the north and south of Europe as the Almande and the Balletto Tedesco, these foreign versions of the dance returned to Germany, where the Tanz itself was still alive. Thus it happened that for a few brief years early in the 17th century, the Tanz, the Almande, and the Balletto, for the only time in their entire history, coexisted together in the same country. Furthermore, all of them existed, to some extent, as both a vocal and an instrumental dance. This period in Germany thus represents the great central moment in the history of these forms. Renaissance ideas are rapidly disappearing, and striking new Baroque concepts are bursting on the scene. In an international exchange of ideas, the forms interact, and eventually crystallize again in new ways appropriate to the spirit of a new era.

There were two waves of influence in Germany at this time. The first came mainly from Italy and affected events in Nuremberg, the city where we encountered the first Deutscher Tanz in 1540. The other was from England and acted mainly at the courts and cities in the north of Germany.

The Tanz and the Ballett in Southern Germany

A transition took place in Nuremberg from 1598 until around 1618 in which the Deutscher Tanz changed its principal medium from lute to ensemble and its name from *Tanz* to *Ballett*. At first voices and instruments were both employed, in the manner of Gastoldi's Balletti. Then the voices and texts were omitted, leaving a purely instrumental ensemble. Nos. 12–14, 16, and 18 in Volume II illustrate this development.

During the last quarter of the 16th century, Italian vocal music exerted a strong influence in Germany, and titles often reveal a conscious importation of styles. Jacob Regnart published in 1574 his *Kurtzweilige teutsche Lieder zu dreyen Stimmen, nach Art der Neapolitanen oder Welschen Villanellen*. This brought the traits of the lighter Italian forms into the German Lied, which often thereafter had its melody in the upper voice and a much less contrapuntal style. Later in the century there was interest in the serious and more contrapuntal madrigal as well as in the lighter forms, as in Hans Leo Hassler's *Neüe teütsche Gesang nach Art der welschen Madrigalien und Canzonetten* (Augsburg, 1596).

Sometimes vocal works by Italian composers were provided, as they were in England, with texts in the native language. Between 1606 and 1610 Valentin Haussmann wrote free translations or, in some cases, new German texts for works of Marenzio, Vecchi, and Gastoldi. In 1609 Morley's Balletts appeared in Nuremberg with German texts by Haussmann, who refers in the title of the book only to Morley's edition in Italian. Plate XIV shows the *cantus* part of *Ich hab ein Ton vernommen*, which can be compared with its English and Italian versions in Plate XXIV. Gastoldi's Balletti, on the other hand, were apparently never translated into German, but they were published in Nuremberg with the original Italian texts.[1] His *Balletti a 5* came out in 1600 and again in 1606, the *Balletti a 3* in 1600. The title page of the latter omits, as the Flemish editions do, any mention of a lute tablature.[2] Unlike those published in Amsterdam, it does retain the words *cantare, sonare, & ballare*. As in England, however, it was the five-voice Balletti of Gastoldi that were most influential in Germany. No. 12 is a German lute arrangement of one of them – a sort of "dittiles" Balletto, to use Charles Butler's expression.

The transition in Germany from a purely instrumental dance to one that included singing seems to have progressed in stages. First of all, instruments were increasingly mentioned in the titles of vocal collections. In 1585, even before Gastoldi's *Balletti a 5*, Johann Pühler published in Munich *Schöner, ausserlessner, geistlicher und weltlicher teutscher Lieder . . . gantz lieblich zu singen, und auff allerley Instrumenten artlich und lustig zugebrauchen*. Similar references to "all sorts of instruments" occur from 1592, 1596, and 1597 in collections of Lieder or *Canzonetten* composed by Haussmann, reflecting an increasing German interest in ensemble playing. In 1598 Haussmann combined singing and dancing in *Neue liebliche Melodien . . . dess mehrern theils zum Tantze zugebrauchen* (Nuremberg). Finally, he joined dancing, singing, and playing together in a book published in Nuremberg the same year: *Neue artige und liebliche Täntze, zum theil mit Texten, dass man kan mit menschlicher Stimme zu Instrumenten singen, zum theil ohne Text gesetzt*.

The dances in this book are important for our history not only because they represent the first sung Tanz, but also because they provide the first Tanz played by an instrumental ensemble. The collection includes twenty-one *Täntze nach teutscher und polnischer Art mit Texten*, of which eleven have a *Nach Tantz* (those, presumably, *nach teutscher Art*), and twenty-five *Täntze nach teutscher und polnischer Art ohne Text*, ten of which possess a Nachtanz.[3] All are for four voices, and No. 13 shows an example of each type. Many traits from the earlier Deutscher Tanz are apparent in both examples: the *Nach Tantz* is a triple transformation of the music of the *Tantz*; both *Tantz* and *Nach Tantz* have two sections, each to be immediately repeated; and there is a steady and insistent rhythmic pulse of four or three beats per measure. In No. 13a there are typical cadences in the middle and end of the second duple section. Those with text are strophic, with two or three lines in the *Tantz* and two or three lines of different text in the *Nach Tantz*. The number of lines in a *Tantz* is not necessarily the same in its *Nach Tantz*. The repetition of a musical section is accompanied by a repetition of the text. Those with text are very chordal, whereas those without are somewhat more contrapuntal and flowing (compare Nos. 13a and 13b).

The next step in the German development was the use of the term *Balletto*. This occurs in Hassler's *Lustgarten neuer teutscher Gesäng, Balletti, Galliarden und Intraden* (Nuremberg, 1601). The word *Balletto* does not occur within the book, however, but five of the five-voice works are listed in the index as *Tantz*. They all have a *Proportio* following the duple dance and four of them have *fa-la* refrains (see Plate XIII). None of the other pieces in the book has a Nachtanz, but four of them do have *fa-las*.[4] Those labeled *Tantz* have two or three sections, and sometimes only the last *fa-las* are repeated from the second section. Two of them conclude with elaborate *fa-las* in which a sequence of rising three-note motives, as in the excerpt from Gastoldi's Balletto in Ex. 34b, occurs in canon between the two outer voices; the phrases end with the typical Tanz cadence.[5] These particular *fa-la* sections seem complex enough to suggest influence from the English Ballett. Each *Tantz* has one stanza of text written under the notes, others printed below (as in Plate XIII). The corresponding Nachtanz, unlike those of Haussmann, repeats the words of the opening stanza of the duple dance. In Plate XIII, therefore, the repetition of the first section of the music of the *Proportio* is sung to the second line of text.

Collections of Tänze or Balletti then continued to appear throughout the first decade of the century. Some examples, such as those of Demantius and Hasz, are very conservative in the simplicity of their chordal homophony. Christoph Demantius published at Nuremberg in 1601 *Sieben und siebentzig . . . polnischer und teutscher Art Täntze, mit und ohne Texten, zu 4. und 5. Stimmen*. The *quinta vox* is optional, so each dance can be performed in either four or five voices. Twelve of the twenty-three with text have a Nachtanz, but none of the untexted dances does. Perhaps a Nachtanz for the latter could have been improvised, if needed. This is the first indication, however, that the Nachtanz is starting to become less important. All the dances in the book have two or three sections, some only four bars long. There are many Tanz cadences and frequent use of sequence in the melodies.

The dances of Georg Hasz (see No. 14) are likewise simple, chordal, and concise, and are filled with Tanz cadences (no less than five in No. 14) and regular phrase structure. All the dances are texted in his *Neue fröliche und liebliche Täntz . . . nicht allein zu singen, sondern auch auf allerhand Instrumenten zugebrauchen, mit vier Stimmen* (Nuremberg, 1602). None of them has a triple

Nachtanz, but many of them have twice as many lines of text for the opening section as for the second, thus creating the traditional German Bar form. Although I show only a single strophe in No. 14, this example actually has eight lines of text in the first section, four in the second. Sung dances such as this one were no doubt performed on Sunday afternoons at the fortnightly meetings of the musical society which was established by Hasz and eleven other citizens of Nuremberg and which met from 1588 to 1602. Hasz was an amateur musician and wrote both music and texts. The second edition of his book in 1610 (now apparently lost) also includes twelve Balletti "mit und ohne Text" by "D.H.N."

The earliest dated German ensemble Ballett without text, however, seems to occur in Staden's *Neue teutsche Lieder, nach Art der Villanellen, beyneben etlicher Balletti oder Täntz, Couranten, Galliarden und Pavanen* (Nuremberg, 1606). The heading preceding the dances states that they are "ohne Text, fürnehmlichen auff Instrumenten zugebrauchen." They are all in four voices and without Nachtänze. The uncertainty over nomenclature on the title page continues within the book itself, for No. 16, which is one of the *Balletti oder Täntz*, has the plural title of *Balli* above the actual music. Staden's melodies are somewhat more constructive, as shown by No. 16. Here he begins by repeating one-bar units in sequence, then extracts the upward-fourth interval from the opening measure and uses it in sequence. This sequentially generated melody moves at the end of both sections, as well as the end of the penultimate phrase, to a typical Tanz cadence.

There are also other collections of Tänze from this period. Melchior Franck published a number of such books in Coburg and Nuremberg between 1604 and 1623, all containing pieces with and without text, "vocaliter und instrumentaliter zugebrauchen."[6] Paul Peuerl's *Newe Padouan, Intrada, Däntz unnd Galliarda*, which appeared in Nuremberg in 1611, contains only instrumental dances "auff allen musicalischen Saitenspielen" or stringed instruments.[7] The dances are arranged in suites, usually in the same order mentioned in the title. The *Däntze* are brief and chordal, with two or three sections and no Nachtanz. Ex. 54 shows two of the melodies, the first involving no conspicuous internal repetition, the second being highly organized, with parallel phrases at the beginning, sequence in the second section, and a third section constructed from material in the first.[8] Haussmann had mentioned the use of viols in his work published in Nuremberg in 1604, the *Neue Intrade . . . fürnemlich auff Fiolen lieblich zugebrauchen*, a collection that contains also "etliche englische Paduan und Galliarde," but, as far as I know, no English Almains. Erasmus Widmann's *Gantz neue Cantzon, Intraden, Balletten, und Couranten* (Nuremberg, 1618), however, are to be performed "auff allerley musicalischen Instrumenten, sonderlich auff Violen." As in Peuerl's book of 1611, no texts are provided and singing is no longer mentioned. No. 20 is an example from this collection. For the repetition of each section, the two upper

Ex. 54: Melodies from *Däntze* of Peuerl, 1611.

(a) *Dantz* from the first suite.

(b) *Dantz* from the ninth suite.

voices are simply reversed. A canonic sequence like Gastoldi's *fa-las* in Ex. 34 ends the first section; another sequence concludes the second.

This piece represents, in a sense, the extent of the transition that took place in southern Germany from 1598 to 1618. Before this time the principal medium for the Deutscher Tanz was the lute. The lute manuscript dated 1603–4 and copied for Philipp Hainhofer, the Augsburg patrician, contains not only the arrangement in No. 12 of Gastoldi's Balletto, but also a number of "deutsche Däntz mit ihren darunder geschrieben Texten." Two of those supplied with text have familiar melodies. *Gut Gesell du musst wandern* (Ex. 2f, Nos. 10b and 76) is the title and incipit for one *Deutscher Dantz*, and two others present texts for the tune that in Flemish sources is called *Don Frederico* (Ex. 2d; No. 7a and Plate XVIII in Volume II).[9] This manuscript marks the end of the German lute sources. Ensembles of voices and instruments replace this instrument, as we have seen, and eventually the vocal type ceases, leaving the purely instrumental ensemble, especially of viols, as the preferred type. In this process, the style becomes more contrapuntal, and the melodies and basses more organized. The number of voices varies between four and five, representing influence, I presume, from the earlier Deutscher Tanz and Gastoldi's *Balletti a 5*, respectively. The familiar tunes from the 16th century no longer appear. The Nachtanz disappears gradually, possibly being improvised when still needed. This suggests that the choreography may also have changed, perhaps, at least in vocal examples, involving pantomimic portrayal of the text rather than the pattern of dance steps we have seen earlier.

The new German Ballett therefore has a sound quite different from that of the parent Tanz. Several features remain, however, to constitute a link with the past: the duple meter; the sectional structure, with each section repeated;

the strong emphasis on the quarter-note, especially at the beginnings of sections; and, perhaps most conspicuous of all, the typical cadence toward which all the melodic activity flows. The transformation of the Tanz into the Ballett proceeded mainly from the Italian influence of Gastoldi. We have also noted the Balletts of Morley and the emergence, finally, of a preference for ensembles of viols. English influence was far stronger, however, in the north, and there we will find both the Ballett and the Allmand.

The Allmand and the Ballett in the North of Germany

English influence was brought directly to northern Germany by the presence of actor–musicians, as well as instrumentalists such as William Brade and Thomas Simpson.[10] These two played the viol, composed and published music, and attached themselves from time to time to the courts of Brandenburg, Brunswick, or Copenhagen, or to the imperial city of Hamburg. Brade seems to have traveled continually, spending only a year or so at each position. He was also an early performer on the violin. The publications of Brade and Simpson from 1609 to 1621 brought to Germany the music of the English masque. The Allmand appears in 1609, the Ballett in 1617.

In 1609 Brade published dances of the sort used in the *measures* and *revels* of the English masque in his *Newe ausserlesene Paduanen, Galliarden, Cantzonen, Allmand und Coranten . . . auff allen musicalischen Instrumenten lieblich zu gebrauchen* (Hamburg). Nos. 17a and 17b are two of the Allmanden, the first in two sections, the second in three, the last section ending with motivic activity. There are no Nachtänze, but the dances are, for the first time, arranged clearly in numbered suites. No. 17a is the last dance in the third suite, preceded by a *Paduana* and *Galliard*; No. 17b concludes the eighteenth group consisting of *Coranta, Allmand, Coranta*, and *Allmand*. We have already noted Peuerl's suites of 1611, which group together *Padouan, Intrada* (in triple meter), *Dantz*, and *Galliarda*.[11] Neither Brade nor Peuerl follows the order of dances suggested by the *measures* and *revels* of the masque, where all the slow duple dances precede the faster triple ones. In the suites of both composers there is sometimes a similarity in the opening notes of the dances of a group, but by no means the sort of exact transformation seen in the Nachtanz.

Brade published in 1617 his *Newe ausserlesene liebliche Branden, Intraden, Mascharaden, Balletten, All'manden, Couranten, Volten, Auffzüge und frembde Täntze . . . auff allerley musicalischen Instrumenten, insonderheit auff Fiolen zu gebrauchen* (Hamburg and Lübeck). A few of the dances in this book come from the *measures* and *revels*, but most are the dances of the masquers. Many of them concord with music in GB-Lbm MS Add. 10444, the main English source of masque music.[12] The two outer parts of the *All'mand* by Robert Bateman (No. 19) appear in Add. 10444, but attributed there to Stephen Thomas. Brade also changes titles, so that *The Second of the Lords* in the English manuscript (referring to the second or main dance of the masquers) becomes *Der Königinnen Intrada*. *The Nymphs' Dance* (an antimasque dance) becomes *Mascharada der Edel Frawen*, *The First* (or entry dance) *of the Lords* becomes *Ballet*, *The First of the Temple* changes to *Auffzug der Kauffleute*, *The Second of the Temple* to *Der Irlender Tantz*, *Gray's Inn, the Second* to *Comoedianten Tantz*, and *The First of the Prince's* to *Der erste Mascharada der Pfaltzgraffen*. The three dances of the masquers are thus named, apparently indiscriminately, by the terms *Intrada*, *Mascharada*, *Ballet*, *Auffzug*, or simply *Tantz*.

Praetorius, in the third part of his *Syntagma musicum* (Wolfenbüttel, 1618), casts some light on these terms. In his chart of all the musical forms, he places *Balletti* among the works that have text and are of a social nature and for entertainment; *Allemanden* and *Mascheraden* are among dances composed without text and without unique dance steps. Chapter VI, entitled *Von den Gesängen, welche in . . . Mummerien gebraucht werden: Als Giustiniani, Serenata und Balletti*, includes his definition of *Balli* or *Balletti*. The first type consists, he says, of songs composed by Gastoldi and Morley for dancing. The other type has no text and includes special dances made for mummeries (*Mummereyen*) and processions (*Auffzüge*) that are played for the masquerade (*Mascarada*). The *Ballet*, Praetorius continues, has three parts: (1) the *Intrada*, when the persons in the mummery make their entrance; (2) the main part consisting of figures which the masked persons make while standing, walking, exchanging places, or forming letters in a circle, triangle, quadrangle, hexagon, or other shape; and (3) the *Retrajecte* or exit, with which the entire *Ballet* ends. Praetorius further defines *Mascherada* as a mummery that "belongs to the Balletten described above," where several people in masks and costumes perform to music at a banquet or gathering of distinguished persons.[13]

Praetorius thus uses the terms *Ballet*, *Mummery*, and *Mascherada*, *Mascharada*, or *Mascarada* to refer to a quasi-theatrical social event in which masked and costumed persons perform three dances. He seems to reserve the word *Intrada* for the entry dance, although *Auffzug* could refer, presumably, to either entry or exit. The three dances correspond, of course, to the three dances of the masquers in England. Neither the German *Mascarada* nor the French ballet, however, includes dancing with the spectators as an integral part of the event, as the masque did in England.

Brade does not use terminology as carefully as Praetorius, for he calls one of the second or main dances *Intrada*. We have noted these terms earlier in Nörmiger's keyboard collection of 1598, which contains *erster*, *ander*, *dritter*, and, in one case, even a *vierder Mummerey Tantz*, as well as dances entitled *Auftzugkh* and *Intrada*.[14] Most of these terms, especially *Intrada*, *Auffzug*, and *Mascarada*, continue to appear in the titles of books and single pieces until late in the 17th century. The word *Intrada* may, perhaps, like the French *entrée*, refer on occasion to a main dance rather than an entering procession. Besard mentions *Intradae, seu Balleta*, as we have seen, in reference to his lute Ballets.

The three movements described by Praetorius seem to occur in the *Balletto detto l'Ardito gracioso*, a *balletto concertato* for nine instruments performed by nine noblemen and nine ladies in Vienna on the 2nd of March 1615 and included at the end of Pietro Paolo Melli's *Intavolatura di liuto attiorbato, Libro quarto* (Venice, 1616). Melli served from 1612 until 1619 in the court orchestra of Holy Roman emperor Matthias. The music (see No. 86) is essentially a trio for violin, flute, and basso continuo, with the latter realized by a harpsichord and five plucked-string instruments. The brief, separate movements are entitled *Intrada, Balletto*, and *Corrente*. The first two are duple and have repeated sections; the *Corrente* consists of a single section in triple meter. The *Intrada* begins on a D-minor chord and ends on B-flat major; the *Balletto* commences on F and ends on B-flat; and the *Corrente* both begins and ends on F. This work by an Italian composer suggests, of course, influence from Italy in connection with this genre, although the interacting sequences in the two upper voices during the second section of the *Balletto* remind one of the motivic counterpoint in the English Balletts.

One wonders, then, how the Italian word *Ballo* or *Balletto* came to be the principal name for the *Mascarada* or *Mummerey* in Germany. With Praetorius it is the term for the entire production, with Brade the title for only an entry dance, with Melli the name for both the main dance and the complete cycle. Perhaps, like the French *ballet*, the word could refer to the entire event as well as to a component part. The word may have come from Italian works such as Melli's. It may have come from the French ballet. It might also have come from Nuremberg, where, as we have already seen, the Gastoldi and Morley Balletti had influenced a German development, resulting in untexted *Balli* or *Balletti* (Nos. 16 and 20). Gastoldi's *Balletti a 5*, we must remember, were also danced, probably by costumed performers within the context of a unified, quasi-dramatic event. If this sort of production accompanied the form to Nuremberg, then it might have given its name to the new *Mascarada* brought to northern Germany by the Englishmen. The term *Ballett* was never employed, as far as I know, in the English masque. In north German sources we find the terms *Intrada, Auffzug*, and *Mascarada*, as well as *Ballett*. All are separate instrumental dances; all are usually duple and look very much alike musically. However, I have never found the *Intrada, Ballett*, and *Auffzug* grouped together in a north German source, to correspond to Praetorius' tripartite division.[15]

Nos. 18a and 18b show both an Allmand and a Ballett from Simpson's collection published in Hamburg in 1617. The Allmand shows unmistakable influence from the English Almain, not only in its ensemble of five instruments, but in the motivic structure in the last four bars of each section, which reminds one of the English *fa-las*. The Ballett in No. 18b starts with a similar melody and has a similar spirit and rhythmic pulse, but the *fa-la* motives are missing. The piece ends, however, with a typical cadence in the top voice. A *Ballet a 4* by Christian Töpffer (No. 21) appears in Simpson's 1621 book. It has three sections and a typical cadence at the end, but the sixteenth-notes and the use of

132   *The Transition*

basso continuo reveal that it belongs to the new Baroque development of the form.

Influence between the North and the South

New and old traits continue, however, to live in German examples through the 1620's. Schein's *Banchetto musicale* (Leipzig, 1617) contains twenty suites, each consisting of *Padouana, Gagliarda, Courente,* and *Allemande*. They are all related tonally and musically, and the last dance is followed by its *Tripla,* a faithful transformation of the *Allemande* into triple meter.[16] Although the Allmand came to Germany chiefly from England, the Almain never had a Nachtanz. Schein's addition of a *Tripla* seems therefore to be a recognition that the imported dance was the equivalent of the Deutscher Tanz. Except for Kargel and Lais' *Almanda, Teutscher Tantz* and its *Reprinse* for cittern in 1575 and 1578 (No. 8) and Schmid's *Alemando novelle, Ein guter neuer Dantz* and its *Proportz* for keyboard in 1577, Schein's pieces are the only examples, as far as I know, of German Allmanden that have Nachtänze. Schein's *Allemanden* are essentially chordal in style, with voices activated occasionally with eighth-notes. Ex. 55 shows three of his melodies, which are often highly constructive.[17] In Ex. 55b, every phrase has the same rhythm, with the first and third beginning with a rising scale and the second and fourth descending. The second section of Ex. 55a displays sequential treatment of a two-bar figure. In Ex. 55c, the two phrases of the first section have a similar beginning, and the second and third sections are constructed sequentially on two-bar patterns. In addition, all three examples contain one or more typical cadences. Scheidt, another northern German composer, includes three dances entitled *Alamande* in his *Paduana, Galliarda, Couranta, Alemande, Intrada . . .* (Hamburg, 1621). They have four voices and a basso continuo, but possess no Nachtanz and do not belong to suites.[18]

Some of the ideas seen in these northern works also appear finally in southern sources as well – the arrangement of dances in a suite, the use of a continuo, and titles such as *Auffzug* and *Intrada* from the *Mascarada*. Southern sources, however, ignore the Allmand and confine themselves to the Ballett or occasionally still the *Tantz* or *Dantz*. Peuerl published a book in Nuremberg in 1620 that contains fourteen suites consisting of a *Padovan,* a triple dance (*Couranta, Intrada,* or *Galliarda*), and a *Dantz*.[19] In 1625 his *Gantz neue Padouanen, Auffzüg, Balleten, Couranten, Intraden und Däntz* (Nuremberg) includes six pieces with the title *Ballet* and one called *Dantz;* all of them are for two instruments and continuo.[20] Isaac Posch's *Musicalische Ehrenfreudt* (Regensburg, 1618) includes four dances entitled *Balleta,* as well as fifteen suites consisting of a *Gagliarda* or *Couranta,* and a *Tantz* followed by its *Proportio*. Excerpts from one *Balleta* in Ex. 56 exhibit imitation, *fa-la* motives in dialogue, and a highly contrapuntal texture.[21] Posch states on the title page that the music is to be performed at the tables of distinguished men and at banquets, weddings, and

Ex. 55: Melodies from *Allemanden* of Schein, 1617.

(a) *Allemande* from the sixth suite.

(b) *Allemande* from the nineteenth suite.

(c) *Allemande* from the fifth suite.

other such gatherings.[22] He explains further in a preface that the *Balleten* are suitable while at the table, whereas the suites can be played either at the table or afterwards for dancing. He also complains that most composers omit the Nachtanz and leave it up to the musicians, thus leading to confusion. Therefore, he provides the proper Nachtanz for each Tanz, as the most distinguished dancers are accustomed to at that time.[23] Praetorius, as we have seen, also mentions banquets and gatherings of distinguished persons as the social setting for the Balletti. Similar purpose is implied by titles such as Schein's *Banchetto musicale*, Simpson's *Taffel Consort*, and Posch's *Musicalische Tafelfreudt*.

Carlo Farina, an Italian composer at the court of Dresden, published there in 1627 a book that contains the *Balletto allemanno a 4* in No. 22, which is one of the "etliche teutsche Täntze" mentioned in the title of the book. The name *Balletto allemanno* reminds one of similar titles in the Italian lute examples of the 16th century (Nos. 72–76, 79, and 81). The piece possesses a very late example of the Nachtanz. In his book of the following year, Farina uses the title *Balletto* for pieces like No. 23a, which remind one strongly of Gastoldi, or like No. 23b, which are simple and full of typical cadences. Instead of a Nachtanz, No. 23a has an independent third section in triple meter.

Ex. 56: Posch, *Balleta I*, 1618, beginning and end of the third section.

Only rarely are vocal versions found this late. Johann Steffens' *Newe teutsche weltliche Madrigalia und Balletten* (Hamburg, 1619) represents the direct influence of the earlier vocal Ballett from Nuremberg. It contains texts with *fa-las*, accompanied often by streams of sequence.[24] In addition, in a manuscript in Berlin there is a rare example of a texted Allmand for voice and lute, dated the 29th of January, 1601.[25] Furthermore, Scheidt includes two *Allemanden* in the second part of his *Tabulatura nova* (Hamburg, 1624) which are sets of variations on melodies identified by the opening words of a text.[26] Curiously, Praetorius mentions a vocal origin in his description of the *Alemande*. His definition consists mainly of a translation from Morley's *Plaine and Easie Introduction* of 1597. He begins, however, by stating that the "Alemande heist so viel als ein deutsches Liedlein oder Tänzlein" (a little German song or dance).[27] He seems not to be familiar with the Franco-Flemish Almande of the 16th century or with the English Almain and its importation into northern Germany. His "Liedlein" may refer to texted Deutsche Tänze such as those we encountered in the Hainhofer manuscript. It seems strange, nevertheless, that he could describe the Balletti in such detail, and yet seem so uninformed about the Allmand.

These rare glimpses of a vocal Allmand, then, complete the description of the German development during the early years of the 17th century. It is a period of confusing variety, with a vocal as well as an instrumental version of the Tanz, the Ballett, and even the Allmand coexisting, for the only time in the entire history of the forms, in the same country at the same time. In addition to the converging international influences, however, this period also represents a transition between two great eras in music history, with Baroque ideas gradually replacing those of the Renaissance. Therefore, we find great variety not only in the medium of performance, but also in musical style and in the requirements of the social setting.

Variety in the medium meant not only voices or instruments, but the number of parts (usually four or five) and occasionally the addition of a basso continuo. Variety in style involved at least three different textures: (1) chordal homophony in which, as in the Deutscher Tanz of the 16th century, there was little internal melodic organization (compare Peuerl's melody in Ex. 54a, for example, with most of the Tänze in Ex. 2, or Haussmann's settings in No. 13 with those of Ammerbach in No. 10); (2) chordal homophony in which, as in the Franco-Flemish Almande, there is extensive repetition and sequence in the melodic construction (compare the melodies of Peuerl in Ex. 54b and Schein in Ex. 55 with the Almande melodies in Exx. 22 and 23); and (3) motivic polyphony, as it occurs in the English sources, especially the *fa-la* music (compare Widmann's piece in No. 20 with the Almain for three viols in No. 141). Variety in the social requirements of the dance must account for the increasing lack of a Nachtanz and the occasional replacement of this arrangement by groups of three or more dances in a suite, and an apparent change from social dancing with fixed patterns of steps to rehearsed, semi-theatrical events danced by more highly skilled performers at formal banquets and weddings.

In the south, we find the vocal Tanz (Nos. 13a and 14) and Ballett (Plate XIII) evolving into purely instrumental forms (Nos. 13b and 16). In the north we have the instrumental Allmand (Nos. 17 and 19) and other dances from the English masque, now called *Balletti* (No. 18b). *Tanz* as a title is in the process of disappearing, for it was, as titles such as that of No. 16 shows, synonymous in the south with *Ballett*. Later southern Balletten, such as Widmann's in No. 20, look very much like those from the north (No. 21). Furthermore, northern Allmanden and Balletten also seem much alike (compare Nos. 18a and 21). Therefore, all the instrumental forms that survive in Germany are almost indistinguishable from one another. This is perhaps not surprising when one remembers that the influence in the south as well as in the north, although tracing somewhat different courses of evolution, came principally from the English love of ensemble playing, especially in viol consorts, and the special style of motivic counterpoint developed therein. A few sources contain both forms – Simpson's book of 1617, which includes the pieces in No. 18 that we have already seen, and also a manuscript from early in the century that contains rare keyboard examples which again display sequences (No. 15a) and *fa-la* motives (15b).

Although dances by native German composers never seem to reflect

Praetorius' tripartite format, they are, as we have noted, sometimes arranged in suites. Here each dance just seems to contrast in spirit, meter, and perhaps tempo with those that surround it. There are also such groups of dances in Italy, however, and it is to this country, and to the vocal and quasi-dramatic forms that succeed Gastoldi's Balletti, that we will next turn our attention.

8 THE VOCAL AND INSTRUMENTAL BALLETTO IN ITALY 1615–1640

WE HAVE SEEN the development of the Balletto for vocal and instrumental ensemble from the untexted *Todescha* of Mainerio in 1578 (Plate XX) to Gastoldi's *Balletti a 5* of 1591 (Plate XXII). Concurrently evolving were examples for lute and voices, such as Vecchi's *Tedesca* and *Aria* in 1590 (No. 77) and Gastoldi's *Balletti a 3* of 1594 (No. 80). The latter was reprinted at least three times in Venice between 1598 and 1611, and the tenth impression of the *Balletti a 5* appeared in 1613. The vocal Balletto flourished in Italy, then, for several decades after the turn of the century. It was often involved in small, semi-dramatic productions in several movements. The word *Ballo* or *Balletto* could refer to the entire event, to a single movement, or to both. The solo singer with instrumental accompaniment was eventually preferred over the vocal ensemble, and the purely instrumental Balletto, especially in trio style with two upper voices and basso continuo, was finally favored over the vocal. These trends are evident in a book published by Antonio Brunelli at Venice in 1616.

Brunelli and the Vocal Balletto

Brunelli was *maestro di cappella* of the Grand Duke of Tuscany to the religious order of the Cavalieri di S. Stefano in Pisa from 1612 until at least 1627. Cosimo II de' Medici was the Grand Duke from 1609 to 1621, and Tuscany was a region that included not only Florence, but also cities such as Pisa and Siena. The Grand Duke was in Pisa every year from Carnival to Holy Week, and the court entertainments included *intermedi* and *mascherate*,[1] as well as the longer dramatic form eventually called *opera*, which had been recently emerging in Florence.

Brunelli's *Scherzi, Arie, Canzonette, e Madrigali . . . per cantare sul chitarrone, & stromenti simili, Libro terzo* includes several works entitled *Ballo* or *Balletto* that were performed at court on specific occasions. First, there is a *Balletto, cioè Gagliarda a 5. voci ridotta a 3. per commodità de cantori, fatta per i Serenissimi di*

138 *The Transition*

Toscana, al Signor Agnolo Ricci Aiutante di Camera, & Maestro di Ballar di S.A. Serenissima. This is a simple, strophic piece in triple meter for two texted voices and a figured bass. It is followed by an arrangement for two voices of *il medesimo Ballo in Gagliarda per sonare solo senza cantare.* This, in turn, is followed by *Altro Ballo per sonare solo senza cantare a 3. danzato da i medesimi Serenissimi, al medesimo Signor Agnolo Ricci.* This dance (see No. 88c) is for two treble instruments and continuo – the trio format that becomes the favored chamber combination in Italy during the Baroque period. It is highly organized musically, beginning with two parallel phrases and continuing with eighth-note figures reminiscent of those in the second measure. Although no sectional divisions are marked by Brunelli, I have indicated in my transcription where a second section seems to commence. The most conspicuous parts of the music, however, are the *fa-la*-like passages at the end of the first section and the middle of the second. Here we see again the three-note motive we first encountered in Gastoldi's Balletti (Ex. 34).

Later in the book Brunelli includes a *Balletto a 5, Danzato alle nobilissime Gentildonne Pisane,* consisting of *Prima parte, Ballo grave, Seconda parte in Gagliarda,* and *Terza parte in Corrente.* This is immediately followed by *Il medesimo Ballo per sonare solo senza cantare,* which includes the same three parts arranged for a melody instrument and continuo. I have included the *Ballo grave* from both the vocal and instrumental versions in Nos. 88a and 88b. The first setting is for five texted voices. However, Brunelli adds a note stating that although the Balletto is in five voices, it is possible to sing it with one voice (the *canto primo*) or with two (both *canto* parts), which can also be sung an octave lower.[2] In such solo or duet performances, the parts not sung were presumably played on instruments.

The *Ballo grave* in No. 88a consists of seven three-bar phrases, each ending with a repeated chord. The phrases are so uniform rhythmically that the bass is completely isorhythmic and the other voices very nearly so. The last two phrases end with the Tanz cadence, but modified by dotting one of its notes. Both the cadences and the repeated chords were frequently present, as we have seen, in the Balletto, the Tanz, and the Almande of the 16th century. Ex. 57 shows the relationship in the opening two phrases of the *canto primo* between the *Ballo grave* and the succeeding two movements. Although the three-bar phrases of the *prima parte* have been adjusted to two or four bars in the other parts, the melodic transformation is exactly the same as in the German Nachtanz, which, as we noted, was by this time in the process of disappearing in Germany itself. Succeeding Italian examples, however, usually obtain unity between dances in less obvious ways.

No. 88b shows the same *Ballo* in a setting for one solo instrument and continuo. The top line seems to be a sort of ornamental fusion of the two upper voices of the other version. In this case, the upper voice has the same rhythm in each phrase, while the bass is slightly varied. Brunelli seems to employ the

Ex. 57: Melodic relationship between the three parts of Brunelli's vocal Balletto, 1616, opening two phrases of *canto primo* (see Nos. 88a and b).

(a) *Prima parte, Ballo grave*

(b) *Seconda parte in Gagliarda*

(c) *Terza parte in Corrente*

word *Ballo* for the instrumental settings and *Balletto* for the vocal; he also uses *Ballo* for the *prima parte* of both versions of the three-part work. Thus the instrumental arrangement of the latter has the term *Ballo* in the comprehensive title as well as in the title of the first part.

These examples of Brunelli give some idea, then, of court entertainment in Italy early in the century. Dances could be duple or triple. They could be, like the earlier Tänze and Balletti "mit und ohne Text" from Nuremberg (see No. 13), for either voices or instruments. They could occur separately, like No. 88c, or in a multi-movement format, as in Nos. 88a and b. The three-movement plan reminds one of Praetorius' Balletti, but Brunelli does not seem to relate them as entry, main, and exit dances. His Balli thus seem to represent the same sort of experimentation and variety in medium, style, and structure that we saw at the turn of the century in Germany.

In 1621 Lamoretti published the *Balletto a 5* in No. 94 for instrumental ensemble. Plate XXIII, however, shows how the piece appears in the basso continuo partbook. Not only is the bass part given, but also the *Aria del Balletto da Cantare*, which is the same melodically as the *canto primo* in No. 94, but here provided with text for a solo singer. There are two additional stanzas, and at the end of the score appear the words "al Ritornello" to indicate that an instrumental interlude should intervene between strophes. Since no special music is provided for a *ritornello*, the last four bars (following the rest) could perhaps be played once or twice by the instruments alone, in the manner indicated by Gastoldi for some of his *Balletti a 3* (*Il Tedesco*, for example, in No. 80b). A number of other features remind one of Gastoldi and the forms from early in the 17th century: the essentially chordal texture, which emphasizes the four beats in a measure; the repeated chords at the end of each section; the shorter repeated chords before the last phrase (like those in Gastoldi's Balletto in No. 80c); and the two typical cadences in the second section. There is no influence here of *fa-la* polyphony at all.

There are a few later examples of brief and separate Balletti for solo voice and continuo. Carlo Millanuzzi's *Terzo scherzo delle ariose vaghezze* (Venice, 1623) contains seven strophic Balletti with basso continuo and guitar chord-letters.[3] Martino Pesenti has a similar type of Balletto in his *Correnti alla francese, Gagliarde, e Balletti* (Venice, 1639).[4] This book includes vocal *gagliarde* and *correnti* as well.

The words *Ballo* and *Balletto* are also associated sometimes with larger dramatic works that include soloists, choruses, and instrumentalists. Monteverdi, in his *Scherzi musicali a tre voci* (Venice, 1607), has a *Balletto* with the text *De la Bellezza le dovute lodi*. It consists of an instrumental *Entrata* followed by many sections for three voices alone that contrast in texture and meter.[5] Marco da Gagliano was *maestro di cappella* to the Grand Duke of Tuscany from 1609 to 1643, and his *Musiche a una, dua a tre voci* (Venice, 1615) includes a lengthy *Ballo di Donne Turche . . . danzato nel Real Palazzo de Pitti al'Altezze di Toscana Il Carneval dell'Anno 1614* (actually on February 26, 1615). This is a multi-movement work with stage directions, including solo sections in monody, vocal ensembles, and instrumental music for dancing.[6] In *Le musiche e balli a quattro voci* (Venice, 1621), which Sigismondo d'India composed in four vocal parts and continuo for the wedding of Vittorio Amadeo, Prince of Savoy, and Christiana of France, the word *Balletto* refers either to a brief, separate piece or to a series of six to eight *arie*. The *Balletto d'aure* and the *Balletto per la festa del Serenissimo Prencipe Cardinale* are both brief strophic pieces. The *Balletto de i Re della China . . . per il dì Natale di Madama Christiana* consists of a series of six brief *arie*, the *Balletto de Sciti* of eight.[7]

Monteverdi concludes his *Madrigali guerrieri* in 1638 with a *Ballo a 5 voci con doi violini*. In the middle there is a cadence and a pause, with the instructions to dance "un canario o passo e mezzo od altro balletto, a beneplacito senza canto." The last piece of the *Madrigali amorosi* is the lengthy *Il Ballo dell'Ingrate, in genere rappresentativo*. This, however, is a more elaborate work for soloists designated with the names of characters, and instrumental music for an *Entrata, Sinfonia*, and dances.[8]

The word *balletto* thus does not seem to confine itself to any definite structural form in Italian vocal music. All it seems to signify is some sort of dancing, or perhaps pantomime. Often, however, there is some sort of dramatic intent, and many of the sources, as we have seen, derive from court entertainments. It is not accidental, of course, that some of the same composers were involved at the same time with the development of opera. We must remember that until 1637, when the first public opera house opened in Venice, operas were exclusively a form of entertainment at the Italian courts. Thus the Balli and Balletti, although on a much smaller scale and usually far less narrative in nature, shared the same courtly milieu with the more elaborate form of opera.

It is difficult, however, to discover in most of the vocal Balletti after the time of Brunelli any specific musical features that connect them with the Tanz, the

Almande, and the Balletto Tedesco of the 16th century. On the other hand, Brunelli also included in his book of 1616, as we have seen, some *Balli per sonare solo senza cantare*, and it is this purely instrumental Ballo or Balletto that forms the link with the instrumental forms of the preceding century and becomes, finally, far more important in Italy than the vocal type.

The Instrumental Balletto

One year before Brunelli's book appeared, Johann Hieronymus Kapsberger published his *Libro primo de Balli, Gagliarde et Correnti a quattro voci* (Rome, 1615), which contains, as far as I know, the first Italian Ballo exclusively for instrumental ensemble. Kapsberger was a *nobile alemanno*, a German nobleman, who was born in Italy and apparently spent all his life there, first in Venice and then, after around 1604, in Rome. He must have maintained an interest in German music, however, for the influence of the most conservative elements from Nuremberg seems strong in his music. His book contains eight Balli, each consisting of an *Uscita* and a *Ballo*. The *Ballo terzo*, transcribed as No. 87, thus has two movements: the *Uscita* (from *uscire*, to come out or to leave) and the *Ballo* (presumably the main dance, since it has the same name as the entire group). The terminology suggests the format described for the Balletto by Praetorius. In fact, if the *Uscita* were repeated again after the *Ballo*, then we would have the three-movement form, with entry, main, and exit dances. This may not happen in this particular example, however, since the group as a whole is centered upon D and the *Uscita* ends on an F-major triad.

Musically, both movements have the same meter, the same heavy chordal texture, and typical Tanz cadences. The *Ballo* proper has three sections, and its phrase structure seems to be conceived mostly in two-bar rhythmic units, most of which conclude with repeated notes in the lower voices. There is not much organization in the melody, and all these traits seem to suggest influence from earlier Tanz composers such as Ammerbach (see No. 10c) or Haussmann (No. 13b).[9]

Lorenzo Allegri published dances from Florentine court productions in *Il primo libro delle musiche* (Venice, 1618). He was a musician at the Medici court from 1604 until 1648, serving as a lutenist and eventually as director of the singers, players, and dancers who performed in the court entertainments. His book contains eight Balli or instrumental suites, each consisting of two to five dances and, in the case of the last one, also two *Ritornelli*. No. 90 is the opening movement of the Ballo that was danced in *La notte d'Amore*, an entertainment at a wedding in 1608.[10] Curiously, the word *alemana* appears above the beginning of the second section of score, perhaps as the title for the entire dance. The music sounds like a majestic overture, with its dotted rhythms and the complex contrapuntal interplay of six voices. The opening movement is followed by *Gagliarda Seconda Parte* and *Corrente Terza, & Ultima Parte*.

Piccinini, in addition to the *Partite* on the melody of *Almande Nonette* mentioned in Chapter 3, includes in his book of 1623 also a *Balletto in diverse partite* for lute. He states that this work was written for a specific nobleman and was danced by sixteen men with scenery and very beautiful costumes in the great hall of the gentleman's home in Bologna.[11] The work has ten movements: three called *In aria di Balletto*, another duple one marked *In aria grave di passo'e mezo*, and five triple sections entitled *In aria di corrente* or *Tempi di gagliarda*. All are related musically.

This work of Piccinini, like those of Allegri (No. 90), Melli (No. 86), and Brunelli (No. 88), derives, as we have seen, from actual entertainments. Kapsberger's *Balli* also seem closely related to specific social requirements. These examples exhibit considerable variety in number of voices (three, four, five, or six), in number of dances involved (one, two, three, four, or five), and in the style of the music. It was in the works of Biagio Marini, however, that the Italian instrumental Balletto finally achieved a form sufficiently definite and viable that it could embark on its own unique path of evolution. In examples from 1617 to 1655 Marini created a Balletto that reached back beyond the vocal and theatrical experiments of Brunelli and Allegri and formed a link with the Balletto Tedesco of the previous century. At the same time, he incorporated the progressive elements that had originated largely in England and which had been cultivated in Germany.

Strong ties with the 16th-century development can be seen in examples such as No. 95b. The expression *Baletto alemano* suggests kinship with the *Bal todescho* of Gorzanis (Nos. 72–75), the *Baletto todesco* of Barbetta (No. 76), and the *Ballo alemano* of Terzi (No. 81). There is a strong insistence in all the voices on the quarter beat, and both sections end with repeated notes. The texture is chordal and homophonic, with no special melodic repetition except for the three typical Tanz cadences. The *Corrente*, like a true Nachtanz, consists of a triple version of the opening music. The title *Balletto alemano* occurs also in No. 89b (and, as we noted before, in Farina's piece, No. 22, published in Dresden), the Nachtanz also in No. 93, and repeated chords at ends of phrases in No. 95a. In addition, No. 89b includes a varied repeat following each section.

All of these traits provide a strong sense of continuity with the evolution of the past. At the same time, Marini also includes a greater degree of organization, as in the parallelism between the opening three bars and the opening two phrases of No. 95a. He also includes motivic counterpoint of the sort we have seen in Gastoldi and Morley, and in subsequent works influenced by them, as in the canonic sequences in the second and fourth sections of No. 89a, and the second section of Nos. 89b and 93. Although he seems to be experimenting with a new multi-sectional format in No. 89a, which has an internal triple section, others, such as Nos. 89b and 95a, are not associated in any way with a triple movement. Marini sometimes adds a descriptive, or perhaps dedicatory, title, as in Nos. 89a, 89b, and 93.

One of the most important of the progressive features of Marini's Balletti, however, is the trio texture. Of the five examples in Nos. 89, 93, and 95, only one is not in three voices (No. 89b for two). The trio style involves two melody instruments in the same treble range (usually two violins) supported by a basso continuo. The latter is performed ordinarily by two instruments, one (a bass viol or other bass instrument) to play the line as written, the other (keyboard or plucked-string instrument) to realize the harmony as well as play the written line (see Nos. 93 and 95). In both examples of No. 89, however, Marini gives two bass lines (which I show in my transcriptions by upward and downward stems), the most active to be played by the bass, the other by the realizing instrument. In some cases, as in the third section of No. 89a, the bass instrument is silent for a few bars.

This trio arrangement becomes the main chamber combination in Italian Baroque music. The two upper voices contrast in range and in tone quality with the continuo instruments. The three written lines can contrast with each other, yet they are fused together by the continuo harmonies. Each voice can easily be heard and distinguished from the others. Therefore, this transparent texture is ideal for the new type of counterpoint. Voices are frequently in dialogue (No. 89a, section 4) or canon (section 2), and the *fa-la*-type counterpoint is projected with clarity. At the same time, there is rich sonority from the continuo realization and often from the upper voices moving in parallel thirds (No. 93, beginning of the second section) or sixths (first section). The upper voices sometimes cross (No. 93, penultimate bar of the duple dance, for example) or exchange positions (No. 89a, the repeats of the first two sections). The trio style tends to be less heavy-footed than the four-voice texture of the 16th century. Although some Balletti, such as No. 95b, continue the older texture with a chord on every quarter beat, the trio style, in general, tends to encourage more variety of note values between the voices and leads eventually, as we will see, to fully developed Baroque polyphony.

Marini thus brought a certain clarity of purpose and style to the Balletto. After the period of experimentation early in the century, the Italian ensemble Balletto becomes a separate dance, usually in two sections and usually for two violins and continuo. It becomes increasingly contrapuntal as the century progresses and eventually is associated with other dances in a suite. Marini has some later examples as well, but we will discuss them in the chapter devoted to the later Italian development.

The period from the last decade of the 16th century to 1630 or 1640 seems, in a sense, like an experimental but temporary diversion in the history of the Tanz, the Almande, and the Balletto. The vocal and theatrical elements introduced by Vecchi and Gastoldi spread, as we have seen, to England and Germany, and had their equivalent manifestation in the French ballet. All of this coincided with the declining years of the Renaissance style and the emergence of the Baroque. International influences and counter-influences were widespread and difficult sometimes to identify precisely. Out of the great variety of styles and structures of this period, however, finally emerged specific forms that could point the way to the future. These forms displayed some of the traits from this period of transition, but they also reached back and formed a link with the instrumental dances of the 16th century. One of these forms was the trio Balletto of Marini. Another was the new French Baroque Allemande, which developed as part of a new school of lutenists, and which finally influenced every country in Europe. Before returning to the Italian forms, we will first explore the Baroque Allemande and its development in France.

PART III

The Baroque Period

9 THE ALLEMANDE FOR LUTE, CLAVECIN, GUITAR, VIOL, AND ENSEMBLE IN FRANCE 1630–1731

THE LAST EXAMPLES of the Franco-Flemish Almande occur in the large lute anthologies of Besard, Vallet, and Fuhrmann published in Germany and the Low Countries during the first two decades of the 17th century and in Valerius' *Neder-landtsche gedenck-clanck* of 1626. Here we find the last concordances for the familiar melodies from the previous century. The Almande was thus a Renaissance form and simply ceased to exist when the ideals of this era declined. The same sources contain also the lute Ballet, the form that reflects the French involvement with vocal and dramatic elements during the period of transition. This form did not continue, however, after around 1620. The creation of a French Baroque Allemande occurred in the new school of French lute composers, who seem to have begun producing music during the 1630's. Most of their works were not published and hence are undated. Pierre Ballard, however, includes examples from their works in his *Tablature de luth* of 1631, and we can see that by this time a new style, as well as a new kind of Allemande, had already been established. Both the lute style and the Allemande spread to clavecin music and later to works for guitar and viola da gamba. Although there are a few examples for chamber groups, the Baroque Allemande occurs in France mainly in music for solo instruments.

Musical and Social Function

We have seen how closely the Renaissance Almande was involved with the social life of the times. The choreography of Arbeau and literary references all testify to its popularity as a social dance. Perhaps some of the most virtuosic of the solo Almandes functioned only as instrumental music, but throughout the entire eighty years or so of its history, the Almande was apparently danced both socially and professionally. It is a matter of some surprise, therefore, to discover that the Baroque Allemande, during the very period when it became one of the most frequent and popular movements in the instrumental suite, was, in general, no longer danced in France.

148   *The Baroque Period*

Mersenne makes this unmistakably clear in 1636: "The Allemande is a German dance, which is measured like the Pavan, but it is not used as much in France [as the *passemezze* and the *pavanne*] . . . one is content today to play it on instruments without dancing . . . if it is not in the ballet."[1] Sources of music show that it is also very rare in the ballet. As early as 1600 it is lacking in Francisque's *Le trésor d'Orphée* published in Paris. In 1612 Praetorius omits it completely from his *Terpsichore*, which is a comprehensive anthology of French dances of the period. The Philidor volume that contains ballet and opera melodies from 1654 to 1691 has only four Allemandes: an anonymous one in 1656, the others by Lully in 1665, Dumanoir in 1666, and Lalande in 1691.[2] In the *Chronologisch–thematisches Verzeichnis sämtlicher Werke von Jean-Baptiste Lully*, Herbert Schneider lists four other Allemandes by Lully.[3] In 1664 Dumanoir's reply to some rebellious dancers in *Le mariage de la musique avec la dance* seems to imply that the Allemande is not a dance: "Would you even dare to think that their majesties, who know marvelously how to value all things and to discriminate, would have wanted to set any kind of dance next to these charming motets, these refined Allemandes, these beautiful, diverse songs that they honor every day by their attention and their esteem?"[4] In the third edition of Brossard's *Dictionaire de musique*, the Allemande is not a dance at all, but a "*symphonie grave*."[5]

Lope de Vega in Spain also mentions the disappearance of the social dance of the *alemana*. Although he mentions in *El maestro de danzar* of 1594 that "una alemana es muy buena,"[6] he later writes in *La noche de San Juan* (1631): "Sad dances of Spain, [which have] already died . . . What has happened to *gallardas* and *pavanas*? And *alemanas* and *brandos en saraos*, why do they have to disappear everywhere?"[7] In *La Dorotea* (1632) he complains that because of the invention of the five-course guitar, "the old instruments are already forgotten, like the old dances . . . Alas, *alemana* and *pie de gibao*, you who for so many years graced the *saraos* [danced entertainments]."[8] There are, however, a few Spanish sources that refer to the *alemana* in connection with instruction[9] or social dancing.[10] Apparently some places in Spain preserved older traditions, while others followed French practice. Curiously, Spain, which had so much to offer to the early history of other dances such as the saraband, the chaconne, and the folia, seems to contribute very little to the history we are tracing, beyond imitating fashion elsewhere. I have therefore included no examples from Spain in Volume II.

Only a single choreography for a French Allemande exists, as far as I know, from this period. It is a complex stage work that occurs in at least two sources. *L'Allemande, Dance nouvelle*, with choreography by Pécour, was published in 1702 by Feuillet.[11] It was danced by Mr. Ballon and Mlle. de Subligny in the *Ballet des fragments de Mr. de Lully*. The choreography, occupying ten pages, includes the melody,[12] the track notation that Feuillet had used in his *Chorégraphie* of 1700, several illustrations of two dancers, and occasional verbal instructions. The melody is marked *gaiment* and moves mostly in quarter-notes and a few eighths – therefore not at all like the usual slow and grave French Allemande that developed at the same time in instrumental music. The choreography also appears in Pierre Rameau's *Abbrégé de la nouvelle méthode* (Paris, 1725).[13] It is clear, however, that this was a stage presentation by professional performers and not a social dance.

There is abundant evidence, on the other hand, that the other dances which eventually joined the Allemande as standard movements in the Baroque suite were popular social dances. The dance choreographies of Feuillet, as well as musical sources such as the Philidor collection, show that the sarabande was danced throughout the entire period, with the courante mainly before 1672, the gigue after 1672.[14] These were all dances that had become popular in France after the turn of the century. The Allemande, on the contrary, was, by comparison, a very ancient dance. Actually, there seem to be no Almandes published in Paris after 1564, although Arbeau's description comes from Langres in 1588. Most of the ballet Almandes in the Philidor volume that spans from 1575 to 1620 bear dates between 1575 and 1583; there is only a single later example from 1601. The latest ensemble Almandes of Phalèse (the younger) and Bellère were also published in 1583. If the ensemble (as in the Phalèse publications) or the orchestra (as it was emerging in the *ballet de cour*) represents the medium used to accompany social and stage dances, then the later lute Almandes from the Low Countries between around 1584 and 1615 must have been instrumental pieces. In this case, the Almande transmitted to the new French school of Baroque lutenists was perhaps, even at that time, a purely instrumental composition.

It thus seems clear that the Baroque French Allemande was seldom danced and certainly was not one of the currently popular stage and social dances.[15] This is even more astonishing when one realizes that the French seemed to dance to anything the orchestra could play, even if it was previously, like the *passacaille*, not a dance at all.[16] The Baroque Allemande in France usually became instead, as Brossard stated, a *symphonie grave* – a slow and stately piece for a solo instrument that could stand as an introduction or overture to a suite or could act, on occasion, as a memorial *tombeau*. The musical traits that evolve, especially in lute and then in clavecin music, reenforce the solemn and majestic affections appropriate to this form. Lighter and livelier types also developed after 1677, as we will see, but usually utilizing the same rhythmic figures.

The French Baroque Style

The new *style luthé* was essentially a "broken" style or *style brisé*, in which individual tones tended, in general, to be played successively rather than simultaneously. This resulted not only in the arpeggiation of chords, as in the concluding measure of No. 57, but also in a sort of rambling syncopation. In Mesangeau's lute Allemande in No. 56, the fourth measure consists of a succession of single notes, and only two are ever struck together in measures 5–9. Tiny rhythmic motives, of the type that had occurred earlier in English keyboard music, appear from time to time in various voices and create a sense of rhythmic counterpoint. The main melody, however, is basically in the upper voice, although it is now almost completely lacking in internal organization. In each section of No. 56, the melody flows without interruption to its concluding cadence, and even the thirteen bars of the second section are not obviously divided into smaller phrase units. The sections are not parallel in any way, and no memorable musical unit recurs during the course of the melody. The melody is thus not tuneful and organized as it was in the 16th-century Almande, and hence is not the main element to attract the listener's attention.

This kind of music has two fundamental purposes: (1) the creation of a tonal design, most often in the standard binary dances by reaching at the end of the first section an area different from the opening center (usually from a major key, the dominant, and from a minor key, the dominant or the mediant) and by returning during the second section to the opening tonality; and (2) the inclusion of rhythmic motives that express a unified mood. The first section of the Renaissance Almande could sometimes, as in No. 34b, end on the dominant, but such a tonal plan was not an objective at that time, since in many examples, such as Nos. 37b and 42 (*Almande Nonette*), the opening section concludes with the same tonic chord with which it began. The tonal design of the French Baroque Allemande becomes one of the main generating forces of the music. Although the chordal progressions seem to wander rather aimlessly in the earliest examples, they later become more purposeful as the concept of the tonal system is more firmly established. Consequently, the unfolding of the tonal drama, especially the approach to cadences, becomes increasingly more apparent to the listener.

More conspicuous, however, are the rhythmic motives, for they represent the affective content of the piece and act at the same time as the main source of unity. Like tonality, this is an element that increases in importance and intensity as the period progresses. The rhythmic figures and other musical elements related to time become in France the chief means of expressing the affections. Each type of piece or dance is thus distinguished from the others by the tempo, accentuations, and motives appropriate to it. These rhythmic elements dominate a texture in which melody itself recedes into the background. In the earliest examples of the *style brisé*, melody contains no element of organization at all. Later, brief sequences sometimes occur momentarily, but it is not until the 18th century that the Italian concept of melodic organization influences French music.

All French dances thus involve the *style brisé* and its special approach to tonality and rhythm. They also share elements of external form. All usually have two sections, each immediately repeated. A section or a complete dance may be followed by a *double*, a varied repetition, and occasionally the last few bars of a dance are repeated as a *petite reprise*. In addition, most of the dances experience a slowing of tempo during the course of the period, with a consequent increase in the number of notes per measure. The notes themselves involve increasingly smaller values, with first sixteenth-notes and then thirty-second-notes becoming more numerous. Related to these smaller note values are also the diverse ornaments or *agréments* which increase in complexity and frequency as time progresses.

General Traits of the French Allemande

Almost all French Allemandes have two sections. I know of only three early lute examples that have three.[17] Seldom is a *double* included.[18] A *petite reprise* is occasionally written out or indicated by signs (see Nos. 62 and 65). It was presumably to be played following the repetition of the second section. There are examples for lute by Mesangeau[19] and for keyboard by Louis Couperin[20] and Gaspard Le Roux.[21]

There is great diversity, as in most French dances except for the sarabande, in the number of bars in each section, and usually there is a different number in the two halves of a single Allemande. The earlier examples range from five to sixteen measures per section, with the second often one or two measures longer than the first. Some typical plans can be seen in the pieces of Volume II, where No. 56 has 9+13, No. 57: 6+8, No. 58: 10+9, No. 59: 10+12, No. 60: 14+16, No. 61: 6+9, No. 62: 13+15, etc. In very late examples a section can be as long as twenty-five measures or so.[22] This irregularity, in sharp contrast to the regular four-, six-, or eight-bar phrases and sections of the Renaissance Almande, tends to blur one's comprehension of formal structure and encourages one to fasten the attention instead on those elements that are immediately perceived – primarily the rhythmic patterns.

The Allemande gradually incorporates those musical motives that project a noble, solemn, and majestic affection. These same figures eventually filled the French versions of the sarabande, the folia, the passacaglia, and the chaconne, as well as the opening duple section of the French overture. The motives involve sixteenth-notes in configurations that produce a powerful forward thrust toward the following note. Some of the most common are shown in Ex. 58. The first three occur in No. 56, for example, the first four in No. 57, (e) in No. 65, and (f) in No. 59. The trend, which can be seen by comparing the early example in No. 56 with the later one in No. 65, is for sixteenth-notes to increase, for each measure to contain more notes, and for the motivic patterns to become more systematically employed.

One important way the motives become more closely associated is in a

Ex. 58: Rhythmic motives in the French Baroque Allemande.

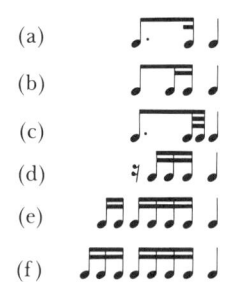

(a) ♪. ♬ ♩
(b) ♫ ♬ ♩
(c) ♪. ♬ ♩
(d) 𝄾 ♬♬ ♩
(e) ♬ ♬♬ ♩
(f) ♬♬ ♬♬ ♩

Ex. 59: Rhythm in the opening measure of the French Baroque Allemande.

(a) (♪)| ♩. ♪ ♬ ♬ | ♩
(b) (♪)| ♩. ♪ ♬ ♪. ♬ | ♩
(c) (♪)| ♩ ♬♬ ♬ ♪. ♬ | ♩
(d) (♪)| ♩ 𝄾♬♬ ♬ ♪. ♬ | ♫ (𝄾)

stereotyped rhythm which often occurs in the opening measure. Ex. 59 shows some of the possibilities.[23] The effect in almost all Allemandes is to throw a strong accentuation onto the first beats of the first two measures. The opening beat of the first bar receives an agogic accent usually by being at least one full quarter beat in duration and sometimes by being preceded by an anacrusis of an eighth, or sometimes a sixteenth or quarter beat in duration. The succeeding notes of this measure then represent various patterns that act together as a grand and powerful anacrusis to the opening note of the second measure. Commonly occurring within this configuration are the three sixteenth-notes (the motive in Ex. 58d) on the second beat and the dotted eighth and sixteenth (Ex. 58a) on the last beat. Sometimes these last two rhythms occur separately: the three sixteenth-notes in No. 59 or 65, for example, or the dotted eighth and sixteenth in No. 57 or 61. Many times, however, the complete pattern is present, as in No. 67.[24] Harmonically the rhythmic units in Ex. 59 are sometimes accompanied by a single tonic chord or a tonic pedal point. At other times the anacrusic effect of the rhythm is reenforced by a movement to the dominant (in root position or first inversion) on the third or fourth beat, with the return to the tonic coinciding with the accent at the beginning of the next measure.

No. 67 also shows the usual way in which the rhythmic energy flows on past the opening note of the second bar. In other late examples such as No. 65, however, the opening rhythmic pattern receives a sense of termination through a downward third, which is sometimes followed by a rest (Ex. 59d).

Although not occurring in the earlier lute pieces, it appears without the rest in an isolated keyboard piece of Louis Couperin.[25] It is far more frequent, however, with François Couperin, whose later works include the third followed by a rest.[26] We previously noted the downward third at the ends of phrases in Gastoldi's Balletti (Exx. 33a, b, and d) and will see it even more frequently in the Italian sources discussed in the next chapter.

The patterns of Ex. 59, or some variant thereof, thus announce the type of affective rhythm that will maintain itself, in general, throughout the entire Allemande. The rhythmic motives of Ex. 58 usually recur at random in the earlier examples, with groups of sixteenth-note patterns often driving vigorously from time to time toward accentuated notes of longer value, as in the second bar of No. 57. Earlier lute Allemandes, such as No. 56 and 57, show no obvious rhythmic or melodic organization of any sort. This is a subtle type of music which changes continually and deliberately avoids the obvious repetitions and parallelisms that were so abundant in the 16th-century Almande.

Even the beginning of the second section is seldom parallel in any way to the opening of the first. Occasionally, however, very modest and momentary motivic repetition in the form of imitation or sequence may appear in later examples. In No. 58 a rising figure of three eighth-notes occurs in imitation in measures 7 and 8 and again in the first three bars of the second section. No. 59 commences with the rhythm and melody of the right hand in the first measure echoed in the second bar by the left. Brief sequences of two or three units sometimes occur, as in No. 62 (measures 8 and 9) or No. 69 (the first two bars of the second section). During the 17th century, this is, for the most part, the extent of any sort of formal organization in French Allemandes. This type of momentary repetition, in company often with brief and extreme changes in note value, reminds one of a similar procedure that had for a long time been characteristic of preludes and toccatas. In these latter two forms also, brief passages of imitation, dialogue, or sequence occur, but the listener is not expected to store the motives in his memory, for they pass by quickly and do not ordinarily reappear later for purposes of unification.[27]

Marin Marais' Allemande of 1701 in No. 65, however, displays the influence of earlier Italian developments in its unified organization of rhythm and melody, and clarity of phrase and tonality. No. 67 shows this fully mature Baroque style even more clearly. Here sixteenth-notes have increased to the point where they fill almost every beat in an endless succession. Every line is intricately organized with motives that relate in a highly unified manner. Sometimes the bass has simply running eighth-notes to emphasize the motoristic rhythm. This new style, although most prevalent perhaps in chamber Allemandes such as those for one or two solo instruments and continuo in F. Couperin's books from 1722 to 1726,[28] occurs also in later keyboard works, from 1716 on, by Couperin[29] and Rameau.[30]

154 *The Baroque Period*

Ex. 60: The typical cadence during the Baroque period.

(a)

(b)

(c)

(d)

(e)

(f)

The Cadences

Although in many conspicuous features the French Baroque Allemande is thus totally different from the Renaissance Almande, one device that does continue is the typical cadence. It occurs throughout the entire history of the French Allemande and in works for all media. It is now usually modified, as shown in Exx. 60d, e, and f, by diminution, by ornamentation (usually trills), and by adding dots on the first or third notes, thus creating motives like Ex. 58a. Ex. 60c is rare, and Ex. 60e, as might be expected, occurs later than Ex. 60b, and Ex. 60f later than Ex. 60e. The latter, however, becomes the most popular version of the typical cadence in France.

The diminution was part of an historical process in which the basic pulse changed to successively smaller note values. As we have already seen, the typical cadence was notated until around 1580 in minims or half-notes, although I have transcribed it in quarter-notes in Volume II for the convenience of the modern reader. Plate XVIII shows an ensemble Almande from Phalèse (ii) and Bellère's book of 1583 in which typical cadences move in half-notes in the middle of the second line to *d'''*, two-thirds through the third line to *b'*-flat, and at the end of the fourth line to *g'*. At the end of the piece, as part of the process of coloration, is a diminished form of the cadence which is notated in quarter-notes (which I would transcribe in eighth-notes). Plate XX, on the other hand, is from Mainerio's ensemble book of 1578, and here the basic pulse, as well as the typical cadence at the end of the *Todescha*, is notated in semiminims or quarter-notes. Most later examples, such as those of Adriaenssen, Denss, and Besard (Nos. 47–49), also employ the quarter-note, which early in the 17th century becomes the standard notation for the basic pulse.

As the French Baroque Allemande evolves, more and more sixteenth-notes are added, the number of notes per measure increases, and the tempo slows down. There is one Allemande by Bouvier in Ballard's 1631 book that ends with the cadence of Ex. 60a (with the opening note replaced by a rest and a trill on the final 7),[31] but most of the typical cadences in the French lute and keyboard Allemandes occur in one of the diminished versions shown in Exx. 60d and e. They are notated in eighth-notes and, since the barring does not change as it did in the transition from half- to quarter-notes, the cadential approach to the final tonic chord now occupies only half a measure. The tempo, however, apparently had slowed down by this time to a point where the pace of the eighth-note corresponded roughly to that previously associated with the quarter-note.

In the later examples, perhaps one barred measure did, in fact, finally amount to two actual measures. A few Allemandes begin on or with an anacrusis to the third beat of the bar. Occasionally, the material in this opening incomplete measure will sound like a long anacrusis to the first beat of the first full measure, especially if it is confined to a single melodic line and additional voices are added on the opening beat of the full measure.[32] In most cases, however, such Allemandes commence with the same sort of accentuation on the third beat as at the beginning of the following measure. In these cases, I cannot imagine a listener perceiving the opening accent on the third beat as anything but the first beat of a metrical unit.[33] There are a few examples in works by Ennemond Gaultier[34] and Le Roux.[35] Many also occur in F. Couperin's chamber works,[36] which show heavy influence from Italy, where we will find even earlier and more numerous examples of such a third-beat beginning. Couperin sometimes adds, in effect, a bar-line in the middle of the long 4/4 measures, so that he has one keyboard Allemande in 4/8, another in 2/4.[37]

French Allemandes almost always conclude each section with the final tonic chord on the opening beat of the last measure. Only a few, such as the lute pieces in Nos. 54 and 55a, reach the concluding tonic chord on the third beat. In the final bar of examples for lute, theorbo, and viola da gamba, the melody tone is usually repeated again on the third beat (see the ends of Nos. 56, 65, and 68, for example), reminding one of the repeated chords in the 16th-century Tanz, Almande, and Balletto Tedesco. Sometimes the repeated tone on beat 3 is preceded by an eighth-note on the same or a neighboring tone (see the end of Nos. 57 and 63). In almost all keyboard Allemandes, however, the melody in the final bar sustains a single tone, while the arpeggiation of the tonic chord below it continues the rhythmic movement of the piece (Nos. 58 and 59). Some guitar works include the repetition on the third beat (Nos. 61 and 62), and others augment this pattern with the repetition at the beginning of a second measure (Nos. 60 and 64), while the latest examples, including the works of De Visée and Campion (No. 71), end, like the keyboard Allemandes, with a single sustained tone in the melody.

Although the repetition over the final tonic chord divides the last measure into two halves, as it did in the 16th-century examples, the typical cadence is now almost always diminished to eighth-notes. Its tempo, however, is prob-

156 *The Baroque Period*

ably similar to earlier ones in quarter-notes. Ex. 60e, without trills and with the opening note tied over from the previous beat, appears in the middle of the first section of two lute Allemandes of Ennemond Gaultier (d. 1651), where it acts to give a slight sense of phrasing within an otherwise shapeless flow of *style brisé*.[38] The works of Dubut (father and son) include a lute example whose first section concludes with Ex. 60d, with a trill on the last eighth-note, as well as others in which Ex. 60e, with or without a trill on the dotted note, appears at the end or middle of a section.[39] The cadence is also modified several times in the middle of a section so that a quarter-note on scale degree 8 replaces the opening two eighth-notes in Ex. 60e.[40]

Typical cadences are even more numerous in clavecin music. The first section of a keyboard example by the lutenist John Mercure, whose works date probably from around 1640 or 1650, concludes with a version of Ex. 60e in which a rest replaces the first eighth-note.[41] Most of Chambonnières' typical cadences follow Ex. 60e, with the opening eighth-note beat occupied usually by scale degree 7, but once by 5 and once by a rest, and trills either absent or occurring on the dotted note or on both the first and the dotted note.[42] In one example a mordent appears on the second eighth-note, followed by a trill on the dotted note.[43] Of course, *agréments* were no doubt often added by the performer even when not notated in the score. Chambonnières also has one instance of Ex. 60f, with both trills included, and with scale degree 2 on the first eighth-note beat.[44] Louis Couperin also has numerous cadences like Ex. 60e, commencing usually with 7, but several times with 2, and sometimes including trills.[45] One of his Allemandes has such a cadence in the middle of the first section and the end of the second, and also Ex. 60a in the middle of the second section.[46]

Some Allemandes of Lebègue in 1687 also display the cadence of Ex. 60e, beginning with 7 or occasionally 2, and sometimes with trills on the first note or on the first and the dotted note.[47] Ex. 60f occurs in two of his pieces.[48] D'Anglebert (1689) has a single example of Ex. 60e beginning with 5.[49] Dieupart (1701) has a few examples of Ex. 60e, one with the opening note tied as in the E. Gaultier Allemandes already mentioned.[50] More frequent in his works, however, is the ornamental version in Ex. 61d.[51] Le Roux in 1705 has examples of Ex. 60e, all beginning with 7,[52] and one ornamented as in Ex. 61e.[53] The typical cadences diminish in frequency in later keyboard works, but isolated examples of Ex. 60e may be found occasionally in works of F. Couperin[54] and Rameau.[55] One keyboard work of Couperin from 1730 concludes with a diminished version of Ex. 60f.[56]

The cadences occur also in Allemandes for other media. Ex. 60e, beginning with scale degree 6, appears at the end of the first section of Marais' gamba Allemande in No. 65. Although lacking in the later chamber music of F. Couperin, the cadence appears in the two Allemandes published by Robert Ballard (iii) in 1665 in *Pièces pour le violon à quatre parties*. The first section of the

Ex. 61: Further modification of the typical cadence during the Baroque period.

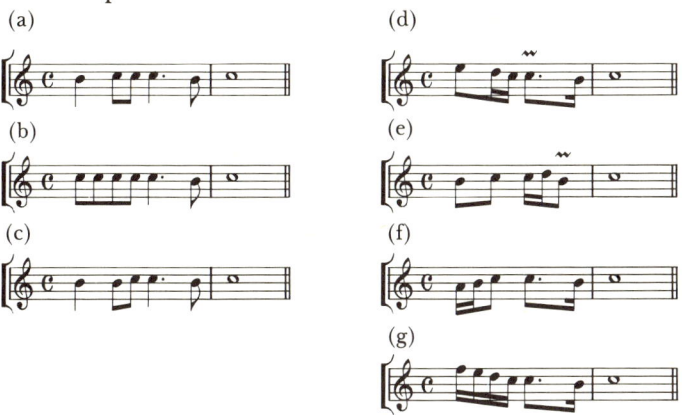

(a)

(b)

(c)

(d)

(e)

(f)

(g)

Allemande cromatique ends with Ex. 60e, the second section of the *Allemande de Monsieur Mayeu* with the quarter-note version shown in Ex. 61a.[57] The undiminished versions in Exx. 60a–c and 61a–c are more frequent, however, in French music for the five-course Spanish guitar. This instrument was brought to France by Italian composers such as Francesco Corbetta, who published two books of guitar music in Paris in 1671 and 1674. Around this time, the guitar generally replaced the lute in France, as it had in Italy three-quarters of a century earlier. French guitar Allemandes tend to have more quarter- and eighth-notes and fewer sixteenth-notes than contemporary examples for other media. Thus, although Ex. 60e may occasionally appear (see the end of the opening section of No. 61), most typical cadences have a quarter-note pulse.

Ex. 60a occurs a few times, as in the middle of the second section of No. 60 and isolated works of Corbetta[58] and De Visée.[59] The most frequent pattern by far, however, is Ex. 60b, which corresponds to the most popular of the diminished versions in Ex. 60e. It occurs at the end of No. 60, concludes the opening section of No. 64, and appears in a number of works of Corbetta.[60] Plate XIX, the opening page of Corbetta's vocal version of the Allemande in No. 62, shows the cadence of Ex. 60b in the upper voice part in measure 4; it recurs also at the end of the piece.[61] De Visée also has many examples.[62] Occasionally Corbetta uses a more ornamented version, as in Ex. 61b or 61c,[63] or the cadence with two dotted notes (Ex. 60c).[64]

The two favored forms of the typical cadence are thus Exx. 60b and e, with the first occurring in the guitar Allemandes, which begin around 1671 and continue a tradition begun in Italy, and the diminished version in the lute and clavecin Allemandes, which represent an exclusively French development that began around 1630. The cadences appear, as we have seen, not only at the end of a section or a piece, but also sometimes as an internal point of articulation within a section. In this case, however, the music is usually flowing onward in one voice or another even during the course of the cadence, so that the effect is far more subtle than a similar cadence in the Renaissance Almande. When tonality is fully established, however, such internal cadences become bolder and more conspicuous.

Ex. 60e is by far the most frequent, and I have found only one in other French duple dances.[65] There are, on the other hand, a few examples of Ex. 60b in the solo *gavotte* and *bourrée*, both fast duple dances that became popular at court around 1650.[66] There are considerably more examples of Ex. 60b in ballet *gavottes* and *bourrées* from 1656 to 1672.[67] The cadence ceases abruptly in the ballet examples of these two dances, however, after 1672, which is almost precisely the time it commences in the French guitar Allemande. Cadences in the later *gavotte* and *bourrée* tend to favor a 2-1 resolution or occasionally some other form of 7-1. The Allemande also uses 2-1 sometimes, but there are a sufficient number of typical cadences, I think, to give the impression that they are a special trait of the Allemande and form a link between the French Baroque examples and the long history that precedes them.

Types, Titles, and Tempo

Descriptive titles occur as early as Ennemond Gaultier and become more numerous in the later keyboard works of François Couperin. I have included some in notes 29–64 on pp. 236–37. They may refer to a person, a place, an event, or perhaps something fanciful. *La Marianne* of John Mercure may refer to a woman,[68] Bocquet's *La Polonoise Allemande* to someone from Poland,[69] and L. Couperin's *Allemande de la Paix* to a contemporary event.[70] Chambonnières' title *Allemande la Rare*[71] may be the equivalent of Le Roux's *Allemande l'Incomparable*[72] and Jean-Nicolas Geoffroy's *Allemande la sans pareille*.[73] Henry Du Mont has a *Belle Allemande*[74] and Corbetta an *Allemande amoureuse*.[75] Corbetta also has one for the Duke of York (No. 62) and an *Allemande aymée de son Altesse* (no doubt the King of England, to whom his 1671 book is dedicated), as well as an *Allemande aymée de l'auteur*.[76] A number, such as F. Couperin's *L'Auguste*, *La Laborieuse*, and *La Ténébreuse*,[77] refer, like many of Gastoldi's Balletti, to someone in a particular mood. In this case, the title can help to suggest the tempo and manner of performance of the piece.

A special category of Allemande is the *tombeau*, a lament for someone who has died. The earliest are E. Gaultier's *Le tombeau de l'Enclos, Allemande* and *Tombeau de Mezangeau*,[78] the latter also called *Allemande* by Perrine in his *Pièces de luth en musique* (Paris, 1680).[79] Later, Corbetta in 1671 has an *Allemande sur la mort du Duc de Glocester*,[80] Jacques Gallot an *Allemande le bout de l'an de Mr. [Denis] Gautier* (No. 63), and De Visée in 1682 an *Allemande, Tombeau de Mr. Francisque* [Corbetta].[81] Some titles, like Geoffroy's *Tombeau en forme d'allemande*[82] and Campion's *Allemande, tombeau* (No. 71b), do not mention any particular person. In addition, the idea of a lament seems to be present in E. Gaultier's *The Loss of the Golden Rose Lute*,[83] Chambonnières' *Allemande dit[e] l'Affligée*,[84] and Corbetta's *Allemande faite sur l'emprisonnement du Duc de Bouquingam*.[85]

The *tombeaux* and some of the other titles suggest a very slow tempo and a solemn manner, and most Allemandes seem to fit Brossard's definition as a *symphonie grave*. Chambonnières marks *lentement* on his *Allemande dit[e] l'Affligée* mentioned above, Louis Couperin indicates for one Allemande that "il faut jouer cette pièce fort lentement,"[86] and Corbetta marks one example *lento*.[87] The title *Allemande grave* appears in a work of Louis Couperin[88] and in succeeding examples by Du Mont,[89] Geoffroy,[90] and Le Roux.[91] Three of those by Du Mont commence with a dotted half-note, so that the title may be a warning not to go too fast. The two examples of Le Roux move mostly in quarter- and eighth-notes and, like only one other in the same book, have a meter of **2** instead of 4/4. Geoffroy also has a *Petite allemande* marked *gravement*,[92] and Du Mont a piece called *Allemande lente*.[93]

In 1677 an *Allemande gaye* appears in Lebègue's collection[94] and apparently establishes another type of Allemande, presumably with a mood opposite to the *Allemande grave*. D'Anglebert has an Allemande in 1689 marked *gaiement*,[95] Geoffroy one called *Allemande de la plaisante gaye*,[96] and Le Roux in 1705 two entitled *Allemande gaye*.[97] In his collections of chamber music, François Couperin has an *Allemande fuguée, gayement* from 1722,[98] as well as two from 1724 marked *gayement*.[99] Most of these gay Allemandes display the same sixteenth-note and dotted rhythms we have seen in the Allemande generally. The tempo no doubt is faster and perhaps the touch is lighter.

F. Couperin has a chamber example marked *vivement*,[100] and he indicates that a number of his keyboard and chamber Allemandes are to be played lightly. The Allemande in *L'Art de toucher le clavecin* is marked *légèrement*, perhaps because it is filled with a constant stream of sixteenth-notes in one hand or the other or both.[101] His *Allemande L'Ausoniéne* is to be *légèrement, et marqué*,[102] and *Le Point du jour* should be played *d'une légèreté modérée*.[103] His chamber works include an *Allemande légère*, as well as one marked *plus légère* and another called *Allemande à 4 tems légèrs, vivement et les croches égales et marquées*.[104]

In addition, Couperin has others in which he seems to want to avoid the extremely slow tempo apparently previously associated with the *Allemande grave*. His Allemande for keyboard called *La Logiviére* is to be performed *majestueusement, sans lenteur*, and the *Allemande La Laborieuse* should be *sans lenteur, et les doubles croches un tant-soit-peu pointées* (without slowness, and the double eighth-notes slightly dotted).[105] He marks two chamber works *fièrement* (proudly), *sans lenteur* and *noblement, et sans lenteur*.[106]

There are occasionally other moods, such as *tendrement* (No. 71a) or *gracieusement*.[107] The Allemande is sometimes combined with fugue, as in F. Couperin's *Allemande fuguée* in the *Concerts royaux* of 1722[108] and Nicolas

Gigault's *Allemande par fugue* for keyboard.[109] It also unexpectedly serves at times as the music for a gigue. E. Gaultier has one piece that appears in some sources as *Allemande* or *Les dernières paroles, ou Testament de Mezangeau*, in others as *Gigue*. He has another that is called variously *La Poste, Gigue, Gigue en Allemande*, or *Allemande giguée*.[110] Both of these pieces were also printed by Perrine in keyboard notation in his *Pièces de luth en musique* (1680). In each case, music entitled *Allemande* appears first, followed by the note: "cette pièce se joüe encore en gigue. Tournez." Upon turning the page, one finds substantially the same music repeated, but this time with the title *Gigue*, the meter changed from C to ₵, and the first note of some of the groups of two eighth-notes dotted.[111] Presumably when played as a gigue, the piece was actually performed faster and perhaps in 12/8, with a dotted eighth followed by a sixteenth played with the first note twice instead of three times as long as the second, producing a triple unit. There are also two keyboard Allemandes in the Bauyn manuscript by Joseph La Barre which appear later in the same source with the title *Gigue*.[112]

Although the Allemande could thus, on occasion, be played faster as in a *gigue* or an *Allemande gaye*, it was usually throughout most of its history slow and solid, and in any case grand and majestic. The rhythmic motives and affective content are particularly arresting and catch a listener's attention. This is the reason it often stands, like the French overture, at the beginning of a series of musical events. In many sources the Allemande thus comes first in a set of dances in a single key, preceded only, on occasion, by a *prélude*. The Allemande is associated with the *courante* and the *sarabande* in the *Tablature de mandore* of Chancy in 1629,[113] and in succeeding lute sources pieces seem to be grouped together according to tuning. Beginning in 1666 suites consisting of *Allemande–courante–sarabande–gigue* (and sometimes other dances added at the end) appear in collections for solo viol by Du Buisson, Machy, Heudelinne, and Morel. Keyboard collections, starting with Lebègue in 1677, group dances by key center. In some sources, such as Dieupart's *Six suittes de clavessin* of 1701, the sets are conceived with a uniform order, in this case *Overture, Allemande, Courante, Sarabande, Gavotte, Menuet* (or *Passepied*) and *Gigue*. At the other extreme, however, are the *ordres* of François Couperin, each with up to twenty-two pieces. Whether grouped together for performance in a suite, or simply as a convenient arrangement for publication, almost all of these French sets of pieces commence either with an Allemande or with a *prélude* followed by an Allemande. Compared to the other dance movements, the Allemande is almost always far more complex and far more contrapuntal.

Thus the Allemande became one of the most important of the French dance movements, equalled only by the *sarabande*, and perhaps by the *courante*, in the continuity and extent of its presence. This is all the more remarkable when we remember that it alone among the dances was no longer actually danced. It developed a style that was distinctively French in nature and almost totally different from the Renaissance Almande. Yet, at the same time, the sectional structure, the duple meter, and, above all, the typical cadences, modified to fit the new affective environment, survived from the past and acted to give a sense of historical continuity. We have noted Italian influence in the later Allemandes of France. In its turn, however, the French Baroque Allemande influenced developments in both Italy and Germany. We will turn first to Italy, where the Baroque Alemanda and the Baroque Balletto developed concurrently.

10 THE BALLETTO AND ALEMANDA FOR GUITAR, KEYBOARD, AND ENSEMBLE IN ITALY 1640–1730

THE MAIN Italian developments during the Baroque period take place in guitar and chamber music. The Balletto is the leading form in chamber music, although the Alemanda and French ideas appear shortly after mid-century. Both chamber forms exhibit the rhythmic ideas of the French Allemande, but at the same time achieve a motivic and melodic unity which, as we have already seen, later influenced the French development. In guitar music, on the other hand, there are only a few Balletti, for it is the Alemanda that dominates throughout the entire century. French influence comes earlier to guitar music and is more thorough in its effect. In both guitar and chamber music, however, the Balletto and the Alemanda, although often occurring together in the same sources, emerge as two forms that are indistinguishable from each other musically and functionally.

The Alemanda and Balletto for Guitar

We have already noted in Chapter 3 the *rasgueado* examples of the *Balletto tedesco*, the *Balletto alemano*, and the *Alemana*. In Exx. 27 and 28, which show progressions that fit the Almandes *Prince* and *Nonette*, I have indicated triads by their root tones. I have fully transcribed the *Alemana* in No. 97, however, since it contains some "dissonant" chords as well as triads. This actually depicts the strumming of all five courses of the guitar more clearly and shows, in addition, the peculiar inversions that occur when the lowest course simply plays the tone of the chord nearest to its open pitch. As in cittern music of the 16th century (see Nos. 9, 41, and 43), such chords do not necessarily act as functional inversions, but are simply a curious circumstance of the style. Even more curious is the survival of these strange inversions in the new styles that emerge around 1640 in which *rasgueado* chords (like the last one in No. 125) are mixed with *punteado* notes (single tones on selected courses) or in which all the notes are *punteado* (see the opening chord of No. 105b). This, I think, was the result of a fierce rivalry between lute and guitar supporters and the desire of each group to retain traits unique to its own instrument.[1]

Most of the guitar activity centered in northern Italy, particularly in Bologna. Several of the most famous guitarists, however, traveled extensively in France, England, and the Low Countries. French influence is evident not only in Sanseverino's *Alemana* of 1620 in Ex. 28, but also in such titles as *Balletto franzese* and *Zarabanda franzese* in Foscarini's book of 1629 or *Alemanda, Baletto frances* (No. 98a) in one of his later undated books. The latter piece appears as *Alemanda francese* in the index to *Li cinque libri* published in Rome in 1640.[2] Granata uses the same title in No. 105b, as well as *Balletto francese* in No. 105a. In 1640 Carbonchi published in Florence his *Sonate di chitarra con intavolatura franzese*. Foscarini spent time in Flanders and had an intimate knowledge of French lute style.[3] Corbetta was in Paris from time to time beginning around 1640.[4] Three of his Italian publications still exist, and we have already seen the influence of his last two Parisian books on the French guitar composers (see No. 62 and Plate XIX). Similarly, Bartolotti, after publishing two guitar books in Italy, moved to Paris and became a part of the French development (No. 60). In his second Italian book from around 1655 he uses French spelling for all the titles. There was thus a vigorous interaction between the Italian guitarists and the French style, beginning with the influence of the French lutenists in the 1630's and continuing throughout the entire century, even after the Italian guitarists had, in effect, ousted the lute from France as they had earlier in Italy.

The *rasgueado* texture, illustrated by No. 97, was clearly a reaction against the style that had previously dominated Italian lute music for a century. Its almost complete victory was no doubt due to the fact that it enabled an untrained amateur to play, with a minimum of effort, popular songs and dances based on the standard chordal schemes. During the 1630's, however, the Renaissance dance style was rapidly declining in popularity and, as new Baroque ideas were emerging on all sides, serious musicians became interested in the guitar. In order to fashion a new style, however, they could not look back to the Italian lute tradition against which they had so vigorously reacted and toward which they were still so hostile. Instead, they found an acceptable guide in the newly developing *style brisé* of the French lutenists. Even so, there was great resistance to the introduction of *punteado* notes in guitar music. Foscarini, who seems to have been the earliest composer to publish examples in the new style, apologizes for pieces such as No. 98a (in mixed style) and especially 98b (completely *punteado*) by admitting they are more appropriate for the lute than for the guitar.[5] Nos. 98a and 99a and b represent the earlier stages of this transformation in style. Late examples, such as those of Granata in No. 121a and Roncalli in No. 125, show that the usual guitar style that emerges is a combination of French *style brisé* and *rasgueado* chords. Occasionally pieces such as Nos. 105a and b are completely *punteado*.

I have not contrapuntalized the guitar transcriptions as I have the lute pieces in Volume II, since the strummed chords and the texture in general do not lend themselves to this sort of treatment. With a little patience, however,

Ex. 62: Opening of *Alemanda* by Granata, 1674.

the reader can get from the guitar scores, I think, a sense of the rhythmic strength of the music and of the subtle melodic lines that weave in and out. The bass line often seems partly or totally absent. Ex. 62 shows the beginning of an ensemble Alemanda in which the violin points out the melody in the guitar texture and the continuo provides the missing or hidden bass line.[6]

Along with the *style brisé*, the Italian guitarists also borrowed from the French such musical forms as the *prélude*, the Allemande, and the dances currently popular in France. The Alemanda seems to become a favorite form for the guitar composers, for many sources contain an unusual number of examples. At the same time a few Italian Balletti are included in the same books and take on the same musical characteristics. Table 2 shows the number of examples of each form occurring in the main Italian guitar sources from 1640 to 1692. Occasionally the forms are completely separate, either within a random mixture of dances (as in Foscarini's earlier book or Granata's book of 1646) or within a group of like dances (as in the eleven Alemande grouped together in Granata's 1674 work). Most often, however, different forms are grouped together by key or by tuning. Such groups usually vary in number, type, and order of movements. The earliest, in Foscarini's fifth book of 1640, contain two or three movements such as *Preludio–Alemanda–Corrente*, *Toccatta et Alemanda*, *Alemanda e' Sarabanda*, or the *Baletto et Alemanda* in No. 99. The Alemanda is usually the first dance of a group, sometimes preceded by an introductory non-dance piece.[7]

Occasionally the groups take on a relatively fixed order, as in Corbetta's 1643 book.[8] The group *Almanda–Corrente–Sarabanda* (A–C–S) occurs seven times, and an eighth group adds a second *corrente*. The pieces are grouped first of all by key, with the *Almanda del 4° tuono*, for example, followed by *Sua Corrente* and *Sarabanda*. The final group begins with an *Almanda per nuova acordatura*, with instructions for a new tuning. Similarly, Bartolotti has six A–C–C–S groups in his 1640 book, and Roncalli in 1692 has many that include a *preludio* followed by A–C–G–S (where G = *gigua* or gigue). In some cases, as in Bartolotti's later book and Granata's work of 1674, the groups become, like François Couperin's *ordres*, so long and formless that they seem to be more a

Table 2. *Incidence of the Alemanda and Balletto in Italian Guitar Sources*

Source	Number of Alemande	Number of Balletti
Foscarini, 1640	15	1
Bartolotti, 1640	6	0
Corbetta, 1643	8	0
Granata, 1646	7	3
Corbetta, 1648	4	0
Pellegrini, 1650	4	1
Granata, 1651	7	0
Bartolotti, c. 1655	23	0
Granata, 1659	15	4
Bottazzari, 1663	17	0
Granata, 1674	26	1
Granata, 1680	23	4
Granata, 1684	18	6
Roncalli, 1692	10	0

convenient arrangement for publication than a unified multi-movement work.

Even in such groups, however, the Alemanda is almost always the first dance, preceded sometimes by a *preludio*. The few Balletti in the same books are sometimes separate pieces (Nos. 104 and 105a), but sometimes, like the Alemanda, they appear as the first dance of a group. No. 108a opens the series B–C–C–S. Granata in 1680 has several B–G pairs, from which No. 121a comes. In a few cases the Alemanda and Balletto are even paired together; in No. 99, the Balletto takes the lead position, whereas in Granata's 1674 book the order is reversed.

Both the Alemanda and the Balletto gradually take on the rhythmic qualities of the French Allemande. Although some of the earlier examples move mainly in even quarter- or eighth-notes (Nos. 98b, 104, 105b), the motives of Ex. 58 begin to appear in the works of Foscarini (No. 98a) and Corbetta (No. 106). After mid-century, Alemande such as those of Granata (Nos. 114b and 121b) and Roncalli (No. 125) are filled with sixteenth-note motives and often contain the opening rhythmic patterns of Ex. 59. Even early examples sometimes include the dotted quarter-note preceded (No. 99b) or not (No. 98a) by an eighth-note anacrusis. Corbetta's *Almanda* in No. 106 begins with Ex. 59b, and Granata's ensemble piece in Ex. 62 commences like Ex. 59c, except for the tie on the first sixteenth-note. Most examples commence with an anacrusis of an eighth-note or a dotted eighth and sixteenth. Most, like the French lute Allemande, end with the final tonic on the first beat of the concluding measure and with the melody tone repeated on the third beat (Nos. 106, 114a and b, 121a, and 125). Only occasionally does a piece end with a single sustained tone (Nos. 105a, 108a, and 121b).

Nos. 99, 105, 108, and 121 each include a Balletto and an Alemanda from the same source, in order to demonstrate the similarity of the two forms. The Balletto in No. 114c lacks the sixteenth-note motives found in the Alemanda of No. 114b with which it is grouped, but another Balletto in the same publication (No. 114a) displays them in abundance. The pair in No. 121 are both in the same key and begin with the same rhythm and even the same melody. Within one source, one Alemanda may differ occasionally from a particular Balletto. In general, however, the two forms seem, as far as I can tell, to have the same musical traits.

Formal construction also follows the French model. There are two sections, each to be repeated and each containing four to sixteen measures. Frequently there are an odd number of bars, and often the second section has one to five bars more than the first. No. 99b, on the other hand, has a longer opening section (17 + 13 bars), whereas Nos. 108b and 114c have equal sections, of five and sixteen bars respectively. No. 108a has a varied repeat following each section. In No. 98b both sections begin with the same melody and rhythm, and in No. 114a the third-from-last bars of each section are almost the same. The two phrases in the opening section of No. 104 begin with a parallel idea, and in No. 99a they conclude with the same construction, including a typical cadence (but shifted so that the bar-line falls between the two appearances of scale degree 1). Usually, however, phrases and sections are not parallel to any extent, and the piece either has no conspicuous recurring elements (see No. 125) or includes sequential passages that act only momentarily. Although sequences dominate the second section of No. 98a, they usually pass by more quickly, as at the beginning of the second section of No. 105b, measures 5 and 6 in the second half of No. 108a, measures 6-8 in section 1 and measures 3 and 4 in section 2 of No. 114a, measures 5-7 in the second section of No. 121a, and the end of the first section and middle of the second section of No. 121b. The first section usually ends on the dominant (see the Balletti in Nos. 104, 105a, and 121a, and the Alemande in Nos. 98b, 99b, 105b, 106, 108b, 121b, and 125), but in a few cases remains in the opening tonality (the Balletto and Alemanda in No. 114).

There seem to be no tempo markings or descriptive titles for either form in the Italian guitar sources. Most, however, follow the French Allemande in other respects. Thus, when Corbetta and other Italian guitarists performed in Paris and published books of music there, they were offering to the French people the forms and style of music already well known to them. The guitar itself, according to Pierre Trichet in the "Traité des instruments de musique" from around 1640, was "widely used among the French and Italians."[9] He describes the Spanish performers who play "their *sarabandes, gaillardes, espagnolettes, passemezes, passecailles, pavanes, alemandes,* and *romanesques* with a thousand gestures and body movements so grotesque and ridiculous that their playing is bizarre and confused."[10] Foscarini, on the other hand, says that "pieces in the French style, such as *correnti*, *balletti*, and *gagliarde*, should be played quietly."[11] Trichet considers the lute and its quiet style more suitable for the French, but notes that "there are nevertheless some in our nation who abandon it completely in order to take up and learn how to play the guitar."[12] Thirty years later the guitar had taken over almost completely in France, although it had, as we have seen, borrowed much from the forms and style of the lute.

The Chamber Forms

The development of the Italian Baroque chamber forms also took place in northern Italy – mainly, again, in Bologna, and also in nearby cities such as Modena and Ferrara. The principal form now is the Balletto, and French influence is less continuous and less pervasive.

Until 1656 there is a continuation of the types related to Praetorius' cycle of entry, main, and exit dances. Thus the multi-sectional form of Marini's *Il Vendramino* of 1617 in No. 89a, with its changing meters and textures, seems to recur in Fantini's *Balletto detto il Cavalca* for trumpet and continuo in 1638 (No. 96).[13] The multi-movement format, which we first encountered in Kapsberger's *Uscita* and *Ballo* of 1615 (No. 87), continues in works by Zanetti (see the *Intrata*, *Balletto*, and *La sua Gagliarda* from 1645 in No. 103a) and Marini (see Nos. 107a and 111a). Marini's *Balletto secondo* of 1655 in No. 111a consists of *Entrata*, *Balletto*, *Gagliarda*, *Corrente*, and *Retirata*. The two pieces in No. 107 are part of another Balletto of Marini (1649) that contains *Entrata*, *Balletto prima parte*, *Seconda parte Gagliarda*, *Retirata*, *Terza parte Corrente prima*, *Retirata*, *Corrente seconda*, *Retirata*, *Quinta parte Allemana*, and *Retirata*. Each *Retirata* has the same music, but the other sections are not related musically. As in the earlier examples by Melli (see Chapter 7) and Kapsberger (Chapter 8), movements of a single Balletto may be in different keys: the *Balletto* in A minor and the *Allemana* in G major in No. 107 are from the same work, and the piece in G major in No. 111a belongs to a Balletto that includes movements in E minor, A minor, and D minor. The first section of a movement may, like most earlier Italian examples of the 17th century, end in the same tonality with which it begins (Nos. 107a and b and No. 111b); it may also occasionally conclude in a different key (see No. 111a, which goes to the subdominant).

The Nachtanz, such as Marini includes in his earlier books (Nos. 93 and 95b), seems to exist no longer, although the triple section of No. 112b begins as a melodic transformation of the duple music. Separate Balletti, however, such as No. 95a, continue with examples by Marini in 1655 (No. 111b) and Francesco Todeschini in 1650 (No. 110).[14] Salvador Gandini includes in his book of 1655 three types: the *Balletto all'italiana* (No. 112a), which with its repeated notes and *fa-la*-like passages reminds one of Gastoldi; the *Balletto all'allemana* (No. 112b), which with its triple section suggests Marini and the 16th-century lute development; and the *Balletto alla francese* (No. 112c) which with its less organized melodies and less significant inner voice may mirror qualities of contemporary French dances. Some of Gandini's Balletti are separate and some are followed by a *corrente*; some are duple and some triple. Francesco Boccella, in his *Primavera di vaghi fiori musicali . . . con diverse Correnti, Sarabande, e Balletti alla francese* (Ancona, 1653), includes examples with titles such as *Le gran Balletto, Balletto del Prencipe*, and *La Moscheni, Balletto*, some followed by a piece labeled *Segue la sua Corrente*.[15] Todeschini's example in No. 110, on the other hand, comes from a group of six Balletti, each entitled simply *Balletto primo, secondo*, etc.

All of these diverse types seem to coexist around 1655. After this date, however, the groups that begin with an *Entrata* disappear. Triple meter and descriptive titles are rare. Occasionally the term *Ballo* appears. The Balletto now occurs in one of two formats: either as a separate piece within a set of Balletti (often six or twelve), or grouped with dances currently popular in France. At first the Balletto is paired exclusively with a *corrente*; around 1670 it could precede a *corrente* or a *giga*. Late in the 1670's the group could include three dances, and later even four. Sometimes the Balletto was preceded by an *Introdutione* or a *Sinfonia*. Occasionally a standard succession such as B–C–S–G, B–C–G–S, B–C–G–M (where S = *sarabanda* and M = *menuet*) emerges, but more often a single source will include a varied assortment of two-, three-, and four-movement groups.

The movements in a group are now in the same key. The opening section may end in the main tonality or a different one (usually the dominant), but the main key is preferred in both the Balletto and the Alemanda, even in works from the end of the century. Pieces in which the first section ends in the tonic (see Nos. 115a, 122a, and 127a, for example) are usually mixed in the same sources with others in which it does not (Nos. 115b, 122b, and 127b). In view of the overwhelming preference in France and (as we will see) also in Germany for a different tonality at this point, it is striking to note how many of the Italian ensemble pieces between Nos. 112 and 128a conclude their opening section on the tonic. Such compositions, of course, trace their own tonal design, with other keys appearing in the middle of a section or at the beginning of the second. Within a single suite, the other dances may or may not follow the Balletto or the Alemanda in regard to the manner of concluding the opening section.

The Balletto is almost always the first dance of a group, and its increasingly central importance is indicated by the titles of the books. The word *Balletto* is the third dance listed in the title of Todeschini's book of 1650, and second in Cazzati's *Correnti e Balletti* of 1651 and 1654. Priuli reverses the order in his *Balletti et Correnti* of 1665, and after 1674 most titles name the Balletto first. In

Table 3. *Incidence of the Balletto and Alemanda in Selective Italian Chamber Sources*

Source	Number of Alemande	Number of Balletti
Todeschini, 1650	0	6
Legrenzi, 1656	3	6
Cazzati, 1662	0	11
Vitali, 1666	0	12
Vitali, 1667	0	10
Vitali, 1668	2	5
Bononcini, 1671	7	0
P. Degli Antoni, 1671	1	5
G. B. Degli Antoni, c. 1680	0	12
Gabrielli, 1684	3	12
Corelli, 1685	12	0
Torelli, 1686	11	12
Laurenti, 1691	6	3
Buoni, 1693	0	12
Griffoni, 1700	6	6

the 1660's the expression *da* or *per camera* begins to appear also in titles, and after 1685 the lists of dances disappear in favor of general titles such as *Sonate da camera, Concerto da camera, Allettamenti per camera, Divertimenti da camera*, and *Trattenimenti da camera*. Occasionally a book, such as Tonini's in 1690, that contains only one dance form will be called *Balletti da camera*.

Table 3 shows the incidence of the Balletto and Alemanda in the sources from which the examples in Volume II were drawn, as well as a few others. This represents about a quarter of the chamber sources which still exist. Some collections omit the Alemanda altogether, some include a few. In the latter case, the Balletti are named first in the title of the book, with the Alemande usually mentioned fourth, following the *correnti* and *gighe*. In Volume II, Nos. 113, 118, 122, 123, 124, 127, and 128 each include a Balletto and an Alemanda from the same source, for comparison. As in guitar music, however, the two forms seem musically the same in most cases. The Alemanda, on the other hand, seems to have been favored by Bononcini in books from 1669, 1671, 1675, and 1677, and by Corelli, who excludes the Balletto completely.[16] Some of the later composers, such as Torelli in 1686 and Griffoni in 1700, give almost equal attention to the two forms. Many books, however, even from the 1680's and 1690's include only Ballctti.[17]

The expression *da camera* seems to be used in 1667 to distinguish purely chamber music from music for dancing, or *per ballare*. Bononcini published in this year his *Sonate da camera, e da ballo*, with the implication that all the dances therein were either for listening or for dancing. Vitali in the same year, however, makes a distinction in his title *Balletti, Correnti alla francese, Gagliarde, e Brando per ballare; Balletti, Correnti, e Sinfonie da camera*. The pieces in the book are entitled either *per ballare* (see No. 117a) or *per camera* (No. 117b), but the only difference between them seems to be that the *Balletti per camera* are together in a group, whereas each *Balletto per ballare* is followed by *Sua Corrente alla francese*. Thus the grouping of dances seems to continue to reflect social requirements, as it did earlier with the Praetorius type. Legrenzi in 1656 makes a distinction between *Sonate da chiesa* and *da camera*, although the Balletto and Alemanda in No. 113 are not part of either type of sonata. Perhaps the separate dances at the end of the book fall into a third category that Bononcini and Vitali describe as *da ballo* or *per ballare* – that is, functional dance music. The continuation of the expression *da camera* and the complete disappearance of *per ballare* after 1667, however, may suggest that the music was no longer used for dance accompaniment after this date.[18]

Although there seems to be little information concerning the dancing of the Balletto in Italy at this time, Giambatista Dufort, in his *Trattato del ballo nobile* (Naples, 1728), mentions that binary meter is used, for the most part, in "those dances which should be danced quickly and with swiftness such as, for example, the *Giga*, the *Gavotta*, the *Burè*, the *Rigodone*, the *Alamanda*, and other similar dances."[19] We have seen in the last chapter how an *Allemande gaye* developed in France after 1677, with a mood contrasting to the more usual *Allemande grave*. We have also seen diversity in earlier Italian Balletti, with Brunelli's *Ballo grave* from 1616 in No. 88a and Marini's Balletti in 1649 and 1655 (Nos. 107a and 111a) both marked *allegro*. Giovanni Scipione, in the preface to his *Intavolatura di cembalo, et organo* (Rome, 1650), says that "in the Corrente and Balletti one should observe the tempo *allegro* in order that they appear with greater charm and grace."[20]

Tempo markings are fairly frequent from the 1660's on, and they regularly indicate slow and fast versions of both the Alemanda and the Balletto. Cazzati's piece in No. 115a is marked *largo*, but other Balletti in the same source are *vivace, allegro*, or *adaggio*. Vitali's *Balletto per ballare* in No. 117a is *largo*, but others are *allegro* or *presto*; the *Balletto per camera* in No. 117b is *allegro*, whereas others are *largo*. Vitali's Alemanda in No. 118b is *largo*, the other one in the same book is *allegro*; his Balletto in No. 118a is *allegro*, whereas others are *largo* or *prestissimo*. Clemente Monari includes eight different markings for the twelve Balletti in his book of 1686.[21] Salvatore Mazzella in 1689 even has a *Ballo* in which the opening section is *largo* and the second *presto*, and another such example that returns at the end to *largo*.[22] There is perhaps a tendency for the later Balletto to be fast, since none of the examples by Brevi and Buoni in 1693 and Griffoni in 1700 is marked "slow." Similarly, most of the later Alemande in the violin sonatas of Giovanni Antonio Piani are marked *allegro* or *allegro ma non presto*,[23] most of those in the violin and trio sonatas of Vivaldi *allegro* or *allegro non molto*.[24]

Composers usually exhibit, however, a variety of tempos even within the same book, ranging from *largo, e con affetto* and *largo, ma spiritoso* to *presto assai*, *prestissimo*, and *vivace*. This is true for the Alemanda and the Balletto, as well as for pieces *da camera* and those *per ballare*. Furthermore, regardless of name, type, or function, and regardless of tempo, all these dances look alike. When the tempo is not marked, there are thus no clues to guide the performer. Perhaps in such cases the work could be played on different occasions with a different tempo and spirit.

In any case, an examination of the Italian chamber examples from Legrenzi's pieces of 1656 in No. 113 on will show that the sixteenth-note figures of Ex. 58, which we have seen already in France and in the Italian guitar pieces, come gradually to dominate the music. Those pieces that commence with a full measure (preceded usually by a quarter- or eighth-note of anacrusis), often display the opening rhythms of Ex. 59. Ex. 59b occurs in Vitali's Balletto in No. 116. In his work in No. 118a the last beat has been filled in with sixteenth-notes, and in No. 118b the first eighth-note is replaced by two sixteenths. The pattern of Ex. 59c, but without the tie, opens Cazzati's Balletto in No. 115a. The rest and the three sixteenth-notes appear in Buoni's piece from 1693 in No. 126.

Italian ensemble examples may begin on beat 1 or 3, and with or without a brief anacrusis of a sixteenth-, eighth-, or quarter-note in duration. In those that commence on the first beat, the final tonic chord usually falls on the first beat of the last measure (see No. 115a, for example), but may occur on the third (No. 122a). Those beginning on the third beat almost always end with the final tonic on a first beat (No. 113a and b); only in rare cases does it fall on the third (No. 119b). A section of an ensemble piece usually ends with a sustained and unrepeated tone in the melody.

We noted in the last chapter a few French Allemandes that begin on the third beat. This is far more common, however, in Italian ensemble music. It seems to lead to different opening rhythms, often looking like the second half of the patterns in Ex. 59. No. 113a, for example, begins like Ex. 59a when the opening dotted quarter-note is omitted. The dotted eighth-note in the second half of Ex. 59b sometimes appears in such cases on the third beat rather than the fourth (No. 120) or on both beats (No. 117a). Other examples in Volume II that commence on the third beat are Nos. 113b, 119b, 122b, and 128a and b. As noted in the last chapter, the diminished note values tend to make each barred measure sound like two, especially in pieces that begin like Ex. 63, where a repetition takes place, but out of phase with the opening statement.[25] A similar effect takes place when a piece that begins on the first beat, opens the second section with the same melody shifted to the third beat (see No. 123a). This avoids the long dotted half-note at the end of the first section of examples such as Nos. 115a, 116, and 117b. The way in which No. 123a ends seems to require that the repetition of the second section commence, as I have shown,

172   *The Baroque Period*

Ex. 63: Beginning of *cantus* part from *Alemanda detta la Bentivoglia* by Cazzati, 1669.

with one measure of 2/4. I have similarly included bars of 2/4 in Nos. 119a and 126. Pieces that begin on beat 3, of course, simply hold the last note of the opening section a dotted quarter and then begin the second section, like the first, on beat 3. This may suggest the rhythmic reason for the origin of the third-beat type. In any event, pieces that have the first accent on beat 3 seem simply mixed at random with others in the same sources that begin on the first beat. Both types appear in the Alemanda as well as the Balletto, in pieces *da camera* and *per ballare*, and in pieces marked *largo* or *allegro*.

Although the sixteenth-note figures of Exx. 58 and 59 create a sort of continuous and affective rhythmic flow, as they did in the French Allemande, the Italian chamber forms differ markedly from French examples and from Italian guitar pieces in their special concern for inner organization and unity. In the 16th century, as we have seen, it was the French who applied this sort of constructive attitude far more than the Germans and Italians. Now the roles are reversed, and it is in Italy that the constructive devices and rigorous motivic unity that we associate with the late Baroque style are cultivated and refined.

Exact repetition may operate in several ways. Phrases may be immediately repeated, as in measures 1 and 3 of No. 115a. A rounded binary form may result, as in Nos. 124b and 126. A *petite reprise* may occur at the end of a piece (No. 123a) or the end of each section (Nos. 122a, 123b, and 124b). They are usually marked *P.* or *piano*, although the example at the end of No. 122a returns to *forte* in the final bar. The two sections may become parallel by beginning with the same rhythm (No. 118a), with the first few notes of the opening melody transposed to a new key (No. 117b), or with a substantial transposition of an opening theme (Nos. 123a, 124b, and 126). Less often, the two sections may end in a similar fashion (No. 120).

On a more detailed level, motivic ostinato may occur (see measures 5 and 6 of No. 115a). More common, however, are the motivic sequences which occur in many of the pieces in Volume II: see, for example, No. 119b (measures 5–6, counting the opening incomplete bar), No. 124b (first in the top voice in measures 5–6, then in the bass in measures 7–8), and No. 128b (measures 1–5 and 9–12 of the second section). Canonic sequences, often of the type we saw in the *fa-la* passages of Gastoldi and Morley and the forms later influenced by them, occur in Nos. 117b (middle of each section), 118a (second section), 122a (measures 4 and 5 of the second section), 127a (measures 6–10 of the second section), and 127b (measures 7 and 8 of the last section). More extensive canon between voices occurs in measures 4–7 of No. 118b.

The downward third, which we have seen before in Gastoldi's Balletti and the French Allemande, occurs now far more frequently and acts often as a source of unity within a piece. It occurs usually in eighth-notes on the opening beat of a measure, where it marks the end of a phrase, especially when followed by a rest. In No. 117a it occurs without a rest on the opening beat of measures 4, 10, 13, and 14. In No. 120 it is followed by a rest in measures 2, 4, 10, 12, and 14. In measure 7 it appears on the third beat. Similarly, No. 123a has downward thirds followed by a rest in measures 6, 9, 19, and 23. Occasionally a different interval has almost the same effect, as the second in the eleventh bar of No. 123a or the fifth in the third bar of No. 113a. The downward third often occurs on the two eighth-notes at the end of Ex. 59d, to mark the end of the opening rhythmic pattern. This happens without a rest in No. 118a, and with a rest, but without some of the conventional rhythms of Ex. 59, in No. 122a. It may also occur in pieces that start on the third beat, either followed by a rest (No. 120) or not (No. 122b). The tiny motive of the downward third thus acts as a termination for small internal phrases and, at the same time, provides rhythmic energy that propels the music beyond the following rest. It can act, as we have seen, to unify an individual work, and its appearance in many examples helps to unify them as a type.

Sections sometimes begin with imitation (No. 119b, each section) or more extensive canon (No. 118b, second section). Later examples, however, display fugal techniques. No. 127a presents a substantial theme and its fugal exposition. The second section opens with the imitation of a new motive that seems related in its pitches to the theme of the first section. The sequences that begin eight measures from the end are drawn rhythmically from the beginning of the section. No. 124a seems like an invention, with many entrances of the opening theme filling almost every measure of both sections. In the fourth bar of the second there is a return to the tonic and a repetition of the opening measure to round the form out. No. 123b, finally, is a real fugue, with a memorable theme, its exposition, an initial counter-subject (seen most clearly in the middle voice of measure 8, beginning on d'' and ending on b'-flat in the next measure), and a second counter-subject, which has a rhythm similar to Ex. 59d (first heard in the top voice at the beginning of the second section).

Thus, all the power and energy of Baroque counterpoint was brought to the Balletto and the Alemanda. Opening melodies are no longer, as they were in the typical French lute and clavecin Allemande, subservient to an endless rhythmic flow, but are now themes to be remembered and to be related to events that happen later. Motivic unity and parallelism pervade every measure. In No. 126 the first six measures of each section correspond, so that material in the opening section is simply moved to new tonal levels in the second. In No. 128a a motivic consistency unifies the piece. No. 123a shows the strong rhythmic effect of the basso continuo. The Italian chamber Balletti and Alemande, even though restricted, like all the dance forms, to two relatively brief sections of music, thus proved capable of displaying all the splendor and complexity of the late Baroque style.

The Cadences

Although we noted typical cadences with the form of Ex. 60b and occasionally Ex. 60a in the guitar Allemandes of France, they are considerably less frequent in Italian guitar pieces. Ex. 60a occurs in No. 99a at the end of the first phrase and the first section, each time with the bar-line between the two repeated notes. The diminished form in Ex. 60d is in the opening phrase of No. 98a, in the fourth bar of the second section of No. 125, and, although surrounded by *rasgueado* chords, at the end of the first section of No. 106. Ex. 60e similarly occurs, with a voice added above the dotted note, at the end of the opening section of No. 121a.

This relative neglect in guitar music is more than compensated for by the abundance of typical cadences in the chamber works. The earlier examples utilize the quarter-note versions, mainly Ex. 60a, which occurs at the end of the first section and in measures 3, 5, and 7 of the second section of Todeschini's Balletto of 1650 (No. 110). An augmented form of Ex. 61f concludes Marini's piece in No. 107a, and its opening section ends with an ornamented version of Ex. 60b. Legrenzi's Balletto in No. 113a concludes each section with a statement of Ex. 60d in the middle voice, followed by Ex. 60a in the bass. Two examples of Ex. 60d occur in the first section of Vitali's piece in No. 117b from 1667, and the second section includes three appearances of Ex. 60e.

As in France, the diminished version in which the second of the repeated notes is dotted (Ex. 60e) becomes most popular in the later examples. Most often it is approached, as shown in Ex. 60e, by scale degree 7, but may substitute also 5, 6, 1, a rest, or some ornamental sixteenth-notes at this point. Ex. 60e occurs at the end of Cazzati's Balletto in No. 115a, in measures 1, 3, and 8 of the first section of Vitali's work in No. 116 and twice in the middle voice at the end of the second, twice in each section of his later piece in No. 118a, four times in the opening section of Gabrielli's Balletto in No. 122a, and three times in each section of Buoni's piece in No. 126. This cadence becomes part of the opening phrase in Nos. 116, 118b, and 119b.

The ornamental cadence in Ex. 61f appears in bars 3 and 5 of the second section of Vitali's Alemanda in No. 118b, the second bar of G. B. Degli Antoni's *Ballo* in No. 120, and at the end of Laurenti's Alemanda in No. 124b. No. 123a contains several cadences like Ex. 61g, both in the top voice (measure 11) and in the middle (measures 2 and 14). Still other ornamental versions occur in Griffoni's work in No. 127b (see the seventh and final measures). The

Ex. 64: End of the opening section of the *Balletto detto Il Ferrari* of Placuzzi, 1682.

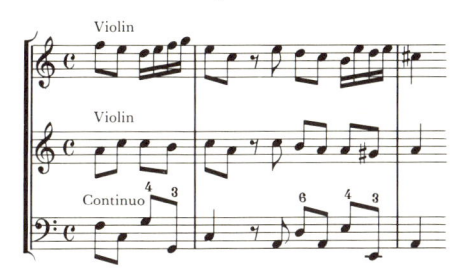

Ex. 65: Excerpt from the second section of *Allemanda prima* by Polaroli, 1673.

cadence with two dotted notes (Ex. 60f) appears, finally, in No. 128a, once in the opening section, twice in the second.

The typical cadence occurs with great frequency in the Italian chamber Balletto and Alemanda. It may appear in either of the upper voices. It may occur in more conspicuous places such as the end of the opening phrase or the end of a section, or it may emerge subtly in the middle of a section, often to mark a passing tonality. It may recur many times, as we have seen, within a single work. Occasionally two will appear in immediate succession, as in the middle voice of Ex. 64,[26] or even four, as in the upper voice in Ex. 65.[27] It occurs with such frequency in the Italian chamber forms of the second half of the century that it constitutes a conspicuous source of unity between individual examples and becomes a characteristic mark of identity of the two forms. Only in the very latest Alemande, such as those in the violin sonatas of Mascitti (Paris, 1714) and Veracini (Dresden, 1721), are the cadences lacking.[28]

During the first half of the century the cadence also appears in vocal monody as one of the possible types of "unaccented" cadence – a cadence in which an unaccented final syllable of text is sung to a shorter, unaccented note. Ex. 66 shows examples that begin in 1600 with Peri's *Euridice*,[29] seem to reach a high point of frequency with Monteverdi[30] and Cesti[31] during the 1640's, and survive even as late as *Il pomo d'oro* of 1668.[32] Exx. 66a, b, and d are regular, augmented, and diminished forms of Ex. 60b, whereas Ex. 66c matches Ex. 60c and Ex. 66e is an augmentation of Ex. 61f. The typical cadences also occur

176 *The Baroque Period*

Ex. 66: Unaccented cadences in Italian opera.

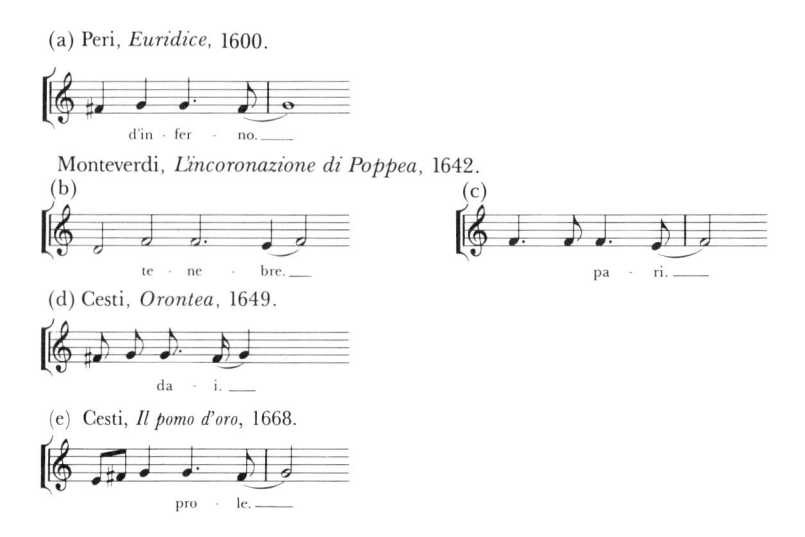

(a) Peri, *Euridice*, 1600.

[music: d'in-fer-no.]

Monteverdi, *L'incoronazione di Poppea*, 1642.
(b)   (c)

[music: te-ne-bre.]   [music: pa-ri.]

(d) Cesti, *Orontea*, 1649.

[music: da-i.]

(e) Cesti, *Il pomo d'oro*, 1668.

[music: pro-le.]

occasionally in keyboard *passamezzi* from the first half of the century,[33] as well as in a few later chamber examples of the *gavotta*, *sinfonia*, or *preludio*.[34]

Although the main Italian developments take place in guitar and chamber music, there are a few examples for other media. Frescobaldi pairs the Balletto three times with a *corrente* and once with a *ciaccona* in his *Toccate d'intavolatura di cimbalo et organo* of 1637.[35] Martino Pesenti's Balletti for keyboard in Nos. 101 and 102, with their typical cadences and occasional imitation, seem to show influence from chamber music. There are several sets of variations: the keyboard Balletto in No. 100b is followed by six variations; Bernardo Storace, in his book of 1664, includes a Balletto and five variations for keyboard, the last labeled *corrente*;[36] Bernardo Gianoncelli has a lute Balletto with two typical cadences and four variations;[37] Marini and Uccellini both have sets for chamber groups.[38] A Balletto occurs as the third section of the *Sinfonia avanti l'opera* in Alessandro Scarlatti's first opera, *Gli equivoci nel sembiante*, in 1679. It is filled with dotted eighth-notes, and the second section contains three appearances of the cadence in Ex. 60f.[39] Bernardo Pasquini, finally, exhibits French influence in his keyboard Alemande, nine of which include one, two, or three typical cadences.[40] He also has a set of variations entitled *Partite diversi sopra Alemanda*.[41]

It was in the chamber works, however, particularly those of Legrenzi, Cazzati, and Vitali, that the constructive attitude of the Italian composers attained its complete fulfillment. This is where the Balletto and the Alemanda became superlatively unified through the counterpoint of rhythmic motives and through the sequences and cadences of a recently crystallized tonal system. A few composers, such as Bononcini and Corelli, reveal more French influence in their preference for the Alemanda, and Italian guitar composers were content to follow the endless and essentially unorganized rhythmic flow of the French Allemande. Both the French Allemande, however, and the Italian Balletto and Alemanda play a role, finally, in shaping the development of these forms in Germany.

11 THE ALLEMANDE AND BALLETT FOR ENSEMBLE AND KEYBOARD IN GERMANY AND ENGLAND 1636–1750

THERE ARE few German sources for two decades after the events described in Chapter 7. The Thirty Years War from 1618 to 1648 involved not only a struggle between the Protestant princes and the Catholic emperor, but also the invasion of Germany at various times by armies from Denmark, Sweden, and France. Following the Peace of Westphalia, Germany was left with a decreased population, with agriculture, commerce, and industry in ruin, and with the central authority of the emperor considerably reduced. After mid-century, however, a more active musical life resumed and publications increased in number. The Allemande and the Ballett flourished at the Viennese court under Leopold I, emperor from 1658 to 1705, and at other southern cities such as Salzburg and Augsburg, as well as at Leipzig in central Germany, Hamburg and Bremen in the north.

The two lines of development that are important in the evolution of the forms during the Baroque period in Germany are involved with two different media: the chamber or orchestral ensemble on the one hand, and the solo instrument, especially the keyboard, on the other. The ensemble examples, in spite of the interruption of the Thirty Years War, continue evolving from the chamber forms we noted in Chapter 7 and thrive at court banquets and theatrical entertainments until the end of the century. The keyboard examples, on the other hand, first emerge around mid-century and then continue, as the final manifestation of the two forms, until the end of the German Baroque period around 1750.

The German Allemanda and Ballett for Instrumental Ensemble

The dominating influence on the German Baroque ensemble forms comes from previous German tradition. Occasionally after 1660 the rhythmic organization of the French Allemande may occur, and even later, but only rarely, the constructive and contrapuntal style of the Italian Alemanda and

Balletto for instrumental trio. Most of the German ensemble forms seem to be involved with the type of Balletto described by Praetorius and often occur in the same sources that contain the *Intrada*, the *Retirada*, and the *Mascarada*. They are characterized mainly by a lack of the kind of uniformity that crystallized in the Baroque forms of Italy and France. Before 1660 they display, as they did earlier in the century, variety in meter, with a separate section occasionally triple, and in number of sections, which may sometimes be three or more instead of the usual two. The opening section continues, as in the earlier Renaissance forms, to end on either the tonic or some other chord. The style tends to be homophonic, but may vary from an endless, totally unorganized texture to one in which imitation or sequence occurs momentarily. There is a tendency throughout the period to emphasize quarter- and eighth-notes as the basic rhythmic values, although after 1660 the French sixteenth-note figures sometimes appear. This variety of note values leads also to variety in the versions of the typical cadence. During most of the period there is variety in the number of voices, the instrumentation, and the number of instruments on a part. In some cases it is difficult to determine whether a work was meant to be performed as chamber or orchestral music.

Before 1660 surviving examples come from northern and central Germany, and a few even date from the period of the Thirty Years War. Andreas Hammerschmidt published at Freiberg in 1636 the *Erster Fleiss allerhand neuer Paduanen, Galliarden, Balletten, Mascharaden, französischen Arien, Courenten und Sarabanden* for five viols, followed by the *Ander Theil* in 1639. The two books contain twenty-one separate Balletten. Most are paired with a *Courente* or a *Sarabande*, but two of them are repeated in a three-voice version followed by a *Canzon* based on its melody, and one, which is in three voices, serves as a theme for seventeen variations. Most have three sections, some have two, and one has five. Most are in duple meter, but sometimes the third section changes to triple. One has the marking *geschwinde und alle mal geschwinder*; two others have *langsam* and *geschwind* within the same section.[1] The quarter-note is the basic pulse, ornamented occasionally with eighth-notes. Some show little internal organization, whereas others have phrases that begin alike,[2] sections that end alike,[3] or brief passages in sequence, either canonic[4] or not.[5] Cadences are often those in Exx. 41a[6] and 41b,[7] which we previously noted in English Almains and French Ballets.

Another early source is the set of books for one to three instruments, especially viols, published by Paulus Matthysz in Amsterdam: *Der goden fluit-hemel* (1644), *'t Uitnement kabinet, Erste deel* (1646) and *'t Uitnemend kabinet, Tweede deel* (1649).[8] These three books contain relatively simple Balletten and Allemanden for two or three melody instruments or for one or two melody instruments and bass, probably for amateur musicians to play at home. Included are five Balletten by C.v.E. and four by B. F. de Bruin, Allemanden by Matthysz himself and by the French composer Louis Constantin, a *Ballet*

Ex. 67: Top voice of the second section of *Vierde Ballet* by B. F. de Bruin, 1644, with four typical cadences.

and eight Allemanden by Johann Schop of Hamburg, an *Almande* by I.K., and several anonymous examples including the *Almande maschera*. Sections sometimes commence with imitation, as in the Balletten by C.v.E.[9] and in some of the Allemanden by Constantin[10] and Schop.[11] *Fa-la*-type motives set off by rests occur in an *Allemande* of Matthysz and a *Ballet* by Schop.[12] Canonic sequence of the type we saw previously in the English vocal Ballett occurs in one of Constantin's Allemanden.[13] The basic pulse is usually the quarter-note, varied sometimes by eighth-notes or even, occasionally, by sixteenth-note figures. The typical cadences, accordingly, are likewise based on the quarter-note. Ex. 67 shows a series of four such cadences in the upper voice of the second section of a *Ballet* by De Bruin; the first three are like Ex. 5e, the last adds an eighth-note on the opening beat to create a rhythm like Ex. $5b_1$.[14] Schop utilizes Ex. $5b_1$ itself in one *Allemande*,[15] Exx. 5a and b in others.[16] Only in one *Allemande* of Constantin does the diminished form in Ex. 60d occur.[17]

Although most the examples in these collections have two sections in duple meter, Constantin has one *Allemande* with three duple sections, and another which seems to be one large section with triple meter in the middle.[18] One of Schop's Allemanden has three sections, with the third triple, and each followed by a varied repeat.[19] He has others in two sections in which the second is triple or both duple and triple.[20] The same sort of variety occurs also in Schop's *Newer Paduanen, Galliarden, Allmanden, Balletten, Couranten, Canzonen, Erster Theil* (Hamburg, 1633) and *Ander Theil* (1635). Examples are for four or five voices in the *Erster Theil*; five of the Allemanden have two sections, seven have three. All of them are in duple meter throughout, except one whose third section is triple. The same book contains two Balletten with four and eight sections, in which one or part of one section is triple. In the later *Ander Theil*, however, all five of the Allemanden have two sections, although the middle of the opening section of one changes briefly to triple meter. One Ballett has four sections, alternately duple and triple, but two others have only two duple sections.[21]

Variety in meter and number of sections continues as late as mid-century in two manuscripts containing ensemble music played and composed by imported French musicians at the courts of Kassel and Stockholm.[22] The two manuscripts have similar contents, and there is concordance between seven of the twenty Allemanden from Kassel and the thirty-eight from Stockholm. The composers include Gustaf, Peter, and Andreas Düben, Pierre Verdier, Jacques de Belleville, Philippe de la Hire, Michel Mazuel, and Louis Constantin, whose works from *'t Uitnement kabinet* are mentioned above. The names of several of these composers appear in both manuscripts. Queen Christina, who reigned from 1644 to 1654, established a resident French orchestra in Stockholm in 1646 to perform ballets. The Kassel manuscript contains a *Ballet à 5* by Nau, which consists of six pieces, each in two sections of duple or triple meter; a *Ballet des Inconstans* with three parts, each entitled *Ballet* and each in two duple sections; and a *Ballet à 4 zu Stockholm getanzt*, a work with tempo markings from *presto, allegro,* and *geschwindt* to *langsamb* and *langsamer,* and with seventeen movements, two of which are entitled *Sarabande*.[23]

More important for our history, however, are the substantial number of Allemanden in the manuscripts. French influence manifests itself not only through an orchestra based mainly on the sound of violins, but also through an increase in the number of eighth-notes, which are occasionally dotted. We must remember, however, that the Allemande was not danced in France itself at this time and was hence not a part of the repertoire of dances played by Parisian ballet orchestras. The development of the French Allemande took place, as we have seen, in lute and clavecin music, so the two ensemble Allemandes published by Ballard in 1665 were rare examples for this medium. Therefore, instead of the sixteenth-note figures of contemporary French lute and clavecin music, the Allemanden in the manuscripts, although more contrapuntal, usually display the solid quarter- and eighth-note movement from German tradition. I see no reason to suppose that these Allemanden were not danced at Kassel and Stockholm, and that the French composers did not simply study previous German and English Allemanden, such as those by Brade, Simpson, Widmann, and others in Nos. 17 through 21, in order to imitate the style.

Two of the Kassel Allemanden have three sections; the third section of one has a middle portion in triple meter. The other manuscript has six examples with three sections, but they are exclusively duple.[24] The texture is usually the continuous sound of four or five voices, relieved, on occasion, only by the occurrence of momentary imitation or sequence. Sections sometimes begin imitatively,[25] and there is occasionally a brief motivic passage in dialogue, sequence, or canon that reminds one of the *fa-la* style.[26] Very rarely is unity achieved through the sort of repetition that occurs in the French Renaissance Almande or the Italian 17th-century Alemanda and Balletto.[27] Opening rhythms vary considerably, but pieces often begin with a dotted half-note and no anacrusis. Only five times does an Allemanda commence with the rhythm of Ex. 59a and twice with Ex. 59b.[28] French influence is also suggested by the appearance of a number of typical cadences with diminished values and with the second repeated note dotted (Ex. 60e).[29] Less frequent are the diminished form without the dot (Ex. 60d),[30] the undiminished type with the dot (Ex. 60b),[31] and the ornamented version in Ex. 61f, which is a dotted diminution of Ex. 5b$_1$.[32] In both manuscripts the pieces are arranged in groups with a common tonal center, although there is no uniformity in the names and number of dances grouped together. Often the Allemanda stands first, but it may occur later, and there may be more than one in a suite. Although a few in the Stockholm manuscript end the opening section on the tonic, most of the others move to a new tonality at this point. In the Kassel manuscript the name is spelled *Allemande*, in the Stockholm manuscript *Allemanda*.

Between the time of these manuscripts and examples from the Viennese court beginning in 1665, the Allemanda and the Ballett occur in a number of books published in the north. Hans Hake includes seven Balletten in his book of 1654 from Stade, three with three sections, four with two. In one of his binary examples, the second section is in triple meter; in one ternary work, the middle section is triple (No. 27). In another, the second duple section begins *adagio*, changes to *presto*, then is followed by a third section in triple meter.[33] Still another has a duple first section, a triple second section, and a third section that begins in duple meter, marked first *lento* and then *praesto*, and concludes with a *praestissimo* triple passage.[34] Such variety in tempo and meter suggests the sort of theatrical function mentioned by Praetorius. They are all *a 3* and homophonic, with continuous music in all the voices. No. 27 begins with the general rhythm of Ex. 59a, but for the most part emphasizes quarter-note movement. Although this piece exhibits very little internal organization, others in the collection sometimes include brief sequences in passing. Each Ballett is preceded in the collection by a *Pavan* and followed by a *Courant* and a *Saraband*.

Johann Rosenmüller includes five-voice Allemanden in his *Studentenmusik* (Leipzig, 1654) that utilize a dense and continuous texture almost completely devoid of internal repetition. One has the diminished typical cadence of Ex. 60d.[35] Johann Jakob Löwe von Eisenach has three Balletten and two Allemanden in his book of 1657 published in Bremen. No. 28 presents an example of each from the same suite, which includes a *Synfonie, Allamand, Aria, Galliarda,* and *Ballet*. Although five voices are provided, the two viola parts are optional. No. 28a commences with the rhythm of Ex. 59a. It has a continually dense texture, but does include a brief sequence in the upper voice in the fourth and fifth measures of the second section, echoed a bar later in the bass. In No. 28b the second section opens with imitation, and there is a *petite reprise* marked *piano* at the end of each section. The diminished cadence of Ex. 60d appears in the second violin part in the second measure, and the dotted version (Ex. 60e) twice in the top voice at the end. Another Ballett of Löwe has one- or two-measure echo effects marked *fort* and *pian*.[36]

Lüder Knop includes the Allemanda and Ballett of No. 29 in his book of 1660 from Bremen. The style is simple and predominantly in quarter-notes, with short, clear phrases. No. 29a commences with two phrases that begin alike; the second section opens with a series of similar two-bar phrases. No. 29b has a typical cadence in quarter-notes in the fifth measure, and a number of his other Allemanden and Balletten also contain such cadences. Although the first sections of both pieces in No. 29 end on the tonic of the main key, other pieces in the same book move to a different key. One Allemanda has *forte* and *pian* echoes at the end of the second section.[37] Each Allemanda and Ballett is followed by a *Courante* or *Saraband*. At the end of the book, Knop adds six *Balli a 2*, each consisting of five to nine movements, some untitled, others labeled *Courante, Saraband,* or *Bataglia*. These are even simpler pieces, and the untitled ones are themselves referred to as *Balletten* in the list of errata. We have previously noted the practice with Melli and others to refer to individual dances, as well as the complete cycle of movements, as a *Balletto*. Knop requests in the preface to his book that "the Paduanen, Galliarden, and Arien be played with a somewhat slow beat," and that "the Balletten, Couranten, and Sarabanden, especially the last Balletten, which I call *Ballo*, [and which] after the French manner are provided with a bass and discant, [be played] with a merry tempo."[38]

After 1654 almost all examples are in duple meter and have two sections. Other factors, however, continue to vary. The number of voices may be three, four, or five. The texture tends to be continuous and unorganized, in general, although occasionally sequences may occur. The music tends to be homophonic, although imitation may sometimes appear. Movement tends to emphasize quarter- and eighth-notes, but sometimes sixteenth-note figures are included. In general, therefore, the style of the German ensemble Allemanden and Balletten after mid-century continues to be essentially conservative, forming a link with earlier German examples rather than reflecting influence from Italy or France. In isolated cases or in certain locations, however, German examples sometimes mirror traits of other countries. Matthias Kelz, for example, has an Allemanda published at Augsburg in 1658 that is filled with dotted eighth-notes and has three cadences with dotted notes like Ex. 60f.[39]

A series of manuscripts in the Österreichische Nationalbibliothek and in the St. Mořic Archive at Kroměříž (formerly Kremsier, now in Czechoslovakia) contains dates, descriptions, and musical scores for ballet music performed at the Viennese court beginning in 1665.[40] Leopold I, in addition to repelling invasions of the Empire from the Turks on one side and Louis XIV on the other, encouraged lavish theatrical and musical entertainments and was himself a competent composer.[41] A Viennese *Ballett* or *Balletto* consists of two to seven movements, often opening, as Praetorius had described earlier, with an *Intrada*, sometimes concluding with a *Retirada*, and including dances such as *Gagliarde, Bourrée, Sarabande, Gigue, Gavotte, Trezza, Courente, Ciaccona, Allemande,* or *Balletto*, as well as movements entitled *Aria*. These Balletti were

184   *The Baroque Period*

performed on birthdays and name days of distinguished persons, at festivals during *Fasching*, during comedies or operas, or in outdoor equestrian events known as *Rossballetten*. One entry, for example, reads: "Balletto 1mo zu den Geburtsdag Ihro May̆. der verwitibten Kheÿserin den 18. November Anno 1668" and is provided with music for a *Sarabanda (per la intrada delle Serenissime)*, *Allemanda (Intrada delle Dame)*, *Aria*, *Gavotte*, and *Retirada* (see Plate XV for the *Sarabanda* and the *Allemanda*).[42] A *Balletto 2do zu dem Geburtstag Ihro May̆. der Regierenden Khaÿserin Margarita den 12. July año 1670* includes *Intrada, Balletto, Borea*, and *Sarabande*.[43] The entries sometimes give the name of a nobleman or lady who danced in the Balletto.

Composers were imported from Italy to provide most of the music for the operas and other dramatic musical works. Italian influence therefore predominated, and extended even to the use of Italian for words such as *Balletto* and *Intrada delle Dame* in the entries above. The dance music, however, even in operas by Italian composers, was written mainly by native German composers and in the same conservative German style we have already seen in the earlier Balletten and Allemanden. Most important were Johann Heinrich Schmelzer, who died in 1680, and his son Andreas Anton, who took over the duties from 1680 until 1693. J. H. Schmelzer often included the Allemanda and the Balletto as separate dances within a Balletto.[44] In fact, in one case, the same music that is called *Allemanda* in the Kroměříž Archive is entitled *Balletto* in the Vienna manuscript.[45] By the time of A. A. Schmelzer, however, both forms are rare, for he has but a single Allemanda and uses the word *Balletto* solely as a title for a complete cycle of movements. Ferdinand Tobias Richter, however, is named as the composer of *Balletti a cinque* in 1685 that consists of *Sonata, Allemande, Menuet, Sarabande, Ballo, Aria*, and *Gigue*, and his *Balletti a 7* in the same manuscript also includes an *Allemande*.[46] Occasionally, as in these last two cycles, the word *Balletti* occurs in later sources in the plural, as though each movement, in addition to its title, were also a *Balletto*. There are Allemanden also by Johann Jacob Prinner and Johann Michael Zacher in 1676[47] and by Alessandro Poglietti, an Italian-born composer who was active at the court between 1661 and his death during the Turkish siege of Vienna in 1683.[48]

The marriage of Leopold I to Margaretha Theresia of Spain in 1667 was the occasion for special entertainments. Cesti's opera *Il pomo d'oro*, which was composed for this purpose (although apparently not actually performed until the following year), included at least two Balletti by J. H. Schmelzer. One contains a *Courente, Allemanda, Aria Viennesa, Gigue*, and *Retirada*; the other, *Gran Ballo, Aria, Branle di Morsetti, Sarabanda per la terra, Balletto per il mare, Trezza, Aria Viennense*, and *Gigue*.[49] Both are for first and second violins, violas, and continuo. The Allemanda and the Balli are all in the constantly changing and dense homophonic style preferred in Germany. The *Gran Ballo* opens with the rhythm of Ex. 59b, the Allemanda with a variant of Ex. 59a. The opening section of the latter, however, ends with the dotted-quarter-note cadence of

Ex. 60b, which, curiously, is very similar to the cadence (see Ex. 66c) being sung by the singers in the same opera. In both Balletti for *Il pomo d'oro*, as in many of the Viennese Balletti, the first and last movements are in the same tonality, but one or more of the other dances are in different keys. The Balletto on Plate XV, for example, includes movements in C (the *Sarabanda*), E minor (the *Allemanda*), A minor, F, and C. This contrast of tonalities seems to be an Italian influence confined, for the most part, to Vienna. In most other German examples, the dances of a single group, following French practice, are all in the same key. In the Viennese Balletti, however, as in most German works after 1660, the music moves at the end of the opening section to the dominant (the *Sarabanda* in Plate XV, for example) or the mediant (the *Allemanda* on the same plate).

Another grand event for the celebration of Leopold's wedding was an equestrian ballet called *La contesa dell'aria e dell'acqua*, which was staged in a specially built outdoor structure and which involved participants both marching and riding on horses.[50] The music, composed by J. H. Schmelzer, was published in Vienna in 1667 with the title and descriptions in Italian: *Arie per il Balletto a cavallo, nella festa rappresentata per le gloriosissime nozze delle SS.CC.MM.tà di Leopoldo primo, imperatore augustissimo, et di Margherita, Infanta di Spagna*. The work consists of a *Corrente*, *Giga*, *Follia* (not related musically to the standard folia scheme), *Allemanda*, and *Sarabanda*. The *Allemanda* was introduced by Leopold himself and other riders "per gl'intrecci e figure di passegio grave" and was played by five-part strings.[51] Its music is again continuous and homophonic. Although including many dotted eighth-notes and sixteenths, the cadence at the end of each section is, again, the one with a dotted quarter-note (Ex. 60b). This cadence also occurs in measures 7 and 8 of the second section, but shifted so that the bar-line comes between the two repeated notes.[52]

The *Balletti francesi* that J. H. Schmelzer wrote for Cesti's *Nettuno e Flora festeggianti* in 1669 also includes an Allemanda in the same general style, with a dotted-quarter-note cadence in the second and third full measures of the second section.[53] The fourth Balletto that Schmelzer composed for Draghi's *Creso* in 1678 commences with an Allemanda marked *adagio*.[54] It begins with an imitation in the top voice that resembles a typical cadence, and a one-bar figure recurs as an echo during the second section. There are many dotted-eighth-note figures, but it is again the dotted-quarter-note cadence, rather than the dotted-eighth-note cadence preferred in France and Italy, that occurs in an inner voice at the end of the opening section. Ex. 68 shows the successive intervals of the second created by the counterpoint of the upper voice in this cadence as it falls to meet the typical cadence below. In the cadence at the end of the first section of Schmelzer's Allemanda in Plate XV, the repetition of scale degree 1 is a dotted quarter-note, but the preceding note has been reduced to an eighth. The diminished forms of the cadence do appear

Ex. 68: Upper voices at the end of the first section of an Allemanda by J. H. Schmelzer (the top voice forming consecutive seconds with the typical cadence in the alto).

in one Balletto of Schmelzer, with the undotted type (Ex. 60d) at the end of the first section, the dotted (Ex. 60e) at the end of the second.[55] Ex. 60e also concludes an Allemanda composed by Leopold I.[56] It occurs also in the opening measure of an Allemanda from 1673 by Jan Křtitel Tolar, who was at the court in Kroměříž of the Prince-Bishop of Olmütz.[57]

Another flourishing musical center in Austria was the court of the Prince-Archbishop in Salzburg. Heinrich Ignaz Franz von Biber was associated with the music here from 1670 until his death in 1704. Georg Muffat was connected with the court from 1678 to 1690, except for a visit during the 1680's to Italy, where he acquired a taste for the Italian style. In addition, Andreas Christophorus Clamer seems to have been at the court around 1682. Biber continues the German type of multi-movement Balletto, with its *Intrada*, *Retirada*, and dances including the Allemanda, Balletto, and Ballo. Both Biber and Clamer use the word *Tafel* (or its Latin equivalent *mensa*) in titles such as *Trombet undt musicalischer Taffeldienst* (Biber, c. 1673), *Mensa sonora* (Biber, 1680), and *Mensa harmonica* (Clamer, 1682), thus indicating the continuation of the tradition of performing these quasi-theatrical dance cycles at banquets and other social gatherings.

The Allemanden and Balletten from Salzburg display far more of the French sixteenth-note figures and the Italian method of construction than most other German ensemble examples of the period. Biber's earlier works from the 1670's show some motivic unity and occasionally imitation,[58] more continuous eighth-note movement (sometimes even in the bass line),[59] occasional sixteenth-note figures,[60] and diminished cadences with a dotted eighth-note (Ex. 60e).[61] His examples from 1680, on the other hand, show considerably more Italian influence in their motivic and melodic unity. The two Allemanden, especially, show an increase in sixteenth- and even thirty-second-note activity; the diminished cadence at the end of each section of one of them has been modified by reducing the first of the repeated notes to a thirty-second-note.[62] Two Balletti from the same source show less sixteenth-note movement, and three others are marked *alla breve*, moving mainly in quarter- and eighth-notes and with quarter-note cadences.[63] In some of the pieces the opening measures of each section have the same or similar rhythm.[64] One of the Balletti commences with two phrases that begin with the same three measures.[65] Another Balletto includes some imitation, and the last eight bars of each section are exactly parallel, but in different keys.⁶⁶ In still another, the melody of the opening bar is repeated three measures from the end of the second, creating a rounded binary form.⁶⁷

All of the examples of Biber which we have discussed so far have been for four voices. His *Harmonia artificiosa-ariosa*, published posthumously in Nuremberg in 1712, however, contains Allemanden and Balletten in the Italian trio style *a 3*. These are even more contrapuntal and motivic, with momentary imitation and sequence. Pieces are arranged in a group called *Partia*, consisting of a *Sonata* or *Praeludium* followed by dance movements. The Allemanden display many sixteenth-notes. Two of the Balletti move mainly in eighth-notes and are marked *allegro* or *presto*. Another does have sixteenth-notes, but is in three sections.⁶⁸ Clamer has a similar collection *a 3* in 1682, with some of the *Partite* beginning with an *Intrada* and two of them including a Balletto. Both Balletti are *alla breve* and thus are notated, when compared to the usual notation, with values doubled and twice as many bar-lines. The advantage of this type of notation becomes evident in Clamer's examples, for the nine measures in each section of the first one and the eleven measures in the second section of the other could have been accommodated in the regular notation only by beginning the section on the third beat.⁶⁹ The Balletti occasionally exhibit momentary motivic repetition, sequence, and *fa-la*-type imitation.⁷⁰ Cadences occur in which the opening repeated note is reduced in value, as in Ex. 61g, but with doubled values in *alla breve*.⁷¹

It is in the works of Georg Muffat, however, that the Italian style is most evident. Movements called *Allemanda, Ballo, Balet*, or *Balletto* are included in his *Concerti grossi* of 1682 and 1701, as well as in the orchestral suites of the *Florilegium primum* of 1695. In the concerti, the Allemanden are *grave, grave e forte*, or *largo*, contrasting to a *Ballo* marked *allegro*.⁷² In the orchestral suites, the Allemanda is notated, like both forms in the concerti, in the usual way; but one *Balet* has a time signature of 2 and begins on the third beat, and the other two are in cut time (₵).⁷³ In the 1682 works, a *petite reprise* of two or three measures occurs at the end of either the first or the second section.⁷⁴ Unifying repetition appears in the form of phrases with parallel rhythm⁷⁵ and sections that begin with the same rhythm⁷⁶ or end with the same music transposed to a different key.⁷⁷ Momentary repetition occurs as imitation,⁷⁸ sequence,⁷⁹ or *fa-la* motives.⁸⁰ Two of the Allemanden conclude with the diminished and dotted cadence of Ex. 60e.⁸¹

The two most important courts of Austria thus represent two opposite stylistic points of view. In the Viennese Allemanden and Balletten there is almost no trace of the Italian style, and the forms gradually disappear after around 1680. In Salzburg, on the other hand, there was eventually strong Italian influence, which increased considerably after 1680 in the later works of Biber and Muffat. Most of the other examples from southern cities seem to be in the thick four-voice texture, which, although including the usual sixteenth-note figures, tends to be more homophonic, with main interest in the top voice. This is shown by an Allemanda published by Hieronymus Gradenthaler in 1675 at Nuremberg, a city which had not regained its former musical importance following the Thirty Years War.[82] Johann Pachelbel has two Allemanden and a Ballett in his *Musicalische Ergötzung* (Nuremberg, 1695) that are in the Italian trio style and include numerous examples of the dotted and diminished cadence (Ex. 60e).[83] However, they display continuous homophony rather than the Italian melodic and constructive style. Rupert Ignaz Mayr, at the court in Munich, has Allemanden *a 4* from 1692, one *alla breve* with three dotted-quarter-note cadences (Ex. 60b),[84] and others in the usual notation that show the results of his study in Paris with Lully. One is labeled *adagio*, another *allegro*.[85] Johann Abraham Schmierer from Augsburg has Allemanden in 1698 with regular notation marked *grave* and Balletten in cut time (¢) labeled *presto*. The Balletten display almost continuous dotted rhythm and note-against-note homophony. The Allemanden contrast completely, with energetic sixteenth- and thirty-second-note figures and occasionally formal organization and a more contrapuntal texture.[86]

Central German sources reveal the same contrasts in style seen in the south. Esaias Reusner published Allemanden in 1670 which, although for four voices and essentially homophonic, display the rhythms, downward thirds, inner organization, and diminished cadences of the Italian forms.[87] Rosenmüller, on the other hand, continues in his *Sonate da camera* (Venice, 1667) the conservative style and dense, unchanging five-voice texture that we noted in his earlier *Studentenmusik*, even though he lived in Italy from 1658 on. The thirteen Allemanden include few sixteenth-note figures and exhibit very little internal organization. The four *Balli* have, in general, more sixteenth-notes and display more sequence and motivic unity.[88] Two of them, however, lack sixteenth-notes and are marked *presto*. In two others, the last two bars of each section are *adagio*.[89] Both Allemanden and Balli have a number of typical cadences in one of the two upper voices, usually diminished and either dotted or not, except for the undiminished ones that accompany the *adagio* endings mentioned above.[90] A number of Rosenmüller's Allemanden, both in this publication and his book of 1654, conclude the opening section in the same key in which they begin.[91]

Elements of the Italian style were more successfully incorporated by Johann Christoph Pezel, a *Ratsmusiker* (town musician) and eventually *Stadtpfeifer* at Leipzig. He includes numerous examples of both forms in his publications of 1669 (all *a 4*), 1675 (all in Italian trio style *a 3*), 1678 (again *a 4*), and 1685 (music *a 5* for cornetts and trombones, of the type played twice a day from the tower of the city hall in Leipzig). The works from 1669 are more homophonic and note-against-note, and emphasize dotted rhythms, especially in the Balletti,[92] and dotted-quarter-note cadences.[93] The trio style in his 1675 book provides a lighter texture (see the *Allemande* and *Ballo* in No. 30) and, although

Ex. 69: Excerpts from works by Pezel, 1675

(a) Opening section of *Ballo* (piece No. 35 in his book).

(b) Opening measures of *Allemanda* (piece No. 38).

(c) Opening phrase of *Ballo* (piece No. 15 in the Appendix of his book).

still homophonic, with the melody on top and a basic note-against-note feeling, has a more buoyant and contrapuntal quality (see the three excerpts in Ex. 69).[94] The figure with three sixteenth-notes sometimes occurs, as in the fourth measure of No. 30a, or the rhythm of Ex. 59d, which is at the beginning of Ex. 69b. The figure of two sixteenth-notes followed by an eighth unifies the section in Ex. 69a and leads to the ornamented version of the diminished and dotted cadence of Ex. 61f. The same motive unifies the second section of No. 30b and again leads to the same cadence. This form of the cadence also occurs at the end of the excerpt in Ex. 69c. Other diminished cadences appear, with Ex. 60e in the top voice in the third bar of the second section of No. 30a, and in the middle voice at the end of each section. In the second measure of the second section is an ornamented version with the rhythm of Ex. 61f. There are many other examples of the cadences in Pezel's publications. Ex. 70 shows the outer

190   *The Baroque Period*

Ex. 70: Outer voices for the first section of an Allemanda by Pezel, 1678, which is constructed largely from the typical cadence in Ex. 60e.

Ex. 71: Beginning of *Allmand a 4* by Becker, 1668, for two violins, viola, & continuo.

voices of the opening section of an Allemanda from 1678 which is almost completely constructed from a dotted diminished cadence (Ex. 60e): first it is integrated into the opening rhythm of Ex. 59d; then it makes a half-cadence in measure 3, forms a sequence in measures 4 and 5, and finally makes a full cadence again at the end.[95] This example almost rivals the melody in Ex. 67 for its exuberant involvement with the typical cadence. The tower music in the 1685 book is, as would be expected, far simpler and emphasizes longer note values and undiminished cadences as well as diminished ones.[96] Pezel indicates *adagio* for three Allemanden in 1669, one in 1675, and all five in 1678.

Northern examples decrease considerably in number after 1660. They sometimes continue the four- or five-voice homophony used by Löwe in No. 28. The excerpt by Dietrich Becker in Ex. 71 shows, however, that even in this dense texture the upper voice can begin with a memorable melody such as we saw earlier in the Italian forms.[97] One can compare Ex. 71 with the opening bars of Legrenzi's Balletto of 1656 in No. 113a or Vitali's example from 1667 in No. 117a. Both Becker's piece and the Balletto by Vitali in No. 118a from the same year display the downward third, then a measure later the dotted and diminished typical cadence (compare also the beginning of G. B. Degli

Ex. 72: Opening phrases of two Allemanden by Meister, 1695.

(a) *Allemanda* from *La musica decima*.

(b) *Allemanda* from *La musica duodecima*.

Antoni's piece in No. 120). In Ex. 71 the cadence is in the alto, with the upper voice forming consecutive seconds with it, as in Ex. 68. The same cadence occurs in the tenor at the end of the first section, in the alto again in the middle of the second, and in the top voice at the end of the piece.

Italian influence is most evident, however, in *Il giardino del piacere overo Raccolta de diversi fiori musicali* (Hamburg, 1695) of Johann Friedrich Meister from Flensburg. The whole of the title page, including the name of the composer, is in Italian, and the contents are in the Italian trio style for two violins and continuo. The *Ballo* in No. 32b has the continuous dotted figure that we have noted before in Balletti by A. Scarlatti and Pezel.[98] The Allemanda in No. 32a, however, exhibits the motivic counterpoint that had developed earlier in Italy. Compare the unifying effect of the motivic imitation and sequences in No. 32a with Italian examples such as No. 115a of Cazzati and No. 117b by Vitali. Ex. 72 shows the opening phrases of two other Allemanden by Meister. Both move to an ornamented version of the dotted diminished cadence, which in Ex. 72a is in the top voice, in Ex. 72b in the middle. The dotted and diminished cadence occurs in the fourth-from-last measure of No. 32a in the inner voice; in No. 32b it is in the top voice three measures from the end and in the middle voice in the final measure. Meister sometimes concludes an introductory *Sonata* or a brief *adagio* passage on the dominant or mediant chord, to lead into the succeeding movement. Otherwise, all the movements, as was the general practice in all countries by this time, are in the same key.

192 *The Baroque Period*

Telemann's *Sonates Corellisantes* (Hamburg, 1735) contains two trio Allemanden, marked *presto* and *allegro*, that imitate the style of Corelli.[99] These Allemanden and the works of Meister, however, are isolated examples of such intense Italian influence in German ensemble music.[100] For the most part, the chamber and orchestral pieces were apparently intended as functional dance music, incorporated within the multi-movement Balletti described by Praetorius in 1618 and indicated even earlier by the terminology in Nörmiger's keyboard book of 1598. For a century, then, the Allemanda and Ballett occurred within this context as part of the small-scale, quasi-dramatic entertainments at banquets, weddings, and birthdays, as well as within operas, equestrian events, and other larger productions. The two forms thus displayed the conservative nature common to functional social music. They tended to retain an unchanging style within a four- or five-voice texture. They start on the first beat, with or without a brief anacrusis, reach the final tonic chord on either the first or third beat of the last measure, and conclude the melody with a sustained and unrepeated tone. Earlier experiments with sequences (see Staden's piece from 1606 in No. 16), with *fa-la* motives (Widmann's example from 1618 to No. 20), or with counterpoint (Posch's Balletten of 1618 in Ex. 56) did not lead to a new style. Perhaps these more constructive ideas might have continued if the musical development had not been interrupted by the conflict of the Thirty Years War. The ensemble music from the second half of the century was, for the most part, unobtrusive background music for danced and costumed court entertainments, and in this role it is perhaps not surprising that the Allemanden and Balletten, in general, did not embrace the highly conspicuous and constructive elements from the Italian Baroque style.

The German Allemande and Ballett for Keyboard

The Allemanden and Balletten for keyboard and other solo instruments developed separately from those for ensemble. They were, like the French lute and keyboard forms, completely independent instrumental pieces, not associated with dancing or any other traditional form of entertainment. Furthermore, there seems to be a gap between the 16th-century keyboard examples and those from the Baroque, which begin only around 1640. The style of the German keyboard forms was therefore not determined by a special social function nor by the perpetuation of a tradition. Influence was predominantly from France, and the German evolution paralleled and interacted with the development in French lute and clavecin music.

As in France, the style eventually involved sixteenth-note rhythmic figures disposed in a relatively unmelodic texture derived from the *style brisé* of lute music. German sources, however, include the Ballett as well as the Allemande, and the style that finally emerges usually involves a continuous flow of

The Allemande and Ballett in Germany and England 193

sixteenth-notes arranged within a highly unified system of motivic organization. As in France, there seems to be also in Germany a direct influence from lute music. The lute manuscripts at Kremsmünster contain many Allemanden, as well as a few Balletti, from the early 17th to the early 18th centuries.[101] Two manuscripts at Darmstadt dated 1672 and 1674 contain keyboard transcriptions of Allemanden for lute and other plucked-string instruments. One piece is entitled at the beginning *Allemande von der Lauten abgesetzt*, and at the end *Allemande Gautier*.[102]

Early German sources include a manuscript from Copenhagen around 1639 (see No. 24), examples (mostly Balletten) by Johann Erasmus Kindermann from around 1640,[103] and the manuscript keyboard book of Regina Clara Imhoff dated 1649 (see No. 25). Examples of the Ballett and Allemande from these early sources are relatively simple pieces, only occasionally displaying sixteenth-notes (opening statement of No. 24), motivic figures, sequences (measures 6–8 of the second section of No. 25b), or imitation (measures 2–3 and 4–5 in the second section of No. 24). They all have a basic eighth-note flow, and the Balletten seem very much like the Allemanden. German keyboard examples, in contrast to those for ensemble, usually follow the practice we noted in French lute Allemandes (but not those for clavecin) of repeating the final melody pitch from the first beat of the last measure again on the third (see Nos. 24 and 26).

The Allemande in No. 24 also has a *variatio* or *double* in which the original harmonic/melodic framework has been filled with an almost endless flow of sixteenth-notes. In the last four measures of the second section, the sixteenth-notes are arranged in patterns that echo back and forth between the voices and create the sort of motivic order and unity that characterizes the general style of the later examples. The Allemande by Johann Jacob Froberger in No. 26 has a similar *double*, but here the continuous stream of sixteenth-notes provides a unity for the entire piece by emphasizing the motive with three sixteenth-notes. Froberger is the first German composer of major significance in the history of the keyboard Allemande, and it is in his examples that the French style emerges most clearly. He traveled to France, England, and the Low Countries, studied with Frescobaldi, and was court organist for the Emperor Ferdinand III in Vienna. His Allemanden are contained in manuscripts dated 1649 and 1656[104] and in the undated Bauyn manuscript, which also includes works of Chambonnières, Louis Couperin, and other French composers such as Richard and Du Mont (see Nos. 58 and 59).[105] No. 26 is an Allemande by Froberger from the Bauyn manuscript, showing, in comparison with the earlier examples in Nos. 24 and 25, the greater complexity of the quasi-contrapuntal texture, the increasing number of notes per measure, and the more majestic pace of the eighth-note, allowing for occasional sixteenth-note figures. The three-sixteenth-note motive occurs three times in the last four bars and, as we have noted, completely dominates the *double* that follows. Matthias

Weckmann, a contemporary of Froberger, has examples that emphasize sixteenth-notes and the broken style.[106]

A comparison of the later Allemanden in Nos. 31 and 33a with the *doubles* of Nos. 24 and 26 reveals a striking similarity. The strength of unity that finally characterizes the German keyboard Allemande seems to occur first with examples by Benedict Schultheiss in 1679. In No. 31, the opening anacrusis and succeeding five quarter-note beats present, in a rhythm similar to one of the typical French patterns in Ex. 59d, a brief, finite, and impressive statement of the affective content of the piece. It is not particularly melodic and does not recur later as a theme, but it gives the listener an immediate sense of phrase structure and orderly purpose. The three-sixteenth-note motive is then extracted from the opening measure and recurs in dialogue between the voices as a modulation to the dominant key commences. Imitation and sequence act momentarily to bring the section to a close. The second section begins briefly like the opening one, but turns quickly to a new motive of an eighth and two sixteenths, which independently unifies this section. Every event in the piece seems to flow logically from what precedes. Ex. 73 shows excerpts from other Allemanden by Schultheiss, each beginning with an arresting statement, which in Ex. 73a leads to a typical cadence.[107] He states in the preface to his book that the *Allemanden* and *Sarabanden* should be played rather slowly, the *Couranten* and *Giquen* somewhat faster and more exuberantly.[108]

The same style can be seen in more elaborate form in Fischer's later Allemande in No. 33a, in which the three-sixteenth-note motive in the second half of each section reminds one of the *fa-la* counterpoint from a century earlier. This sort of Allemande became so popular that Friedrich Erhard Niedt models examples on it in his *Handleitung zur Variation, wie man den General-Bass und darüber gesetzte Zahlen variiren, artige Inventiones machen, und aus einen schlechten General-Bass Praeludia, Ciaconen, Allemanden, Couranten, Sarabanden, Menueten, Giquen und dergleichen leichtlich verfertigen könne* (Hamburg, 1706). Ex. 74a shows the first four measures of the figured bass which he uses for all the forms. He explains that the bass must be divided into two parts when making an Allemande, with the first part ending on the fifth degree. He then constructs an Allemande that begins as shown in Ex. 74b. After remarking that another Allemande, or indeed hundreds of them, can be made over the same bass, he includes another example that begins as in Ex. 74c.[109] Comparison, then, of the *doubles* in Nos. 24 and 26, the Allemanden in Nos. 31 and 33a, and the instructive models of Niedt in Ex. 74 shows the evolution of the principal type of German Allemande for keyboard.

Between the time of Schultheiss' Allemanden from 1679 and Fischer's from 1698, there are a number of examples by other composers, some following their model, others with some different construction. Poglietti, one of the few composers who wrote Allemanden for both ensemble and keyboard, has one in which each section is highly unified by many repetitions of a melodic motive,

Ex. 73: Excerpts from keyboard Allemanden by Schultheiss, 1679.

(a) *Allemande* on p. 32 of his book.

(b) *Allemande* on p. 2.

(c) *Allemande* on p. 22.

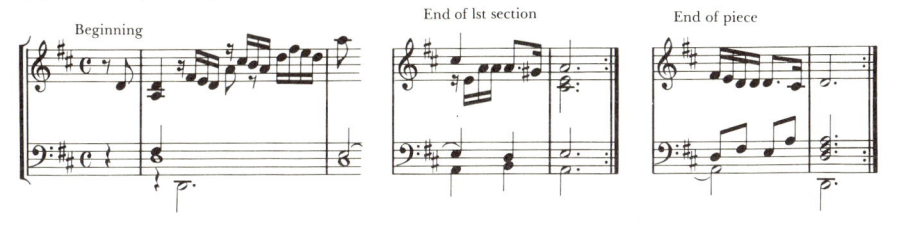

and another, *La Prisonnie* from his suite *sopra la ribellione di Ungheria*, which includes thirty-second-notes within a highly rhapsodic flow of changing rhythms and syncopations.[110] Most of Pachelbel's Allemanden are simpler, often with mainly eighths or dotted eighths, and usually without extensive unifying features. A few, however, are, like Niedt's models, based on sixteenth-note movement, and one contains a lengthy canonic sequence in the second section.[111] More consistently filled with sixteenth-notes are those of Buxtehude, many of which are unified by the three-sixteenth-note motive. They display the *style brisé* more intensely and occasionally exhibit momentary sequences. He also has an *Allemande d'Amour*, but it seems to have no relation to the 16th-century Almande of the same name.[112] Richter, another composer

Ex. 74: Excerpts from demonstration Allemanden by Niedt, 1706.

(a) Beginning of the *General-Bass.*

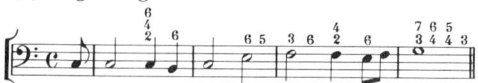

(b) Beginning of the first Allemande.

(c) Beginning of the second Allemande.

who, like Poglietti, also wrote ensemble Balletti for Leopold's court in Vienna, has two keyboard Allemanden which, for the most part, move in sixteenth-notes.[113] Adam Reincken has two examples that follow Niedt's models faithfully, and another that is confined to slower note values.[114] Most of those in Johann Kuhnau's books of 1689 and 1692 are based on a continuous flow of sixteenth-notes, varied occasionally by thirty-second-note figures.[115]

Around the turn of the century, then, the German keyboard Allemande, heavily influenced by its French counterpart, usually takes a form similar to Fischer's work in No. 33a, in which endless sixteenth-note movement is disposed in recurring rhythmic motives. Such a piece is essentially unmelodic, unthematic, and not formally organized in any conspicuous way. What repetition may occur in the form of sequences or similar beginnings of sections is usually brief and of momentary significance. Johann Krieger in 1697, however, not only gives the title page of his *Sechs musicalische Partien* in both German and Italian, but also displays the Italian melodic and constructive approach in his Allemanden. He sometimes begins with melodic motives like trumpet calls that are easily remembered when they recur.[116] Often the second section starts like the first, with the parallelism extending as far as five measures,[117] or involving the inversion of a thematic motive.[118] He also has some that are less melodic,[119] and some with thirty-second-note figures,[120] but they are all filled with an energetic and exuberant application of the *style brisé*.

Although the melodic, constructive, and contrapuntal techniques that we saw in the Italian trio forms sometimes become conspicuous elements during the 18th century in other German keyboard forms, they seldom occur in the Allemanden. The unthematic type of No. 33a thus continues in Mattheson's collection of 1714,[121] in the works of Techelmann,[122] Böhm,[123] and Gottlieb Muffat,[124] and in later examples by Fischer.[125] Somewhat more melodic and highly unified are two examples of Telemann.[126] Italian influence is strongest in the Allemanden of Handel, which are sometimes, like those of Krieger, highly organized and even thematic. Both sections of one begin with imitation, with the motive inverted for the second section.[127] Another has a singing melody with recurring motives, which is transposed up a fifth at the beginning of the second section.[128] Still another is like a two-part invention, with a theme that is introduced in imitation and then recurs frequently throughout the Allemande in different keys.[129] Some of Handel's examples are as unthematic as No. 33a,[130] but one sees even in these the typical keyboard figurations and the running or motivically organized bass line associated with the late Baroque style in general.

The Allemanden in Bach's suites and partitas also exhibit various styles. The rhapsodic, rambling type, essentially unthematic and unmelodic and with much *style brisé*, occurs in the Allemanden of the first English Suite and the first French Suite. An ornate, singing melody in the top voice, accompanied by notes of longer duration in the lower voices, characterizes those in the fourth partita and the second and fifth French Suites. A type like an invention, with both hands equally involved in thematic material and sixteenth-note movement, appears in the second partita, the second and fifth English Suites, and the third French Suite. In this type, sections often commence with imitation (the second partita), and the opening thematic material may be inverted at the beginning of the second section (fifth partita). A few seem to combine a melodic upper voice with considerable sixteenth-note activity in the lower voices (the third and fourth English Suites). Still another type occurs in the first partita and the fourth French Suite, where an essentially harmonic effect is achieved by arpeggiating chords in the right hand in a continuous flow of sixteenth-notes. Bach sometimes includes many thirty-second-notes (see the third partita especially) or a triplet to replace two sixteenth-notes (the fifth partita and the fourth English Suite), thus continuing the historic process of diminishing the note values.

Almost all of the German keyboard Allemanden occur in suites. Apparently Schultheiss was the first to adopt the standard order of the four main dances, with the *Allemande, Courante, Sarabande*, and *Gigue* sometimes preceded by a *Praeludium*. Later, optional dance movements were also added. The keyboard Allemande is always in two sections and always in duple meter. It is occasionally followed by a *double*, as we have seen in Nos. 24 and 26. There are isolated examples in works of Poglietti, Pachelbel, Buxtehude, Kuhnau, and Mattheson.[131] A *petite reprise* is very rare, with an isolated example written out and marked *piano* by Kuhnau, and three, four, or (in one case) six bars regularly indicated by sign at the end of the second section in all the Allemanden of Gottlieb Muffat's *Componimenti musicali*.[132] Almost always the opening section ends, as in French examples, in a new tonality. Froberger's piece in No. 26, which concludes both sections with a D major chord, is, in this regard, unique even among his own Allemanden. Occasionally in later keyboard suites, one of the shorter and simpler dances may end both sections in this manner, but the older dances, including the Allemande, almost invariably move at the end of the first section to a new chord or key as an essential element of the tonal design.

Tempo is almost never marked in keyboard examples. As we have previously seen, there was by 1677 a fast Allemande in France as well as the more common grave one, and there were Alemande both fast and slow in Italy. All these influences are evident in German ensemble music, but examples from 1669 to 1701 by Pezel, J. H. Schmelzer, Georg Muffat, and Schmierer that are marked *adagio, largo*, or *Allemande grave* far outnumber the few, which show mainly Italian influence, that are *presto* or *allegro*. The few indications we have, indicate that keyboard Allemanden also favor a slow tempo. Schultheiss, as we have noted, mentions in his preface that they should be played "rather slowly." Gottlieb Muffat marks five of his examples *affettuoso*, one *spirituoso*.[133] Mattheson, in *Der vollkommene Capellmeister* (Hamburg, 1739), states that "the Allemande is now an arpeggiated [referring, presumably, to the *style brisé*], serious, and well-constructed harmony which conveys the image of a contented and satisfied spirit that takes delight in good order and repose."[134] Walther says in his *Musicalisches Lexicon* of 1732 that it is composed gravely and seriously and should be played in the same manner.[135]

The Ballett is relatively rare in German keyboard sources and occurs here far less often than in ensemble music. Most were written by composers who also composed ensemble Balletten for court entertainments. The Ballett in No. 25b comes from a manuscript source that also includes pieces called *Mascaraden*. Kindermann, who has nine keyboard Balletten, also composed many ensemble Balletten and a few Allemanden.[136] These earlier keyboard Balletten are much like the contemporary Allemanden. Later keyboard

Balletten, however, are simpler than the Allemanden, with longer note values and often continuous dotted-eighth-and-sixteenth motives. The same difference we noted between the ensemble *Allemanda* and *Ballo* of Meister in No. 32 exists in Fischer's examples in No. 33. The same contrast appears also in Reusner's lute Ballett and Allemanden.[137] Reusner's Ballett, as well as one by Pachelbel,[138] is inserted as an optional dance into a suite that commences with an Allemande. Fischer's *Ballet* in No. 33b, as well as two others in his book of 1738,[139] is marked, like the few ensemble examples that indicate tempo, to be played fast. In addition, it takes the place, immediately following the *Praeludium*, which is usually occupied by an Allemande. The suite containing No. 33b includes *Praeludium II, Ballett, Menuet, Rondeau, Canaries,* and *Passepied*, whereas No. 33a occurs in the group *Praeludium VI, Allemande, Courante, Sarabande, Gigue, Bourée,* and *Menuet*. In addition, Reincken uses a Ballett as a theme for a set of eleven variations.[140]

The evolution of the German keyboard forms was a unified development that included composers from north, south, and central Germany. It was influenced largely by the French Allemande and only very slightly by German ensemble music and Italian chamber examples. The same style spread finally to other solo instruments such as violin, cello, and lute. Buxtehude has an *Allamanda* for violin and continuo;[141] Bach has examples in the suites for lute and for solo cello and the partitas for solo violin. The *style brisé* is evident in lute Allemanden by Johann Gotthard Peyer, Jan Antonin Losy, and Laurent de Saint-Luc.[142] The fully developed French style emerges in the eight Allemanden and one Ballett from the lute suites of Reusner from 1667 and 1676.[143] There was some discontent among lutenists, however, with the French *style brisé* and an interest in more melodic music. Ernst Gottlieb Baron writes in 1727 that "they [the French] too often change voices, so that one cannot even recognize the melody, and . . . there is little *cantabile* to be found, particularly because they regard it as very fashionable to brush back chords on the lute with the right hand, just as on the guitar; a constant hopping around is required to give spirit and life to the pieces . . . Mattheson is absolutely right when he satirizes the scratching away at Allemandes in the Parisian style."[144] The Italian melodic and constructive style emerges finally in the late Baroque works of Silvius Leopold Weiss.[145]

We have already noted Allemanden by Saint-Luc for lute, violin, and bass, and the examples for string ensemble by Reusner. The solo and ensemble developments in Germany, however, were in general almost totally separate. The ensemble pieces, in response to social conditions and local traditions, display great variety in their musical characteristics. The solo works, on the other hand, show more consistency of style, and changes, guided almost exclusively by artistic purposes, tended to occur in a more orderly fashion. Although ensemble and keyboard examples both commence ordinarily on the first beat, the final tonic chord in the ensemble examples may occur on beat 1

200 *The Baroque Period*

Ex. 75: The usual cadences in German Baroque keyboard Allemanden.

BASIC TYPES

VARIANTS

(the first note is sometimes tied over from the preceding beat)

or 3, whereas in the keyboard examples it regularly falls on the first beat. Diverse forms of the typical cadence appear in ensemble music, as we have seen, with diminished and undiminished, dotted and undotted versions coexisting in examples both early and late. The typical cadences in the solo Allemande and Ballett are more numerous, more uniform, and more purposeful in the way they are ornamented.

The most frequent keyboard cadence, shown at the top of the left column of Ex. 75, is the diminished version with the second repeated note dotted – the same cadence that was most important, as we have seen, in French lute and clavecin pieces and in Italian chamber works. Below the cadence in Ex. 75 are set variants that replace the opening eighth-note of the basic cadence with two sixteenth-notes. The effect of this pattern is to throw an agogic accent onto the first repeated note, which, in turn, increases the accentuation on the second repeated note. At the top of the right column is the basic diminished cadence with the first repeated note reduced to a sixteenth-note. In the variants below it, the entire first quarter-note beat is filled with sixteenth-notes. Although the second repeated note still receives accentuation due to its greater length, the angular effect of the cadences in the left column is considerably softened. In

The Allemande and Ballett in Germany and England 201

Ex. 76: Rare cadences in German Baroque keyboard examples

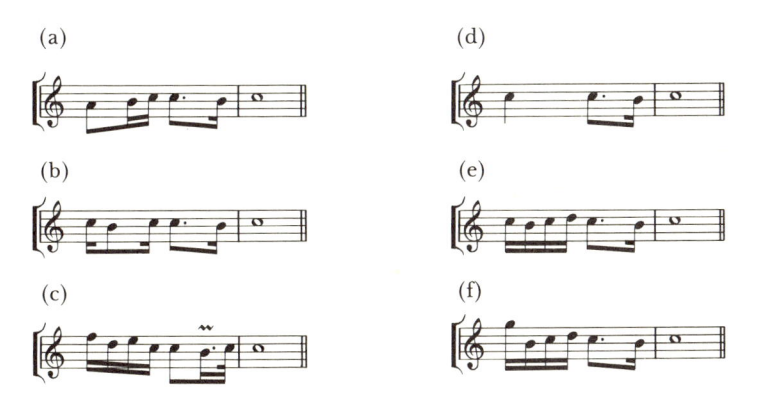

(a)

(b)

(c)

(d)

(e)

(f)

addition, the four sixteenth-notes in most of the cadences in the right column blend in with the continuous sixteenth-note movement that characterizes the Allemande in general. It is significant, of course, that the dotted rhythms in the two basic cadences, as well as the sixteenth-note figures on the first quarter-note beats of the variants in both columns, fit the affective nature of the Allemande and, indeed, are the very figures that one finds elsewhere in the music.

The first note of each pattern in both columns is occasionally tied over from the previous beat. A trill is sometimes indicated for the second repeated note. Ex. 76 shows some of the modifications of the cadence that do not become popular. Although Exx. 76a and b are closely related to the variants in the right column of Ex. 75 by simply omitting the second or third sixteenth-note from the first beat, these patterns occur very rarely.[146] In Ex. 76c an anticipation of the final note occurs.[147] The first repeated note in Ex. 76d is lengthened to a quarter-note.[148] The cadences in Exx. 76e and f included the sixteenth-note rhythm of some of the variants in Ex. 75, but the first repeated note occurs here as the third sixteenth-note, followed by an upper neighbor.[149] This is also very rare, so it must have seemed to composers of the time that this sort of ornamentation, which eliminates the two immediately adjacent repeated notes, destroys an essential element of the cadence. The experiments in Ex. 76 are therefore important for demonstrating which of the possible variants of the cadence were generally considered to be less effective.

The undiminished and undotted cadences occur only in the earliest works. The *Ballet* from the Imhoff manuscript in No. 25b has one in the fifth measure of the second section, as well as at the end. The same piece, however, has a diminished and dotted cadence in the fourth measure of the opening section and the third measure of the second. An undiminished cadence without a dot appears at the end of a *Ballet* by Kindermann; one with a dot concludes an Allemande by Kuhnau and another by Pachelbel.[150]

The main keyboard cadence, however, is the dotted and diminished one at

202 *The Baroque Period*

Ex. 77: Final cadence of an Allemande by Froberger.

(a) From the Bauyn MS (see No. 26) without a typical cadence.

(b) From other sources with a dotted & diminished typical cadence.

the left of the top line in Ex. 75. It occurs in works by most of the composers discussed above. Ex. 77 shows how the Allemande by Froberger in No. 26 ends in the Bauyn manuscript without a typical cadence (a) and in other sources with a dotted and diminished cadence (b), with its opening note tied over from the previous beat. There are also other examples of this cadence in the works of Froberger.[151] Schultheiss includes it in the third bar of the second section of No. 31, as well as at the end of the phrase in Ex. 73a and the end of the piece in Ex. 73b. Other examples occur in the works of Poglietti,[152] Pachelbel,[153] Buxtehude,[154] Richter,[155] Reincken,[156] Krieger,[157] Kuhnau,[158] Mattheson,[159] and Techelmann.[160]

Occasionally the variants shown in the left column of Ex. 75 occur. They differ from each other only in the pitches of the opening three notes. We previously encountered the first variant, with the pitches 6-7-8, in Italian chamber compositions; rare examples appear in the works of Buxtehude.[161] The opening figure 2-5-1 occurs in a piece by Richter,[162] 7-5-1 in works by Pachelbel and Krieger,[163] 7-2-1 in an example by Krieger,[164] and 3-5-1 in Allemanden by Techelmann and Böhm.[165] In addition to the variants in Ex. 75, others sometimes occur, such as the figure 2-3-1 in a piece by Kuhnau[166] and the Allemande by Schultheiss in Ex. 73b (end of the first section). The pitches 1-5-1 occur with this rhythmic pattern in an Allemande by Kuhnau.[167]

The cadence with two dotted notes at the top of the right column in Ex. 75 appears occasionally in works by Reusner,[168] Pachelbel,[169] Richter,[170] and Techelmann.[171] More frequent, however, are the variants shown below this cadence. The first one, with 3, 1, or a rest on the opening sixteenth-note beat followed by 3-2-1, is most common. Kuhnau begins the figure with scale degree 3,[172] Froberger with 1 tied over from the previous beat,[173] Reincken with 3 or 1 tied over,[174] Buxtehude with a rest.[175] The 7-5-1-1 figure below this one in Ex. 75 is used by Weckmann, Pachelbel, and Böhm,[176] 5-3-2-1 by

Richter,[177] 2-4-7-1 by Buxtehude,[178] and 2-3-2-1 by Reincken.[179] Other figures not shown in Ex. 75 may occur with the opening four sixteenth-notes: 3-2-1-1 at the end of the Schultheiss Allemande shown in Ex. 73c, 6-2-5-1 in a piece by Reincken,[180] and 3-1-6-1 and 1-2-7-1 in works of Buxtehude.[181] Krieger uses a version in which 2 and 1 appear on the second and fourth sixteenth-note beats, with rests on the first and third.[182]

These typical cadences may occur in a conspicuous location at the end of a section or a piece, or in the middle of a section to articulate an internal phrase. Most frequent by far is the dotted and diminished cadence at the top and left of Ex. 75. The cadence with two dots appears only occasionally. More numerous are the variant forms, especially those in the right column. With the gradual increase in the number of sixteenth- and thirty-second-notes in the Allemande generally, it is not surprising that the cadences most preferred are those with the maximum number of sixteenth-notes. In some of the latest examples, however, the typical cadences disappear altogether. In the works of Handel I have discovered only one (Ex. 76c). I have found none in the keyboard pieces of Gottlieb Muffat or Fischer, or in the lute examples of Weiss.

Although they seem to be missing also in the solo violin, cello, and keyboard works of Bach, he does have a single example at the end of the opening section of his E-minor Allemande for lute.[183] The last two bars of this section, given in Ex. 78, show that the cadence matches the variant in the last line of the right column in Ex. 75. Ex. 79 reveals another occasion on which Bach was involved with these cadences. Ex. 79a shows the opening and final measures of an ensemble Allemande by Reincken, Ex. 79b Bach's keyboard transcription of these same measures.[184] Reincken's piece ends with the first variant in the right column of Ex. 75, with the figure of four sixteenth-notes and the pitches 3-3-2-1. Although Bach retains the sixteenth-note figure, he removes the second repeated note, thereby deliberately rejecting an essential feature of the typical cadence.

The cadences of Ex. 75, however, occur abundantly, as we have seen, in German Baroque keyboard Allemanden in general. Along with the uniformity of rhythmic figures, of meter, number of sections, and general style, they contribute to a sense of unity and stability that was not equaled by the more varied Balletten and Allemanden for ensemble. Late Baroque writers could therefore describe the form rather precisely. Niedt states that the Allemande

Ex. 78: Allemande from Suite in E minor for lute by Bach, end of first section.

204   *The Baroque Period*

Ex. 79: Opening and concluding bars of an Allemande by Reincken transcribed by Bach.

(a) Reincken, *Allemand* from *Hortus musicus*, 1687, for two violins, viola da gamba, & continuo.

(b) J. S. Bach, transcription for keyboard (BWV 966).

"has two repeated sections and begins with an anacrusis in duple meter."[185] According to Walther, it "has 4/4 meter, two repeated sections of almost the same length, and begins in the first as well as the second section with a short anacrusis, usually an eighth- or sixteenth-note, sometimes also with three sixteenth-notes."[186] Mattheson says that "in keyboard, lute, and viola da gamba music, the Allemande, as a genuine German invention, goes before the *Courante*, as the latter before the *Sarabande* and *Gigue*, which succession of movements one calls a suite."[187] When Walther describes the Allemande as "the proposition from which the rest of the suite flows,"[188] he may be referring to the melodic similarity which occasionally links the Allemande with the opening notes of the other dances, especially the *Courante*. On the other hand, he may be simply describing the arresting, introductory quality which the Allemande projects by virtue of its majestic rhythmic motives and its position as the first of the dances.

References to a vocal origin derive most likely from Praetorius, for Niedt mentions "ein Deutscher Gesang oder Deutsches Lied," Walther a "schwäbisches Lied."[189] Both authors, however, know the Allemande of their time mainly as an instrumental piece that is neither sung nor danced. For Niedt, it is a song which "nur auff Instrumenten gespielet wird"; for Walther it is "ein Teutsches Kling-Stück." Mattheson says that Allemanden are not sung, but that he himself has added words for singing the Allemande dance. He also mentions that in addition to the types for solo instrument in Germany and for violin in Italy there is also "a special dance with which the name of Allemande is associated, although it looks more like a *Rigaudon* than a real Allemande."[190] He may be referring here to the social ensemble Allemanda of the court and *Tafel*, which, as we have seen, often, like the newer dance called *Rigaudon*, used longer note values than its keyboard counterpart. Walther mentions dancing only near the end of his article; stating that the Germans surpass the other nations in the composition of the type of Allemande he has been describing, he adds enigmatically in parentheses that this is especially true if it is to be danced.[191]

The *Ballo* is defined by Niedt as a German and Italian dance which is set in two repeated sections of four or eight measures in duple meter.[192] Walther refers to Niedt in his entry on the *Balletto*, and adds that it is for instruments and begins with an eighth-note anacrusis. He also mentions the sung Balletti of Gastoldi and Morley, but not those of Hassler nor the ensemble development that followed.[193]

The Ensemble Almain and the Keyboard Almand in England

Events in the history of the English Almain run remarkably parallel to those in Germany during this period, with the separate development of ensemble and keyboard versions. The ensemble Almain continued to evolve as an accompaniment to dancing in the masque. Mace, as we have already seen in Chapter 5, described the Almain in 1676 as "ayrey and lively." In *The Art of Dancing* (London, 1735), Kellom Tomlinson characterizes the *Allemaigne*, along with the *Gavot*, *Bouree*, and *Rigadoon*, as lighter and less solemn (see Mattheson's comments above, in which he compares the danced Allemande to the *Rigadon*).[194] The example by Christopher Simpson in No. 142 shows traits that we have noted in earlier Almains, especially imitation and brief motives in canonic sequence. Later examples, however, are far simpler and more homophonic, as shown in No. 143 by William Lawes,[195] No. 146 by Charles Coleman, and No. 147 by Benjamin Rogers. These three examples were all published in 1662 by John Playford in *Courtly Masquing Ayres*. They move mainly in quarter- and eighth-notes, thus suggesting the light and lively mood described by Mace and Tomlinson. A few Almains were also composed later by Matthew Locke.[196] Although the theaters were closed by law from 1642 to 1660 and the court eliminated by 1649, there are reports of social dancing during this period, and the Almain presumably continued to serve this function without interruption into the 18th century.

As in Germany, a purely instrumental keyboard Almand also emerged in England that was strikingly different from the ensemble dance accompaniment. A comparison of the early example by John Roberts in No. 145 with the *Allemande* in No. 58 of Richard and the *Alamand* in No. 25c from the Imhoff manuscript reveals a parallelism with the French and German developments.

The same manuscript from which No. 145 comes contains Almands also by Thomas Heardson, Benjamin Rogers, John Cobb, Christopher Gibbons, and Albertus Bryne, as well as Monsieur Tresor and John Mercure. The latter was a lutenist at the English court of Charles I, and the transcription of two of his Almands in this manuscript was part of the evolution, as we have already seen in Germany and in France itself, of the keyboard style from lute music. A slightly later period is represented by the Almains in Matthew Locke's *Melothesia* (London, 1673).[197] Four are by Locke himself,[198] others by Christopher Preston, William Gregory, John Moss, John Roberts, and Gerhard Diessener (a German composer living in England).[199] These works display more sixteenth-notes and occasionally even thirty-second-notes.[200] Imitation sometimes occurs, as well as *fa-la* sequences and, in one case, a fugal theme. One example by Moss is entitled *A Jig–Almain*, a combination of terms we noted also in French keyboard examples in Chapter 9.[201]

Later examples, from around the turn of the century, seem much like those from Germany, with continuous sixteenth-note figures in a highly organized, but essentially unthematic and unmelodic texture. Jeremiah Clarke's Almand in No. 150 thus displays the same general type of construction used by Fischer in No. 33a and Niedt in Ex. 74. Each section of Clarke's work is rigorously and separately unified by a common motive, which occurs in sequence and in dialogue between the voices.[202] Croft's Almand in No. 151 shows how the continuing process of diminution, which we also noted in German sources, involves eventually many thirty-second-notes.[203] A slow tempo is sometimes indicated, as in the title of No. 151 and in Purcell's *Almand, very slow*, published in 1696 (the year following his death) in *A Choice Collection of Lessons for the Harpsichord or Spinnet*.[204] Most of the eight Almands from the suites in this publication, as well as three others by Purcell,[205] display the same sixteenth-note or dotted figures, and occasionally thirty-second-notes, that dominate Nos. 150 and 151. There are numerous keyboard Almands from around 1700. In the manuscript that contains No. 150 there are others by George Holmes, Philip Hart, and John Blow.[206] Other composers from the same period are Robert King, Daniel Purcell (brother of Henry), Francis Piggott, and John Barrett.[207] Printed Almands appeared in publications such as *A Choice Collection of Ayres* (1700) or *Choice Lessons for the Harpsichord or Spinet* (1711). The Italian melodic style is evident, finally, in the works of Maurice Greene[208] and, as we have already seen, in examples by Handel, who published some of his suites in England. Although earlier keyboard examples such as No. 145 retain the name *Almain*, most later ones prefer the title *Almand*.

There are also examples for other solo instruments such as lyra viol and violin. No. 144 shows two simple Almains for solo viol, the second exhibiting the dialogue motives that came originally from Gastoldi's *fa-las* and earlier occurred in ensemble Almains. An instructional Almand for violin and continuo by Nicola Matteis, an Italian composer resident in England, appears in No. 149b, and a Ballett in No. 149a.

The instrumental Ballett, however, is extremely rare in England at any time. James Grassineau, in *A Musical Dictionary* (London, 1740), quotes Brossard's *Dictionaire de musique* of 1703 when he writes that the "Balletto is what we call a Balet, a sort of dance, the air whereof begins with a quaver, the hand rising; it has two strains of four or eight bars each, and is beat in two or four times quick."[209] He also distinguishes between the "*Almain*, a sort of air that moves in common time," the "*Almanda*, a certain air or tune where the measure is in common time, and movement slow," and the "*Allemand*, a sort of grave and solemn music, whose measure is full and moving."[210] He defines *Suonata di camera* as "properly a series of little short pieces named from the dances which may be put to them, yet not designed for dancing, tho' a master of that art may have a mind to apply certain positions, and steps thereto, which by his Judgment are made to agree with their motions. They usually begin with a prelude or little *Sonata*, serving as an introduction to all the rest; afterwards come the *Allemand*, *Pavan*, *Courant*, and other serious dances; after them jiggs, gavots, minuets, chacones, passecailles, and gayer airs, the whole composed in the same tone or mode."[211]

In England, as in Germany, the ensemble pieces commence on beat 1 (with or without a brief anacrusis), reach the final tonic chord on beat 1 or 3, and do not repeat the final melody pitch (see Nos. 143, 146, and 147). Keyboard examples, like those in Germany, commence usually on beat 1, resolve to the final tonic on beat 1 of the last measure, and repeat the chord or melody pitch on the third beat (Nos. 145 and 150). At the end of each section of the lyra-viol piece in No. 144b, the final tonic chord falls on the third beat, and the violin Ballett in No. 149a commences on beat 3. The opening sections of almost all English keyboard Almands, like those in Germany, end on the dominant chord or key (Nos. 145, 150, and 151) or, if in the minor mode, sometimes the mediant chord or the relative major key. Although ensemble examples usually follow the same procedure (Nos. 140–143 and 147), they may sometimes conclude both sections on the main tonic chord (Nos. 139 and 146), as do the two lyra-viol pieces in No. 144.

The ensemble Almains in England occasionally use the dotted and diminished version of the typical cadence, as at the end of Coleman's piece in No. 146.[212] Matteis' example for violin and continuo in No. 149b includes it at the end of the opening section, with undotted cadences in the third measure and again at the end. The cadences are more abundant, however, in the keyboard Almands, where the versions are much like those shown in Ex. 75 for German keyboard music. Here again, the basic dotted and diminished cadence at the top of the left column of Ex. 75 is the most frequent, appearing, for example, at the end of Diessener's Balletto in No. 148 and Croft's Almand in No. 151.[213] The variant below this cadence in Ex. 75 occurs at the end of the first section of Diessener's Balletto (No. 148) and again in the fourth bar of the second. The third variant (with the first repeated note approached by pitches 7 and 5) appears in an Almand by the same composer.[214]

208 *The Baroque Period*

As in German keyboard music, the most frequent variants, however, are those, in the right column of Ex. 75, in which the first repeated note is reduced to a sixteenth-note. The basic type on the top line appears only a few times in works of Locke, Purcell, and Croft.[215] More numerous are the variants in which the first repeated note is preceded by three sixteenth-notes (as in the variants of the right-hand column of Ex. 75),[216] by an eighth and one sixteenth (as in Ex. 76a),[217] by a sixteenth and an eighth (as in Ex. 76b),[218] by two sixteenths and a rest,[219] by a rest and two sixteenth-notes,[220] or by a sixteenth-note between two rests.[221] Clarke's Almand in No. 150 concludes with a rare type of cadence in which the two repeated notes on 1 are interrupted by scale degree 2, as in Exx. 76e and f. I have not considered this to be a real typical cadence, since the two "repeated" notes are not adjacent and hence no longer repeated. However, the trill that is often marked over the second repeated note begins itself with 2 and hence momentarily breaks the repetition of 1. Less common versions of the typical cadence are shown in Ex. 80, where the Purcell example in (a) reduces the first repeated note to a sixteenth, but extends the second one to a dotted quarter.[222] Exx. 80b and c involve thirty-second-notes, applied first to the note preceding the first repeated tone,[223] then to the repeated note itself.[224]

Ex. 81a shows an internal cadence from a published *Alman* by Purcell, and below it, the corresponding measures from two manuscript versions of the same piece.[225] In the manuscripts, tied notes are sometimes replaced by rests or vice versa, and ornamental figures added or replaced by signs. Occasionally notes written as an inner part are moved to the upper voice. The opening note *d'* in Exx. 81b and c, for example, actually appears on the first beat of Ex. 81a, but as a quarter-note in an inner voice. These sorts of changes suggest that the manuscript versions were written down from hearing the work and not from seeing it in notation. One of the most striking changes, however, is the dotting

Ex. 80: Rare cadences in English Baroque keyboard Almands (transposed to C major).

(a) Purcell, *Almand*, end of first section.

(b) Locke, *Almain*, fourth measure of second section.

(c) Moss, *Almain*, end.

Ex. 81: Versions from three sources of the cadence in the fifth bar of the second section of the Almand from Purcell's fourth suite.

(a) *A Choice Collection of Lessons for the Harpsichord or Spinnet*, 1696.

(b) GB-Och, MS 1177.

(c) F-Pc, MS Rés. 1186 *bis*, Part I.

of many of the odd-numbered sixteenth-notes in the manuscripts. This is an application of the general Baroque principle of inequality[226] and, for the Almand, a continuation of the same process that earlier produced dotted eighth-notes. Ex. 81c shows the first and third sixteenth-notes dotted, producing, of course, thirty-second-notes on the second and fourth notes of the group. As in Ex. 80c, the first repeated note has here been reduced to a thirty-second-note.

There are not many examples of this in written notation, however, but these manuscripts suggest that the performer was permitted, or perhaps expected, to dot the sixteenth-notes. This also suggests that the tempo has continued the historic process of slowing down, for the one Almand from *A Choice Collection* of 1696 which is filled with dotted sixteenths (sometimes even on the second and fourth sixteenth-notes, producing a rhythm like the Scotch snap) is marked *very slow* by Purcell. In any event, it is clear from Ex. 81 that whatever changes occur from version to version, the essential elements of the typical cadence remain intact. In all three versions an initial appearance of scale degree 1, reduced now to a sixteenth- or thirty-second-note, acts as an anacrusis to the repetition of 1 on a beat that is accented due to both its greater rhythmic length and to its dissonant relationship to the dominant chord below it.

After around 1750 the word *Allemande* referred to a new dance that became popular in Europe. Jacques Lacombe describes it in 1752 as a dance from Germany in sixteen measures of two beats each.[227] Pablo Minguet y Yrol, in *Arte de danzar a la francesa* (Madrid, 1758), gives a melody in cut time (¢) for *la alemana*, one of four related *contredanses*. In his prose description, he mentions four couples, a *rasgueado* guitar accompaniment, and a step called *alemanda*.[228] La Cuisse speaks of "contredanses allemandes" in *Le répertoire des bals* (Paris,

210   *The Baroque Period*

1762) and the interlacing of arms which the French army had brought back from Germany.[229] Giovanni Andrea Gallini, in *A Treatise on the Art of Dancing* (London, 1762) says that "the Germans have a dance called the *Allemande*, in which the men and women form a ring. Each man holding his partner round the waist, makes her whirl round with an almost inconceivable rapidity . . ."[230] In Charles Compan's *Dictionnaire de danse* (Paris, 1787), the Allemande is a dance of much gaiety from Switzerland and Germany.[231]

Dictionaries from around the end of the century thus have several meanings for the word *Allemande*. Thomas Busby, in *A Complete Dictionary of Music* (London, c. 1801), contrasts the slow, obsolete type, which had four quarter-notes in a bar and was found in Handel's harpsichord lessons, with the dance, still alive in Germany and Switzerland, which has two quarter-notes per bar.[232] German sources from this period describe the old type in 4/4 from the keyboard suite as serious and thoughtful, the contemporary dance in 2/4 as merry, lively, and with leaping movements, and a third type as a folk dance in triple meter popular in Switzerland and in Swabia (a region in southwest Germany).[233]

These new Allemandes, however, belong to new types that seem unrelated to the Renaissance and Baroque forms we have been tracing.[234] The unified history of the Deutscher Tanz, the Balletto Tedesco, and the Allemande ends, for the most part, with the disappearance of Baroque ideas in each country. The French Allemande and the Italian Alemanda and Balletto live to around 1730, when the Classic forms and style begin to dominate. Most of the German ensemble Balletti and Allemanden occur before the turn of the century, and it is the German keyboard Allemande that lives on into the 18th century. Although the later sources are not precisely dated, the English keyboard Almand probably lives as long or perhaps longer than its German counterpart. In any event, they both survive until the end of the Baroque period in both those countries around 1750. They represent the final examples of the forms and mark the end of the history of the Renaissance and Baroque Allemande, Balletto, and Deutscher Tanz.

THE CADENCE

From 1540, then, when the Deutscher Tanz first emerges in Nuremberg, until about 1750, when Classic concepts finally replace Baroque ideas, a fairly unified evolution unfolds that involves the Allemande, the Balletto, and the Tanz in most of the countries of western Europe. Changes occur as the form moves from country to country, and as it moves from the Renaissance, through a time of transition, to the Baroque period. Features emerge, however, that unify the development within a certain country or within a period of time, and some traits act more broadly to unify the entire history.

During the Renaissance, the Deutscher Tanz in Germany, the Almande in France and the Low Countries, the Balletto Tedesco in Italy, and the Almain in England share a general homophonic style and a particular rhythmic emphasis on each of four beats in a measure. They are performed by plucked-string instruments, especially the lute, and, in particular countries, by ensembles and keyboard instruments. They borrow familiar melodies, such as those of the *Printzentantz*, the *Almain Monsieur*, or the Almandes *d'amour*, *Nonette*, *Loraine*, or *Bruynsmedelijn*. The main dance is duple, but it is usually paired with a Nachtanz in which the same music is transformed into triple meter. There are usually two or three sections, each with an even number of bars to match a choreographic unit of two measures in which three walking steps are followed by another movement in place. Most examples seem closely connected with the functional social situation and, although possibly performed independently on occasion, are probably intended primarily as an accompaniment to dancing. Like the other dances of the Renaissance, they have a style that is conspicuously different from the imitative polyphony of the contemporary art music.

From 1590 until 1630 or 1640, the forms undergo extensive and dramatic alterations. They are subjected to the same theatrical and vocal trends that produce opera in art music. Vecchi and Gastoldi include both elements in the Tedesca and Balletto, which inspire Morley to compose vocal Balletti that are not associated with dancing. At the same time in England, the Almain serves a theatrical function in the masque, and in France lute Ballets are derived somehow from vocal pieces in the larger form of the same name. All of these forms from Italy, England, and France then move back to Germany, where the Tanz itself is still alive. In Germany and Italy the vocal element is gradually abandoned, leaving a multi-sectional or multi-movement Balletto for instrumental ensemble that serves a function at occasions such as banquets, weddings, and birthdays as a tiny quasi-theatrical event. Such Balletti continue until mid-century in Italy and until the end of the century in Germany, and may include a Balletto or an Allmand as a separate movement. During the course of this transition period, the Tanz, the Nachtanz, the familiar melodies, and most of the other Renaissance traits disappear and new Baroque concepts take their place. It is also during this period that rhythmic, motivic, and other elements from the popular dances are incorporated into art music.

The new Baroque style emerges in the lute and clavecin Allemandes in France, in the guitar and chamber Alemande and Balletti in Italy, and in the keyboard Allemanden and Balletten of Germany and England. Most of these, except for some of the Italian chamber pieces, are grouped with other dances in the same key. Apparently none of them, except for a few Italian chamber examples before 1668, is intended as a dance accompaniment. The primary unifying element in the Baroque development, however, is the association of the forms with a particular affection that is expressed by means of certain sixteenth-note motives. In the French pieces, the motives, as they contrast with one another, create a sort of rhythmic homogeneity within an energetic broken texture derived from the *style brisé* of lute music. Later keyboard examples from Germany and England generally display a more motoristic flow of sixteenth-notes and a more consistent use of the motives to achieve a powerful sense of unity. It is in the Italian ensemble forms, however, that the motives are incorporated into the far more melodious, contrapuntal, and constructive texture that we know from the works of Bach and Handel as the fully developed Baroque style. Unlike the Renaissance forms, which have a style different from that of the contemporary art music, the Italian Baroque ensemble Alemanda and Balletto participate fully in the style of the main Baroque art forms.

The Italian ideas came to Germany more easily in forms such as the concerto, which did not have to compete with a native tradition that was already established. Even in German keyboard music, forms such as the prelude or fugue exhibit more of the Italian style than the Allemande and Ballett. When Walther, as we noted in the previous chapter, points with pride to the German keyboard Allemande as an achievement unequaled by any other nation, he is confirming that the Allemande was one of the serious and substantial compositional forms of his time. However, it seems to me, without intending to pass an artistic value judgement, that the special golden period in the entire history of these forms occurs in the Italian ensemble Alemanda and Balletto, usually for one or two violins and continuo, from around 1656 to the end of the century. This involves the works of Legrenzi, Cazzati, Vitali, Torelli, and many others, and most of the examples in Volume II from No. 113 to No. 128. This is the only time between 1540 and 1750 when the full force of the contemporary art style was brought to bear upon the forms. With each of the four beats of a measure enlarged to include four sixteenth-notes, the forms had a more extended structure than the other dances. Compared to the concerto or the movements of a *sonata da chiesa*, of course, they were miniature. The Italian chamber Alemanda and Balletto present probably the most concise expression possible of the full Baroque style. Although they are not as well known to music lovers or historians today as the German and French examples, they were composed in great numbers during the second half of the century, and obviously with great enthusiasm. They constitute, it seems to me, the climax of this story.

As we survey the complete history of the forms, then, examples from the three periods of the Renaissance, the transition, and the Baroque reveal some differences in style, function, and approach. There are also some similarities, however. During all three periods they consist of a series of repeated sections, with the possibility of a varied repeat. They can at any time have only two sections, although before 1650 one or more of the sections might be triple. The repetition of the final tonic chord, which occurred sometimes in the Renaissance forms, continues in Italian vocal and instrumental ensemble pieces of the transition period and in French lute, as well as German and English keyboard examples of the Baroque. Most of the time they are grouped with one or more dances of a different type, in the Renaissance with a Nachtanz directly related musically, in the Baroque with two, three, or more other dances related by key, but only occasionally by a few notes of similarity at the beginning.

The most important thread of unity in the history of the Allemande, the Balletto, and the Tanz, however, consists of the presence of the typical cadence. The cadence first appears in examples, such as the *Printzentantz* (see No. 3), from Heckel's lute book of 1556. The latest dated examples that I can find occur in Mattheson's *Pièces de clavecin* of 1714. Ex. 82a shows the usual Renaissance version, with its note values quartered to facilitate comparison with the Baroque type in Ex. 82b. These two examples from the beginning and end of the history (from Nos. 4 and 151) reveal the essential features of the cadence: an accented scale degree 1 placed two basic beats before the final tonic chord, with this note preceded by the same pitch and followed by a resolution to 7, and with neither the first repeated note nor the 7 exceeding the value of the basic pulse. The accentuation of the second repeated note is usually strengthened by its dissonant relationship with a V chord (see Exx.

214 *The Cadence*

Ex. 82: The most popular Renaissance and Baroque versions of the cadence.

(a) Ammerbach, 1571: end of *Wer das Töchterlein haben wil* (No. 4) transposed to C minor, note values quartered.

(b) Croft, c. 1700: end of *Slow Almand* (No. 151) transposed to C minor, original note values.

Ex. 83: The evolution of the typical cadence from 1556 to 1714.

6a–d). It specifically does not contain the suspensions characteristic of Renaissance vocal music (Ex. 4a).

Ex. 83 summarizes the evolution of the cadence from 1556 to 1714. The changes involve the diminution of note values, the dotting of notes, and the approach to the first repeated note. The three columns in Ex. 83 represent the historic process of diminution in which the duration of the basic pulse simply changed from a half-note to a quarter-note, and then to an eighth-note

Ex. 84: Relationship of the final repeated notes or chords to the typical cadence.

(a) Renaissance

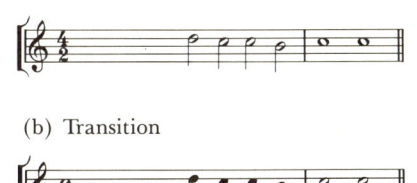

[musical notation]

(b) Transition

[musical notation]

(c) Baroque

[musical notation]

(keeping in mind that I have changed the basic half-note to a quarter in my transcriptions of the Renaissance examples in Volume II). The barring matches the change from the half-note to the quarter, but for the next diminution the bar-lines continue to mark off four quarter-notes, so that the four eighth-notes at the beginning of the cadences in the third column constitute only the last half of a full measure. These changes are, for the most part, merely a matter of notation. It is curious to note, however, that the diminutions match precisely the same periods that are significant in the history of our forms, for the half-note is the notated pulse, generally, during the Renaissance, the quarter-note during the transition, and the eighth-note during the Baroque. Occasionally, as we have seen, the quarter-note cadence continues during the Baroque period in German ensemble or French guitar examples. Curiously, the repeated tonic chords that sometimes occur as whole-notes at the end of a section during the Renaissance (see Ex. 84a), appear during both the transition (Ex. 84b) and the Baroque period (Ex. 84c) as half-notes, and thus do not participate in the second diminution shown in Ex. 83.

In the Renaissance cadences the march-like strength of even notes fitted the simple choreography of a processional dance. The Baroque cadences, on the other hand, reflect the affective content of the forms. The evolution of the dotted motives commences in the quarter-note cadences in the second column of Ex. 83, but completes itself in the various eighth-note versions in the third column. Almost always present in the Baroque cadence is the dot on the second repeated note, and usually also a trill, both of which act to increase the accentuation on that note. Occasionally the tone before the first repeated note is also dotted, producing two affective motives in succession consisting of a sixteenth-note falling to an eighth.

During the Renaissance the approach to the first repeated note was most often by a note of basic pulse on scale degree 2, or sometimes 5 or 6. Occasionally, however, the quarter-note beat was filled by two smaller notes on 6 and 7. This not only produces a pleasing melodic approach, but also adds to the accentuation of the first repeated note and hence also of the second. Although not occurring at any time in history with great frequency, this version of the cadence, shown on the third line of Ex. 83, is one of the few that appear during all three periods. The most popular of the Baroque cadences, shown on the second line of the third column, includes before the first repeated note a pitch of basic pulse on scale degree 7. Often, however, the duration of the first repeated note is reduced to a sixteenth-note to allow formation of the affective figures shown on the bottom three lines. During the later years thirty-second-notes are also introduced, and it is clear that if the Allemande, the Balletto, and the Baroque period had survived another fifty years or so, another diminution of note values would have placed the basic pulse on the sixteenth-note. Ex. 85 shows three rare examples of typical cadences based on a sixteenth-note pulse. Ex. 85a is a further diminution of the version on the first line of the third column in Ex. 83,[1] Ex. 85b a diminution of the second cadence in this column,[2] and Ex. 85c a diminution of the fourth.[3] In all three cases, the music before the bar-line represents only a single quarter-note beat. As in Ex. 82b, I have omitted the concluding arpeggiation of the final tonic chord.

The modifications that occur in the cadence thus reflect the influence of broad historical events that affected music far beyond the Tanz, the Allemande, and the Balletto. A sense of the tenacious survival of certain cadential features over a very long period of time, however, becomes apparent by comparing Exx. 85a and 82a, the latter being the version at the head of the left column in Ex. 83. Bach demonstrates the process by which musical ideas are transmitted when he transcribes an Allemande by Reincken, as we have noted in the previous chapter, and consciously rejects its typical cadence (Ex. 79). On another occasion, however, he does include it in his own lute Allemande (Ex. 78). The evolution of a musical form is determined by the cumulative effect of many composers, over a long period of time, individually studying models of the form by previous composers, and then deciding which elements of the form to retain in order that the new work be identified as belonging to the type, and which elements to alter in order that the work be recognized as a new composition. When one sees how easily Bach rejected Reincken's cadence, it seems all the more remarkable that the cadence survived with such tenacity for over one hundred and fifty years. If just one generation of composers had rejected the cadence, it would no doubt have completely disappeared.

At no period in its history was the cadence absolutely required in order for a piece to be a Tanz, an Allemande, or a Balletto. On the other hand, the cadence occasionally appeared in other duple compositions by the same composers. We have already noted its presence in some German, French, and

Ex. 85: Typical cadences based on a sixteenth-note pulse, transposed to C.

(a) Froberger, end of *Allemande*, c. 1650.

(b) Poglietti, end of first section of *Allemande. La Prisonnie*, 1671.

(c) F. Couperin, end of Allemande *Le Point du jour*, 1730.

Italian *passamezzi* from the second half of the 16th century, in a few *branles* between 1571 and 1669, and in a number of *gavottes*, *bourrées*, and *Intraden* from the second half of the 17th century. It occurs on rare occasions in non-dance forms such as the *preludio*, *sinfonia*, or *sonata*, and is one of the "unaccented" cadences in vocal music. Most of the examples from the 17th century, however, involve a quarter-note cadence from the middle column of Ex. 83 at a time when the main Baroque Allemande and Balletto are utilizing the diminished cadences of the third column. I know of no other form that displays the cadence with such frequency, and over such a long period of time, as the Tanz, the Allemande, and the Balletto. Therefore, it seems to me that it is indeed a special property of these dances, and the one, finally, that provides the most conspicuous thread of unity in their history.

Germany provides the geographical center for the history, for it is here that the forms begin, here that they survive the longest, and only here that they all coexist together during a brief period at the midpoint of this evolution. The development in Germany would not have been the same, however, if the forms had not also traveled to France, Italy, England, and the Low Countries, and been enriched there with new ideas. As they move back and forth across the map of western Europe, the forms create a fascinating choreography that is the source of both unity and diversity. The cadence persists as the chief symbol of unity in the development. Yet it is remarkable, I think, that it occurs in such diverse works as a Deutscher Tanz by Ammerbach, a Balletto with a *fa-la* refrain by Gastoldi, an Allmand by Emperor Leopold I for a court Balletto, an Italian Alemanda or Balletto for chamber ensemble, or an Allemande in a suite by Froberger, François Couperin, or Bach.

Some works are brief and modest from a musical point of view and do not pretend to be anything more than inconspicuous dance accompaniments. Others are substantial compositions that can stand on their own as works of art. Such works can be enjoyed exclusively for their own individual artistic qualities. I believe, however, that a richness is added to the experience when one understands the history of the form. Then, when one hears the typical cadence, for example, in an Allemande, a Balletto, or a Deutscher Tanz, one can remember the evolving tradition of which the piece is a part, and the long and eventful history that began in 1540 in the city of Nuremberg.

NOTES

Preface

1 This is the section entitled "Instrumental" in the article "Balletto" in *New Grove*, II, 91–92.
2 The terms *ballo* and *balletto* occur in dance treatises from the 15th century by Domenico da Piacenza, Guglielmo Ebreo da Pesaro, and Antonio Cornazano. See W. Thomas Marrocco, *Inventory of 15th Century Bassedanze, Balli, & Balletti in Italian Dance Manuals* (New York: Congress on Research in Dance, *Dance Research Annual* XIII, 1981). In addition, *La Allemande* appears as the title of a *bace dance* in the translation by Robert Coplande, published in 1521, of a French dance manual; see the article "Allemande" by Meredith Ellis Little and Suzanne G. Cusick in *New Grove*, I, 276.

Chapter 1. The Deutscher Tanz for Lute, Cittern, and Keyboard in Germany 1540–1603

1 Concerning the *Hoftanz*, see Daniel Heartz's article in *New Grove*, VIII, 637–638, and Otto Gombosi, "Der Hoftanz," *Acta musicologica*, VII (1935), 50–61, as well as the numerous musical examples printed in Wilhelm Merian, *Der Tanz in den deutschen Tabulaturbüchern* (Leipzig: Breitkopf und Härtel, 1927; reprint, Hildesheim: Georg Olms, 1968).
2 Elias Nikolaus Ammerbach, in his *Orgel oder Instrument Tabulatur* (Leipzig, 1571), copy at GB-Cu, includes it at the end of the first *Passametzo* and its *Reprisa* on fol. M$_4$^{v} (printed in *HAM*, No. 154 on p. 171) and *La Reprisa* of the *Passametzo Dangleterre* on fol. O$_3$^{r} (Howard Mayer Brown apparently consulted an edition that had continuous arabic foliation, for he cites the same pieces differently on p. 253 of his *Instrumental Music Printed Before 1600*). Bernhard Schmid (i) has one at the end of the *Passomezo comun* on fol. X$_3$^{r} of his *Zwey Bücher* (Strassburg, 1577).
3 In Ex. 7, (a) and (d) are on fols. K$_2$^{v} and L$_1$^{r} of Ammerbach's *Orgel oder Instrument Tabulatur* of 1571. The others come from works in Volume II of the present set.
4 In *De preceptis artis musicae*, p. 293 in Edmond de Coussemaker, *Scriptorum de musica medii aevi, Nova series*, Vol. III (Paris, 1869), and p. 39 in Albert Seay, *Corpus scriptorum de musica*, Vol. XI (American Institute of Musicology, 1965). Ernest Trumble includes a translation of this part of the treatise in *Fauxbourdon, An Historical Survey*, Vol. I (*Musicological Studies*, No. 3 [Institute of Mediaeval Music, 1959]), 47. I applied Guilelmus Monachus' rules of harmonization to the folia melody in "The Folia, Fedele, and Falsobordone," *The Musical Quarterly*, LVIII (1972), pp. 403–404, and Ex. 4 on p. 400.
5 For a description of the process of chordal variation, see my article "Chordal Aspects of the Italian Dance Style 1500–1650," *Journal of the Lute Society of America*, III (1970), 35–52. I give a brief summary of the Renaissance chord-rows on pp. 365–367 of "The Ripresa, the Ritornello, and the Passacaglia," *Journal of the American Musicological Society*, XXIV (1971), and discuss Scheme V in particular in "The Folia Melodies," *Acta musicologica*, XLV (1973), 98–119.
6 See Howard Mayer Brown, *Music in the Renaissance* (Englewood Cliffs, New Jersey: Prentice-Hall, 1976), p. 56.

220   *Notes to pages 13–27*

7 *Ibid.*, pp. 212–213 and Example 8–1.
8 See Willi Apel, *The Notation of Polyphonic Music 900–1600* (*The Medieval Academy of America, Publication* No. 38 [Cambridge, Mass., 4th ed., 1953]), p. 33.
9 *Ibid.*, pp. 156–157. The notation on the last line of p. 156 is exactly the sort encountered in the Tanz and Nachtanz.
10 *Orgel oder Instrument Tabulatur*, fols. L_1^v-M_1^r: *deutsche Dentze* Nos. 9, 10, and 11.
11 *Ibid.*, No. 5: *Ein kurtzer Dantz*, fols. K_2^v-K_3^r.
12 *Das ander Buch newerlessner kunstlicher Lautenstück* (Strassburg: Bernhard Jobin, 1573), copy at A-Wn. The first two are on fols. G_1 and H_2, the other on fols. G_1^v-G_2^r.
13 Sixt Kargel, *Renovata cythara* (Strassburg, 1578), copy in D-B, pieces No. 92 and 93: *Almande nova* and *Reprinse*, fols. L_3^v-L_4^r.
14 The piece by Jobin is on fols. G_1^v-G_2^r of the work cited in footnote 12. The Neusidler version is transcribed as No. 7a.
15 *Dantz* No. 11 on fols. L_3^v-L_4^r of his *Orgel oder Instrument Tabulatur* of 1571, and piece No. 126 on pp. 191–192 in his *Orgel oder Instrument Tabulaturbuch* (Nuremberg, 1583), copy at D-Mbs.
16 For more information on these two books, as well as Gerle's works, see Brown's *Instrumental Music Printed before 1600*.
17 For further examples, see Merian's *Der Tanz in den deutschen Tabulaturbüchern*. This anthology includes keyboard works of Bernhard Schmid the elder (Strassburg: Bernhard Jobin, 1577), Jakob Paix (Lauingen, 1583), and August Nörmiger (a manuscript, now lost), as well as anonymous works in manuscripts from 1593 and 1585 (one owned by the Nuremberg politician Christoph Loeffelholtz von Colberg). Since Merian has quartered the original note values, his eighth-notes correspond to the quarter-notes in my transcriptions. This should be taken into account when considering coloration, since his smaller values tend to make the music look more ornate than it really is.
18 Printed in *Ludwig Senfl, Sämtliche Werke*, Vol. V (1949), ed. Arnold Geering and Wilhelm Altwegg, pp. 64–65.
19 Printed in *Publikation älterer praktischer und theoretischer Musikwerke*, Jahrgang XXXIII, Vol. 29 (1905), p. 27 (No. 16).
20 *Ein newes Lautenbüchlein*, copy at A-Wn, fols. B_2^v-B_3^r.
21 Ernst Radecke, "Das deutsche weltliche Lied in der Lautenmusik des sechzehnten Jahrhunderts," *Vierteljahrsschrift für Musikwissenschaft*, VII (1891), 285–336.
22 From Georg Forster's *Ein Ausszug guter alter und newer teutscher Liedlein, einer rechten teutschen Art* (Nuremberg, 1539); transcribed by Kurt Gudewill in *EDM*, Erste Reihe, Vol. 20, No. 43, pp. 61–62; also in *DTÖ*, Jahrgang XXXVII/2, Vol. 72: *Das deutsche Gesellschaftslied in Österreich von 1480–1550*, ed. Leopold Nowak, p. 42. Adolf Koczirz transcribes ten instrumental versions of *Nach willen dein*, as well as intabulations of many other Lieder, on pp. 75–97 of the latter source.
23 Hans Neusidler, *Ein newgeordent künstlich Lautenbuch* (Nuremberg, 1536), copy at US-Wc, fol. e_4^v.
24 Hans Neusidler, *Ein newes Lautenbüchlein* (Nuremberg, 1540), fol. E_1^v.
25 Hans Neusidler, *Der ander Theil des Lautenbuchs* (Nuremberg, 1536), copy in D-W, fol. Gg_1^r. The complete piece is transcribed by Helmut Mönkemeyer in *Die Tabulatur*, No. 9 (1966), pp. 14–15.
26 Printed by Eduard Bernoulli and Hans Joachim Moser in *Das Liederbuch des Arnt von Aich* (Kassel: Bärenreiter, 1930), No. 45, p. 83.
27 Facsimile of the copy at D-LEm published by Zentralantiquariat der Deutschen Demokratischen Republik (Leipzig, 1977), p. 67.
28 From Forster's work cited in note 22. See *EDM*, Erste Reihe, Vol. 20, p. 163 (No. 117), and *DTÖ*, Jahrgang XXXVII/2, Vol. 72, pp. 31 and 80.
29 *Orgel oder Instrument Tabulatur* (Leipzig, 1571), piece No. 43 on fols. H_4^v-I_1^r.
30 In his 1571 book Ammerbach includes other cadences like the first one in Ex. 14b at the end of the pieces numbered 7, 10, 14, 18, 22, 34, 35, 41, and 44. For the other cadences in Ex. 14b, see the end of Nos. 20, 30, 33, 36, 39, and 40.
31 Hans Neusidler, *Ein newgeordent künstlich Lautenbuch* (Nuremberg, 1536) copy at US-Wc, fol. i_3^v, and *Das ander Buch* (Nuremberg, 1549), copy at D-Ngm, fol. k_2^v. The latter is transcribed by Wilhelm Back in *Lieder, Tänze und Präambeln* (Neuhausen–Stuttgart: Hänssler, 1975), pp. 23–24. Arnold Geering and Wilhelm Altwegg include other intabulations of this Lied in *Ludwig Senfl, Sämtliche Werke*, Vol. VII (1960), pp. 6–10: two examples from *Trium vocum carmina* (Nuremberg:

Hieronymus Formschneider, 1538), pp. 28–34: keyboard versions from the books of Sicher and Kleber and from an anonymous manuscript from Warsaw, and pp. 37–38: a piece for two lutes from Wolff Heckel's *Lautten Buch* (Strassburg, 1556). An arrangement also appears in Hans Gerle's *Tabulatur auff die Lauden* (Nuremberg, 1533). Numerous vocal versions of this popular Lied also exist.

32 Printed in Claudin de Sermisy, *Opera omnia* (*Corpus mensurabilis musicae*, LII [American Institute of Musicology]), Vol. III (1974), ed. Isabelle Cazeaux, pp. 67–69 (No. 43).

33 *Das erst Buch* (Nuremberg, 1544), copy at D-KA, fols. F_1^v-F_2^r.

34 *Ein newes Lautenbüchlein*, fols. G_2^r-G_3^r.

35 *Neuf Basses Dances, deux Branles, vingt et cinq Pavennes avec quinze Gaillardes* (Paris: Pierre Attaingnant, 1530), fol. 11^r. It is printed by Friedrich Blume in *Studien zur Vorgeschichte der Orchestersuite im 15. und 16. Jahrhundert* (Leipzig, 1925), Beispiel 3^a. *Het derde musyck boexken* (Antwerp: Tielman Susato, 1551) contains *Bergerette Dont vient cela* followed by *Reprise* (Blume's Beispiel 12^a), and *Reprise Cest a grant tort* (see my Ex. 16), each a Sermisy chanson arranged as a basse danse.

36 Sermisy, *Opera omnia*, Vol. III, pp. 33–35 (No. 22).

37 *Ein newes Lautenbüchlein*, fols. G_3^v-G_4^r. See note 35 for a later source of the same music used as a basse danse in France.

38 *Das ander Buch*, fols. t_3^v-t_4^r.

39 Sermisy, *Opera omnia*, Vol. III, pp. 78–79 (No. 49), and Neusidler, *Das erst Buch*, fols. G_3^v-G_4^r.

40 See *Preludes, Chansons and Dances for Lute Published by Pierre Attaingnant, Paris (1529–1530)* (*Publications de la Société de Musique d'Autrefois, Textes musicaux*, II [Neuilly-sur-Seine, 1964]), ed. by Daniel Heartz. *Languir me fais*, No. 14 on p. 21, shows almost continuous coloration in one voice or another. *D'où vient cela*, No. 23 on pp. 32–33, is somewhat simpler.

41 Pierre Attaingnant, *Transcriptions of Chansons for Keyboard* (*Corpus mensurabilis musicae*, XX [American Institute of Musicology, 1961]), ed. by Albert Seay. See *Dont vient cela* on pp. 187–189, *Cest à grant tort*, pp. 114–115.

42 *Tant que vivray* (Sermisy, *Opera omnia*, Vol. IV, pp. 99–100) has such a cadence at the end of the first and third phrases. Since this work at least begins like a textbook definition of a Parisian chanson, it is often quoted. See, for example, Howard M. Brown, *Music in the Renaissance* (1976), p. 212. See also the repeated middle section of *Au joly boys* (Sermisy, *Opera omnia*, Vol. III, p. 18) and the opening phrase of *Il me souffit* (Vol. III, p. 98).

43 Concerning the monophonic chanson, see Howard Brown, "The *Chanson rustique*: Popular Elements in the 15th- and 16th-century Chanson," *Journal of the American Musicological Society*, XII (1959), 16–26.

44 Théodore Gérold, *Le manuscrit de Bayeux* (Paris, 1921), p. 52 (No. XLIV).

45 Gaston Paris, *Chansons du XVe siècle publiées d'après le manuscrit de la Bibliothèque Nationale de Paris* (Paris, 1875). The melodies are transcribed by Auguste Gevaert at the end of the book. Ex. 19a occurs in Nos. 8, 15, 16, 20, 49, 123, and 130; (b) in Nos. 29, 50, 69, and 80. Ex. 19c is approached from 3 in Nos. 21, 52, 69, and 143, and from 7-1 in Nos. 50 and 71. Ex. 19d occurs in Nos. 77 and 115, (e) in 39, 104, and 132.

46 Monophonic chanson No. 22 from the source in note 45 appears with different text in three polyphonic settings of *Je suis d'Alemagne*. Two of them include cadences like Ex. 19b. The music is printed by Howard Mayer Brown in *Theatrical Chansons of the Fifteenth and Early Sixteenth Centuries* (Cambridge, Mass.: Harvard University Press, 1963), Nos. 40 and 41 on pp. 118–120. See also the same author's *Music in the French Secular Theater, 1400–1550* (Cambridge, Mass., 1963), p. 241, where he names many other sources for this melody. The cadence of Ex. 19c occurs in Nos. 50 and 57 of *Theatrical Chansons*.

47 *Ein newes Lautenbüchlein*, fol. E_4.

48 *Ein newgeordent künstlich Lautenbuch* (1536), fol. t_1: *Hie folget ein welscher Tantz Wascha mesa*, and *Ein newes Lautenbüchlein* (1540), fol. F_4^v: *Passa mesa, Ein welscher Tantz*.

49 *Das ander Buch* (1544), fol. G_3^r: *Ein welsch Tentzlein Clira Cassa*. The scheme occurs here without the opening i chord, in a form that was extremely popular in a number of different forms during the Renaissance.

50 Giovanni Antonio Casteliono, *Intabolatura de leuto de diversi autori*, copy at A-Wn. See, for example, *Pavana chiamata la Malcontenta* and its *saltarello* on fols. 14^r-15^v. Here, one measure of the triple

version matches one of the duple. This pair, as well as some others in the same book, is by Pietro Paolo Borrono.

51 *Ein newgeordent künstlich Lautenbuch. Der recht artlich Hofftantz im Abzug* and its *Hupff auff* on fols. t$_3$^{v}-t$_4$^{v} and *Ein geringer Hoff Tantz* and *Der Hupff auff* on fols. u$_1$^{r}-u$_2$^{r} seem to commence with similar melodies and chords. Here, each bar of triple seems to match one of duple. *Ein ser guter Hoff Tantz mit durch Straichen*, fols. u$_2$^{r}-u$_4$^{v}, however, shows much less relationship with its *Hupff auff*.

52 Sources given in full in Volume II are cited here only by composer, year, and, in some cases, a brief title. I do not give folio or page numbers for those pieces which have distinctive titles and can therefore be easily located by means of one of the following books:

Brown = *Instrumental Music Printed before 1600* by Howard Mayer Brown. A splendid source for locating concordances. The contents of each book are listed in detail, and the many indexes are enormously helpful.

Dieckmann = *Die in deutscher Lautentabulatur überlieferten Tänze des 16. Jahrhunderts* by Jenny Dieckmann (Kassel: Bärenreiter, 1931). She lists the dances of each source in detail. Since Brown's book is more complete for printed works, Dieckmann's is now valuable mainly for manuscript sources.

DTÖ, Jahrgang XVIII/2, Vol. 37 = *Österreichische Lautenmusik im XVI. Jahrhundert* (1911, reprint 1959) by Adolf Koczirz. This volume includes transcriptions of selected lute pieces from both printed and manuscript sources.

Merian = *Der Tanz in den deutschen Tabulaturbüchern* by Wilhelm Merian (Leipzig, 1927; reprint, Hildesheim: Georg Olms, 1968). This includes transcriptions of keyboard examples from both printed books and manuscripts.

Moe = "Dance Music in Printed Italian Lute Tablatures from 1507 to 1611" by Lawrence H. Moe (unpublished Ph.D. dissertation, Harvard University, 1956). Moe gives concordances from all European countries.

53 In *The Dublin Virginal Manuscript* (*The Wellesley Edition*, No. 3 [1954]), p. 50. The chanson is printed in Sermisy, *Opera omnia*, Vol. III, p. 18.

54 From Georg Forster, *Der ander Theil, kurtzweiliger guter frischer teutscher Liedlein* (Nuremberg, 1540), printed by Kurt Gudewill and Hinrich Siuts in *EDM*, Erste Reihe, Vol. 60, p. 115 (No. 74).

55 A modern facsimile of Hondius' *Nova Europae descriptio* was published jointly by the Royal Geographical Society, London, and John Bartholomew & Son Ltd., Edinburgh; the facsimile was taken from a copy (later sold) in the Bartholomew family's private collection. I am indebted to Francis Herbert, librarian in the Map Room of the Royal Geographical Society, for aid in identifying the original source of the facsimile and for obtaining information for me from Kenneth Winch, Librarian of John Bartholomew & Son Ltd.

56 Some regions that were under the rule of the emperor were not considered part of the Empire, whereas others that were not controlled by the emperor did belong. In the prose description of Germany in the Mercator atlases, the author explains how confusing it is to determine what is and what is not in the Empire. In an attempt to clarify the situation, he quotes from an official document which lists all those who hold political power, from the emperor to the specific princes and nobles, the members of the clergy, and all the free imperial cities. See the English edition published at Amsterdam in 1636, and reprinted as *Mercator–Hondius–Janssonius Atlas or a Geographicke Description of the World*, in *Theatrum Orbis Terrarum: Series of Atlases in Facsimile*, 4th series, Vol. II (Amsterdam: Theatrum Orbis Terrarum, 1968), pp. 117–126.

57 This painting, in the Stadtbibliothek at Nuremberg, is reproduced in *MGG*, Vol. IX (1961), *Abb.* 1 on *Tafel* 111, following col. 1760. Daniel Heartz, in his article on the *Hoftanz* in *New Grove*, VIII, 637, includes a painting from 1522 that also portrays a processional dance for couples, accompanied by an ensemble of instrumentalists.

58 See Gerald Strauss, *Nuremberg in the Sixteenth Century*, rev. ed. (Bloomington and London: Indiana University Press, 1976), especially p. 24 (description of the Great Hall), p. 79 (definition of "patricians" as those families formally invited to dance at the City Hall), and pp. 262–269 (on music printing and music making). I have corresponded with Prof. Strauss, who wrote me that he has "no doubt that the dance itself, and the circumstances of its use in the city, can be documented from the sources." This, however, would require detailed searching of the archives by someone sufficiently skilled in the language. This has not yet been done to my knowledge, although most of the entries concerning dance in Franz Krautwurst's *Das Schrifttum zur Musikgeschichte der Stadt Nürnberg* (1964) are, unfortunately, not available to me.

59 *Journal de voyage*, Vol. I, in *Oeuvres complètes*, ed. A. Armaingaud, Vol. VII (1928), p. 93: "Nous vismes aussi la danse de cet' assemblée: ce ne furent qu'*Alemandes*: ils les rompent à chaque bout de champ, et ramènent seoir les dames qui sont assises en des bancs qui sont par les costés de la sale ... Après avoir faict une petite pose, il les vont reprendre ..."

Chapter 2. The Almande for Lute, Guitar, Cittern, and Instrumental Ensemble in France and the Low Countries 1546–1603

1 Transcribed by Ernst Mohr in *Die Allemande* (1932), II. *Teil*, p. 5 (No. 7).
2 NL-Lu, Thysius lute book, fol. 503^v, melody printed by J. P. N. Land in "Het Luitboek van Thysius," *Tijdschrift der Vereeniging voor Noord-Nederlands Muziekgeschiedenis*, II (1887), 283.
3 GB-Lbm, MS Add. 29485, fol. 12^v, printed by Alan Curtis in *MMN*, Vol. III: *Dutch Keyboard Music of the 16th and 17th Centuries* (1961), pp. 24–25.
4 See John Ward, *The Dublin Virginal Manuscript*, p. 48.
5 Curtis, in *MMN*, Vol. III, p. 6.
6 Land II, pp. 292–293.
7 Printed by John Wendland in *Acta musicologica*, XLVIII (1976), 203.
8 *Monuments of Music and Music Literature in Facsimile*, Second Series – *Music Literature*, Vol. LXIII (New York: Broude Brothers, 1974), p. 180. See also the modern edition with introduction by P. J. Meertens, N. B. Tenhaeff, and A. Komter-Kuipers (Amsterdam and Antwerp, 1947), p. 176.
9 Besard's publications seem to confirm that the Renaissance Almande ceased to exist shortly after 1603. His book from this date contains many Almandes, including the *Allemande Une jeune fillette*. His *Novus partus* (Augsburg, 1617), however, includes no Almandes at all, but does have a setting of *Une jeune filette*. See Julia Sutton, "Jean-Baptiste Besard's *Novus partus* of 1617," Ph.D. dissertation, Eastman School of Music, 1962, Vol. I, pp. 150ff.
10 Complete piece printed in Mohr II, No. 6 on p. 5.
11 Land I, p. 163.
12 *Ibid.*
13 Curtis, in *MMN*, Vol. III, pp. 22–23.
14 Complete piece in Mohr II, p. 9.
15 The Denss example is printed by Adalbert Quadt in *Lautenmusik aus der Renaissance* (1967), Vol. I, p. 8; the other in Land II, 285.
16 Curtis, *MMN*, Vol. III, p. 25. The expression *Alemana de amor* appears also a number of times in Spanish sources, although it may not refer here to the specific melody. Cotarelo y Mori includes three references to it in his *Colección de entremeses*, Vol. I. On p. clxxviii he quotes a contract from 1626 in which a dancing instructor certifies that he will teach a certain person "doce mudanzas de Pavana ... quatro de Villano ... y Alemana de amor." In *Las fiestas bacanales* (1656) on p. clxvi, a character mentions "Alemana, Alemana de amor," whereupon six women dance an *alemana* while singing. Finally, in Calderón's *Mujer, llora y venceras* (p. ccxxxiii), one German gentleman says, "What will they play?"; another replies, "La Gallarda ..."; and a third person says, "Isn't an *Alemana de amor* better? You are both one, aren't you?" – that is "a German in love" (¿Qué tocarán? La Gallarda ... ¿No es mejor una *Alemana de amor*, pues vos lo sois?).
17 F-Pn, MS Rés.F.496, p. 3. The complete piece is in Mohr II, p. 18.
18 Land II, pp. 283–284 (No. 295).
19 Fol. 130^r, bottom piece.
20 Mohr II, p. 15.
21 Printed in Quadt, *Lautenmusik aus der Renaissance*, Vol. I, p. 7, but with the original title changed to simply *Allemande*.
22 Fol. 100^v.
23 Mohr II, p. 12.
24 Fol. 85^v.
25 Land II, p. 295.
26 F-Pn, MS Rés.F.496, p. 4, and Mohr II, p. 18.
27 Concordances also exist between less well-known examples of the Tanz and the Almande. In the lute collection of Denss in 1594, the *Allemandes* on fols. 88^r (the second one) and 90^r set the same melodies as the ninth and eleventh *Tantz* in Waissel's book of 1591. A number of the *Allemandes* in

Besard's 1603 book correspond to Tänze: fol. 129ᵛ is a *Deutscher Dantz* in the Hainhofer MS at D-W (*Vierter Thail*, fol. 27ᵛ), fol. 131ʳ (first one) is a *Dantz* in Jobin's book of 1573 (fol. H₂), and fol. 134ʳ (top), included as No. 49a in Volume II, equates with Waissel's twenty-fifth *Tantz* of 1591 and *Tanz. Frolich in allen Ehren* in a Berlin tablature of 1593 (Merian, p. 208).

28 Merian, p. 129.
29 Printed by Henry Expert in *Les maîtres musiciens de la Renaissance française*, Vol. XXIII (1948), pp. 46–47; facsimile edition in *Six livres de danseries*, with introduction by François Lesure (Geneva: Minkoff, 1977), *Troisième livre*, fol. 16ᵛ: *Almande I*. The opening section is almost identical to that of *Almande VIII: Et d'où venez vous, ma dame Lucette*. Concerning this melody, see Howard Mayer Brown, *Music in the French Secular Theater, 1400–1550*, pp. 214–215.
30 Mohr II, p. 9.
31 Fol. 31ᵛ, printed in Adrian Le Roy, *Premier livre de tablature de luth* (1551), ed. André Souris and Richard de Morcourt (Paris: CNRS, n.d.), pp. 57–59. See also the concordances given by Daniel Heartz on p. xx.
32 Fol. 67ᵛ.
33 Fol. 24ʳ.
34 Land II, p. 290.
35 Curtis, *MMN*, Vol. III, p. 52.
36 From Adriaen Valerius, *Neder-landtsche gedenck-clanck* (Haarlem, 1626), p. 74; also on p. 86 of the modern edition cited in note 8 of this chapter.
37 For the top voice, see Mohr I, p. 44.
38 Land II, pp. 295–296.
39 Land II, p. 287.
40 Copy at A-Wn, pp. 99 and 108.
41 P. 286 (modern edition, p. 270).
42 Mohr II, p. 14.
43 Modern edition in *Nicolas Vallet, Le Secret des Muses*, ed. André Souris and Monique Rollin (Paris: CNRS, 1970), pp. 109–113.
44 Land I, p. 239.
45 Only a few typical cadences seem to appear in other duple forms of the period. In Phalèse and Bellère's ensemble collection of 1571, see the end of the second *bransle* on fol. 20ᵛ and the third on fol. 22ʳ. A diminished form of the cadence concludes the *Passomezo d'Anvers* on fol. 7ᵛ.
46 See Mohr II, pp. 3–19.
47 Both printed in Mohr II, p. 5.
48 Mohr II, p. 15.
49 The transcription of the first Almande in Mohr I, p. 18, lacks the opening section, as one can see by comparing the triple portion.
50 Curtis, *MMN*, Vol. III, p. 24.
51 Modern edition published by Sociedad de Bibliófilos Españoles, *Segunda época*, Vol. VIII (Madrid, 1930).
52 *Ibid.*, p. 51: "todos en muy buena orden y dançando una dança alemana con tanto concierto y compás que era hermosa cosa de verlos." See Daniel Heartz, "Un divertissement de palais pour Charles Quint à Binche," in *Les fêtes de la Renaissance*, Vol. II: *Fêtes et cérémonies au temps de Charles Quint* (Paris, 1960), pp. 331 and 341.
53 Calvete, p. 395: ". . . entraron los dioses y ninfas con los menestriles dançando una alemana . . ."
54 *Ibid.*, pp. 399–400: "Entraron con los menestriles dançando una alemana, con hachas de cera blanca encendidas en las manos. Desta manera dieron una vuelta por la sala dançando, y dejadas las hachas, dançaron todos con las damas."
55 François Rabelais, *Le cinquiesme et dernier livre des faicts edicts héroïques du son Pantagruel* (published posthumously in 1562), in *Les oeuvres*, ed. Ch. Marty-Laveaux (Paris, 1873), Vol. III, p. 222. See Nan Cooke Carpenter, *Rabelais and Music* (Chapel Hill: University of North Carolina Press, 1954), pp. 36 and 69.
56 La Sociedad de Bibliófilos Españoles, Vol. XXXII: *Relaciones históricas al los siglos XVI y XVII* (Madrid, 1896), p. 58: "Comenzó Don Diego de Córdoba el sarao y sacó á Doña Ana Fajardo; danzaron una *pavana* y *una alta* y tras él salió el Duque y danzó una *alemana* con Doña Isabel Manrique; luego bajó el duque del Infantazgo y danzó otra con madama de Monpensier y tras

ellos salieron todas las damas españolas y francesas á danzar el *alemana* . . ." See also Cotarelo y Mori, *Colección de entremeses*, Vol. I, p. clxviii.
57 Cited by Cotarelo y Mori in *Colección de entremeses*, Vol. I, p. clxviii.
58 Land II, p. 294.
59 On pp. 74, 114, and 180, respectively. In the modern edition cited in note 8 in this chapter, these three Almandes are on pp. 86, 120, and 176.
60 Thoinot Arbeau, *Orchésographie* (Langres, 1589; facsimile reprint, Bologna: Forni, 1969), fol. 67^r: "L'allemande est une dance plaine de médiocre gravité, familière aux Allemands, & croy qu'elle soit de noz plus anciennes, car nous sommes descendus des Allemands: Vous la pourrez dancer en compagnie: Car ayant une damoiselle en main, plusieurs aultres se pourront planter derrier vous, chacun tenant la sienne, & dancerez tous ensemble, en marchant en avant, & quand on veult en rétrogradant, par mesure binaire, trois pas & une grève, ou pied en l'air sans sault, & en quelques endroits par un pas & une grève, ou pied en l'air: Et quand vous aurez marché jusques au bout de la salle, pourrez dancer en tornant, sans lascher vostre damoiselle: Les aultres danceurs qui vous suyuront en seront de mesme quand ils seront au dit bout de la salle: Et quand les joueurs d'instruments cesseront ceste première partie, chacun s'arrestera & devisera avec sa damoiselle, & recommencerez comme auparavant pour la secunde partie: Et quand viendra à la troisième partie vous la dancerez par la mesme mesure binaire plus légiere & concitée, & par les mesmes pas, en y adjoustant des petits saults comme à la Courante: Ce que vous entendrez facilement par la tabulature, laquelle ne seroit quasi point nécessaire, attendu qu'il n'y a guieres de diversitez de mouvements, toutesfois afin que vous voyez le tout plus clairement, je n'espargneray la peine de la vous donner par escript." See also the English translation by Mary Stewart Evans, with a new introduction and notes by Julia Sutton (New York: Dover Publications, 1967), pp. 125–128. Julia Sutton, in the article on Arbeau in *New Grove*, I, 544, gives the date of the first edition as 1588.
61 Arbeau, *Orchésographie*, fol. 45^r: "comme s'il vouloit donner un coup de pied à quelcun."
62 *Ibid.*, fol. 45^r: "Et quand treuverez en ladicte tabulature ce mot grève, le dit mouvement se debura faire fort eslevé & hardiment."
63 *Ibid.*, fol. 68^v: "Les minimes blanches qui sont icy a vuyde, tiennent lieu de souspirs & pauses, ou de petits saults, comme dit a esté en la Courante."
64 In *New Grove*, I, 277, it seems to me that Ex. 1 includes twice as many steps for each measure as Arbeau indicates.
65 Arbeau, *Orchésographie*, fol. 68^v: "En dançant l'Allemande les jeunes hommes quelquesfois dérobent les damoiselles, les ostant de la main de ceulx qui les meynent, & celuy qui est spolié se travaille d'en r'avoir une aultre. Mais je n'appreuve point ceste façon de faire, parce qu'elle peult engendrer des querelles & mescontentements."
66 *Ibid.*, fol. 30^r-32^v. The first page is reproduced in the article "Pavan" in *New Grove*, XIV, 311.
67 *Ibid.*, fol. 28^v.
68 *Ibid.*, fol. 29^v.
69 *Ibid.*, fol. 29^v.
70 *Ibid.*, fol. 33^v.

Chapter 3. The Balletto Tedesco for Lute, Keyboard, and Ensemble in Italy 1561–1615

1 On pp. 35 and 240 of the manuscript. They are printed in Oscar Chilesotti, *Da un codice Lauten-buch del cinquecento* (Leipzig: Breitkopf und Härtel, [1890]), pp. 16 and 101.
2 Lucca, Biblioteca Statale, MS 774, fols. 18^v and 31^r (Moe, p. 259).
3 Transcribed by Gerald Lefkoff in *Five Sixteenth Century Venetian Lute Books* (Washington, D.C.: Catholic University of America Press, 1960), p. 141.
4 Pietro Millioni, *Quarta impressione del primo, secondo et terzo libro d'intavolatura di chitarra spagnola* (Rome, 1627), copy at I-Bc, p. 30.
5 Giovanni Ambrosio Colonna, *Intavolatura di chitarra spagnuola* (Milan, 1620), copy at GB-Lbm, p. 56. Ex. 27 actually presents only the first half of the piece. The entire chord progression, with some small changes, recurs a second time.
6 This is further confirmed by the many appearances in Italy of the *monica*, referring to the text on

the same subject as the French *Nonette* or *Une jeune fillette* concerning a girl who does not want to be a nun. The Italian text appears with the melody first in 1610 in a manuscript collection of canzonettas and madrigals assembled by Michele Pario at Parma (I-BRq, MS L.IV.99, fol. 16ʳ); it is printed by John Wendland in *Acta musicologica*, XLVIII (1976), p. 197, and I have included the melody on the top staff of Ex. 28. The guitar works from the first half of the 17th century include many examples of the *monica*, sometimes followed by a triple version. The word *ballo* or *balletto*, however, never occurs, as far as I know, together with the word *monica* in a title. *La monica* does appear in Girolamo Montesardo's *Nuova inventione d'intavolatura per sonare li balletti sopra la chitarra spagniuola* (Florence, 1606), but here the word *balletti* refers to dances in general. When associated with dance in the guitar books, the *monica* melody seems usually to be entitled *Alemana*, another indication of French or Flemish influence. Benedetto Sanseverino, in his *Intavolatura facile* (Milan, 1620) for the Spanish guitar, includes three pieces that utilize a *rasgueado* chordal scheme that matches the melody: *Alemana* (p. 37), *Aria sopra É tanto tempo hormai* in triple meter (p. 41), and *Madre non mi far monica* (p. 64). See pp. 186–187 and 195 in Wendland's article.

7 *Monuments of Music and Music Literature in Facsimile*, Second Series – *Music Literature*, Vol. XLVI (New York: Broude Brothers, 1967), fol. 135ʳ.
8 Transcribed by Oscar Chilesotti in *Biblioteca di rarità musicali*, Vol. I, reprinted as *Danze del secolo XVI* (*Bibliotheca musica bononiensis*, Sezione IV N.22 [Bologna: Forni, 1969]), p. 8.
9 At US-SFsc, on p. 55.
10 Alessandro Piccinini, *Intavolatura di liuto, et di chitarrone, Libro primo* (Bologna, 1623), pp. 104–106. See also the *Corrente fatta sopra l'aria francese* for lute on pp. 84–85 and the *Corrente sopra l'Alemana* for chitarrone on p. 107. A facsimile edition appears in the set *Antiquae musicae italicae, Monumenta bononiensia, I maestri del liuto* (Bologna, 1962).
11 Benedetto Sanseverino, *Intavolatura facile* (Milan, 1620), copy at GB-Lbm, p. 37.
12 Carlo Calvi, *Intavolatura di chitarra, e chitarriglia* (Bologna, 1646), copy at I-Bc, p. 34.
13 In the latter, on fols. 18ᵛ, 16ᵛ (in Mohr II, p. 12), and 19ᵛ, respectively; in Mainerio, pp. 10, 21, and 15. Mainerio's entire book is printed in a modern edition by Manfred Schuler as Vol. V of *Musikalische Denkmäler* (Mainz, 1961); see pp. 22, 45, and 32.
14 I-MOe, MS C311, fol. 30ʳ (No. 75), transcribed by Carol MacClintock in *The Wellesley Edition*, No. 8: *The Bottegari Lutebook* (1965), p. 94. See also the *Ballo tedesco* in the lute tablatures at Kremsmünster in Austria, transcribed and compared to Mainerio's version by Rudolf Flotzinger on the unnumbered page following p. 191 in "Die Lautentabulaturen des Stiftes Kremsmünster," Ph.D. dissertation, Universität Wien, 1964.
15 Facsimile edition, fols. 53ʳ-53ᵛ.
16 Chilesotti, *Biblioteca di rarità musicali*, Vol. I (see note 8 for the reprint), p. 43.
17 Modern edition in *Marco Facoli, Collected Works*, edited by Willi Apel as No. 2 (1963) of *CEKM*, p. 35.
18 *Ibid.*, pp. 34–35; in Facoli's book, fols. 33ʳ-33ᵛ.
19 They appear in Mainerio on pp. 19 and 1, respectively, and in Schuler's modern edition on pp. 40 and 1.
20 On p. 144 of the manuscript and pp. 55–56 of *Da un codice Lauten-buch del cinquecento*.
21 On p. 240 of the manuscript and p. 100 of the modern edition.
22 Giovanni Picchi, *Intavolatura di balli d'arpicordo* (Venice, 1621), facsimile edition in *Bibliotheca musica bononiensis*, Sezione IV N.36 (Bologna: Forni, 1968), pp. 46–48. The piece is transcribed in *CEKM*, No. 38 (1977): *Giovanni Picchi, Collected Keyboard Works*, ed. J. Evan Kreider, pp. 21–22.
23 One concludes the *Pavana detta la bella Andronica* from Borrono's *Intavolatura di liuto* (Venice, 1548), transcribed by Gerald Lefkoff from the 1563 edition in *Five Sixteenth Century Venetian Lute Books* (Washington, D.C.: Catholic University of America Press, 1960), p. 84. Mainerio includes them not only in his *tedesche*, but also in *passemezzi* and other works; see Schuler's modern edition, the *Pass'e mezzo antico* on pp. 4 (line 2), 5 (line 3), and 7 (lines 1 and 2); *Pass'e mezzo della Paganina* on p. 10 (two on line 2, two on line 3); *Pass'e mezzo moderno*, pp. 26 (two on line 4), 27 (one on line 3, two on line 4), 28 (in diminution end of the second line, regular form on line 4), and 29 (lines 1 and 2); *Caro ortolano*, p. 12 (two on line 3); *Schiarazula Marazula*, p. 31 (two on line 2); *La Parma*, p. 38 (line 3); and *Ballo anglese*, p. 43 (lines 2 and 3). In addition, Simone Molinaro, in his *Intavolatura di liuto* (Venice, 1599), has a typical cadence in the second measure of one *pass'e mezo* and five bars from the end of the *prima parte* of another; printed in Oscar Chilesotti, *Lautenspieler des XVI. Jahrhunderts* (Leipzig: Breitkopf und Härtel, [1891]), pp. 147 and 153.

24 See Marc Southard and Suzana Cooper, "A Translation of Hans Newsidler's *Ein newgeordent künstlich Lautenbuch* (1536)," *Journal of the Lute Society of America*, XI (1978), pp. 7–8.
25 Facsimile reprint by Forni in *Bibliotheca musica bononiensis*, Sezione II N. 104 (Bologna, 1969).
26 For the reconstruction of this choreography I am deeply indebted to Carolann Busch, graduate student in the Dance Department at UCLA. She has made it clear, however, that there may indeed be other possible ways to realize portions of the dance. Considering the imprecision of Negri's instructions, however, some solution like this seems to be the best one can do.
27 Described by Negri on pp. 104–113. Some of these movements are explained also by Putnam Aldrich in *Rhythm in Seventeenth-Century Italian Monody* (New York: Norton, 1966), pp. 78ff.
28 Juan de Esquivel Navarro, in *Discursos sobre el arte del dançado* (Seville, 1642; reprinted 1947 as Vol. IV of the *Publicaciones de la Asociación de Libreros y Amigos del Libro*), seems to be describing on fol. 17^r a similar dance step when he defines the *subtenido*, which one does "by raising the body above the points of the toes . . . It is a grave movement, which is employed in the *torneo*, . . . *alemana*, and other dances for the *mascaras* and *saraos*" (levantando el cuerpo sobre las puntas de los pies . . . Es un movimiento grave, que se pratica en Torneo, . . . Alemana, y otras danças . . . para mascaras y saraos).
29 The piece is transcribed literally by Chilesotti in *Biblioteca di rarità musicali*, Vol. I (see note 8 in this chapter for the reprint), p. 60.

Chapter 4. Vecchi, Gastoldi, and the Vocal Balletto in Italy during the 1590s

1 *Intermedii et concerti, fatti per la commedia rappresentata in Firenze* . . . (Venice, 1591). Warren Kirkendale prints Cavalieri's *Ballo* in *L'Aria di Fiorenza, id est Il Ballo del Gran Duca* (Florence, 1972), pp. 87–88, and reports on p. 42 that it is called *Allemande* in D-Bds, Mus. MS. 40316 for keyboard. See also my review of this book in the *Journal of the American Musicological Society*, XXVI (1973), 344–350.
2 I can find only a few Tanz cadences in the frottola literature. From Petrucci's *Strambotti, Ode, Frottole, Sonetti, Libro quarto* (Venice, 1505?), see the end of *A che affligi*, printed on pp. 53–54 of *Publikationen älterer Musik*, Jahrgang 8 (1933/35): *Ottaviano Petrucci – Frottole, Buch I und IV*, ed. Rudolf Schwartz. See *Quasi sempre avanti dì* from Petrucci's *Frottole libro septimo* (Venice, 1507), fols. 36^v-37^r (especially on the text "cucurucu") and *Pregovi frondi fiori aque* by Bartolomeo Tromboncino arranged for one voice and lute (final cadence) by Franciscus Bossinensis in *Tenori e contrabassi intabulati col sopran in canto figurato per cantar e sonar col lauto Libro secundo* (1511), fol. 17^r. Both pieces are printed by Benvenuto Disertori in *Le frottole per canto e liuto intabulate da Franciscus Bossinensis* (*Instituzioni e monumenti dell'arte musicale italiana, Nuova serie*, Vol. III [Milan, 1964]), pp. 128–132 and 488. See also the final cadence of *Poi che son di speranza al tutto privo* by Joannes Lulinus from Petrucci's *Frottole libro undecimo* (Venice, 1514), printed by Alfred Einstein in *The Italian Madrigal* (Princeton University Press, 1949), Vol. III, p. 8.
3 Both versions are printed by Disertori in the work cited in the preceding note, pp. 176–179. The vocal work is in *Petrucci, Harmonice musices odhecaton A*, ed. Helen Hewitt (*Medieval Academy of America, Publication* No. 42, *Studies & Documents*, No. 5 [Cambridge, Mass., 1942; reprint, New York: Da Capo Press, 1978]), pp. 375–376. The lute arrangement is in Francesco Spinacino's *Intabulatura de lauto, Libro primo* (Venice: Petrucci, 1507), fol. 8.
4 Printed in Alfred Einstein, *The Italian Madrigal*, Vol. III, p. 73 (No. 33).
5 See Moe, pp. 144–145. He includes the "dance section" from this piece on p. 145. The manuscript version of the entire *villotta* is printed in Fausto Torrefranca, *Il segreto del quattrocento* (Milan, 1939), pp. 525–526.
6 In Torrefranca's *Il segreto del quattrocento*, see *De la da l'acqua* (last bar of the first line on p. 444), *Donne, venete al ballo* (both lines on p. 446 and the first phrase on p. 447), *Favelami fantina* (two on the bottom system of p. 456; one on p. 457), *La mi fa sol fa re* (two on the top line of p. 472), *L'ultimo dì di Mazo* (end of the top line on p. 486 and end of the first phrase on p. 487), and *Ne par estre vegnu* (end of the opening phrase). In some of these cases the editor has added dotted bar-lines between the two repeated scale degree 1's of the cadence. In addition, six other works included by Torrefranca have typical cadences: see the pieces that begin on pp. 434, 450, 481, 503, 507, and 517.
7 Printed in *Das Chorwerk*, Vol. VIII: *Volkstümliche italienische Lieder*, ed. Erich Hertzmann, lines 2 and 3 on p. 4; the fourth from the last measure on p. 5.

8 Printed in Moe, pp. 337–338 (see also pp. 140–141 concerning the work), and in *Filippo Azzaiolo, Villote del fiore*, ed. Francesco Vatielli (Bologna, 1921), pp. 1–3.
9 All printed in *Pubblicazioni della Biblioteca del Conservatorio G. B. Martini in Bologna, Maestri Bolognesi*, 2: *Filippo Azzaiolo, Il secondo libro de Villote del fiore alla padovana*, ed. Giuseppe Vecchi (Bologna, 1953). See No. 2 (three cadences on pp. 20 and 21), No. 3 (one on p. 22, two on p. 23), No. 4 (end of the first three phrases on p. 24, another on p. 25), and No. 6 (three on p. 28). In some of these, the first or, more commonly, the second repeated note of the cadence is a dotted quarter-note.
10 See Moe, p. 141. *La cara cosa* is one of the popular forms of the 16th century and is based on the Renaissance chordal scheme I call Chord-row V, the one later used by the folia, but without the opening i chord. Moe transcribes *La cara cosa* from Barberiis' *Intabolatura di lauto, Libro nono* (Venice, 1549), on p. 338.
11 Einstein, *The Italian Madrigal*, Vol. III, p. 77.
12 The text is printed by Einstein in *The Italian Madrigal*, Vol. II, pp. 751–752.
13 See Warren Kirkendale, "Franceschina, Girometta, and their Companions in a Madrigal 'a diversi linguaggi' by Luca Marenzio and Orazio Vecchi," *Acta musicologica*, XLIV (1972), 187. The Bottegari manuscript of 1574 also contains a brief, homophonic piece for voice and lute called *Mi stare pone Totesche*, transcribed by Carol MacClintock in *The Wellesley Edition*, No. 8, p. 38 (No. 33).
14 G. Vecchi edition cited in note 9, pp. 33–34 (No. 8).
15 Kirkendale, the article cited in note 13, p. 181. This entire article (pp. 181–235) is devoted to a discussion of this remarkable piece.
16 Cesare Negri, *Le gratie d'amore*, pp. 222–224.
17 See *New Grove*, II, 94, where Suzanne G. Cusick, in our joint article "Balletto," compares the complete melodies of Vecchi and Negri in Ex. 2.
18 *The Wellesley Edition*, No. 8, ed. Carol MacClintock, p. 15 (No. 11).
19 Facsimile edition published by Minkoff (Geneva, 1980), p. 6.
20 From *Convito musicale* (Venice, 1597), which is transcribed in *Capolavori polifonici del secolo XVI* "Bonaventura Somma," Vol. VIII (Rome, 1966). *Chi vuol goder il mondo* is on p. 157 of this modern edition.
21 Modern edition in *LP* 10 (Paris, 1968), ed. Michel Sanvoisin. There are facsimile partbooks of the edition from Venice, 1593, in *Corpus of Early Music* (Brussels: Editions Culture et Civilisation, 1970), No. 30.
22 Einstein, in *The Italian Madrigal*, Vol. II, p. 605, suggests that it might be considered the forerunner of Vecchi's *Amfiparnaso* and other madrigal comedies.
23 Negri, *Le gratie d'amore*, p. 213 (the first of two pages so numbered). Two new sections of music are added following Gastoldi's Balletto.
24 The melody and bass of *La Sirena* (Ex. 33c), as well as a lute part, appear in Valerius' *Neder-landtsche gedenck-clanck* (Haarlem, 1626), pp. 262–263 (modern edition, p. 249), with the title *Ballet. Questa dolce Sirena* (Gastoldi's opening text).
25 See my article "Chordal Aspects of the Italian Dance Style 1500–1650," *Journal of the Lute Society of America*, III (1970), 35–52.
26 Transcribed by Giuseppe Vecchi in *Gian Giacomo Gastoldi, Opera omnia*, Vol. I, Part A2 (*Monumenta musica lombarda* [Milan, 1969]).
27 The melody and bass, entitled with the opening words "Sonatemi un Balletto," appear, along with a lute part, in Valerius' *Neder-landtsche gedenck-clanck*, pp. 278–279 (modern edition, pp. 263–264).
28 The copy at D-Hs has the correct format. In the microfilm copy I received from D-As, however, some of the pages appear to have been moved from their original positions.
29 In my article "The Ripresa, the Ritornello, and the Passacaglia," in the *Journal of the American Musicological Society*, XXIV (1971), see p. 379 concerning the *arie per cantare*.
30 G. Vecchi indicates the same plan of repetition in the modern edition cited in note 26. *Il Tedesco* is on p. 8.
31 G. Giac. Castoldi [sic], *Balletten, lustigh om te zingen, en speelen, met drie stemmen* (Amsterdam, n.d.), copy at NL-DHgm, p. 7 in the *Canto I, Canto II* and *Tenor*. The lowest partbook is missing, so I have supplied this part in Ex. 36 from Gastoldi's original version in No. 80b.

Chapter 5. The Vocal Ballett and the Instrumental Almain for Keyboard, Plucked Strings, and Ensemble in England 1550–1650

1. *Scottish Text Society, Publications*, Series 4, Vol. XI, with introduction by A. M. Stewart (Edinburgh, 1979), p. 52.
2. Randle Cotgrave, *A Dictionarie of the French and English Tongues* (London, 1611), facsimile edition in *English Linguistics 1500–1800*, No. 82 (Menston, England, 1968), under "haye." To "march en haye" is to march by files.
3. GB-Lbm, Royal App. 74 (one of the Lumley Books), fol. 44^r. All voices are transcribed in *New Grove*, I, 277, Ex. 2 in the article "Allemande" (with the source numbered 75 instead of 74), and in *MB*, Vol. XLV: *Elizabethan Consort Music I*, ed. Paul Doe (1979), p. 164.
4. This manuscript is bound at the end of EIRE-Dtc, MS D.3.30 (The Dallis Lutebook). The pieces are transcribed by John Ward in *The Dublin Virginal Manuscript (The Wellesley Edition*, No. 3 [1954]), pp. 18–19, 21, 17–18, and 20–21, respectively.
5. *The Fitzwilliam Virginal Book*, ed. J. A. Fuller Maitland and W. Barclay Squire (Leipzig: Breitkopf und Härtel, 1899; corrected reprint, New York: Dover, 1979), Vol. II, pp. 217–219.
6. *The Complete Works of Anthony Holborne*, ed. Masakata Kanazawa (*Harvard Publications in Music*, 5 [Cambridge, Mass., 1973]), Vol. II, p. 27. Another cittern setting, called *The Queenes Allmaine*, is in GB-Cu, MS Dd.4.23, fol. 31^v, and is transcribed by Andrew J. Sabol in *Four Hundred Songs and Dances from the Stuart Masque* (Providence, R.I.: Brown University Press, 1978), p. 464.
7. *Complete Works*, Vol. II, pp. 36–37. Other settings are listed by Sydney Beck in *The First Book of Consort Lessons, Collected by Thomas Morley 1599 & 1611* (New York Public Library, 1959), pp. 190–191.
8. *Fitzwilliam Virginal Book*, Vol. I, pp. 234–237. Also, see *Mounsiers Allmayne* in *Clement Matchett's Virginal Book (1612)*, ed. Thurston Dart, 2nd, rev. ed. (London: Stainer & Bell, 1969), pp. 6–7. This is probably also the same piece listed on p. 244 of Will Forster's Virginal Book (see *Grove's Dictionary*, 5th ed. [1954], Vol. IX, p. 13). See also *Mounsers Almane* in the Wickhambrook lute manuscript at the John Herrick Jackson Music Library at Yale University, transcribed by Daphne E. R. Stephens in *Collegium musicum*, No. 4 (1963), pp. 98–99 (No. 19).
9. Vol. I, pp. 238–244. Also in Byrd's *My Ladye Nevells Booke*, ed. Hilda Andrews (London: Curwen, 1926; reprint, New York: Dover, 1969), pp. 221–228 (No. 38); see p. xliv for other sources of the piece.
10. *Fitzwilliam Virginal Book*, Vol. II, pp. 146–147.
11. *MB*, Vol. XX: *Orlando Gibbons, Keyboard Music*, ed. Gerald Hendrie, 2nd, rev. ed. (London, 1967), pp. 73–74 and 79. There are four other Almains without descriptive titles.
12. Printed in William Dauney, *Ancient Scottish Melodies from a Manuscript of the Reign of King James VI* (Edinburgh, 1838), p. 239 (see also pp. 280–281). On pp. 368–369 of the same publication is a list of the contents of Robert Gordon of Straloch's manuscript lute book of 1627–29, taken from the *Gentleman's Magazine* for February, 1823. Included are *Ballat, or Almon, The Prince Almon*, and *Queene's Almone, as it is played on a fourteen cord lute*. The manuscript is now lost, and unfortunately the *Almons* are not among the pieces copied by George Farquhar Graham in 1847 in Adv. MS 5.2.18 of the National Library of Scotland in Edinburgh.
13. *An Almaine for the lute* from Barley's book is transcribed by Wilburn W. Newcomb in *Lute Music of Shakespeare's Time* (University Park: Pennsylvania State University Press, 1966), pp. 46–48. The *Almaine by Frauncis Cuttinge* from Jane Pickeringe's Book, GB-Lbm, MS Egerton 2046, is on fols. 31^v-32^r.
14. *Fitzwilliam Virginal Book*, Vol. II, p. 158.
15. *Ibid.*, Vol. I, p. 243, line 5. I have halved the note values.
16. Mohr, in his chapter on the English virginalists (Vol. I, pp. 47–59), discusses in detail the variation technique in the examples from the *Fitzwilliam Virginal Book*.
17. For other keyboard Almains, see *Grove's Dictionary*, 5th edition (1954), Vol. IX, pp. 4–19 (the article "Virginal Music, Collections of"), especially in Will Forster's and Benjamin Cosyn's Books. An *Almayne* from Lady Jean Campbell's Book from around 1635 is printed by Kenneth Elliott in *Early Scottish Keyboard Music*, rev. ed. (London: Stainer & Bell, 1967), p. 22. For other lute examples, see *The Collected Lute Music of John Dowland*, ed. Diana Poulton and Basil Lam, 3rd ed. (London: Faber Music, 1981), pp. 161–177, and *New Grove*, XVII, 745–746 (article "Sources of Lute Music, England").

230   *Notes to pages 102–13*

18 Modern edition in *The English Madrigalists*, ed. Edmund H. Fellowes, rev. by Thurston Dart, Vol. IV (London: Stainer & Bell, 1965).
19 Facsimile reprint by Gregg International, 1971, p. 180.
20 Joseph Kerman, in *The Elizabethan Madrigal* (New York: American Musicological Society, 1962), has a detailed chart on p. 140 showing very clearly the equivalence between Morley and the Italian sources. See also the entire chapter on the Ballett, pp. 136–149.
21 See *New Grove*, II, 94, Ex. 2, in which the Morley and Vecchi melodies are compared.
22 *The English Madrigalists*, ed. by Edmund H. Fellowes, rev. by Thurston Dart, Vol. X (London: Stainer & Bell, 1968).
23 *Ibid.*, Vol. XXXVI (1961), pp. 35–39 of the second paging.
24 *Ibid.*, Vol. XXXIV (1958), pp. 1–14.
25 *Ibid.*, Vol. XVIII (1960), "no" on pp. 93–98, *fa-las* on pp. 29–39, 70–92, 99–111, and 132–138.
26 Copy of the book at GB-Cu, reprinted in *The English Experience*, No. 608 (Amsterdam: Theatrum Orbis Terrarum, and New York: Da Capo, 1973), fols. Q_1^v-Q_2^r, Q_2^v-Q_3^r (the one with "fa-la-ing"), and R_2^v-R_3^r. Modern edition in *The English Madrigalists*, rev. ed., Vol. XXXVI (1961), pp. 1, 2–4, and 11–13 of the third paging.
27 *The English Madrigalists*, rev. ed., Vol. XXVIII (1968), pp. 88–109.
28 *Musical Antiquarian Society, Publications*, Vol. XIII (1844), ed. Joseph Warren, microfiche edition (New York: University Music Editions, 1973).
29 Facsimile edition, with introduction by Gilbert Reaney (New York: Da Capo Press, 1970), p. 2.
30 Facsimile in *English Lute Songs 1597–1632*, Vol. V, ed. David Greer (Menston: Scolar Press, 1971). *Lessons* No. 3 and 8 are Almains for two lyra viols.
31 Facsimile in *English Lute Songs 1597–1632*, Vol. III, ed. David Greer (1970).
32 *Ibid.*
33 *English Lute Songs*, Vol. VIII, ed. Ian Harwood (1970), pieces No. XIII and XIIII.
34 *English Lute Songs*, Vol. VI, ed. Frank Traficante (1969).
35 *Ibid.*
36 The Almains are printed in *Anthony Holborne, Complete Music for Brass*, ed. Robert Paul Block (London: Musica Rara, 1971), Vol. II.
37 *The First Book of Consort Lessons, Collected by Thomas Morley, 1599 & 1611*, ed. Sydney Beck (New York, 1959), pp. 137–140.
38 *MB*, Vol. XL: *Music for Mixed Consort*, ed. Warwick Edwards (1977), pp. 21–23, 24–27, and 66–67.
39 Facsimile edited by Richard Rastall, with commentary by Warwick Edwards, in *Early Music Reprinted*, 1 (Leeds: Boethius Press, 1974).
40 See *MB*, Vol. XXVI: *John Jenkins, Consort Music of Four Parts*, ed. Andrew Ashbee (1969), pp. 96, 109, 159, 163, 165, and 168. See also *MB*, Vol. IX: *Jacobean Consort Music*, ed. Thurston Dart and William Coates (2nd rev. ed., 1971), for examples in four to six voices by Thomas Tomkins (p. 50), Alfonso Ferrabosco (ii) (p. 105), and Martin Peerson (p. 170).
41 The melodies in Ex. 52 are Nos. 8 and 7 (both on the same page) from the earlier pieces at the beginning of MS 24.E.15. Thurston Dart has described the manuscripts in detail in "The Repertory of the Royal Wind Music," *Galpin Society Journal*, IV (1957–58), 70–77. He has also published six of the pieces, including four *Almandes*, in *Suite from the Royal Brass Music of King James I* (Oxford University Press, 1959).
42 *Galpin Society Journal*, IV (1957–58), 75.
43 *MB*, Vol. XLVI: *John Coprario, Fantasia–Suites*, ed. Richard Charteris (1980). There are fifteen Almains in suites for one violin, eight in those for two violins.
44 For much detailed information on the masque, as well as many examples of music, see Andrew J. Sabol, *Four Hundred Songs and Dances from the Stuart Masque* (Providence, R.I.: Brown University Press, 1978). The parts of the masque are listed on p. 7.
45 James P. Cunningham, *Dancing in the Inns of Court* (London: Jordan, 1965), p. 14. See pp. 40–41 for a chart comparing the contents of the six sources, and pp. 23–39 for the complete choreographies of all the dances. The manuscripts, in chronological order, are:

   (1) GB-Ob, Rawl.Poet.108 (the "Gunter MS" from Lincoln's Inn), c. 1570.
   (2) GB-Lbm, Harley 367.
   (3) GB-Ob, Douce 280: "Practise for Dauncinge" (The Middle Temple, John Ramsay's commonplace book), c. 1606.

(4) GB-Ob, Rawl.D.864: "A Copye of the Oulde Measures" (Elias Ashmole), c. 1630.
(5) London, Inner Temple Library, Misc. Vol. XXVII: "The Measures as They are Danced in the Inner Temple Hall" (Butler Buggins), 1640–75.
(6) GB-Lcm, MS 1119: "A Copy of the Old Measures in the Inner Temple" (Butler Buggins), 1640–75.

46 For help in reconstructing the choreographies, I am greatly indebted to the unpublished monograph "Practise for Dauncinge, Some Almans and a Pavan, England 1570–1650, A Manual for Dance Instruction" by Patri J. Pugliese and Joseph Casazza (Cambridge, Mass., 1980). This choreography is on pp. 25–26 (and on p. 26 of Cunningham's *Dancing in the Inns of Court*).

47 Pugliese and Casazza's manual, p. 21, and Cunningham, p. 23. A copy of the manuscript page that contains this choreography appears facing p. 144 of Mabel Dolmetsch's *Dances of England and France from 1450 to 1600*, 2nd ed. (London: Routledge and Kegan Paul, 1959). Since she apparently did not have access to the other manuscripts, her reconstructions of the Almains on pp. 144–158 are incorrect in a number of respects.

48 There are more complex choreographies in the manuscripts. GB-Lcm, MS 1119, for example, gives the melody of *The Black Almaine* in triple meter and the following directions (Cunningham, *Dancing in the Inns of Court*, p. 36):

> Sides 4 Doubles round about the house and close the last Double face to face then part y^r hands and go all in a Double back one from the other and meet a Double againe. Then go a Double to y^r left hand and as much back to your right hand, then all the women stand still and the men set & turne, then all the men stand still and the women set and turne, then hold both hands and change places with a Double and slide four french slides to the mans right hand, change places againe with a Double and slide four french slides to the right hand againe, Then part hands and go back a Double one from another and meet a Double againe. Then all this measure once over and so end . . .

49 Facsimile reprint in *English Linguistics 1500–1800*, No. 82 (Menston, 1968). See Mohr I, p. 48.
50 *The Works of Ben Jonson* (London: George Routledge, 1838), p. 344 (Act I, Scene 1).
51 *The Poetical and Dramatic Works of Sir Charles Sedley*, ed. V. de Sola Pinto, Vol. II (London: Constable, 1928), p. 80 (Act V, Scene 1).
52 Facsimile reprint from 1654 edition (New York & London: Putnam, 1913), Act III, p. 33.
53 *A Plaine and Easie Introduction to Practicall Musicke* (reprint, Gregg International, 1971), p. 181.
54 Thomas Mace, *Musick's Monument* (London, 1676; facsimile, Paris: Centre National de la Recherche Scientifique, 1958), p. 129.
55 From *The Virtuoso*, in *The Works of Thomas Shadwell, Esq.* (London, 1720), Vol. I, p. 362.
56 Cunningham, *Dancing in the Inns of Court*, p. 8.
57 *Fedele and Fortunio . . . Comoedie of two Italian Gentlemen, translated out of Italian* (London, 1585; reprint, Oxford: Malone Society, 1909).
58 *The Araygnement of Paris, A Pastorall Presented before the Queenes Maiestie* (London, 1584), in *The Works of George Peele*, ed. Alexander Dyce (London, 1829), Vol. I, p. 28 (Act II, Scene 2).
59 Facsimile edition (New York: Da Capo Press, 1970), p. 2.
60 Three pages reproduced by John H. Long in *Shakespeare's Use of Music: The Histories and Tragedies* (Gainesville: University of Florida Press, 1971), pp. 273–275, and described on pp. 269–270.

Chapter 6. The Vocal and Instrumental Ballet for Lute in France 1603–1619

1 Facsimile reprint (Geneva: Minkoff, 1975), fol. 140^r: "quibus annectuntur postmodum selectiores quadam Intradae, seu Balleta, prout illi nominant, ingratiam eorum qui saltatorijs cantionibus delectantur."
2 F-Pn, MS Rés.F.496, pp. 58–59.
3 Robert Ballard, *Deuxième livre (1614) et Pièces diverses*, ed. by André Souris, Sylvie Spycket, and Jacques Veyrier (Paris: CNRS, 1964), p. 1. See also the *Étude des concordances* by Monique Rollin on p. ix.
4 *Terpsichore*, ed. by Günther Oberst, Vol. XV in *Gesamtausgabe der musikalischen Werke von Michael Praetorius* (Wolfenbüttel–Berlin, 1928–40), p. 162 (No. CCLXXIII).
5 Georg Leopold Fuhrmann, *Testudo gallo-germanica* ([Nuremberg], 1615), copy at B-Br, pp. 149–150.

6 Robert Ballard, *Premier livre (1611)*, ed. André Souris and Sylvie Spycket (Paris: CNRS, 1963), p. 19 and the concordances by Monique Rollin on p. xvi.
7 F-Pn, MS Rés.F.496, p. 41.
8 *Second livre* (Paris, 1609), facsimile reprint (Geneva: Minkoff, 1980), fols. 6^v-7^r.
9 Copy at US-Wc, fols. 48^v-49^r.
10 F-Pn, MS Rés.F.496, pp. 97–98. The first piece begins in the middle of the first line; the second commences at the double-bar in the second line and concludes on the next page.
11 Gabriel Bataille, *Airs de différents autheurs, mis en tablature de luth, Quatriesme livre* (Paris, 1613; reprint, Geneva: Minkoff, 1980), fols. 53^v-54^r.
12 Robert Ballard, *Deuxième livre* (Paris, 1964), p. 10.
13 Nicolas Vallet, *Het tweede boeck van de luyt-tablatuer* (Amsterdam, 1616), p. 1; modern edition in *Nicolas Vallet, Le secret des muses*, ed. André Souris (Paris, 1970), pp. 202–203: *3. Ballet*. Monique Rollin reports on p. xxxi that the same setting occurs with the title *Balletto* on p. 89 in the *Thesaurus gratiarum* (Frankfurt am Main, 1622), now lost, of Johann Daniel Mylius, and another version, on fol. 9^r of MS Nn.6.36 at Cambridge University Library, is called "A French Toy."
14 Transcribed by Oscar Chilesotti in *Lautenspieler des XVI. Jahrhunderts*, p. 225.
15 Land III, p. 44.
16 Piece No. 12 on fol. 8^r. For incipit and contents of the manuscript, see Bruce Gustafson, *French Harpsichord Music of the 17th Century* (Ann Arbor: UMI Research Press, 1979), Vol. III, p. 219. I am indebted to Prof. David Fuller at the State University of New York, Buffalo, for information concerning this manuscript.
17 US-SFsc, Bentivoglio MS, p. 56.
18 *Thesaurus harmonicus*, fol. 130, second piece.
19 A few typical cadences also appear in other forms from this period in Praetorius' *Terpsichore* of 1612. In the modern edition by Günther Oberst in *Gesamtausgabe der musikalischen Werke*, Vol. XV, see the fifth *gavotte* on p. 6 (end of the first section) and the *bransles* on pp. 11 (end of the first and second sections of the first *Bransle simple de Poictu* and the end of the first section of the second *Bransle*), 23 (end of the second and third sections of the second *Bransle gentil*), 27 (end of the second *Bransle de la Royne*), and 28 (end of the first section of the sixth *Bransle*).
20 MS 33 748. Five of the Ballets are transcribed in *Die Tabulatur*, ed. Helmut Mönkemeyer, No. 25: *Nürnberger Lautenbuch*, Part III, pp. 99, 102–107.
21 The contents are listed in Dieckmann, pp. 101–105, with the Ballets on p. 103.
22 Robert Ballard, *Premier livre (1611)*, ed. André Souris and Sylvie Spycket, p. 11. All six of Mercure's Ballets are transcribed in *Oeuvres des Mercure*, ed. Monique Rollin and Jean-Michel Vaccaro (Paris, 1977), pp. 44–52 (Nos. 18–23). They occur in printed sources such as Fuhrmann's *Testudo gallo-germanica* (1615) and Van den Hove's *Delitiae musicae* (Utrecht, 1612), and in manuscripts at Kassel, Nuremberg, and Skokloster, Sweden, as well as a manuscript formerly at Danzig and now lost. See the concordances on pp. xxvii–xxviii of *Oeuvres des Mercure*.
23 Facsimile reprint (Gregg International, 1971), p. 180.

Chapter 7. The Vocal and Instrumental Tanz, Ballett, and Allmand in Germany 1598–1628

1 On the other hand, the publication *Johann-Jacobi Gastoldi und anderer Autorn Tricinia . . . mit teutschen weltlichen Texten . . . durch Valentinum Haussmann* (Nuremberg, 1617), copy at D-W, does not contain any Balletti by Gastoldi.
2 Repetitions in the music, however, are indicated correctly by sign as in the original Italian publication (see Plate XI), not written out as in the Flemish editions (Plate XII). Only the *tenore* book exists in the unique copy of this Nuremberg edition of the *Balletti a 3* at the Buffalo and Erie County Public Library. Therefore one cannot determine whether the lute tablature was actually omitted from the *cantus* book, as it was in the Flemish editions mentioned in Chapter 4.
3 A modern edition of the instrumental *Täntze* from the 1602 edition is in *DDT, 1. Folge*, Vol. 16: *Melchior Franck, Valentin Haussmann, Ausgewählte Instrumentalwerke*, ed. Franz Bölsche, revised edition by Hans Joachim Moser (Leipzig, 1958), pp. 115–122.
4 A modern edition of the entire book is in *Publikation älterer praktischer und theoretischer Musikwerke*, Jahrgang XV, Vol. 15, ed. Friedrich Zelle (Leipzig, 1887). Those marked *Tantz* are Nos. XVI, XVII, XVIII, XXII, and XXV. Nos. XV, XX, XXI, and XXIII have *fa-las*.

5 *Ibid.*, Nos. XVIII and XXII.
6 See *DDT*, 1. *Folge*, Vol. 16, pp. 40–50.
7 Modern edition by Karl Geiringer in *DTÖ*, Jahrgang XXXVI/2, Vol. 70 (Vienna, 1929), pp. 1–24.
8 *Ibid.*, pp. 4 and 19.
9 D-W, MS Codex Guelferbytanus 18.7.Augusteus 2° and 18.8.Augusteus 2°, *Vierter Thail*, fols. 19^r for the first melody, fols. 20^v-21^r and 33^r-33^v for the other.
10 See Paul Mueller, "The Influence and Activities of English Musicians on the Continent during the Late 16th and Early 17th Centuries," Ph.D. dissertation, Indiana University, 1954.
11 I will deal only briefly in this book with the various ways in which dances are grouped together during the 17th and 18th centuries. For more information, I refer the reader to the detailed and excellently organized article "Suite" by David Fuller in *New Grove*, XVIII, 333–350.
12 A detailed chart of concordances between the two sources is on pp. 34–35 of Andrew J. Sabol's *Four Hundred Songs and Dances from the Stuart Masque*.
13 A facsimile of the 1619 edition of *Syntagma musicum*, III: *Termini musici*, is in *Documenta musicologica*, *Erste Reihe*, Vol. XV (Kassel: Bärenreiter, 1958). The chart is on p. 25, *Balletti* on pp. 18–19, and *Mascherada* on p. 3. On p. 19 Praetorius states, "Der andern Art Balli oder Ballete seynd, welche keinen Text haben . . . Ballet aber sein sonderliche Täntze zu Mummereyen und Uffzügen gemacht, welche zur Mascarada gespielet werden; Dieselbe werden uff ihre sonderliche *Inventiones* gerichtet, unnd hat ein jedes Ballet gemeiniglich drey Theil. 1. Die *Intrada*, wenn die Personen in der Mummerey zum eingang erscheinen. 2. Die *Figuren*, welche die vermascarirten Personen im stehen, tretten, auch umbwechsslung der Örther, und sonsten uff Buchstaben in eim Ringe, Crantze, Triangel, Vierecket, Sechsecket, oder andere Sachen formieren, und sich durch einander winden, darauff dann die gantze *Invention* und Essentia des Ballets bestehet und gerichtet ist. 3. Die *Retrajecte*, das ist der Abzug oder Abtritt, damit die *Invention*, unnd gantz Ballet geendet unnd beschlossen wird . . ." On p. 26: "Mascherada . . . ist uff deutsch ein Mummerey, wenn ihrer etliche mit Larven und Kleidern sich vermummen, und also in Panckcketen, und furnehmer Personen *Collationibus* mit einer Music erscheinen . . . und gehöret zu den Balletten . . ." See also Hans Lampl, "A Translation of Syntagma musicum III by Michael Praetorius," D.M.A. dissertation, University of Southern California, 1957, pp. 24, 56–57, and 71. Demantius repeats the same ideas in his *Isagoge artis musicae* (Freiberg, 1632): "*Balletti* seynd sonderliche Täntze zu Mummereyen und Auffzügen gemacht," and "*Mascherada* seynd sonderliche Auffzüge so in Mummereyen als wie *Ballette* gebraucht werden." See Hans Heinrich Eggebrecht, "Ein Musiklexikon von Christoph Demantius," *Die Musikforschung*, X (1957), 51 and 56.
14 Transcribed in Merian, pp. 234–240.
15 Concerning all these terms, see Margarete Reimann, "Materialien zu einer Definition der Intrada," *Die Musikforschung*, X (1957), 337–364; and Werner Braun, *Britannia abundans: Deutsch–englische Musikbeziehungen zur Shakespearezeit* (Tutzing: Hans Schneider, 1977), especially pp. 71, 153–156, and 169–172.
16 Modern edition in *Johann Hermann Schein, Neue Ausgabe sämtlicher Werke*, Vol. IX, ed. Dieter Krickeberg (Kassel: Bärenreiter, 1967). For a comparison of the opening bars of all the dances in one suite, see Kurt von Fischer's article "Variations" in *New Grove*, XIX, 544, Ex. 10.
17 The complete pieces are printed in *Neue Ausgabe sämtlicher Werke*, Vol. IX, pp. 48, 137, and 38–39, respectively.
18 *Samuel Scheidt, Werke*, Vol. II/III, ed. Gottlieb Harms (Hamburg, 1928), p. 20.
19 Only the tenor book exists today. For incipits, see *DTÖ*, Jahrgang XXXVI/2, Vol. 70, pp. 128–129.
20 *Ibid.*, pp. 61–77.
21 I was unsuccessful in obtaining a microfilm copy of any of the pieces from the unique copy of Posch's 1618 book at D-Rp. This particular *Balleta*, however, appears also in the collection *Amoenitatum musicalium hortulus* (1622), and from this source it is printed in *DTÖ*, Jahrgang XXXVI/2, Vol. 70, p. 131.
22 *Ibid.*, p. 129, from the title page of the reprint of Posch's books of 1618 and 1621 in *Musicalische Ehrn- und Tafelfreudt* (Nuremberg, 1626): "an fürnemer Herrn unnd Potentaten Tafeln, auch auff adelichen Panqueten, und Hochzeiten, und andern ehrlichen Convivijs."
23 *Ibid.*, p. 129 (also from the 1626 edition): "Balletten, welch am tauglichsten über der Tafel musicirt werden mögen. Nach diesem findt etliche Gagliarden und Couranten, deren jeden

innsonderheit ein Tantz darauff gehörig, angehenckt, können beydes zur Tafel gebraucht, oder darnach getantzt werden. Und weilen bisshero eine grosse Unordnung der Proportion daher entstanden, inn dem nemlich, die meisten Componisten, so dergleichen sonst im Druck aussgehen lassen keine oder doch wenig Proportionen ihren Täntzen zugesetzt, und also ein jeder Musicant seines gefallens (es sey recht, oder nicht) dieselbe Proportionirt: Und dann fürs dritte findet man auff einen jeden Tantz seine ordentliche Proportion wie sie jetziger Zeit gebräuchig, unnd die fürnembsten Täntzer darnach zu tantzen pflegen." See p. 339 in David Fuller's article "Suite" in *New Grove*, XVIII.

24 *EDM*, Vol. 29, Steffens' book ed. by Gustav Fock (Wolfenbüttel, 1958), pp. 55ff.
25 D-Bds, Mus.Ms. 40143, reproduced and transcribed by Johannes Wolf in *Handbuch der Notationskunde*, Vol. II (*Kleine Handbücher der Musikgeschichte nach Gattungen*, Vol. VIII [Leipzig: Breitkopf & Härtel, 1919; reprint, Hildesheim: Georg Olms, 1963]), pp. 89–90.
26 *Samuel Scheidt, Werke*, Vol. VI: *Tabulatura nova*, ed. Christhard Mahrenholz (Hamburg, 1953), Teil II, pp. 69–77 on *Soll es sein* and pp. 78–84 on *Also gehts, also stehts*.
27 *Syntagma musicum*, III, p. 25.

Chapter 8. The Vocal and Instrumental Balletto in Italy 1615–1640

1 For a list of *mascherate carnascialesche*, most published during the late 16th and early 17th centuries, see Federico Ghisi, *I canti carnascialeschi* (Florence: Leo S. Olschki, 1937), pp. 155–160.
2 The note is on p. 25 of Brunelli's book: "Questo Balletto se bene è a 5. si può cantare a una voce sola cioè il primo soprano, o a 2. cioè i dua soprani quali si possono cantare ancora in Tenore." Contents of the book are listed by Claudio Sartori in *Bibliografia della musica strumentale italiana*, Vol. I (Florence: Leo S. Olschki, 1952), pp. 220–222.
3 Copy at D-Hs, pp. 15, 19, 21, 23, 29, 31, and 33.
4 Copy at CH-E, p. 18. Two others are listed in the *Tavola*, but the pages are missing in this unique copy of the work.
5 Printed in *Tutte le opere di Claudio Monteverdi*, ed. G. Francesco Malipiero, Vol. X (1929), pp. 62–68.
6 Copy at I-Fn, pp. 34–45. Concerning the date of the *Ballo*, see the article on Gagliano by Edmond Strainchamps in *New Grove*, VII, 85.
7 Copy at GB-Och, pp. 21, 6, 1–3, and 22–25, respectively.
8 *Madrigali guerrieri, et amorosi* (Venice, 1638), printed in Malipiero's *Tutte le opere*, Vol. VIII, pp. 162–177 and 314–347.
9 Kapsberger later includes two other *Uscita–Ballo* pairs in his *Libro quarto d'intavolatura di chitarone* (Rome, 1640), copy at GB-Lbm, pp. 39 and 41.
10 See Edmond Strainchamps' article on Allegri in *New Grove*, I, 267.
11 *Intavolatura di liuto, et di chitarrone, Libro primo* (Bologna, 1623), pp. 52–54: "Balletto in diverse partite fatto a requisitione dell'Illustrissimo Signor Conte Alessandro Bentivogli, e ballato da essi Signori al numero de sedici, con apparato, & habiti bellissimi nella sua gran Sala in Bologna." See *Alexandri Piccinini, Opera* (*Antiquae musicae italicae, Monumenta bononiensia, I maestri del liuto* [Bologna, 1962–65]), Vol. I (facsimile) and Vol. II, transcribed by Mirko Caffagni on pp. 51–56.

Chapter 9. The Allemande for Lute, Clavecin, Guitar, Viol, and Ensemble in France 1630–1731

1 Marin Mersenne, *Harmonie universelle* (Paris, 1636), facsimile of the copy at Bibliothèque des Arts et Métiers, with introduction by François Lesure (Paris, 1963), Vol. II, pp. 164–165 of the first paging (*Livre second des chants*): "L'Allemande est une dance d'Allemagne, qui est mesurée comme la Pavanne, mais elle n'a pas esté si usitée en France que les précédentes . . . on se contente auiourd'huy de la jouër sur les instrumens sans la dancer . . . si ce n'est aux Balets."
2 F-Pn, MS Vm^6.5, fols. 3^v, 34^v, 44^r, and 345^v.
3 (Tutzing: Hans Schneider, 1981), Nos. 31/12, 35/1 and 75/19–21 on pp. 125, 140, and 499–500, respectively. He lists six more on pp. 519–521 as falsely attributed. Wendy Hilton, in *Dance of Court and Theater: The French Noble Style 1690–1725* (Princeton Book Company, 1981), says on p. 37, after describing the most popular dances, "Lully wrote an occasional pavane and allemande."

4 Modern edition by J. Gallay (Paris: Librairie des Bibliophiles, 1870), pp. 69–70: "oseriez-vous mesme avoir dans l'idée que leurs Majestez, qui sçavent merveilleusement donner le prix à toutes choses et en faire aussi toutes les différences, voulussent mettre en paralèlle quelque Dance que ce puisse estre avec ces charmants motets, avec ces fines Alemandes, avec ces autres beaux chants diversifiez qu'elles honnorent chaque jour de leur attention et de leur estime?"

5 Sébastien de Brossard, *Dictionaire de musique*, 3rd ed. (Amsterdam, n.d.). The word "Allemande" is not in the first edition published at Paris in 1703. Both are reprinted on microfiche from copies at US-Wc in *Musical Dictionaries*, Series I (Washington, D.C.: Brookhaven Press, 1976).

6 *Obras de Lope de Vega, Nueva edición, Obras dramáticas* (Madrid: Rivadeneyra, 1930), Vol. XII, p. 482.

7 Lope de Vega, *La Dorotea*, ed. Edwin S. Morby (Berkeley and Los Angeles: University of California Press, 1958), pp. 116–117, footnote 142: "Tristes danzas de España, ya murieron . . . ¿Qué se hicieron gallardas y pavanas . . . ? . . . y alemanas y brandos en saraos, ¿por qué se han de dejar de todo punto?"

8 *Ibid.*, p. 116: "ya se van oluidando los instrumentos nobles, como las danças antiguas . . . ¡Ay de ti, alemana y pie de gibao, que tantos años estuuistes honrando los saraos!"

9 According to Juan de Esquivel Navarro, on fol. 26ᵛ of *Discursos sobre el arte del dançado* (Seville, 1642; reprinted, Madrid, 1947, as Vol. IV of the *Publicaciones de la Asociación de Libreros y Amigos del Libro*), "Enseñase comunmente el Alta, quatro mudanças de Pavana, seis passeos de Gallarda, quatro mudanças de Folias, dos de Rey, dos de Villano, Chacona, Rastro, Canario, Torneo, Pie de gibado, y Alemana." See also the contract from 1626 mentioned in note 16 of Chapter 2.

10 Cotarelo y Mori, in *Colección de entremeses*, Vol. I, p. clxix, mentions the dancing of an *alemana* by the *infanta* and her ladies in 1648. See also the quotations from Calderón (probably between 1630 and 1650) and *Las fiestas bacanales* (1656) in note 16 of Chapter 2.

11 F-Po, Rés. 841: *Recüeilles de toutes les dances de bal qui ont été gravées depuis l'année 1700 jusqua la fin de l'année 1720*, Vol. I, pp. 59–70.

12 This melody by Lully appears in an arrangement for keyboard in F-Pn, MS Vm⁷.6307⁽²⁾ (*olim* 2750) and two other manuscript sources listed by Bruce Gustafson, together with the incipit, in *French Harpsichord Music of the 17th Century*, Vol. III, pp. 104–105.

13 Facsimile edition (Gregg International, 1972), pp. 58–64. The seven pages correspond to pp. 62–64, 66–68, and 70 in F-Po, Rés. 841.

14 See Hilton, *Dance of Court and Theater*, p. 37.

15 The article "Allemande" in *New Grove*, I, 279, is therefore misleading, I think, when it states that "the allemande apparently continued to be performed as a dance throughout the 17th and 18th centuries."

16 See *Passacaglio and Ciaccona: From Guitar Music to Italian Keyboard Variations in the 17th Century*, a publication of my Ph.D. dissertation as No. 37 of *Studies in Musicology* (Ann Arbor: UMI Research Press, 1981), p. 281.

17 *Oeuvres de Chancy, Bouvier, Belleville, Dubuisson, Chevalier*, ed. André Souris and Monique Rollin (Paris: CNRS, 1967), pp. 10–11 by Chancy and pp. 66–67 by Dubuisson from Pierre Ballard's *Tablature de luth* (1631), and pp. 16–17 by Chancy from Mersenne's *Harmonie universelle* (1636).

18 For a lute example in which each section is followed by a *double*, see *Oeuvres des Dubut*, ed. Monique Rollin and Jean-Michel Vaccaro (Paris: CNRS, 1979), pp. 13–15. For a separate keyboard *double*, see *Le Moutier, Allemande de Mʳ de Chambonnières* and *Double du Moutier par Mʳ Couperin*, printed in *Jacques Champion de Chambonnières, Oeuvres complètes*, ed. Paul Brunold and André Tessier (Paris, 1925; reprint, New York: Broude Brothers, 1967), pp. 54–55, and also in *LP 18: Louis Couperin, Pièces de clavecin*, ed. Alan Curtis (Paris, 1970), pp. 48–51.

19 *Oeuvres de René Mesangeau*, ed. André Souris and Monique Rollin (Paris: CNRS, 1971), pp. 40–41 (written out with variations).

20 *LP 18: Pièces de clavecin*, ed. Alan Curtis, p. 9: *Allemande l'Amiable* (an almost exact repeat of the end of the second section).

21 *Pieces for Harpsichord*, ed. Albert Fuller (New York: Alpeg Editions, 1959). Those on pp. 13 (in the *Allemande l'Incomparable*), 20, and 37 (*Allemande gaye*) are indicated by signs; that on p. 36 is written out with slight variations.

22 See *Musique et musiciens au XVIIᵉ siècle, Correspondance et oeuvre musicales de Constantin Huygens*, ed. W. J. A. Jonckbloet and J. P. N. Land (Leiden: E. J. Brill, 1882), pp. 23–24. Huygens, in a letter to Henry Du Mont dated 6 April 1655, questions the composer about an Allemande that has

twenty-four measures in its opening section, but only seventeen in the second. He mentions a rule that the two sections should be equal, or at least the second one longer. He says he follows in his own pieces certain great composers who confine themselves to twelve measures in each section. However, I have been able to locate only a single example with twelve bars per section – *L'encyclopédie, Allemande* in *Oeuvres des Dubut*, ed. Monique Rollin and Jean-Michel Vaccaro (Paris, 1979), pp. 26–27.

23 For many keyboard examples, see Gustafson, *French Harpsichord Music of the 17th Century*, Vols. II and III, which include one-measure incipits for each piece.
24 See, for example, every single Allemande in *Nicolas Lebègue, Oeuvres de clavecin*, ed. Norbert Dufourcq (Monaco: Éditions de l'Oiseau-lyre, 1956).
25 *LP* 18: *Pièces de clavecin*, ed. Alan Curtis (Paris, 1970), p. 38.
26 The four books of his *Pièces de clavecin* are edited by Kenneth Gilbert in *LP* 21–24 (Paris, 1969–72). For the third without a rest, see the *Premier livre* (1713), pp. 2 (*Allemande l'Auguste*) and 78 (*La Ténébreuse*). For examples followed by a rest, see the *Second livre* (1716–17), p. 58 (*Allemande à deux clavecins*), and the *Troisième livre* (1722), p. 72 (*Allemande La Verneüil*). In addition, Couperin's *L'Art de toucher le clavecin* (1717) contains an Allemande which, although not commencing with the rhythms in Ex. 59, does include many examples of tiny phrases concluded by the downward third. It is on p. 40 of Couperin's *Oeuvres complètes*, ed. Maurice Cauchie, Vol. I (Paris: L'Oiseau-Lyre, 1933). See also the chamber examples in *Oeuvres complètes*, ed. Maurice Cauchie, Vol. VIII, p. 193, and Vol. X, p. 117; an example without a rest is in Vol. IX, p. 251.
27 In *HAM*, Vol. I, see measures 3–5 of No. 84g: *Praeambulum in fa* from Kotter's tablature (c. 1520); measures 14–16 in No. 135: Andrea Gabrieli's *Intonazione settimo tono*; and measures 14–15 of No. 153, a toccata of Merulo. In *HAM*, Vol. II, see the toccata by Frescobaldi (No. 193), measures 4–6 and 7–8; and the *praeludia* by Scheidemann (No. 195a, bars 2–3, and No. 195b, bars 6–8).
28 *Oeuvres complètes*, ed. Maurice Cauchie, Vols. VII, VIII, and IX.
29 See the Allemande from *L'Art de toucher le clavecin* cited in note 26, as well as *Allemande L'Ausoniéne* from his *Second livre* of 1716–17 (p. 40 in *LP* 22), *Allemande La Verneüil* from the *Troisième livre* of 1722 (*LP* 23, p. 72), and *Le Point du jour* and *L'Exquise* from the *Quatrième livre* of 1730 (*LP* 24, pp. 30 and 112).
30 *LP* 59: *Jean-Philippe Rameau, Pièces de clavecin*, ed. Kenneth Gilbert (Paris, 1979), p. 20 from the 1724 book, and p. 62 from around 1728.
31 *Oeuvres de Chancy, Bouvier, Belleville, Dubuisson, Chevalier*, ed. André Souris and Monique Rollin (Paris, 1967), p. 30.
32 See *Oeuvres des Dubut*, ed. Monique Rollin and Jean-Michel Vaccaro (Paris, 1979), especially p. 24, but also perhaps pp. 26: *L'encyclopédie, Allemande*, and 28: *Caprice*.
33 The idea may have been borrowed from the *gavotte*, which, as a duple court dance introduced around mid-century, regularly commences on the third beat. In this case, however, the dance steps begin only on the first beat of the following measure. The Allemande, on the other hand, has no choreography to clarify the rhythm, since, as we have seen, it was not a social dance at that time. See Meredith Ellis Little's article "Gavotte" in *New Grove*, VII, 201.
34 *Oeuvres du vieux Gautier*, ed. André Souris and Monique Rollin (Paris: CNRS, 1966), p. 13: *Tombeau de Mezangeau*.
35 *Gaspard Le Roux, Pieces for Harpsichord*, ed. Albert Fuller (New York: Alpeg, 1959), p. 42.
36 *Oeuvres complètes*, ed. Maurice Cauchie (Paris, 1933), Vol. VII, pp. 14, 31, 55, and 82; Vol. VIII, pp. 11, 31, 50, 145, 149, and 193; and Vol. X, p. 117.
37 *Allemande L'Ausoniéne* from the *Second livre* in *LP* 22, p. 40, and *Le Point du jour* from the *Quatrième livre* in *LP* 24, p. 30.
38 *Oeuvres du vieux Gautier*, ed. André Souris and Monique Rollin (Paris, 1966), pp. 6 and 8: *Allemande le languetock ou la Pompe funèbre ou bien le Bucentaure*.
39 *Oeuvres des Dubut*, ed. Monique Rollin and Jean-Michel Vaccaro (Paris, 1979), p. 18 (Ex. 60e at end of the first line), p. 36 (Ex. 60d at end of the first section; Ex. 60e end of the second), and p. 41 (Ex. 60e in the middle of the first section).
40 *Ibid.*, p. 18, beginning of the last line to a'; p. 19, middle line to d'; and p. 25, end of the first line and the beginning of the second, to e'.
41 *Oeuvres des Mercure*, ed. Monique Rollin and Jean-Michel Vaccaro (Paris: CNRS, 1977), p. 111.
42 *Oeuvres complètes*, ed. Paul Brunold and André Tessier (Paris, 1925; reprint, New York: Broude

Brothers, 1967), pp. 6: *Allemande La Dunquerque* (middle and end of the second section), 10: *Allemande La Loureuse* (middle and end of the first section), 17 (end), and 75: *Allemande La Mignonne* (middle of second section).
43 *Ibid.*, p. 10 (end of first section).
44 *Ibid.*, p. 37 (end of piece).
45 *LP* 18: *Pièces de clavecin*, ed. Alan Curtis (Paris, 1970), pp. 9: *Allemande l'Amiable* (middle and end of second section), 78 (end), 103: *Allemande de la Paix* (middle and end of the first section, middle of second), and 122 (end of first section).
46 *Ibid.*, p. 33, line 5.
47 *Oeuvres de clavecin*, ed. Norbert Dufourcq (Monaco: Éditions de l'Oiseau-lyre, 1956), pp. 53 (end of first line), 62 (end of first section, middle and end of the second), and 79 (end of first section).
48 *Ibid.*, p. 54, line 4, and p. 79, line 6.
49 *LP* 54: *Pièces de clavecin*, ed. Kenneth Gilbert (Paris, 1975), p. 147 (middle of second section).
50 *Six suites pour clavecin*, ed. Paul Brunold (Paris: Éditions de l'Oiseau-lyre, 1934), pp. 4 (end of first section, with first note tied over), 25 (middle of first section), and 34–35 (end).
51 *Ibid.*, pp. 15 (end of first section), 25 (middle and end of each section), and 34 (end of the first bar and the first section).
52 *Pieces for Harpsichord*, ed. Albert Fuller (New York: Alpeg, 1959), pp. 3: *Allemande La Vauvert* (middle and end of the first section), 20: *Allemande gaye* (end), and 37: *Allemande gaye* (end of first section).
53 *Ibid.*, p. 43 (end of first section).
54 *LP* 22: *Second livre*, ed. Kenneth Gilbert (Paris, 1969), p. 60: *Allemande à deux clavecins* (middle of second section). This cadence reflects the increasing number of *agréments* in keyboard music: the opening note has a trill, the second a mordent, and the dotted note a trill.
55 *LP* 59: *Pièces de clavecin*, ed. Kenneth Gilbert (Paris, 1979), p. 5 (first and third bars of the second section, both with 5 on the first eighth-note beat).
56 *LP* 24: *Quatrième livre*, ed. Kenneth Gilbert (Paris, 1970), pp. 30–31: *Le Point du jour*.
57 *Publications de la Société Française de Musicologie, Première série*, Vol. XIX, ed. Martine Roche (Paris, 1971), pp. 36 and 24, respectively.
58 Richard T. Pinnell, *Francesco Corbetta and the Baroque Guitar* (*Studies in Musicology*, No. 25 [Ann Arbor: UMI Research Press, 1980]), Vol. II, pp. 293: *Allemande La Royalle* from the 1671 book (third measure) and 362: *Allemande* from the 1674 book (second measure).
59 *Oeuvres complètes pour guitare*, ed. Robert W. Strizich in *LP* 15 (Paris, 1969), p. 72 (middle of first section).
60 Pinnell, *Francesco Corbetta*, Vol. II, pp. 222: *Allemande aymée de l'auteur* (fourth measure), 270: *Allemande La Canossa* (middle of first section), 282 (end), and 289 (end) from the 1671 book, and p. 341 (fifth measure) from 1674.
61 *Ibid.*, Vol. II, pp. 318–321, for the entire vocal piece.
62 *LP* 15, ed. Robert W. Strizich, pp. 2 (middle of second section), 13: *Allemande La Conversation* (sixth bar of second section), and 38 (end of the opening section) from his 1682 book, and pp. 63 (end) and 73 (middle of first section) from the 1686 book.
63 Pinnell, *Francesco Corbetta*, Vol. II, p. 282 (measure 4) for Ex. 61b, and p. 259 (fourth bar of the second section) for Ex. 61c. A cadence in which 5 and 7 replace the first two eighth-notes of Ex. 61b occurs on p. 225 (end of opening section).
64 *Ibid.*, pp. 213: *Allemande faite sur l'emprisonnement du Duc de Bouquingam* (fourth full bar of the second section) and 289 (end of the first section).
65 *Oeuvres des Dubut*, ed. Monique Rollin and Jean-Michel Vaccaro (Paris, 1979), p. 169: *Gavotte* (end).
66 For examples of Ex. 60b in the *gavotte*, see Dieupart, *Six suites pour clavecin*, ed. Paul Brunold (Paris, 1934), pp. 9 (end of first section), 18 (end), and 49 (end). It is also at the end of the opening section of his *Ouverture* on p. 42, and Ex. 60c occurs at the end of the *Gavotte* on p. 28. Examples of Ex. 60b in the *bourrée* occur in *Nicolas Lebègue, Oeuvres de clavecin*, ed. Norbert Dufourcq (Monaco: Éditions de l'Oiseau-lyre, 1956), p. 87 (end of each section), and in *LP* 15: *Robert de Visée, Oeuvres complètes pour guitare*, ed. Robert W. Strizich (Paris, 1969), pp. 8 (end of first section), 21 (end), and 58–59 (end).
67 See F-Pn, MS Vm^6.5, the end of the first and/or second sections of seven *gavottes* from 1657 to

1667 on fols. 9^r, 25^r, 28^v, 41^r, 43^v, 44^v, and 50^v, and six *bourrées* from 1656 to 1672 on fols. 5^r (first one), 12^v, 28^v, 30^r (first one), 44^r, and 85^r. There is also a *pavanne* on fol. 330^v from 1690 that ends with Ex. 60b.

68 *Oeuvres des Mercure*, ed. Monique Rollin and Jean-Michel Vaccaro (Paris, 1977), p. 81.
69 *Oeuvres des Bocquet*, ed. André Souris and Monique Rollin (Paris: CNRS, 1972), p. 79.
70 *LP* 18: *Pièces de clavecin*, ed. Alan Curtis (Paris, 1970), p. 103.
71 *Oeuvres complètes*, ed. Paul Brunold and André Tessier (Paris, 1925; reprint, New York: Broude Brothers, 1967), p. 1.
72 *Pieces for Harpsichord*, ed. Albert Fuller (New York: Alpeg, 1959), p. 12.
73 Incipit in Gustafson, *French Harpsichord Music of the 17th Century*, Vol. III, p. 63.
74 *Ibid.*, Vol. II, p. 29.
75 Pinnell, *Francesco Corbetta and the Baroque Guitar*, Vol. II, p. 394.
76 *Ibid.*, Vol. II, pp. 276–277 and 222.
77 *LP* 21: *Premier livre*, ed. Kenneth Gilbert (Paris, 1972), pp. 2, 36, and 78.
78 *Oeuvres du vieux Gautier*, ed. André Souris and Monique Rollin (Paris, 1966), pp. 14 and 13.
79 Reprint (Geneva: Minkoff, 1982), p. 3.
80 Pinnell, *Francesco Corbetta*, Vol. II, p. 203.
81 *LP* 15; *Oeuvres complètes pour guitare*, ed. Robert W. Strizich (Paris, 1969), p. 32.
82 Incipit in Gustafson, *French Harpsichord Music of the 17th Century*, Vol. III, p. 66.
83 *Oeuvres du vieux Gautier*, ed. André Souris and Monique Rollin (Paris, 1966), p. 10. See Thurston Dart in *The Galpin Society Journal*, No. 11 (May, 1958), Ex. 69 on pp. 57–58.
84 *Oeuvres complètes*, ed. Paul Brunold and André Tessier (Paris, 1925; reprint, New York: Broude Brothers, 1967), p. 99.
85 Pinnell, *Francesco Corbetta*, Vol. II, p. 212.
86 *LP* 18: *Pièces de clavecin*, ed. Alan Curtis (Paris, 1970), p. 67.
87 Pinnell, *Francesco Corbetta*, Vol. II, p. 382.
88 *LP* 18: *Pièces de clavecin*, ed. Alan Curtis (Paris, 1970), p. 110.
89 See Gustafson, *French Harpsichord Music of the 17th Century*, Vol. II, p. 425 (two examples), and Vol. III, pp. 243 and 249 (for organ, clavecin, or three viols).
90 *Ibid.*, Vol. III, p. 59, with the instruction "il faut couler les nottes."
91 *Pieces for Harpsichord*, ed. Albert Fuller (New York: Alpeg, 1959), pp. 8 and 25.
92 See Gustafson, *French Harpsichord Music of the 17th Century*, Vol. III, p. 56.
93 *Ibid.*, Vol. II, p. 29.
94 *Oeuvres de clavecin*, ed. Norbert Dufourcq (Monaco: Éditions de l'Oiseau-lyre, 1956), p. 14.
95 *LP* 54: *Pièces de clavecin*, ed. Kenneth Gilbert (Paris, 1975), p. 76.
96 See Gustafson, *French Harpsichord Music of the 17th Century*, Vol. III, p. 13.
97 *Pieces for Harpsichord*, ed. Albert Fuller (New York: Alpeg, 1959), pp. 20 and 37.
98 *Oeuvres complètes*, ed. Maurice Cauchie (Paris, 1933), Vol. VII, p. 31.
99 *Ibid.*, Vol. VIII, pp. 11 and 50.
100 *Ibid.*, Vol. VIII, p. 193.
101 *Ibid.*, Vol. I, p. 40.
102 *LP* 22: *Second livre*, ed. Kenneth Gilbert (Paris, 1969), p. 40.
103 *LP* 24: *Quatrième livre*, ed. Kenneth Gilbert (Paris, 1970), p. 30.
104 *Oeuvres complètes*, ed. Maurice Cauchie (Paris, 1933), Vol. X, p. 117, and Vol. VIII, pp. 149 and 31, respectively. The first is also on p. 5 of *LP* 51: *François Couperin, Pièces de violes*, ed. Lucy Robinson (Paris, 1973).
105 *LP* 21: *Premier livre*, ed. Kenneth Gilbert (Paris, 1972), pp. 117 and 36.
106 *Oeuvres complètes*, ed. Maurice Cauchie (Paris, 1933), Vol. VIII, p. 145, and Vol. IX, p. 251.
107 *Ibid.*, Vol. IX, p. 91.
108 *Ibid.*, Vol. VII, p. 31.
109 See Gustafson, *French Harpsichord Music of the 17th Century*, Vol. III, p. 352.
110 *Oeuvres du vieux Gautier*, ed. André Souris and Monique Rollin (Paris, 1966), pp. 76 and 83 for the music, p. XXIV for the concordances for Nos. 57 and 63, p. XXXI for comments, and p. 111 for a second version of *La Poste* on p. 83.
111 Reprint (Geneva: Minkoff, 1982), pp. 5–8 and 16–19.
112 F-Pn, MSS Rés. Vm^7 674 & 675. The Allemande on fol. 27^v of the second numbering corresponds to the gigue on fol. 45^v, that on fol. 28^v to the gigue on fol. 43^r.

113 See David Fuller's article "Suite" in *New Grove*, XVIII, 339. For a *Recherche*, *Allemande*, and *Courante*, see *Oeuvres de Chancy, Bouvier, Belleville, Dubuisson, Chevalier*, ed. André Souris and Monique Rollin (Paris, 1967), pp. 18–20.

Chapter 10. The Balletto and Alemanda for Guitar, Keyboard, and Ensemble in Italy 1640–1730

1 The lutenists, for their part, almost completely avoided the passacaglia, the form most closely identified with the guitar. See Volume III in my set *The Folia, the Saraband, the Passacaglia, and the Chaconne* (American Institute of Musicology, *Musicological Studies & Documents*, No. 35 [Neuhausen–Stuttgart: Hänssler, 1982]), p. xxvii.
2 Copy at I-Vnm. The piece in No. 98a is also on p. 22 of this publication, which is reprinted in *Archivum musicum, Collana di testi rari* 20 (Florence: Studio per Edizioni Scelte, 1979).
3 *Ibid.*, third page of *A' i lettori*.
4 For details concerning Corbetta's travels, influence, and life, as well as information on other guitar composers, see Pinnell, *Francesco Corbetta and the Baroque Guitar*, Vol. I, pp. 93–95, for example.
5 See my dissertation *Passacaglio and Ciaccona: From Guitar Music to Italian Keyboard Variations in the 17th Century* (*Studies in Musicology*, No. 37 [Ann Arbor: UMI Research Press, 1981]), p. 96.
6 Giovanni Battista Granata, *Novi capricci armonici musicali in vari toni* (Bologna, 1674), copy at I-Bc, pp. 6–7.
7 Concerning the Italian guitar literature and influences on it, see my article "The Music in Italian Tablatures for the Five-Course Spanish Guitar," *Journal of the Lute Society of America*, IV (1971), especially Figures 2 and 3 on pp. 26 and 38–39.
8 *Vari capricii per la ghittara spagnuola* (Milan, 1643), copy in I-Bc. The complete book is transcribed by Richard Pinnell in *Francesco Corbetta and the Baroque Guitar*, Vol. II.
9 Pierre Trichet, *Traité des instruments de musique*, modern edition (Paris, 1957; reprint, Geneva: Minkoff, 1978), p. 158: "grandement usité parmi les français et italiens."
10 *Ibid.*, "avec mille gestes et mouvements du corps autant crotesques et ridicules que leur jeu est bigearre et confus."
11 Giovanni Paolo Foscarini, *Li cinque libri* (Rome, 1640), reprinted in *Archivum musicum, Collana di testi rari* 20 (1979), last page of *A' i lettori*: "le Sonate, come Corrente, Balletti, e Gagliarde, che vanno nello stile Francese, si devano sonare quietamente."
12 Trichet, *Traité des instruments de musique* (Paris, 1957; reprint, Geneva: Minkoff, 1978), pp. 158–159: "Toutesfois quelques-uns de nostre nation le quittent tout à faict pour prendre et apprendre le jeu de la guiterre."
13 The *Balletto a 3* by Martino Pesenti, in *Il primo libro delle Correnti alla francese per sonar nel clavicembalo* (Venice, 1635), copy in I-Bc, p. 25, also has a form of contrasting sections, in which the fourth and last section is mostly in triple meter.
14 There are also separate Balletti in Bartolomé de Selma y Salaverde's *Primo libro Canzoni, Fantasie et Correnti* (Venice, 1638), copy at PL-WRu, pieces No. 29 and 30: *Balletto a doi*, and piece No. 42: *Balletto a 3*.
15 The contents of all these Italian chamber works are listed in Claudio Sartori, *Bibliografia della musica strumentale italiana stampata in Italia fino al 1700*, Vols. I and II (Florence, 1952 and 1968). Plucked-string music is not included in this work. For the Boccella book, see Vol. I, pp. 416–417, and Vol. II, pp. 122–123.
16 See *Les oeuvres de Arcangelo Corelli*, ed. J. Joachim and F. Chrysander (London, c. 1890), Vols. I, pp. 73ff, and II, pp. 193ff (trio sonatas), Vol. III, pp. 69ff (violin sonatas), and Vol. V, pp. 171ff (concerti grossi).
17 Most of the works listed in Table 3 are cited in full in Volume II. For this study I also obtained copies of the following works, which are arranged chronologically within three categories: those with only Balletti, those with only Alemande, and those with both. A letter following the year refers to the entry in Sartori's *Bibliografia*.

WORKS WITH BALLETTI:
    Cazzati, Maurizio, *Trattenimenti per camera d'Arie, Correnti, e Balletti a due violini, e violone* (Bologna, 1660a), copy at I-Bc.

Cazzati, Maurizio, *Correnti e Balletti a cinque, alla francese, et all'italiana* (Bologna, 1667b), copy at GB-Ob.
Uccellini, Marco, *Sinfonici concerti . . . con Brandi, e Correnti alla francese, e Balletti al italiana* (Venice, 1667g), copy at I-Bc.
Colombi, Giuseppe, *Balletti, Correnti, Gighe, Sarabande a due violini, e violone o spinetta* (Bologna, 1674c), copy at I-MOe.
Degli Antoni, Giovanni Battista, *Balletti, Correnti, Gighe, e Sarabande da camera a violino, e clavicembalo o violoncello* (Bologna, 1677a), copy at I-Bc.
Bassani, Giovanni Battista, *Balletti, Correnti, Gighe, e Sarabande a violino, e violone, overo spinetta, con il secondo violino a beneplacito* (Bologna, 1677c), copy at I-Bc.
Grossi, Andrea, *Balletti, Correnti, Sarabande, e Gighe a tre, Opera prima* (Bologna, 1678g), copy at GB-Ob; *Opera seconda* (Bologna, 1679a), copy at I-Bc.
Piazzi, Carlo, *Libro primo Balletti, Correnti, Gighe, e Sarabande a tre* (Bologna, 1681b), copy at I-Bc.
Albergati, Pirro, *Balletti, Correnti, Sarabande, e Gighe, a violino e violone, con il secondo violino a beneplacito* (Bologna, 1682e), copy at I-Bc.
Vitali, Giovanni Battista, *Balletti, Correnti, e Capricci per camera a due violini, e violone* (Modena, 1683e), copy at I-Bc.
Vitali, Giovanni Battista, *Balli in stile francese a cinque stromenti* (Modena, 1685j), copy at I-Bc.
Monari, Clemente, *Balletti e Correnti da camera a due violini, con il suo Basso continuo* (Bologna, 1686e), copy at I-Bc.
Marino, Carlo Antonio, *Sonate da camera a tre strumenti* (Bologna, 1687i), copy at I-Bc.
Brasolini, Domenico, *Suonate da camera a tre* (Bologna, 1689n), copy at GB-Ob.
Mazzella, Salvatore, *Balli, Correnti, Gighe, Sarabande, Gavotte, Brande, e Gagliarde* (Rome, 1689a), copy at GB-Lbm.
Vitali, Giovanni Battista, *Artificii musicali* (Modena, 1689i), copy at I-MOe.
Degli Antoni, Giovanni Battista, *Balletti a violino, e violoncello, o clavicembalo* (Bologna, 1690d), copy at GB-Ob.
Belisi, Filippo Carlo, *Balletti, Correnti, Gighe, e Sarabande da camera a due violini, e violoncello, con il suo Basso continuo* (Bologna, 1691c), copy at I-Bc.
Legrenzi, Giovanni, *Balletti e Correnti a cinque stromenti* (Venice, 1691h), copy at GB-Ob.
Vitali, Giovanni Battista, *Sonate da camera a tre* (Modena, 1692d), copy at I-Bc.
Ariosti, Attilio, *Divertimenti da camera a violino, e violoncello* (Bologna, 1695f), copy at I-Bc.
(See also in Sartori, 1651d and 1654a by Cazzati, 1665d by Marieta Morosina Priuli, 1669c by Elzeario Pizzoni, 1673e by Agostino Guerrieri, and 1692g by Carlo Antonio Marino.)

WORKS WITH ALEMANDE:
Bononcini, Giovanni Maria, *Arie, Correnti, Sarabande, Gighe, & Allemande a violino, e violone, over spinetta* (Bologna, 1671e), copy at I-Bc.
Caldara, Antonio, *Suonate da camera a due violini, con il Basso continuo* (Venice, 1699c), copy at I-Bc.
(See also Sartori 1669g, 1671f, 1673i, and 1677f by Bononcini, 1688a by Pietro Sanmartini, and 1693a by Paris Francesco Alghisi.)

WORKS WITH BOTH BALLETTI AND ALEMANDE:
Cazzati, Maurizio, *Varii, e diversi capricci per camera e per chiesa, da sonare con diversi instromenti* (Bologna, 1669a), copy at I-Bc.
Degli Antoni, Pietro, *Arie, Gighe, Balletti, Correnti, Allemande, e Sarabande a violino, e violone, o spinetta, con il secondo violino a beneplacito* (Bologna, 1670b), copy at I-Bc.
Polaroli, Orazio, *Correnti, Balletti, Gighe, Allemande, Arie, etc., overo Suonate da camera a tre* (Bologna, 1673d), copy at GB-Ob.
Legrenzi, Giovanni, *Suonate da chiesa, e da camera, Correnti, Balletti, Allemande, e Sarabande a tre* (Venice, 1682f), copy at A-Wn.
Placuzzi, Gioseffo Maria, *Il numero sonoro* (Bologna, 1682i), copy at GB-Ob.
Torelli, Giuseppe, *Concertino per camera a violino e violoncello* (Bologna, no date: see Sartori, Vol. I, p. 545), copy at I-Bc.
Brevi, Giovanni Battista, *Bizzarie armoniche overo Sonate da camera a tre strumenti* (Bologna, 1693d), copy at I-Bc.

(See also Sartori 1667d and 1675b of Bononcini, 1678c by Giovanni Buonaventura Viviani, 1681d by Tomaso Motta, 1681f by Francesco Ballarotti, and 1700d by Giacomo Cattaneo.)

18 Marco Uccellini also published in 1667 his *Sinfonici concerti . . . per chiesa, e per camera. Con Brandi, e Corenti alla Francese, e Balletti al Italiana, giusta l'uso aprovatissimo della corte di Parma* (Venice), copy at I-Bc. All the *brandi* and *correnti* include the expression *per ballare* in their titles, whereas the *balli* do not. Every *ballo*, however, is in some triple meter, although the entire group is preceded by a duple *Introdutione de' Balli al Italiana*.
19 Reprint (Gregg International, 1972), pp. 22–23: "Il tempo binario s'adopera per lo più in quelle danze, che speditamente, e con prestezza deono esser ballate: come per esemplo la Giga, la Gavotta, la Burè, il Rigodone, l'Alamanda, ed altre simili."
20 All that survives of this work is a copy of the title page and preface. It is printed in Sartori's *Bibliografia*, Vol. I, p. 412: "Nelle Corrente, e Balletti, si dovrà osservare il tempo allegro, acciò apparischino di maggior vaghezza, e leggiadria."
21 *Balletti e Correnti da camera* (Bologna, 1686), copy at I-Bc.
22 *Balli, Correnti, Gighe, Sarabande, Gavotte, Brande, e Gagliarde* (Rome, 1689), copy at GB-Lbm, p. 5: *Ballo secondo*, and pp. 20–21: *Ballo sesto*.
23 See his *Sonate a violino solo e violoncello col cimbalo* (Paris, 1712), modern edition in *Recent Researches in the Music of the Baroque Era*, Vol. XX (Madison, Wisconsin: A-R Editions, 1975), ed. Barbara Garvey Jackson. Although most of the Alemande are notated in the usual way, those on pp. 2 and 114, like the keyboard examples of F. Couperin mentioned in the previous chapter, are in 2/4.
24 See *The Manchester Violin Sonatas* (after 1718), ed. Michael Talbot in *Recent Researches in the Music of the Baroque Era*, Vol. XXVI (1976), and the trio sonatas from 1705 and 1709 in *Le opere di Antonio Vivaldi*, ed. Gian Francesco Malipiero (Rome: Edizioni Ricordi, 1947–), F.XIII, Nos. 17, 19, 20, 22, 23, 25, 26, 32, 35, 38, 40, 43, 44, 45, and 46. Nos. 21 and 34 are *presto*. The Alemanda in the cello sonata F.XIV, No. 9, on the other hand, is marked *andante*.
25 Maurizio Cazzati, *Varii, e diversi capricci per camera, e per chiesa* (Bologna, 1669), copy at I-Bc, p. 42.
26 Gioseffo Placuzzi, *Il numero sonoro* (Bologna, 1682), copy at GB-Ob, p. 4 in each partbook.
27 Orazio Polaroli, *Correnti, Balletti, Gighe, Allemande, Arie* (Bologna, 1673), copy at GB-Ob, p. 7 of the *violino primo* and *secondo* books, p. 6 in the *violone, spinetta, o tiorba* book.
28 See *Michele Mascitti, Psyché*, ed. Frits Noske in the series *Antiqua* (Mainz: Schott, 1959), pp. 18–19: *La noce, Allemanda*; and F. M. Veracini, *Zwölf Sonaten Opus 1*, ed. Walter Kolneder (Leipzig: Peters, 1958), Vol. I, pp. 16–17 and 26–29, and Vol. II, pp. 24–26.
29 Jacopo Peri, *Le musiche sopra l'Euridice* (Florence, 1600), facsimile edition by Enrico Magni Dufflocq (Rome: Reale Accademia d'Italia, 1934), p. 30 (line 4), also printed in *HAM*, Vol. II, p. 1, last line (with note values halved). The cadence concludes the refrain that begins with the word "lacrimate." For other examples, see pp. 12 in the facsimile edition (second line from the end), and 46 (last line). I have included only the final words of the texts in Ex. 66, in order to show how the unaccented syllable fits the music.
30 See Monteverdi's *L'incoronazione di Poppea* in *Tutte le opere*, ed. G. Francesco Malipiero, Vol. XIII (1931). Ex. 66b is on p. 17, Ex. 66c on p. 46. See also pp. 21 (line 4), 22 (line 2), 26 (last bar), and 35 (last bars).
31 See *The Wellesley Edition*, No. 11: *Antonio Cesti, Orontea*, ed. William Holmes (1973). Ex. 66d is on p. 139 (line 2). See also pp. 9 (line 3), 10 (line 4), 70 (line 3), 78 (line 2), 79 (line 1), 93 (last bar), 110 (first line), and 155 (third line).
32 See *DTÖ*, Jahrgang III/2, Vol. VI. Ex. 66e is on p. 14 (line 3). See also p. 78 (last measure).
33 Although Pesenti includes typical cadences in the Balletti of Nos. 101 and 102, they also occur in his 1641 book in the *Passemezzo a doi* (p. 18, lines 4 and 5: Ex. 60e, and p. 19, lines 1 and 2: Exx. 60d and e) and the *Passemezo a tre* (p. 23, last line: Exx. 60e and a). For examples of Ex. 60a in the *passemezzi* of his 1645 book, see pp. 65 (lines 1 and 2), 66 (lines 4 and 5), and 67–69 (one or two examples in each line of the *Parte terza*); Ex. 60d is at the end of p. 65.
34 In Giovanni Battista Vitali's *Balletti, Correnti alla francese . . .* (Bologna, 1667), which contains the *Balletti per ballare* and *per camera* in No. 117, the opening section of the *Sinfonia prima* on p. 23 of the *violino primo* book concludes with an augmented version of Ex. 61f, the second section with Ex. 61a. Laurenti, in his *Sonate per camera* for violin and cello, includes diminished cadences in some of his Alemande (although not in the pieces in No. 124), as well as a slightly ornamented version of Ex.

242 Notes to pages 176-80

60b at the end of the first section of the *Aria di gavotta* on p. 9 of the manuscript copy of his book at I-Bc. Griffoni has numerous examples of the cadences in the Balletti and Alemande of his book of 1700 (including those in No. 127), but he also includes them at the end of the first section of the *gavotte* on pp. 10, 18, 26, and 45 of the *violino primo* book, as well as in the pieces entitled *preludio* on pp. 1 (end of the opening phrase and end of the piece), 8 (the last two bars), 16 (middle), 27 (middle and end), and 43 (end). Most of his cadences are like Ex. 60b or e. Finally, the manuscript from which the pieces in No. 128 come, includes also a *gavotta* on fol. 26^r in which each section ends with Ex. 60f.

35 Girolamo Frescobaldi, *Orgel- und Klavierwerke*, ed. Pierre Pidoux, Vol. III (Kassel: Bärenreiter, 1954), pp. 72, 73, 74, and 90. The second half of the last one is in 6/4 meter.
36 *Selva di varie compositioni d'intavolatura per cimbalo ed organo* (Venice, 1664), copy at I-Nc, pp. 77-79; transcribed by Barton Hudson in *CEKM* 7, pp. 117-121.
37 Transcribed by Oscar Chilesotti in *Lautenspieler des XVI. Jahrhunderts* (Leipzig: Breitkopf und Härtel, [1891]), pp. 228-231.
38 In the same book from 1655 that contains Marini's Balletti in No. 111, the *Balletto primo* presents a theme from his 1626 book, with three variations added. Marco Uccellini, in his *Sonate, Arie, et Correnti* (Venice, 1642), copy at D-Kl, has two sets called *Aria terza* and *Aria sesta sopra un Balletto*.
39 *The Operas of Alessandro Scarlatti*, Vol. VII (*Harvard Publications in Music*, 12), ed. Frank A. D'Accone (1982), p. 33, last line.
40 *CEKM* 5: *Bernardo Pasquini, Collected Works for Keyboard*, ed. Maurice Brooks Haynes, Vol. II, pp. 9 (Ex. 60e at the end of the first section and in the middle of the second), 12 (a variation of Ex. 61g at the end), 14 (Ex. 60f at the end of the first section, Ex. 60e in the middle and at the end of the second), 20 (Ex. 60e in the middle of each section, each time beginning with a rest), 23 (a variation of Ex. 61f at the end), 26 (Ex. 60e in the middle of the second section, with a rest), 29 (Ex. 60e at the end of the first section), 33 (Ex. 60f with a rest at the end of the first section), and 39 (Ex. 60e at the end of both sections).
41 *Ibid.*, Vol. III, pp. 29-42.

Chapter 11. The Allemande and Ballett for Ensemble and Keyboard in Germany and England 1636-1750

1 Modern edition in *EDM*, Vol. 49 (1957), ed. Helmut Mönkemeyer, pp. 35, 12, and 88.
2 *Ibid.*, the opening section on pp. 30 and 40.
3 *Ibid.*, pp. 21 and 75 (end of the first and third sections).
4 *Ibid.*, pp. 14 (second section) and 37 (second).
5 *Ibid.*, pp. 66, 82-83, and 86.
6 *Ibid.*, p. 37 (end of first section).
7 *Ibid.*, pp. 14 (end of the first section), 38 (second), 58-59 (second), 82-83 (first), and 88-89 (end).
8 Modern edition of all three books by Rudi A. Rasch in *'t Uitnement kabinet* (Amsterdam: Muziekuitgeverij Saul B. Groen, 1975). Balletten and Allemanden are in Vols. II, III, IV, VII, and VIII. The last letter of "Uitnement" is "t" in the original *Erste deel*, "d" in the *Tweede*.
9 *Ibid.*, Vol. II, pp. 6-8.
10 *Ibid.*, Vol. III, p. 10. The measures immediately following the opening section are probably a second ending that should replace the last four measures upon repetition of the section.
11 *Ibid.*, Vol. III, pp. 19-21: the *Derde, Vierde*, and *Vijfde Allemande*.
12 *Ibid.*, Vol. II, p. 14 (No. 15b especially), and Vol. VIII, p. 11, measures 4-6.
13 *Ibid.*, Vol. III, p. 14, measures 5-8.
14 *Ibid.*, Vol. II, p. 19.
15 *Ibid.*, Vol. III, p. 20 (end of first section).
16 *Ibid.*, Vol. III, pp. 18-19, end of first section of the *Eerste* and *Derde Allemande*.
17 *Ibid.*, Vol. III, p. 16, line 2.
18 *Ibid.*, Vol. III, pp. 17 and 14-16, respectively.
19 *Ibid.*, Vol. VIII, pp. 26-28.
20 *Ibid.*, Vol. III, pp. 19, 21, and 20.

21 Only the tenor partbooks of Schop's two books were available to me for study. I was unable to obtain microfilm copies of the outer voices from the Evangelisch-Lutherisches Pfarramt at Udestedt über Erfurt. I did obtain copies of the *altus*, *tenor*, and *quinta vox* from the 1640 edition of the *Erster Theil* at CH-Zz.
22 The Kassel manuscript is published in facsimile and transcription by Jules Echorcheville in *Vingt suites d'orchestre du XVIIe siècle français 1640–1670*, Vols. I and II (Paris and Berlin, 1906). The Stockholm manuscript is transcribed by Jaroslav J. S. Mráček in *Monumenta musicae svecicae*, 8: *Musica svecica saeculi XVII*, 5: *Seventeenth-Century Instrumental Dance Music in Uppsala University Library Instr. mus. hs 409* (Stockholm: Reimers, 1976). In the Kassel manuscript, each part is written, as usual, in mensural notation, whereas the music in the other manuscript is notated, curiously, in new German organ tablature.
23 Ecorcheville, Vol. II, pp. 25–30, 212–218, and 235–258.
24 Ecorcheville, Vol. II, pp. 157–159 and 46–48, and Mráček, pp. 6, 38–39, 42–44, 54–55, 94–95, and 241–243.
25 See Ecorcheville, Vol. II, pp. 46, 135 (second section), 172–173 (each section), and 220 (second); and Mráček, pp. 42, 54–55 (first and third sections), 59 (second), 72–73 (each section), 154, 183, 241–242 (both).
26 See Ecorcheville, Vol. II, pp. 19 (measures 7-8), 21 (measures 4-6), 231 (top line); and Mráček, pp. 54 (measures 6-8), 58 (measures 6-9), 95 (last line), and 184 (line 2).
27 For one of the few subtle examples I could find, see Mráček, pp. 54–55, where the motive in the second line of the first section reappears in bars 4-7 of the second.
28 Ex. 59a is in Ecorcheville, Vol. II, pp. 222 and 259 (see also 172), and Mráček, pp. 45, 154, and 241; Ex. 59b in Mráček, pp. 116 and 270.
29 Ecorcheville, Vol. II, pp. 20 (end of the first section), 31 (end of first), 66–69 (bar 9 and the end of the first section, bars 1 and 11 of the second), 86 (bar 4), 94 (end of first section), 135 (end of first), 157 (bar 6) and 261 (end of piece). See also Mráček, pp. 45 (end of first) and 146 (three bars from end).
30 Mráček, pp. 89 (first bar of line 3) and 95 (fourth bar of the second line).
31 Mráček, pp. 77 (fourth bar of line 2) and 137 (end of first section). This undiminished version of the cadence occasionally occurs in other forms in the same manuscripts. In Mráček, see the *bransles* on pp. 60–61 (end of piece), 124 (end of piece), and 185 (end). In Ecorcheville, Vol. II, see the *branles* on pp. 39 (end) and 125 (end of first section), and the *bourrées* on pp. 85 (end of first section) and 184 (end of piece).
32 Mráček, p. 146, first measure.
33 *Ander Theil newer Pavanen, Sonaten* . . . (Stade, 1654), copy at GB-Lbm, piece No. XIV in each partbook.
34 *Ibid.*, piece No. XI.
35 Four are printed in Mohr II, pp. 42–45. Ex. 60d appears on p. 45, the fourth bar of the second section.
36 *Synfonien, Intraden, Gagliarden* . . . (Bremen, 1657), copy in D-W, piece No. XXVII.
37 Printed in Mohr II, pp. 54–55.
38 *Ander Theil newer Paduanen, Galliarden* . . . (Bremen, 1660) copy at F-Pn, page preceding the first page of music, *An den wollmeinenden Leser*: "ist meine freundliche Bitte hiebey, dass . . . die Paduanen, Galliarden und Arien mit einem in etwas langsamen Tact, die Balletten, Couranten und Sarabanden, insonderheit die letzten Balletten die ich Ballo genennet, sind nach der frantzösischen Manier mit einem Bass und Discant gesetzet . . . mit einem lustigem Tact zu streichen."
39 See Mohr II, p. 53, measures 4, 6, and 8. The second section on p. 54 ends with triple meter.
40 Those in Vienna are described by Egon Wellesz in *Die Ballett-Suiten von Johann Heinrich und Anton Andreas Schmelzer* (Sitzungsberichte der Kais. Akademie der Wissenschaften in Wien, Philosophisch–Historische Klasse, Vol. 176, Part 5 [Vienna, 1914]), those at Kroměříž by Paul Nettl in *Studien zur Musikwissenschaft*, VIII (1921), pp. 45–175: "Die Wiener Tanzkomposition in der zweiten Hälfte des siebzehnten Jahrhunderts." Nettl printed examples of the music in *DTÖ*, Jahrgang XXVIII/2, Vol. 56: *Wiener Tanzmusik in der zweiten Hälfte des siebzehnten Jahrhunderts*.
41 See the impressive list of his compositions, including operas, oratorios, and masses, in *New Grove*, X, 680.

42 According to Wellesz, *Die Ballett-Suiten*, p. 36 (entry No. 36), this work was for Draghi's *Atalanta*.
43 *Ibid.*, p. 38 (Nos. 62 and 63).
44 *Ibid.*, the table on pp. 63–73. In sources from 1665 to 1672, J. H. Schmelzer has twelve Allemanden and twenty-seven separate dances called *Balletto*.
45 See the Nettl article, p. 131, entry No. 1.
46 *Ibid.*, p. 156.
47 *Ibid.*, pp. 158–159.
48 *Ibid.*, p. 157.
49 The music is printed by Nettl in *DTÖ*, Jahrgang XXVIII/2, Vol. 56, pp. 5–10. Concerning the date of the first performance of this opera, see Carl B. Schmidt, "Antonio Cesti's *Il pomo d'oro*: A Reexamination of a Famous Hapsburg Court Spectacle," *Journal of the American Musicological Society*, XXIX (1976), 381–390, and the article "Cesti" in *New Grove*, IV, 91–93.
50 For an engraving depicting this event, see *New Grove*, XIX, 97, and the article "Tourney" by Colin Timms. Concerning earlier equestrian Balletti in Italy, see Tim Carter, "A Florentine Wedding of 1608," *Acta musicologica*, Vol. LV (1983), p. 103; and Rudolf Gläsel, *Zur Geschichte der Battaglia* (Leipzig, 1931), pp. 24–26.
51 See Claudio Sartori, *Bibliografia della musica strumentale italiana*, Vol. II, pp. 145–146.
52 The music is printed by Wellesz on pp. 80–82 of his monograph.
53 Printed in *DTÖ*, Jahrgang XXVIII/2, Vol. 56, p. 1.
54 *Ibid.*, p. 40.
55 *Ibid.*, pp. 52–53: Balletto 1.
56 Printed in *Musikalische Werke der Kaiser Ferdinand III, Leopold I und Joseph I*, ed. Guido Adler, Vol. II (Vienna: Artaria, [1893]; reprint, Gregg International, 1972), p. 269. There is another *Allemande* by Leopold on p. 262.
57 *Musica antiqua bohemia*, Vol. XL (1959), pp. 2–3. The Allemanda is preceded by an *Intrada* and followed by a *Sarabanda* and a *Gigue*.
58 See *DTÖ*, Vol. 127, ed. Jiří Sehnal (Vienna, 1976), the *Allamande* on pp. 69–70, for example, in which a tied motive unifies the opening section and imitation begins the second.
59 *Ibid.*, p. 62, opening measure.
60 *Ibid.*, pp. 109–110, which include several examples of three sixteenth-notes moving to a longer note.
61 *Ibid.*, pp. 34 (three bars from the end of the first section), 35 (measure 3), 69 (measure 3 of the second section), and 110 (end). At the end of the *Allamanda* on pp. 91–92 is an ornamented version with pitches like Ex. 61d and rhythm like Ex. 61f.
62 *DTÖ*, Vol. 96: *Mensa sonora* (1680), ed. Erich Schenk (Vienna, 1960), pp. 28–29. The other Allemanda is on pp. 5–6.
63 For the first two, see *ibid.*, pp. 30 and 36. The *alla breve* Balletti are on pp. 14–15, 16–17, and 18. A cadence like Ex. 60b is in the fifth measure of the first section and measures 5 and 7 of the second section on p. 14, and in measure 3 on p. 18. An augmented version of Ex. 61d appears at the end of the Balletto on pp. 14–15.
64 *Ibid.*, pp. 5, 14, 16, 18, and 28.
65 *Ibid.*, p. 14.
66 *Ibid.*, pp. 16–17.
67 *Ibid.*, p. 30.
68 In *DTÖ*, Vol. 92, ed. Paul Nettl and Friedrich Reidinger (Vienna, 1956), see the Allemanden on pp. 7–8, 23, 32–33, 47–48, and 88–89. The Balletto with three sections is on p. 35, the other two on pp. 26–27 and 54–55.
69 *DTÖ*, Vol. 129, *Mensa harmonica*, ed. Rudolf Scholz and Karl Schütz (Graz, 1979), pp. 9–10 and 40.
70 *Ibid.* See the motivic unity in the first four bars of the Balletto on p. 9, and the sequence in the following two measures. *Fa-la* motives recur in the last line on p. 40.
71 *Ibid.*, pp. 9 (end of first section) and 40 (measure 7 of the second section).
72 In *DTÖ*, Vol. 89, ed. Erich Schenk (Vienna, 1953), see the Allemanden that commence on pp. 47, 7, and 106, the Ballo on p. 76.
73 *DTÖ*, Jahrgang I/2, Vol. 2, ed. Heinrich Rietsch (Vienna, 1894), the Balletten on pp. 45, 63, and 79, respectively.

74 *DTÖ*, Vol. 89, pp. 40 and 48 (end of second section) and p. 7 (end of first).
75 *DTÖ*, Jahrgang I/2, Vol. 2, the *Balet* on p. 45, the two phrases of section 1.
76 *DTÖ*, Vol. 89, pp. 47–48 and 106–107 (the rhythm in Ex. 59c).
77 *Ibid.*, pp. 7–8, compare measures 10-12 (or its *petite reprise* in measures 13-15) with measures 25-27 in the second section.
78 *DTÖ*, Jahrgang I/2, Vol. 2, p. 45 (outer voices at beginning), and *DTÖ*, Vol. 89, p. 47 (line 3).
79 *DTÖ*, Vol. 89, pp. 47 (end of first line) and 77 (canonic beginning of the second section).
80 *Ibid.*, pp. 106 (measures 7-8) and 107 (measures 7-8).
81 *Ibid.*, p. 107, and *DTÖ*, Jahrgang I/2, Vol. 2, p. 98.
82 Printed in Mohr II, pp. 52–53.
83 See *Hortus musicus*, Nos. 54–55: *Johann Pachelbel, Triosuiten*, ed. Fritz Zobeley (Kassel: Bärenreiter, 1960–66). In the *Allemand* on p. 3 of No. 54 (the first four bars of which are printed as Ex. 6b in *New Grove*, I, 279), Ex. 60e appears in the first violin part in measures 2 and 4, in the second violin in measure 6 of the first section and measures 4 and 5 and the end of the second. In the *Ballet* on p. 5 of No. 54 it is in the top voice of the second bar of the second section; in the *Allemand* on p. 6 of No. 55, it occurs in the upper voice in measure 5 of the opening section and measure 4 of the second, as well as in the second violin part in the following measure. A modified version of the cadence, in which the first repeated note is preceded by two sixteenth-notes on the pitches 3 and 2, occurs in all three pieces: in No. 54, p. 3, in the second violin in measure 4; in No. 54, p. 5, in the first violin at the end of the *Ballet* and at the end of the first section of the *Variatio*; in No. 55, p. 6, in the second violin at the end of the piece. The same rhythm, with the pitches 7 and 5 before the first repeated note, appears in No. 55, p. 6, in the top voice of measure 4. Note that in *New Grove*, I, 279, Ex. 6b, the two sixteenth-notes on the third beat of the fourth full measure in the second violin part are apparently printed incorrectly on the second half of the beat, where they produce parallel fifths with the top voice; the *Hortus musicus* version shows the sixteenth-notes on the first half of the beat.
84 Mohr II, p. 63, the end of each section and measure 11 of the second.
85 Mohr II, pp. 64–65 and 66.
86 *DDT, 1. Folge*, Vol. 10: *Orchestermusik des XVII. Jahrhunderts*, ed. Ernst von Werra (Graz and Wiesbaden, 1958). The Balletten are on pp. 97–98 and 128, the Allemanden on pp. 104–105, 123–124, and 133–134. Note especially the successive entries on pp. 123 and 124, the similar beginnings of the two sections, and the parallel activity in the second line of each section.
87 Two are printed in Mohr II, pp. 58–61. In the first, note the downward thirds in measures 2, 3, 5, and 6 of the first section, measures 1, 2 and 5 of the second. The diminished and dotted cadence (Ex. 60e) occurs at the end of the first section (ignoring the incorrect measure in brackets) and in the third bar of the second. Ornamented versions also appear in measure 4 of the first section and measure 5 of the second. The other Allemande ends with the cadence of Ex. 60e.
88 In *DDT, 1. Folge*, Vol. 18, ed. Karl Nef, rev. by Hans Joachim Moser (Graz and Wiesbaden, 1957), see especially the *Balli* on pp. 37–38, 56–57, 69–70, and 121–122.
89 *Ibid.* The *Balli* marked *presto* are on pp. 92–93 and 112, those that end *adagio* on pp. 69–70 and 132–133.
90 *Ibid.* Ex. 60e occurs in the top voice, for example, in the second measure of the second section of the Allemanda on p. 44, and at the end of the first section of the *Ballo* on p. 37 and the end of the *Ballo* on p. 122. Ex. 60d is in the next-to-top voice at the end of the first section on p. 34. Ex. 60b is in the next-to-top voice at the end of the *Ballo* on p. 93; it is preceded by a rest in this voice at the end of each section on pp. 70 and 133.
91 *Ibid.*, pp. 33–35, 44–45, and 119–120. For examples from *Studentenmusik* of 1654, see Mohr II, pp. 44 and 45.
92 *DDT, 1. Folge*, Vol. 63, ed. Arnold Schering (Graz and Wiesbaden, 1959). See especially the Balletten on pp. 45 and 61, and also the Allemanden on pp. 44–45 and 65.
93 *Ibid.* Ex. 60b occurs at the end of both sections on p. 65 and the end of the second in the Allemanda on pp. 44–45. A shifted version, with the bar-line between the two repeated notes, is at the end of the first section on pp. 44 and 66. One diminished form appears in the fifth measure of the Allemanda on p. 70.
94 Johann Christoph Pezel, *Bicinia* (Leipzig, 1675), copy at S-Uu, pieces No. 35 and 38 in the front of the book, and No. 15 in the *Appendix*.

246   *Notes to pages 190–5*

95 The complete Allemanda is in *DDT, 1. Folge*, Vol. 63, p. 111.
96 *Ibid*. Undiminished cadences are at the end of each section on p. 28, and in shifted form in measures 4-5 and at the end of the Allemanda on p. 34. Diminished cadences are at the end of the first section of the *Bal* on p. 29, and in measure 2 and the end of both sections of the *Bal* on p. 35. Pezel sometimes includes the cadences in other duple forms as well. See the examples from his 1669 book of the dotted and undiminished cadence (Ex. 60b) in a *Brandl* (p. 46 in *DDT, 1. Folge*, Vol. 63, end of first section), a *Sonata* (p. 63, end of page), and an *Intrade* (p. 70, measure 6). The same volume of *DDT* contains an example from 1685 of Ex. 61f at the end of the first section of an *Intrade* on p. 27, and examples of Ex. 60e at the end of both sections, as well as in measure 5 of the second section, in the *Intrade* on pp. 31–32. His *Bicinia* of 1675 (the work from which No. 30 comes) contains Ex. 60b in a *Sonatina* (end of piece No. 10), as well as examples of Ex. 60e in a *Sonatina* (end of No. 2) and an augmented version of Ex. 61f at the end of an *Aria* (No. 30), a *Gavotte* (No. 58), and two *Intraden* (Nos. 27 and 31 in the *Appendix*).
97 *Musicalische Frülings-früchte* (Hamburg, 1668), copy at GB-Lbm, piece No. 6. The complete Allemanda is transcribed in Mohr II, pp. 46–47.
98 See especially Pezel's Balletten in *DDT, 1. Folge*, Vol. 63, pp. 45 and 61. Scarlatti's Balletto, cited in note 39 of Chapter 10, is in the opening *Sinfonia* of his opera *Gli equivoci*.
99 *Georg Philipp Telemann, Musikalische Werke*, Vol. XXIV, ed. Adolf Hoffmann (Kassel: Bärenreiter, 1974), pp. 75–77 and 94–96.
100 By the time the Italian ideas were fully accepted in Germany very late in the Baroque period, there was little demand for the ensemble Allemanda and Ballett, since they were no longer popular court dances. Bach, for example, did not, as far as I know, include the Allemanda or Ballett in any of his ensemble works. Two Balletten from Francesco Antonio Bonporti's *Invenzioni da camera* (Bologna, 1712) for violin and continuo, however, were printed by error in Vol. XLV of the Bach-Gesellschaft edition of Bach's *Werke*, pp. 173 and 182–183. See Schmieder's *Thematisch–systematisches Verzeichnis*, pp. 643–644 (Anh.173–176), under "Fälschlich zugeschriebene Werke."
101 Incipits are given in Vol. II of Rudolf Flotzinger, "Die Lautentabulaturen des Stiftes Kremsmünster," Ph.D. dissertation, Universität Wien, 1964; see also *ibid*., Vol. I, pp. 200–202.
102 Darmstadt, Hessische Landes- und Hochschulbibliothek, Mus MS 18: "Neue Allemanden, Couranten, Sarabanden, Giquen [spelled, as in some other German sources, with a "q"], Cavoten [*sic*] unnd Canarien mit sonderbahrem Fleiss von der Angelique und Lau[ten] auff das Clavier gesetzt: auff einem Spinet zu spielen," fols. 8^v-9^r. The other source is Mus MS 17: "Allemanden, Couranten, Sarabanden, Giquen, Cavotten auss unterschiedlichen Tonen mit sonderbarem Fleiss von der Lauten und Mandor auff das Spinet von einem beedes der Lauten Mandor und dess Clavier Verständigen abgesetzet." See Gustafson, *French Harpsichord Music of the 17th Century*, Vol. I, p. 42.
103 Printed in *DTB*, Jahrgang XXI-XXIV, Vol. 32, ed. Felix Schreiber and Bertha Antonia Wallner, pp. 29–40 *passim* (nine Balletten and three Allemanden).
104 The works from both manuscripts are printed in *LP* 57: *Johann-Jakob Froberger, Oeuvres complètes pour clavecin*, Vol. I (1979), ed. Howard Schott.
105 *DTÖ*, Jahrgang VI/2, Vol. 13, ed. Guido Adler, pp. 36–81 *passim*. The suites on pp. 1–35 are the same ones in *LP* 57.
106 *EDM, Zweite Reihe*, Vol. 4, ed. Gerhard Ilgner (Leipzig, 1942), pp. 135 and 138.
107 The three Allemanden are on pp. 32, 2, and 22 of Schultheiss' *Muht- und Geist-ermuntrender Clavier-Lust, Erster Theil* (Nuremberg, 1679). I am currently preparing a modern edition of his complete keyboard works for *CEKM*.
108 *Ibid*., fifth page of the *Vorrede*: "Bevorab wann Sie ihnen werden belieben lassen, die Allemanden und Sarrabanden [*sic*] etwas langsam, die Couranten aber und Giquen etwas geschwinder und frischer zu spielen."
109 Microcard (MT 49) of the copy at Sibley Music Library, Eastman School of Music, fols. Q_3^v-S_1^r.
110 *DTÖ*, Jahrgang XIII/2, Vol. 27: *Wiener Klavier- und Orgelwerke aus der zweiten Hälfte des 17. Jahrhunderts*, ed. Hugo Botstiber (Vienna, 1906), pp. 5 (from the so-called *Rossignolo* suite) and 32–33.
111 *Johann Pachelbel, Suiten für Cembalo*, ed. Hans Joachim Moser and Traugott Fedtke (Hamburg: Musikverlag Hans Sikorski, 1968). Simpler ones with eighth-note movement are on pp. 7, 11,

and 14, for example; two with more sixteenth-note motion are on pp. 17 and 28. For the canonic sequence, see p. 35. There are twenty-one Allemanden and one Ballett in this volume.
112 Dietrich Buxtehude, *Klavervaerker*, ed. Emilius Bangert, 2nd ed. (Copenhagen: Wilhelm Hansen, 1944), p. 18. See also p. 45, as an illustration of the unifying effect of the three-sixteenth-note motive.
113 *DTÖ*, Jahrgang XIII/2, Vol. 27, pp. 44 and 47.
114 *Collected Keyboard Works*, ed. Willi Apel in *CEKM* 16 (American Institute of Musicology, 1967), pp. 80–81 and 85–86 for those with sixteenth-note movement, pp. 91–92 for the other.
115 *DDT*, 1. Folge, Vol. 4, ed. Karl Päsler (Leipzig, 1901), pp. 7–60 *passim*.
116 *DTB*, Jahrgang XVIII, Vol. 30, ed. Max Seiffert, pp. 7, 22, and 25.
117 *Ibid.*, p. 22.
118 *Ibid.*, pp. 19 and 25.
119 *Ibid.*, p. 12.
120 *Ibid.*, pp. 7–8.
121 *Monuments of Music and Music Literature in Facsimile*, First Series – *Music*, Vol. V (New York: Broude Brothers, 1965).
122 *DTÖ*, Vol. 115: *Suiten für Tasteninstrumente von und um Franz Mathias Techelmann*, ed. Herwig Knaus (Graz and Vienna, 1966). On pp. 39–40 is an *Alamande dell'Allegrezze alla Liberazione di Vienna*.
123 Georg Böhm, *Sämtliche Werke*, Vol. I, ed. Johannes Wolgast (Leipzig, [1927]).
124 *DTÖ*, Jahrgang III/3, Vol. 7: *Componimenti musicali per il cembalo*, ed. Guido Adler (Graz, 1959).
125 *Musicalischer Parnassus* (Augsburg, 1738), copy at D-As.
126 Both printed in the Bach-Gesellschaft edition of *J.S. Bach, Werke*, Vol. XXXVI, pp. 231–232 from the *Clavierbüchlein vor Wilhelm Friedemann Bach* (unified by a distinctive melodic motive), and Vol. XLII, pp. 255–256.
127 *Klavierwerke*, ed. Walter Serauky (Leipzig: Peters, no date), Vol. I, pp. 6–7 (from the suite in A major).
128 *Ibid.*, pp. 22–23 (from the suite in D minor).
129 *Ibid.*, Vol. III, pp. 8–9 (from the suite in G minor).
130 *Ibid.*, Vol. I, pp. 36 and 41–43, for example.
131 Poglietti has two *doubles* on pp. 5–8 of *DTÖ*, Jahrgang XIII/2, Vol. 27. See also *Pachelbel, Suiten für Cembalo*, pp. 50–51; Buxtehude, *Klavervaerker*, pp. 21–22; Kuhnaus *Klavierwerke* in *DDT*, Erste Folge, Vol. 4, pp. 39–40; and Mattheson's *Pièces de clavecin* (1714), pp. 4–5, 18–19, and 29–30.
132 *Kuhnaus Klavierwerke* in *DDT*, 1. Folge, Vol. 4, p. 11, and Gottlieb Muffat, *DTÖ*, Jahrgang III/3, Vol. 7, pp. 14–15, 24–25, 34–35, 48–49, 61–62, and 71–72.
133 *DTÖ*, Jahrgang III/3, Vol. 7, p. 14, for example, and p. 71.
134 Facsimile edition in *Documenta musicologica*, Erste Reihe, Vol. V (Kassel: Bärenreiter, 1954), p. 232: "Die Allemande nun ist eine gebrochene, ernsthaffte und wol ausgearbeitete Harmonie, welche das Bild eines zufriedenen oder vergnügten Gemüths trägt, das sich an guter Ordnung und Ruhe ergetzet."
135 Facsimile in *Documenta musicologica*, Erste Reihe, Vol. III (Kassel: Bärenreiter, 1953), p. 28: "welches ernsthafft und gravitätisch gesetzet, auch auf gleiche Art executirt werden muss."
136 In *Deliciae Studiosorum* (Nuremberg, 1640–43). See *DTB*, Jahrgang XXI–XXIV, Vol. 32, pp. xxv–xxviii, for a list of the contents of its four volumes. On pp. 56–57 is a transcription of a *Ballet* from the third and only volume still complete.
137 *EDM*, Erste Reihe, Vol. 12: *Lautenmusik des 17./18. Jahrhunderts*, ed. Hans Neemann (Braunschweig, 1939), the *Ballet* on p. 24 and Allemanden on pp. 3, 7, 10, 13, etc.
138 *Johann Pachelbel, Suiten für Cembalo*, p. 44.
139 *Musicalischer Parnassus* (Augsburg, 1738), copy at D-As, pp. 9 (*Balet anglois*) and 22–23 (*Ballet*), both marked *allegro*.
140 *CEKM* 16, pp. 74–79.
141 *DDT*, 1. Folge, Vol. 11: *Dietrich Buxtehude, Instrumentalwerke, Sonaten für Violine, Gambe und Cembalo*, ed. Carl Stiehl, new edition by Hans Joachim Moser (Graz and Wiesbaden, 1957), pp. 160–161.
142 *DTÖ*, Jahrgang XXV/2, Vol. 50: *Österreichische Lautenmusik zwischen 1650 und 1720*, ed. Adolf Koczirz (Graz, 1960), pp. 1 (Peyer), 19 (Losy), and 51 (*Tombeau de Mr. François Ginter* by Saint-Luc). See also the works for violin and lute (with or without a bass instrument): an Allemande by

Ferdinand Ignaz Hinterleithner (1699) on p. 7, an Allemande by Wenzel Ludwig Freiherr von Radolt (1701) on p. 26, two Allemanden and a Ballett by Saint-Luc on pp. 52–53, 64, and 58–59. For a guitar Allemande by Losy, see *Musica antiqua bohemica*, Vol. XXXVIII (Prague, 1965), p. 1.

143 *EDM, Erste Reihe*, Vol. 12: *Lautenmusik des 17./18. Jahrhunderts*, ed. Hans Neemann (Braunschweig, 1939), pp. 3, 7, 10, and 13–14 from 1667, and pp. 20–21, 23, 24, 26, and 29 from 1676.

144 From the translation of *Historisch–theoretisch und practische Untersuchung des Instruments der Lauten* (Nuremberg, 1727) by Douglas Alton Smith in *Study of the Lute by Ernst Gottlieb Baron* (Redondo Beach, Calif.: *Instrumenta Antiqua* Publications, 1976), p. 77.

145 *Sylvius Leopold Weiss, Intavolatura di liuto*, ed. Ruggero Chiesa (Milan, 1967), contains twenty Allemanden. See pp. 106–107 for a highly organized and melodious example.

146 Ex. 76a is in *Dietrich Buxtehude, Klavervaerker*, p. 48 (measure 5 of the second section) and in Johann Mattheson, *Pièces de clavecin*, p. 18 (measure 3 of second section). The same pattern, but with the first three pitches changed from 6-7-8 to 7-8-8, occurs in works of Froberger in *LP* 57, pp. 80 (measure 4) and 93 (end of first section). An example of this rhythm beginning with 1-1-2, and with the first note tied over, appears in *Johann Pachelbel, Suiten für Cembalo*, p. 37 (end of piece). Ex. 76b is in *EDM, Erste Reihe*, Vol. 12, p. 20 (end of the first section of *Allemanda* for lute by Reusner).

147 Händel, *Klavierwerke*, ed. Walter Serauky, Vol. I, p. 22 (end of first section). See also a similar example by Fischer in *Musicalischer Parnassus* (Augsburg, 1738), copy at D-As, *Allemande* on p. 13 (end of first section).

148 See the examples by Krieger in *DTB*, Jahrgang XVIII, Vol. 30, p. 25 (end of first section), and Reusner in *EDM, Erste Reihe*, Vol. 12, p. 23 (sixth bar of the first section, third bar of the second).

149 See *Dietrich Buxtehude, Klavervaerker*, p. 45 (end of first section), *Kuhnaus Klavierwerke*, *DDT, 1. Folge*, Vol. 4, pp. 7 (end), 22 (end), 25 (end of first section), and 53 (measure 3), and *EDM, Erste Reihe*, Vol. 12, p. 29 (end of *Allemanda* for lute by Reusner).

150 *DTB*, Jahrgang XXI–XXIV, Vol. 32, p. 40 (shifted so the bar-line comes between the two repeated notes); *DDT, 1. Folge*, Vol. 4, p. 57; *Pachelbel, Suiten für Cembalo*, p. 54.

151 For the cadence in Ex. 77b, see *DTÖ*, Jahrgang VI/2, Vol. 13, p. 72. For other examples by Froberger, see pp. 57 (measure 10), 60 (first bar of the second section), 64 (end of first section, measure 3 and the end of the second), and 77 (measure 2 and another in measure 3). The Allemande on p. 64 is also printed in *Masterpieces of Music Before 1750*, ed. Carl Parrish and John F. Ohl (New York: Norton, 1951), p. 148. See also *LP* 57, pp. 87 (measure 3) and 93 (end).

152 *DTÖ*, Jahrgang XIII/2, Vol. 27, pp. 5 (end of first section) and 33 (measure 3 of second section).

153 *Suiten für Cembalo*, pp. 10 (end of first section and first measure of the second), 17 (end), 22 (measure 7), 28 (measure 3 of the first section, measure 5 of the second), 37 (first bar of the second section), 40 (end of the first section and measure 3 of the second), 43 (end of first section), 46 (end of *Allemande I* and end of the first section of *Allemande II*), 50 (measure 6 and end of both sections), 54 (measure 3 of the second section), 57 (end of first section), and 60 (end of piece).

154 *Klavervaerker*, pp. 10 (fourth bar of second section), 15 (end of first section), 21 (measure 4 of second), 38 (measure 3), and 51 (measure 3 of the first section, measure 9 of the second).

155 *DTÖ*, Jahrgang XIII/2, Vol. 27, p. 44 (measure 4 of second section).

156 *CEKM* 16, pp. 74 (end), 91–92 (end).

157 *DTB*, Jahrgang XVIII, Vol. 30, pp. 12 (measure 3), 16 (measure 4 of second section), and 25 (measure 8).

158 *DDT, 1. Folge*, Vol. 4, pp. 28–29 (end), 56–57 (measure 2 of second section), and 60 (end).

159 *Pièces de clavecin*, pp. 22 (measure 4) and 38 (end).

160 *DTÖ*, Vol. 115, pp. 25 (end) and 58 (end of first section).

161 *Klavervaerker*, pp. 31 (measure 6, with the opening pitch in an inner voice) and 54 (end).

162 *DTÖ*, Jahrgang XIII/2, Vol. 27, p. 47 (end).

163 Pachelbel in *Johann Pachelbel, Suiten für Cembalo*, p. 35 (end of first section); Krieger in *DTB*, Jahrgang XVIII, Vol. 30, p. 19 (end).

164 *DTB*, Jahrgang XVIII, Vol. 30, p. 19, end of first section.

165 *DTÖ*, Vol. 115, pp. 72–73 (end), and *Georg Böhm, Sämtliche Werke*, Vol. I, p. 41 (measure 4).

166 *DDT, 1. Folge*, Vol. 4, p. 11 (measure 2).

167 *Ibid.*, pp. 48–49 (end of first section).

168 *EDM, Erste Reihe*, Band 12, pp. 10 (measure 5 of second section), 13–14 (measure 3 of each section), 24 (measure 2 of second section), and 26 (measure 4 and the end of the second section).
169 *Suiten für Cembalo*, p. 35 (measure 4 of second section).
170 *DTÖ*, Jahrgang XIII/2, Vol. 27, pp. 44 (measure 3) and 47 (measure 3 of the second section).
171 *DTÖ*, Vol. 115, pp. 62–63 (end of each section).
172 *DDT, 1. Folge*, Vol. 4, pp. 35–36 (end).
173 *DTÖ*, Jahrgang VI/2, Vol. 13, p. 54 (end).
174 *CEKM* 16, pp. 80 (end of first section) and 85 (measure 6).
175 *Klavervaerker*, p. 15 (end).
176 *EDM, Zweite Reihe*, Vol. 4, p. 135 (end of piece); *Johann Pachelbel, Suiten für Cembalo*, p. 35 (end); and *Georg Böhm, Sämtliche Werke*, Vol. I, p. 64 (fourth full measure).
177 *DTÖ*, Jahrgang XIII/2, Vol. 27, p. 44 (end).
178 *Klavervaerker*, p. 10 (end).
179 *CEKM* 16, p. 91 (measure 5).
180 *CEKM* 16, p. 80 (fifth bar of second section).
181 *Klavervaerker*, pp. 7 (end of first section) and 18 (end of piece).
182 *DTB*, Jahrgang XVIII, Vol. 30, p. 12 (end of each section).
183 BWV 996, in the Bach-Gesellschaft edition of the *Werke*, Vol. XLV, p. 151, and in the *Neue Bach-Ausgabe*, Series 5, Vol. X, p. 96.
184 Jean Adam Reinken, *Hortus musicus*, ed. J. C. M. van Riemsdijk (*Vereeniging voor Nederlands Muziekgeschiedenis, Uitgave*, XIII [Amsterdam and Leipzig, 1888]), *Allemand 12ma* on p. 12 of the *violino I* part. The Bach transcription (BWV 966) is in the Bach-Gesellschaft edition of the *Werke*, Vol. XLII, pp. 48–49.
185 *Handleitung zur Variation* (Hamburg, 1706), fol. O$_2$^{v}: "hat zwey Repetitionen, und fängt mit dem Auff-Tacte in schlechten Tacte an."
186 *Musicalisches Lexicon* (Leipzig, 1732), facsimile in *Documenta musicologica, Erste Reihe*, Vol. III (Kassel: Bärenreiter, 1953), p. 28: "hat einen Viertel Tact, zwo Repetitiones von fast gleicher Länge, und hebet so wohl im ersten als zweyten Theile mit einer kurtzen Note, nemlinem Achtel oder Sechzehntheil, bisweilen auch mit drey Sechzehntheilen im Aufschlagen an."
187 *Der vollkommene Capellmeister* (Hamburg, 1739), facsimile in *Documenta musicologica, Erste Reihe*, Vol. V (Kassel: Bärenreiter, 1954), p. 232: "In Clavier, Lauten, und Violdigamben-Sachen gehet die Allemanda, als eine aufrichtige Teutsche Erfindung, vor der Courante, so wie diese vor der Sarabanda und Gique her, welche Folge der Melodien man mit einem Nahmen Suite nennet."
188 Walther, p. 28: "Die Proposition, woraus die übrigen Suiten, als die Courante, Sarabande und Gique, als Partes fliessen."
189 Niedt, fol. O$_2$^{r}; Walther, p. 28.
190 Mattheson, p. 232: "Man hat auch einen sonderlichen Tantz, der mit dem Allemanden-Nahmen beleget wird; ob er wol einem Rigaudon viel ähnlicher siehet, als einer rechten Allemande."
191 Walther, p. 28: "In dieser Gattung, zumahl (wenn darnach getantzet werden soll), übertreffen die Teutschen andere Nationen . . ."
192 Niedt, fol. O$_1$^{r}: "Ballo, Ital: von ballare dantzen: eigentlich ein Dantz, und italiänscher Dantz, welcher in zweyen Repetitionen gesetzet wird, da jede 4. oder 8. Tacte lang ist, wird in schlechten Tacte gesetzet."
193 Walther, p. 67: "Balletto . . . ist ein . . . Tantz auf Instrumente, dessen Melodie mit einem Achtel im Aufheben anfängt . . . Jacobus Gastoldus und Thomas Morley am Ende des 16ten Seculi . . . haben auch Ballette verfertiget, die zum Tantze mit Worten gesungen werden können."
194 Facsimile edition (Gregg International, 1970), pp. 143–144 and 146.
195 For other Almains by Lawes (d. 1645) for various instrumental combinations, see *MB*, Vol. XXI: *William Lawes, Select Consort Music*, ed. Murray Lefkowitz (1963), pp. 57, 63, 64, and 93.
196 *MB*, Vol. XXXI: *Matthew Locke, Chamber Music I*, ed. Michael Tilmouth (1971), pp. 30–31 and 38–39.
197 *Monuments of Music and Music Literature in Facsimile*, Second series, Vol. XXX (New York: Broude Brothers, 1975).
198 Transcribed by Thurston Dart in *Keyboard Suites, Matthew Locke* (London: Stainer & Bell, 1964),

pp. 2–3, 4–5, 6–7, and 9. An *Alman* by Locke from *Musick's Hand-Maid* (1678) is on p. 12.
199 All the keyboard music by other composers is printed by Anthony Kooiker in *The Penn State Music Series*, No. 16: *Keyboard Suites from Melothesia* (University Park: Pennsylvania State University Press, 1968).
200 *Ibid.*, especially the works of Moss on pp. 35–36 and 40–41.
201 *Ibid.*, p. 5 for the title and pp. 40–41 for the music (see also p. 66 of the facsimile edition of *Melothesia*). For imitation, see the beginning of the Almain by Moss on p. 40; for a fugal theme, see its second section on p. 41. For *fa-la* motives, see the second section of Diessener's piece on p. 43, especially the fourth line.
202 For other Almands by Clarke, see *The Contemporaries of Purcell*, ed. J. A. Fuller Maitland (London: Chester, 1921), Vol. V.
203 *Ibid.*, Vols. III and IV contain other examples by Croft. One, on pp. 12–13 of Vol. III, has a refrain heard three times alone in the bass. Another, on pp. 21–22, is uncharacteristically tuneful.
204 Transcribed by Howard Ferguson in *Eight Suites, Henry Purcell* (London: Stainer & Bell, 1964), p. 19. The piece is also in GB-Lbm, MS Add.31465, fols. 18^v-20^r.
205 Two are printed by E. Pauer in the Purcell volume in *Old English Composers for the Virginal & Harpsichord* (London: Augener, [1879]), pp. 152–153 and 166. The other is in *Miscellaneous Keyboard Pieces, Henry Purcell*, ed. Howard Ferguson (London: Stainer & Bell, 1964), pp. 6–7.
206 *The Contemporaries of Purcell*, ed. J. A. Fuller Maitland, Vols. I and II include Almands by Blow.
207 *Ibid.*, Vols. VI and VII contain examples of these four composers.
208 See Maurice Greene, *Voluntaries and Suites for Organ and Harpsichord*, ed. Gwilym Beechey, in *Recent Researches in the Music of the Baroque Era*, Vol. XIX (Madison, Wisconsin: A-R Editions, Inc., 1975), pp. 49–50, 56–57, 61–63, 66–67, and 75–76.
209 For Grassineau, see *Monuments of Music and Music Literature in Facsimile*, Second series, Vol. XL (New York: Broude Brothers, 1966), p. 7. See the first edition of Brossard's work (Paris, 1703), microfiche copy in *Musical Dictionaries*, Series I. Grassineau and Brossard go on to explain that "among the French the word Balet has another signification, for 'tis by them used for a succession of airs, in all sorts of movements whether brisk or slow, with which the dances agree . . ."
210 Grassineau, p. 4.
211 *Ibid.*, p. 231. Except for the reference to dancing, this is essentially a translation from Brossard's first edition of 1703, the article "Suonata."
212 See also in Playford's *Courtly Masquing Ayres* of 1662, the end of the first section of pieces No. 140 and 182.
213 For other examples, see Kooiker's *Keyboard Suites from Melothesia*, works by Preston (p. 8, measure 7 of the second section), Gregory (p. 20, end), Moss (p. 35, end of first section), and Diessener (p. 42, measures 4 and 7 of the first section, measures 7-8 of the second). See also Dart's *Keyboard Suites, Matthew Locke*, p. 12 (third and last measures of the second section), and Fuller Maitland's *The Contemporaries of Purcell*, Vol. I, p. 23 (measure 6 of the *Almaine* by Blow).
214 *Keyboard Suites from Melothesia*, ed. Kooiker, p. 43 (ninth bar of the second section).
215 *Keyboard Suites, Matthew Locke*, ed. Thurston Dart, p. 9 (measure 6 of the first section and end of piece); *Eight Suites, Henry Purcell*, ed. Howard Ferguson, p. 17 (measure 3); and *The Contemporaries of Purcell*, ed. J. A. Fuller Maitland, Vol. III, pp. 15–16 (end of the Almand by Croft).
216 See *Old English Composers for the Virginal & Harpsichord, Henry Purcell*, ed. E. Pauer, p. 166 (end of piece, with pitches 4-3-2-1 on the first quarter-note beat, as in Ex. 61g); *Eight Suites, Henry Purcell*, ed. Howard Ferguson, pp. 17–18 (end, with 1 tied over followed by 1-2-1); *Early Keyboard Music*, ed. Louis Oesterle (New York: G. Schirmer, 1904), Vol. I, p. 121 (measure 2 of second section and the end of the piece, both with 7-5-7-1, and measure 4 of the second section, with 2-7-7-1).
217 See the *Almain* by Preston in *Keyboard Suites from Melothesia*, ed. Anthony Kooiker, pp. 7–8 (end of piece, with pitches 6-2-1). See also *Keyboard Suites, Matthew Locke*, ed. Thurston Dart, pp. 2–3 (end of first section, with 1 tied over followed by 2 and 1). The same pitches occur also in Playford's *Courtly Masquing Ayres* (1662) at the end of the first section of piece No. 150 and the end of the second section of No. 182.
218 *Keyboard Suites from Melothesia*, ed. Anthony Kooiker, p. 7 (measure 7 of Preston's work, with pitches 3-1). See also *The Hunting Almand* on fols. 42^v-43^r of GB-Lbm, MS Add. 31465 (end of piece, with 5-7).

219 *Keyboard Suites, Matthew Locke*, ed. Thurston Dart, pp. 6–7 (end of first section, with 7-5-rest).
220 *Ibid.*, measure 4 of the first section, with rest-2-3.
221 *Early Keyboard Music*, ed. Louis Oesterle, Vol. I, p. 123 (end of the Almand by Blow, with rest-7-rest).
222 *Old English Composers, Henry Purcell*, ed. E. Pauer, p. 166 (end of first section).
223 *Keyboard Suites, Matthew Locke*, ed. Thurston Dart, pp. 4–5, measure 4 of the second section.
224 *Keyboard Suites from Melothesia*, ed. Anthony Kooiker, pp. 40–41 (end of piece).
225 *Eight Suites, Henry Purcell*, ed. Howard Ferguson, p. 11. All three versions are printed together to facilitate comparison.
226 See Robert Donington, *The Interpretation of Early Music*, new version (London: Faber and Faber, 1975), pp. 665–670. Note especially his quotation of excerpts from a Purcell Almand, taken from Howard Ferguson's *Eight Suites*.
227 *Dictionnaire portatif des beaux-arts*, microfiche of the copy at US-Wc in the set *Musical Dictionaries*, Series I (Washington, D.C.: Brookhaven Press, 1976), p. 20: "c'est un air propre à une danse qui vient d'Allemagne. Cet air est composé de seize mesures à deux temps chacune."
228 Copy at E-Mn, the twenty-fourth page of the *Explicación* following numbered page 40 of the opening prose section, entitled *Explica.ⁿ de las 4 contradˢ que llaman Airosas:* "En la 1ª parte todos ocho bailan una de las diferencias, y en la 2ª cada Cavallero con su Dama ha en Alemanda. Esta musica se puede tañer con la Guitarra de rasgueado, y suena bien."
229 Freda Burford, article "Contredanse" in *New Grove*, IV, 704.
230 *Monuments of Music and Music Literature in Facsimile*, Second series, Vol. XLVIII (New York: Broude Brothers, 1967), pp. 192–193.
231 *Ibid.*, Second series, Vol. LXXXIV (1974), p. 8: "Danse fort commune en Suisse & en Allemagne . . . L'Air de cette Danse a beaucoup de gaieté, & se bat à deux temps." For other French descriptions, see Dubois, *Principes d'allemandes* (Paris, 1760) and S. Guillaume, *Almanach dansant, ou Positions et attitudes de l'allemande* (Paris, 1768).
232 Microfiche of the copy at US-Wc in *Musical Dictionaries*, Series I (Washington, D.C.: Brookhaven Press, 1976), the article "Allemande."
233 See *Musikalisches Handwörterbuch* (Weimar, 1786), pp. 10–11, and Georg Friedrich Wolf, *Kurzgefasstes musikalisches Lexikon* (Halle, 1787), pp. 6–7. Both sources are reproduced on microfiche from copies at US-Wc in the set *Musical Dictionaries*, Series I (Washington, D.C.: Brookhaven Press, 1976).
234 For further information concerning the new dance, see Oskar Bie, *Der Tanz*, 2nd ed. (Berlin, 1919), pp. 223–226.

The Cadence

1 The complete piece is in *DTÖ*, Jahrgang VI/2, Vol. 13: *Johann Jakob Froberger, Suiten für Clavier*, ed. Guido Adler (Vienna, 1899), pp. 42–43.
2 *DTÖ*, Jahrgang XIII/2, Vol. 27: *Wiener Klavier- und Orgelwerke aus der zweiten Hälfte des 17. Jahrhunderts*, ed. Hugo Botstiber (Vienna, 1906), pp. 32–33.
3 *Pièces de clavecin, Quatrième livre*, ed. Kenneth Gilbert in *LP* 24, pp. 30–31.

BIBLIOGRAPHY

Arbeau, Thoinot (Tabourot, Jehan). *Orchésographie.* Langres, 1588. Facsimile reprint of 1589 ed., in *Bibliotheca musica bononiensis,* Sezione II N.102, Bologna: Forni, 1969. English translation by Mary Stewart Evans, with introduction and notes by Julia Sutton, New York: Dover, 1967.

Bischoff, Heinz, and Zirnbauer, Heinz. *Lieder und Tänze auf die Lauten (um 1540) aus der Tabulaturhandschrift 1512 der Münchner Staatsbibliothek.* Mainz: Schott, n.d. (*Vorwort* dated 1938).

Brown, Howard Mayer. "The *Chanson rustique*: Popular Elements in the 15th- and 16th-century Chanson." *Journal of the American Musicological Society* XII (1959): 16–26.

——— *Instrumental Music Printed Before 1600: A Bibliography.* Cambridge, Mass.: Harvard University Press, 1965.

——— *Music in the French Secular Theater, 1400–1550.* Cambridge, Mass.: Harvard University Press, 1963.

——— *Theatrical Chansons of the Fifteenth and Early Sixteenth Centuries.* Cambridge, Mass.: Harvard University Press, 1963.

Chilesotti, Oscar. *Da un codice Lauten-buch del cinquecento.* Leipzig: Breitkopf und Härtel, 1890.

——— *Lautenspieler des XVI. Jahrhunderts.* Leipzig: Breitkopf und Härtel, 1891.

Cotarelo y Mori, Emilio. *Colección de entremeses, loas, bailes, jácaras y mojigangas desde fines del siglo XVI á mediados del XVIII.* 2 vols. Madrid: Bailly/Bailliére, 1911. *Nueva biblioteca de autores españoles,* Vols. XVII and XVIII.

Cunningham, James P. *Dancing in the Inns of Court.* London: Jordan, 1965.

Curtis, Alan, *Dutch Keyboard Music of the 16th and 17th Centuries.* Amsterdam: Vereeniging voor Nederlandse Muziekgeschiedenis, 1961. *Monumenta musica neerlandica,* Vol. III.

Cusick, Suzanne G. "Balletto, Vocal." *The New Grove Dictionary of Music and Musicians,* Vol. II, 92–94.

Cusick, Suzanne G., and Little, Meredith Ellis. "Allemande." *The New Grove Dictionary of Music and Musicians,* Vol. I, 276–280.

Dieckmann, Jenny. *Die in deutscher Lautentabulatur überlieferten Tänze des 16. Jahrhunderts.* Kassel: Bärenreiter, 1931.

Ecorcheville, Jules. *Vingt suites d'orchestre du XVIIe siècle français 1640–1670.* 2 vols. Berlin & Paris, 1906.

Einstein, Alfred. *The Italian Madrigal.* 3 vols. Princeton University Press, 1949.

Esquivel Navarro, Juan de. *Discursos sobre el arte del dançado*. Seville, 1642. Reprinted in *Publicaciones de la Asociación de Libreros y Amigos del Libro*, Vol. IV. Madrid, 1947.
Gastoldi, Giovanni Giacomo. *Balletti a cinque voci*. Venice, 1591. Modern ed. by Michel Sanvoisin in *Le pupitre* 10. Paris: Heugel, 1968.
— *Balletti a tre voci*. Venice, 1594. Transcribed by Giuseppe Vecchi in *Monumenta musica lombarda, Gian Giacomo Gastoldi, Opera omnia*, Vol. I, Part A2. Milan: Antiquae Musicae Italicae Studiosi, 1969.
Gérold, Théodore. *Le manuscrit de Bayeux*. Paris, 1921.
Gustafson, Bruce. *French Harpsichord Music of the 17th Century*. 3 vols. Ann Arbor: UMI Research Press, 1979. *Studies in Musicology*, No. 11.
Hudson, Richard. "Balletto, Instrumental." *The New Grove Dictionary of Music and Musicians*, Vol. II, 91–92.
— "Chordal Aspects of the Italian Dance Style 1500–1650." *Journal of the Lute Society of America* III (1970): 35–52.
— "The Folia, Fedele, and Falsobordone." *The Musical Quarterly* LVIII (1972): 398–411.
— *The Folia, the Saraband, the Passacaglia, and the Chaconne: The Historical Evolution of Four Forms that Originated in Music for the Five-Course Spanish Guitar*. 4 vols. Neuhausen–Stuttgart: Hänssler, 1982. American Institute of Musicology, *Musicological Studies & Documents* 35.
— "The Folia Melodies." *Acta musicologica* XLV (1973): 98–119.
— "The Music in Italian Tablatures for the Five-Course Spanish Guitar." *Journal of the Lute Society of America* IV (1971): 21–42.
— *Passacaglio and Ciaccona: From Guitar Music to Italian Keyboard Variations in the 17th Century*. UMI Research Press, 1981. *Studies in Musicology*, No. 37. (revision of Ph.D. dissertation, University of California, Los Angeles, 1967).
— "The Ripresa, the Ritornello, and the Passacaglia." *Journal of the American Musicological Society* XXIV (1971): 364–394.
Kerman, Joseph. *The Elizabethan Madrigal*. New York: American Musicological Society, 1962.
Land, J. P. N. "Het Luitboek van Thysius." *Tijdschrift der Vereeniging voor Noord-Nederlands Muziekgeschiedenis* I–III (1884–88).
MacClintock, Carol. *The Bottegari Lutebook*. Wellesley, Mass.: Wellesley College, 1965. *The Wellesley Edition*, No. 8.
Mattheson, Johann. *Der vollkommene Capellmeister*. Hamburg, 1739. Facsimile ed. in *Documenta musicologica, Erste Reihe*, Vol. V. Kassel: Bärenreiter, 1954.
Merian, Wilhelm. *Der Tanz in den deutschen Tabulaturbüchern*. Leipzig: Breitkopf und Härtel, 1927. Reprint, Hildesheim: Georg Olms, 1968.
Moe, Lawrence, H. "Dance Music in Printed Italian Lute Tablatures from 1507 to 1611." Unpublished Ph.D. dissertation, Harvard University, 1956.
Mohr, Ernst. *Die Allemande: Eine Untersuchung ihrer Entwicklung von den Anfängen bis zu Bach und Händel*. Vol. I: *Text*, Vol. II: *Noten-Beispiele*. Zurich & Leipzig, 1932.
Morley, Thomas. *A Plaine and Easie Introduction to Practicall Musicke*. London, 1597. Reprint, Gregg International, 1971.
Mráček, Jaroslav J. S. *Seventeenth-Century Instrumental Dance Music in Uppsala University Library Instr. mus. hs 409*. Stockholm: Reimers, 1976. *Monumenta musicae svecicae* 8, *Musica svecica saeculi* XVII 5.
Negri, Cesare. *Le gratie d'amore*. Milan, 1602. Facsimile ed., Bologna: Forni, 1969. *Bibliotheca musica bononiensis*, Sezione II N. 104.
Nettl, Paul. "Die Wiener Tanzkomposition in der zweiten Hälfte des siebzehnten Jahrhunderts." *Studien zur Musikwissenschaft* VIiI (1921): 45–175.

Paris, Gaston. *Chansons du XVe siècle publiées d'après le manuscrit de la Bibliothèque Nationale de Paris*. Paris, 1875.

Pinnell, Richard T. *Francesco Corbetta and the Baroque Guitar, with a Transcription of His Works*. 2 vols. Ann Arbor: UMI Research Press, 1980. *Studies in Musicology*, No. 25.

Praetorius, Michael. *Syntagma musicum, Band III: Termini musici*. Wolfenbüttel, 1618. Facsimile of 1619 ed. in *Documenta musicologica, Erste Reihe*, Vol. XV. Kassel: Bärenreiter, 1958.

Pugliese, Patri J., and Casazza, Joseph. "Practise for Dauncinge, Some Almans and a Pavan, England 1570–1650: A Manual for Dance Instruction." Unpublished monograph, Cambridge, Mass., 1980.

Quadt, Adalbert. *Lautenmusik aus der Renaissance*. 2 vols. Leipzig: VEB Deutscher Verlag für Musik, and Vienna: Universal Edition, n.d. (*Vorwort* dated 1967).

Radecke, Ernst. "Das deutsche weltliche Lied in der Lautenmusik des sechzehnten Jahrhunderts." *Vierteljahrsschrift für Musikwissenschaft* VII (1891): 285–336.

Sabol, Andrew J. *Four Hundred Songs and Dances from the Stuart Masque*. Providence, R.I.: Brown University Press, 1978.

Sartori, Claudio. *Bibliografia della musica strumentale italiana stampata in Italia fino al 1700*. 2 vols. Florence: Leo S. Olschki, 1952 and 1968.

Strauss, Gerald. *Nuremberg in the Sixteenth Century*. Rev. ed. Bloomington & London: Indiana University Press, 1976.

Valerius, Adriaen. *Neder-landtsche gedenck-clanck*. Haarlem, 1626. Facsimile ed. New York: Broude Brothers, 1974, in *Monuments of Music and Music Literature in Facsimile*, Second Series – *Music Literature*, Vol. LXIII. Modern ed., Amsterdam & Antwerp: Wereldbibliotheek, 1947, with introduction by P. J. Meertens, N. B. Tenhaeff, and A. Komter-Kuipers.

Walther, Johann Gottfried. *Musicalisches Lexicon*. Leipzig, 1732. Facsimile ed. in *Documenta musicologica, Erste Reihe*, Vol. III. Kassel: Bärenreiter, 1953.

Ward, John. *The Dublin Virginal Manuscript*. Wellesley College, 1954. *The Wellesley Edition*, No. 3.

Wellesz, Egon. *Die Ballett-Suiten von Johann Heinrich und Anton Andreas Schmelzer*. Vienna, 1914. *Sitzungsberichte der Kais. Akademie der Wissenschaften in Wien, Philosophisch–Historische Klasse*, Vol. 176, Part 5.

Wendland, John. "'Madre non mi far Monaca': the Biography of a Renaissance Folksong." *Acta musicologica* XLVIII (1976): 185–204.

INDEX

Separate arabic numbers indicate pages in Volume I. "Ex." refers to a musical example in Volume I, "No." to a composition in Volume II. The Tables are all in Volume I. Plates I–XII are in the first volume, Plates XIII–XXIV in the second.

Adriaenssen, Emanuel, 44, 45, 46, 48, 49, 51, 154, Ex. 23d, No. 47
Aich, Arnt von, 24, Ex. 13
air, English, see *ayre*
air de cour, 119, 120, 122
alemana: Italian, 36, 64, see also *Amore (Alemana d')*;
  Spanish, 53, 54, 209, 227 n. 28, 235 n. 9, see also *Amor (Alemana de)*
Allegri, Lorenzo, 141, 142, No. 90
Allmeyer Dantz, Der, 3, 35
Alten Weiber Tantz, Der, 35, 46, 65, Ex. 2e, No. 7b
Ammerbach, Elias Nikolaus, 3, 10, 19, 21, 26, 35–37, 42, 50, 65, 101, 135, 141, 218, 219 nn. 2, 3, 220 n. 30, Exx. 1c, 2e, 2f, 2g, 7a, 7d, 14b, 82a, Plate II, Nos. 4, 10
Amor, Alemana de, 223 n. 16
Amore, Alemana d', 68–76, Exx. 29, 30, Plates VI–IX, No. 82
Amour(s), Almande (d) (d') (de), 37, 43, 45, 50, 51, 65, 97, 195, 211, Ex. 37, Plate XVII, No. 6, see also *Schena Somer zeytt, Die*
Amsterdam, 54, 86, 90, 93, 179
Antwerp, 43, 50, 52, 53, 54, 86, 90, 93
Arbeau, Thoinot (Tabourot, Jehan), 55–61, 69, 76, 81, 97, 114, 116, 147, 149, 253, Exx. 24, 25, 26, 53b, 53d, Plates IV, V
aria, 93, 137, 139, 140, 142, 179, 182, 183, 184, 226 nn. 6, 10, 227 n. 1, 242 n. 38, Plate XXIII
Attaingnant, Pierre, 21, 27, 29, 31, 33, 122
Aufzug, 42, 129–32

Augsburg, 24, 39–41, 128, 178, 183, 188
ayre (air, aer, aeir), 105, 107, 109–10, 205–7, 250 n. 209
Azzaiolo, Filippo, 83, 107

Bach, Johann Sebastian, 197–98, 199, 203, 212, 216, 218, 246 n. 100, Exx. 78, 79b
Ballard, Pierre, 147, 154, 235 n. 17
Ballard, Robert (ii), 119–21
Ballard, Robert (iii), 156–57, 181
ballet de cour, 119, 122, 130, 131, 143, 148, 149, 212
Barbetta, Giulio Cesare, 62, 63, 65, 67, 95, 142, No. 76
Baron, Ernst Gottlieb, 199
Barrett, John, 206
Bartolotti, Angelo Michele, 163, 164, Table 2, No. 60
basse danse, xi, 3, 33, 60, 221 nn. 35, 37
Bataille, Gabriel, 120, Nos. 50, 51
Bateman, Robert, 110, 129, Nos. 19, 137
battaglia, 183, 244, n. 50
Bauyn MS, 160, 193, 202, Ex. 77a, Nos. 26, 58, 59
Becker, Dietrich, 190, Ex. 71
Bellère, Jean, see Phalèse, Pierre (i & ii) and Bellère, Jean
Belleville, Jacques de, 181
Bentivoglio Lute Book, 64, 121; Vol. II: 246 n. for No. 52
Besard, Jean-Baptiste, 45, 54, 68, 119, 121, 130, 147, 154, 223 nn. 9, 27, Ex. 21f, No. 49
Betler (Bethler, Petler) Tantz, Der, 3, 35, Ex. 2a, No. 1a

257

258 Index

Biber, Heinrich Ignaz Franz von, 186, 187
Bisarde, Almande, 47, 51, Ex. 23c, No. 43b
Blacke Almaine, The, 113, 231 n. 48
Blow, John, 206, 250 n. 213, 251 n. 221
Boccella, Francesco, 168
Böhm, Georg, 197, 202
Bologna, 68, 142, 163, 167
Bononcini, Giovanni Maria, 169, 170, 177, 240–41 n. 17, Table 3
Bottazzari, Giovanni, Table 2
Bottegari Lute MS, 65, 84, 254, 228 n. 13
bourée (borea, buré), 158, 170, 183, 184, 199, 205, 217, 243 n. 31
Brade, William, 129, 130, 131, 181, No. 17
branle (bransle, brando), 119, 129, 170, 217, 224 n. 45, 232 n. 19, 241 n. 18, 243 n. 31, 246 n. 96
Bremen, 178, 182
Brevi, Giovanni Battista, 170, 240 n. 17
Brossard, Sébastien de, 148, 159, 207
Bruin, B. F. de, 179, 180, Ex. 67
Brunelli, Antonio, 137–39, 140, 142, 170, Ex. 57, No. 88
Brunswick (Duke of), Almande, 100, 113
Brussels, 52–53, 54
Bruynsmedelijn, Almande, 37–38, 45, 50, 51, 64, 97, 211, Exx. 2c, 20, 39, Plates XVI, XX, No. 5b
Bryne, Albertus, 206
Bull, John, 100
Buoni, Giorgio, 170, 171, 174, Table 3, No. 126
Busby, Thomas, 210
Butler, Charles, 109, 111, 118, 125
Buxtehude, Dietrich, 195, 198, 199, 202, 203, 248 nn. 146, 149
Byrd, William, 99, 100, Ex. 40c

cadence: typical, xi, 7–9, 13, 49, 65, 66, 82–83, 84, 86, 88, 90, 97, 99, 101, 104, 121, 126–32 *passim*, 142, 154–58, 174–76, 200–3, 207–9, 213–18, 181–92 *passim*, Exx. 3, 5–7, 60, 61, 75–85; unaccented, 175–6, 185, 217, Ex. 66; vocal, 8, 27, 31, 33, 101, Exx. 4, 42; in monophonic chansons, 31–33, Ex. 19; with 2 to 1, 13, 31, 38, 101–2, 121, Ex. 41; with final I on third beat, 155, 171, 207; with repeated notes or chords, 9, 50, 66, 89, 138, 139, 142, 155, 165–66, 193, 207, 215, Ex. 84; tonality at end of first section, 150, 166, 168, 183, 188, 198, 207
Calvete de Estrella, Juan, 53
Calvi, Carlo, 64, No. 104
Campion, François, 155, 158, No. 71
canario, 140, 199, 235 n. 9

canzona (Canzon, Cantzon), 127, 129, 179, 180
canzonetta, 102, 107, 125, 137, 226 n. 6, Plate X
Cara Cosa, La, 33, 83
Carbonchi, Antonio, 163
Caroso, Fabritio, 63–64, 65
Carré, Antoine, Sieur de la Grange, No. 61
Cazzati, Maurizio, 168, 170, 171, 174, 176, 191, 213, 239–40 n. 17, Ex. 63, Table 3, No. 115
Cesti, Antonio, 175, 184–85, Exx. 66d, 66e
chaconne (chacona, ciaccona), 151, 176, 183, 194, 207, 235 n. 9
Chambonnières, Jacques Champion de, 156, 158, 159, 193, 235 n. 18
chanson: intabulations, 27–31, 34; monophonic, 31–33; polyphonic, 52, 53; for solo voice, 122, *see also* Sermisy
Charles V (Holy Roman emperor & king of Spain), 39, 52–53, 68
chorea, 4, 121
Christina (queen of Sweden), 181
Clamer, Andreas Christophorus, 186, 187
Clarke, Jeremiah, 206, 208, No. 150
Cobb, John, 206
Coleman, Charles, 110, 112, 205, 207, No. 146
Colonna, Giovanni Ambrosio, 63, Ex. 27
coloration, 21, 24–26, 29–31, 49, 50, 66, 99–101, 120, 142, Exx. 12, 15, 16, 17
Compan, Charles, 210
concerto, 169, 187, 212, 213
Constantin, Louis, 179, 180, 181
coranto (coranta, corante), 109, 129, *see also corrente, courante*
Corbetta, Francesco, 64, 157, 158, 159, 163, 164, 165, 166, 255, Table 2, Plate XIX, Nos. 62, 97, 106
Corelli, Arcangelo, 169, 177, 192, Table 3
corrente (corente), 131, 138, 140, 141, 142, 164, 167, 168, 169, 170, 176, 185, 226 n. 10, 241 n. 18, Ex. 57c, Nos. 86, 93, 95b, *see also coranto, courante*
Couperin, François, 153–60 *passim*, 164, 218, Ex. 85c
Couperin, Louis, 151, 153, 156, 158, 159, 193, 235 n. 18
courante (courant, couranta, courente, courrent), 55, 57, 59, 121, 127, 129, 132, 149, 160, 179, 180, 182, 183, 184, 194, 198, 199, 204, 207, 239 n. 113, *see also coranto, corrente*
Court, Almande (de), 47, Ex. 23d
Croft, William, 206, 207, 208, Ex. 82b, No. 151

D'Anglebert, Jean-Henri, 156, 159
Degli Antoni, Giovanni Battista, 174, 190–91, 240 n. 17, Table 3, No. 120
Degli Antoni, Pietro, 240 n. 17, Table 3, No. 119
Demantius, Christoph, 126, 233 n. 13
Denss, Adrian, 45, 54, 154, 223 n. 27, No. 48
De Visée, Robert, 155, 157, 158, 237 n. 66, No. 68
Diessener, Gerhard, 206, 207, 250 n. 213, No. 148
Dieupart, Charles, 156, 160, 237 n. 66
Don Frederico, Almande de, 36, 45–46, 50, 128, Ex. 2d, Plate XVIII, No. 7a, see also *Man ledt uns zu der Hochzeit freud*
double: English dance step, 113–16; French varied repeat, 151, 193, 194, 198, 235 n. 18, 247 n. 131, Nos. 26, 37b, see also *variatio*
downward third, 89, 152–53, 173, Exx. 33a, 33b, 33d
Draghi, Antonio, 185
Dresden, 42, 133, 142, 175
Drusina, Benedikt de, 4, 35, 42
Düben, Gustaf, Peter, & Andreas, 181
Dublin Virginal MS, 97–98, 102, 116, 255, Exx. 38, 39, 53
Dubut (father & son), 156, 235 n. 18, 236 nn. 22, 32, 237 n. 65
Dufort, Giambatista, 170
Dumanoir, Guillaume, 148
Du Mont, Henry, 158, 159, 193, 235 n. 22, No. 59

entrata, 140, 167, 168, see also *Intrada*
entrée, 119–20, 130
espagnolette, 166
Esquivel Navarro, Juan de, 254, 227 n. 28, 235 n. 9
Estrée, Jean d', 50, 51, 52, 53, 66, 119, No. 39

Facoli, Marco, 65, 66, Plate XXI
Fa la (referring to an entire piece), 97, 102–4, 107, 108, 109, 111, 118, 122
Falconieri, Andrea, No. 109
Fantini, Girolamo, 167, No. 96
Farina, Carlo, 135, 142, Nos. 22, 23
Ferdinand (Holy Roman emperor & brother of Charles V), 39, 68
Feuillet, Raoul-Auger, 148, 149
Fischer, Johann Caspar Ferdinand, 194, 196, 197, 199, 203, 206, 248 n. 147, No. 33
Fitzwilliam Virginal Book, 99–100

Florence, 68, 81, 83, 137, 141, 163, 244 n. 50
folia (follia), 12, 151, 185, 219 n. 4, 228 n. 10, 235 n. 9
Forster, Georg, 22, 41, 220 nn. 22, 28, 222 n. 54, Exx. 11a, 11c
Fortune hélas pourquoy, Almande, 47–48, 65, Ex. 23e
Foscarini, Giovanni Paolo, 163, 164, 165, 167, Table 2, Nos. 98, 99
Franck, Melchior, 127
Frankfurt an der Oder, 42
Frescobaldi, Girolamo, 176, 193, 236 n. 27
Froberger, Johann Jacob, 193, 194, 198, 202, 218, 248 n. 146, Exx. 77, 85a, No. 26
frottola, 82, Ex. 31
fugue, 159, 173, 206, 212, 250 n. 201
Fuhrmann, Georg Leopold, 119, 120, 121, 147, No. 52

Gabrielli, Domenico, 174, Table 3, No. 122
Gagliano, Marco da, 140
gagliarda, 62, 69, 132, 137–38, 140, 141, 142, 167, 170, 183, Ex. 57b, Plate VIII, Nos. 75, 76, 79, 82, 103a, see also *gaillarde, gallarda, galliard*
gaillarde, 21, 29, 33, 55, 166, see also *gagliarda, gallarda, galliard*
gallarda, 148, 223 n. 16, 235 n. 9, see also *gagliarda, gaillarde, galliard*
galliard (galliarda), 109–10, 112, 117, 121, 126, 127, 129, 132, 179, 180, 182, 183, see also *gagliarda, gaillarde, gallarda*
Gallini, Giovanni Andrea, 210
Gallot, Jacques, 158, No. 63
Gandini, Salvador, 167–68, No. 112
Gastoldi, Giovanni Giacomo, 97, 86–96, 97, 100, 103–7, 122, 124–136 *passim*, 137, 139, 142, 143, 153, 158, 168, 173, 205, 206, 211, 218, 254, Exx. 33, 34, 35, 36, 43a, Plates X, XI, XII, XXII, Nos. 12, 78, 80
Gaultier, Denis, 158, 193, No. 63
Gaultier, Ennemond, 155, 156, 158, 159, 160
gavotte (gavotta, gavot), 158, 160, 170, 176, 183, 205, 207, 217, 232 n. 19, 236 n. 33, 237 n. 66, 246 n. 96
Geoffroy, Jean-Nicolas, 158, 159
Gerle, Hans, 20, 24, 27, 221 n. 31
Gervaise, Claude, 46, 50, 53, Ex. 22a
Gianoncelli, Bernardo, 176
Gibbons, Christopher, 206
Gibbons, Orlando, 100

giga (gigua), 164, 168, 169, 170, 185, see *gigue, jig*
Gigault, Nicolas, 159–60
gigue (gique), 149, 160, 164, 183, 184, 194, 198, 199, 204, 244 n. 57, see *giga, jig*
Gorzanis, Giacomo, 62–65 *passim*, 67, 68, 91, 95, 142, Exx. 1e, 21d, Nos. 72–75
Gradenthaler, Hieronymus, 188
Graff Johan von Nassaw Dantz, 3, 38, see *Wie möcht ich frölich werden*, No. 47
Granata, Giovanni Battista, 163, 164, 165, Ex. 62, Table 2, Nos. 105, 114, 121
Grassineau, James, 207
Greaves, Thomas, 105, Ex. 46
Gregory, William, 206, 250 n. 213
grève, 55–60, 76, 116, Exx. 24, 25, Plate V
Griffoni, Antonio, 169, 170, 174, 242 n. 34, Table 3, No. 127
Guerre, guerre gay, Almande, 47, 55, 98, Ex. 23a, No. 43a
Guilelmus Monachus, 10–13, Ex. 8
Gut Gesell du musst wandern, 22, 35, 46, 65, 128, Ex. 2f, Nos. 10b, 76, see also *Regine Sweden (Almande)*

Hainhofer MS, 35, 36, 128, 134, 224 n. 27, Ex. 2d, No. 12
Hake, Hans, 182, No. 27
Hamburg, 129, 131, 132, 134, 178, 180, 191, 192, 198
Hammerschmidt, Andreas, 179
Handel, George Frideric, 197, 203, 212
Hart, Philip, 206
Hassler, Hans Leo, 125, 126, 205, Plate XIII
Hasz, Georg, 126–27, No. 14
Haussmann, Valentin, 125, 126, 127, 135, 141, Plate XIV, No. 13
Hautemant, No. 69
Heardson, Thomas, 206
Heckel, Wolff, 3, 34–35, 36, 38, 41, 213, 221 n. 31, Ex. 1b, Plate I, No. 3
Heckerling und Haberstro, 37, Ex. 1a, see also *Prince (Almande), Printzentantz, Wer das Töchterlein haben wil*, Plate XVI, Nos. 39c, 73
Hilton, John (ii), 107, Ex. 49
Hofhaimer, Paul, 24–26, Exx. 12a, 14a
Hoftanz, 3, 4, 34, 41, 222 n. 57
Holborne, Anthony, 99, 100, 101, 107, Ex. 40b
Holborne, William, 107
Holmes, George, 206
Holmes, Thomas, No. 132
Hooper, Edmund, No. 131
Hove, Joachim van den 46, 47, 232 n. 22

Hudson, George, No. 144b
Hupffauff, 15, 19, 34, Nos. 1, 2, 7, see also *Nachtanz, Proportio, recoupe, reprinse, Sprung, Tripla*
Huygens, Constantijn, 235–36 n. 22

Ich ging einmal spazieren, 35–36, 44, 63, Exx. 2b, 21b, see also *Jeune fillette (Almande Une), Monica, Nonette, (Almande), Oulde Almain, Queenes Almain, Von Gott will ich nicht lassen*, Nos. 5a, 75, 97
Ich stund an einem Morgen, 22, 27
Ich weiss (mir) ein schöne (stoltze) Müllerin, 22, 27, 36, Ex. 10, No. 1b
Imhoff, Regina Clara, MS Keyboard book, 193, 201, 205, No. 25
Imperial (a), see *Alten Weiber Tantz, Der*
India, Sigismondo d', 140
intermedio, 119, 137, No. 78
Intrada (Intrata), 42, 126, 127, 129–32 *passim*, 167, 179, 183–84, 186, 187, 217, 244 n. 57, 246 n. 96, Nos. 86, 103a, see also *entrata*

James I (king of England), 110, 112
Jenkins, John, 110, No. 140
Jeune fillette, Almande Une, 36, 44–45, 55, 226 n. 6, Ex. 21f, see also *Ich ging einmal spazieren, Monica, Nonette (Almande), Oulde Almain, Queenes Almain, Von Gott will ich nicht lassen*, Nos. 5a, 75, 97
jig (jigg), 109, 206, 207, see also *giga, gigue*
Jobin, Bernhard, 3–4, 19, 35–38, 41, 45, 224 n. 27, No. 5
Johnson, Robert, 100, 110, No. 136

Kapsberger, Johann Hieronymus, 67, 141, 142, 167, Nos. 83, 87
Kargel, Sixt, 4, 19, 35–37, 41, 43, 45, 132, Exx. 2b, 21b. Nos. 8, 9
Kassel, 180–82
Kelz, Matthias, 183
Kindermann, Johann Erasmus, 193, 198, 201
King, Robert, 206
Kits, Almande, 55
Knop, Lüder, 182–83, No. 29
Krieger, Johann, 197, 202, 203, 248 n. 148
Kroměříž (Kremsier), 183, 184, 186
Kuhnau, Johann, 196, 198, 201, 202, 248 n. 149

La Barre, Joseph, 160
Lacomb, Jacques, 209
Lais, Johan Dominico, 4, 41, 43, 132, No. 8
Lalande, Michel-Richard de, 148, No. 70

Lamoretti, Pietro Maria, 139, Plate XXIII, No. 94
Laurenti, Bartolomeo Girolamo, 174, 241–42 n. 34, Table 3, No. 124
Lawes, William, 205, No. 143
Lebègue, Nicolas-Antoine, 156, 159, 160, 236 n. 24, 237 n 66
Legrenzi, Giovanni, 170, 171, 174, 176, 190, 213, 240 n. 17, Table 3, No. 113
Leipzig, 42, 121, 132, 178, 182, 188
Leopold I (Holy Roman emperor), 178, 183–86 *passim*, 196, 218, Plate XV
Le Roux, Gaspard, 151, 155, 156, 158, 159
Le Roy, Adrian, 46, 49, 53, 122, Nos. 36, 37
Locke, Matthew, 112, 205, 206, 208, 250 nn. 213, 217, 251 nn. 219, 220, Ex. 80b
Lope de Vega Carpio, Félix, 148
Loraine (Loreyne), Almande, 46–47, 49, 50, 51, 52, 65, 99–100, 113, 115, 211, Exx. 22, 52, Plate XVII, see also *Tournée (Almande)* & No. 135
Losy, Jan Antonin, 199
Louvain, 43, 50, 53, 54
Löwe von Eisenach, Johann Jakob, 182, 190, No. 28
Lully, Jean-Baptiste, 148, 188

Mace, Thomas, 117, 205
Madre non mi far monaca, see *Monica*
madrigal, 84, 86, 90, 95, 102–8 *passim*, 125, 134, 137, 226 n. 6
Magister Dantz, Der, 36, 65, Ex. 2g, No. 10c, see also *Poussinghe (Almande)*, *tedesca*: *Tedesca dita l'Austria*
Mainerio, Giorgio, 46, 64–65, 66, 67, 68, 81, 84, 89, 137, 154, 226 nn. 12, 23, Plate XX
Mangeant, Jacques, 120
Man ledt uns zu der Hochzeit freud, 36, see also *Don Frederico (Almande de)*
Marais, Marin, 153, 156, No. 65
Marini, Biagio, 142–44, 167–68, 170, 174, 176, Nos. 89, 93, 95, 107, 111
Mary Hofmans, Almande, 55
Mascarada (Mascherada, Mascharada), 129–32, 137, 179, 198
Mascitti, Michele, 175
masque, 110–13, 117, 129–31, 135, 205, 212, 255
Matteis, Nicola, 206, 207, No. 149
Mattheson, Johann, 197, 198, 199, 202, 204–5, 213, 248 n. 146, 254
Matthysz, Paulus, 86, 93, 179–80, Plate X
Mayr, Rupert Ignaz, 188
Mazzella, Salvatore, 170, 240 n. 17

measures, 113, 129
Mein Hertz ist frisch, 36, 46
Meister, Johann Friedrich, 191, 199, Ex. 72, No. 32
Melli, Pietro Paolo, 131, 142, 167, 183, Nos. 85, 86, 92
menuet (minuet), 160, 168, 184, 194, 199, 207
Mercure d'Orléans, 121
Mercure, John, 156, 158, 206
Mersenne, Marin, 148, No. 56
Mertel, Elias, 121
Mesangeau, René, 150, 151, 158, 160, No. 56
Milan, 34, 68
Millioni, Pietro, 63
Minguet y Yrol, Pablo, 209
Monari, Clemente, 170, 240 n. 17
Monica (Monaca), 36, 225–26 n. 6, 255, Ex. 28, see also *Ich ging einmal spazieren*, *Jeune fillette (Almande Une)*, *Nonette (Almande)*, *Oulde Almain*, *Queenes Almain*, *Von Gott will ich nicht lassen*, Nos. 5a, 75, 97
Monsieur, Almande, 47, 55, 99, 100, 101, 109, 110, 211, Ex. 40
Montaigne, Michel de, 41
Montesardo, Girolamo, 226 n. 6
Monteverdi, Claudio, 140, 175, Exx. 66b, 66c, No. 89b
Morlaye, Guillaume, 46, No. 38
Morley, Thomas, 97, 102–8, 111, 116–17, 122, 125, 129, 130, 131, 134, 142, 172, 205, 211, 254, Exx. 43, 44, Plates XIV, XXIV
Moss, John, 206, 250 n. 213, Ex. 80c
Moy, Louis de, No. 53
Muffat, Georg, 186, 187, 198
Muffat, Gottlieb, 197, 198, 203
Mummerey, 42, 130–31
Munich, 188
My bonny lasse (Morley), 103, 107, 111, Ex. 44, Plates XIV, XXIV

Nachtanz, 3, 15–20, 33–34, 50–52, 62, 65, 66–67, 84, 125–29, 132–33, 135, 138, 142, 167, 211, 213, Ex. 9, Nos. 5, 8, 13, 22, 25a, see also *Hupffauff*, *Proportio*, *recoupe*, *reprinse*, *Sprung*, *Tripla*
Naples, 68, 170
Negri, Cesare, 65, 67, 68–76, 84, 86, 114, 116, 254, Exx. 29, 30, 32b, 32c, 53c, Plates VI–IX, No. 82
Neusidler, Hans, 3, 4, 20, 22, 24, 27, 29, 33–34, 35–36, 38, 41, 68, Exx. 11, 12, 15, 16, 17, Nos. 1, 2
Neusidler, Melchior, 19, 22, 35–38, 39–40, Ex. 2h, No. 7

Niedt, Friedrich Erhard, 194, 195, 203, 204, 205, 206, Ex. 74
Nonette, Almande (de) (la), 36, 44–45, 51, 52, 55, 62, 63–64, 67, 81, 98–99, 142, 150, 162, 211, 226 n. 6, Ex. 21, No. 42, see also *Ich ging einmal spazieren, Jeune fillette (Almande Une), Monica, Oulde Almain, Queenes Almain, Von Gott will ich nicht lassen*, Nos. 5a, 75, 97
Nörmiger, August, 36, 37, 42, 192, 220 n. 17
Nunnen Tantz, Der, 3
Nuremberg, ix, 3, 20, 22, 39–41, 86, 90, 121, 124–27, 131–32, 134, 139, 141, 187, 188, 211, 218, 255

Oulde (Old) Almain, The, 99, 101, 113, see also *Ich ging einmal spazieren, Jeune fillette, (Almande Une), Monica, Nonette, (Almande), Queenes Almain, Von Got will ich nicht lassen*, Nos. 5a, 75, 97
overture, 149, 151, 160, 237 n. 66

Pachelbel, Johann, 188, 195, 198, 199, 201, 202, 248 n. 146
padoana, 62, 63, Nos. 73, 74
Padouan (Paduan, Paduana), 127, 129, 132, 179, 180, 183
Paix, Jakob, 37, 38, 41, 46, 220 n. 17
Paris, 43, 50, 53, 86, 149, 158, 163, 175, 181, 188, 199, 209, 210
Partia, 187, 197, see also *Partita*, suite
Partita, 142, 187, 197–98, see also *Partia*, suite
Pasquini, Bernardo, 176
passacaglia (passecaille), 149, 151, 166, 207, 239 n. 1
passamezzo, 33, 64, 66, 121, 140, 142, 148, 166, 176, 217, 219 n 2, 224 n. 45
passepied, 160, 199
pavan, 109–10, 113, 117, 127, 182, 207, 231 n. 46, see also *pavana, pavane*
pavana, 33, 53, 67, 121, 148, 223 n. 16, 226 n. 23, 235 n. 9, see also *pavan, pavane*
pavane, 21, 60–61, 81, 148, 166, 234 n. 3, 238 n. 67, Ex. 26, see also *pavan, pavana*
Pekelharing, Almande, 55
Pellegrini, Domenico, Table 2, No. 108
Peri, Jacopo, 175, Ex. 66a
Perrine, 158, 160
Pesenti, Martino, 140, 176, 239 n. 13, 241 n. 33, Nos. 101, 102
petite reprise, 151, 172, 182, 187, 198, 245 n. 77, Nos. 28b, 62, 65, 122a, 123b, 124b
Peuerl, Paul, 127, 129, 132–33, 135, Ex. 54

Peyer, Johann Gotthard, 199
Pezel, Johann Christoph, 188–90, 191, 198, Exx. 69, 70, No. 30
Phalèse, Pierre (i), 45–47, 52, 54, 63, 122, Ex. 21c, Nos. 34, 35, 40, 42, *see also* Phalèse, Pierre (i) & Bellère, Jean
Phalèse, Pierre (i) & Bellère, Jean, 43–47, 50, 51, 52, 54, 63, 100, 224 n. 45, Exx. 1f, 22b, 37a, Plate XVII, Nos. 44, 45, *see also* Phalèse, Pierre (i), as well as Phalèse, Pierre (ii) & Bellère, Jean
Phalèse, Pierre (ii), Plate XII, *see also* Phalèse, Pierre (ii) & Bellère, Jean
Phalèse, Pierre (ii) & Bellère, Jean, 45–47, 50, 51, 52, 54, 64, 65, 149, 154, Exx. 23b, 23c, 23e, Plate XVIII, No. 46, *see also* Phalèse, Pierre (ii), as well as Phalèse, Pierre (i) & Bellère, Jean
Philidor, Pierre Danican, No. 67
Philidor Collection: F-Pn, MS Rés. F.496 (from 1575 to 1620), 45, 50, 119, 120; F-Pn, MS Vm^6.5 (from 1654 to 1691), 148, 149
Philip II (king of Spain & son of Charles V), 53–54, 60, 68
Philip III (king of Spain & son of Philip II), 68
Piani, Giovanni Antonio, 170
Picchi, Giovanni, 65–66
Piccinini, Alessandro, 64, 142
Pied de cheval, Almande le, 48, 57–58, 98, No. 37a
pied en l'air, see *grève*
Piggott, Francis, 206
Placuzzi, Gioseffo, 240 n. 17, Ex. 64
Playford, John, 205, 250 n. 217
Poglietti, Alessandro, 184, 194–95, 198, 202, Ex. 85b
Polaroli, Orazio, 240 n. 17, Ex. 65
Posch, Isaac, 132–33, 192, Ex. 56
Poussinghe, Almande, 36, 46, 51, 64, 65, No. 46, see also *Magister Dantz, tedesca: Tedesca dita l'Austria*
Praetorius, Michael, 119, 120, 130–31, 133, 134, 136, 139, 141, 148, 167, 170, 179, 182, 183, 192, 204, 231 n. 4, 255
prelude (*Praeludium, prélude, preludio*), 153, 160, 164, 165, 176, 187, 194, 198, 199, 207, 212, 217
Preston, Christopher, 206, 250 nn. 213, 217, 218
Prince, Almande (du), xi, 37, 43–44, 50–52, 59–60, 62, 63, 65, 67, 97, 100, 102, 110, 115–16, 119, 122, 162, 229 n. 12, Exx. 1f, 27, 38, 53, No. 41, see also *Heckerling und Haberstro, Printzentantz, Wer das*

Töchterlein haben wil, Plate XVI, Nos. 39c, 73
Princes Almayne, The, 100, 110, No. 136
Prins de Parma, Almande, 54, 55
Printzentantz, xi, 3–5, 11–13, 15, 33, 36–37, 43, 63, 91, 101, 211, 213, Exx. 1, 8, 9, 35, Plate I, No. 3, see also *Heckerling und Haberstro, Prince (Almande), Wer das Töchterlein haben wil*, Plate XVI, Nos. 39c, 73
Priuli, Marieta Morosina, 168, 240 n. 17
Proficiat ir lieben Herren, 5, 22, 37, 65, Ex. 2h, No. 10d
Proportio (Proportz), 15–19, 132, Plates I, II, Nos. 3, 4, 10, see also *Hupffauff, Nachtanz, recoupe, reprinse, Sprung, Tripla*
punteado, 64, 162, 163
Purcell, Daniel, 206
Purcell, Henry, 206, 208, 209, 250 n. 216, Exx. 80a, 81

Queenes Almain, The, 36, 98–99, 100, 113–14, 117, Exx. 21e, 51, No. 129, see also *Ich ging einmal spazieren, Jeune fillette (Almande Une), Monica, Nonette, (Almande), Oulde Almain, Von Gott will ich nicht lassen*, Nos. 5a, 75, 97
Questa dolce Sirena: Gastoldi, 103, 228, n. 24, Ex. 33c, Plate XXII; Morley, 103, Plate XXIV

Rabelais, François, 53
Rameau, Jean-Philippe, 153, 156
Rameau, Pierre, 149
rasgueado, 63, 162, 174, 209, 226 n. 6, Ex. 27
recoupe, 51, see also *Hupffauff, Nachtanz, Proportio, reprinse, Sprung, Tripla*
Regine Sweden, Almande, 46, 65, see also *Gut Gesell du musst wandern*
Reincken, Adam, 196, 199, 202, 203, 216, Ex. 79a
reprinse, 51–52, 59, 97, 102, 132, 220 n. 13, Ex. 25, Nos. 8, 9, 34, 41, 42, 47, see also *Hupffauff, Nachtanz, Proportio, recoupe, Sprung, Tripla*
repryme, see *double*: English dance step
Retirata (Retirada), 167, 179, 183–84, 186
Reusner, Esaias, 188, 199, 202, 248 n. 149
Richard, Etienne, 193, 205, No. 58
Richter, Ferdinand Tobias, 184, 195–96, 202–3
rigaudon (rigadoon, rigodone), 170, 205
ripresa, 93, see also *ritornello*
ritornello, 91–93, 139, 141, Plate XXIII, see also *ripresa*

Roberts, John, 205, 206, No. 145
Robinson, Thomas, Nos. 133, 134
Rogers, Benjamin, 205, 206, No. 147
romanesca, 13, 33, 88, 166
Rome, 141, 163, 170
Roncalli, Ludovico, 163, 164, 165, Table 2, No. 125
Rosenmüller, Johann, 182, 188
rounded binary form, 172, 187

Saint-Luc, Laurent de, 199
saltarello, 20, 33, 34, 51, 62, 67, Plate XX, No. 72
Salzburg, 178, 186, 187
Sanseverino, Benedetto, 64, 163, 226 n. 6, Ex. 28
sarabande (sarabanda), 149, 151, 160, 164–66, 168, 179, 181, 182–85, 194, 198, 199, 204, 244 n. 57, Plate XV
Scarlatti, Alessandro, 176, 191
Scheidt, Samuel, 132, 134
Schein, Johann Hermann, 132, 133, 135, Ex. 55
Schena Somer zeytt, Die, 37, see also *Amour(s) (Almande d')*
Schlick, Arnolt, 26, Ex. 13
Schmelzer, Andreas Anton, 184, 255
Schmelzer, Johann Heinrich, 184–86, 198, 255, Ex. 68, Plate XV
Schmid, Bernhard (i), 35, 36, 38, 41, 43, 132, 219 n. 2, 220 n. 17
Schmierer, Johann Abraham, 188, 198
Schop, Johann, 180
Schultheiss, Benedict, 194, 198, 202, 203, Ex. 73, No. 31
Scipione, Giovanni, 170
seguito spezzato, 73–76, 116, Exx. 29, 30
Senfl, Ludwig, 22, 24, 36, Ex. 10
Sermisy, Claudin de, 27–31, 33, 38, Exx. 15, 16, 17, 20c
Simpson, Christopher, 205, No. 142
Simpson, Thomas, 129, 131, 133, 135, 181, No. 18
sinfonia, 168, 170, 176, 182, 217, No. 89a
single (English dance step), 113–16
Sirena, La, see *Questa dolce Sirena*
So ben mi c'ha (chi ha) bon tempo, 84, 104, Ex. 32, No. 77b
sonata: introductory movement, 184, 187, 191, 207, 217, 246 n. 96; *da camera*, 169–70, 188, 207; *da chiesa*, 170, 213
Spiers, Almande, 47, Ex. 23b
Sprung, 15, 19, 36, No. 11, see also *Hupffauff, Nachtanz, Proportio, recoupe, reprinse, Tripla*
Staden, Johann, 127, 192, No. 16

Steffens, Johann, 134
Stockholm, 180–82
Storace, Bernardo, 176
Strassburg, 3, 4, 39–41, 43, 121
style brisé, 149–50, 156, 163, 164, 192, 195, 197, 198, 199, 212
suite, 127, 129, 132–33, 135–36, 141, 147, 149, 160, 164–65, 197–98, 204, 212–13, 218, 230 n. 43, see also *Partia*, *Partita*
Susato, Tylman, 37, 38, 43, 45, 50, 51, 52, 53, 65, 221 n. 35, Ex. 20a, Plate XVI
Suzanne van Soldt MS, 44, 45, 47, 49, 51

Techelmann, Franz Matthias, 197, 202
tedesca (*tedesco, todesca, todesco, tedescha, todescha*): German soldier (Landsknecht), 82, 83, 86; *Tedesca dita l'Austria* (Facoli), 65, 226 n. 23, Plate XXI, see also *Poussinghe* (*Almande*); *Il Tedesco* (Gastoldi), 91–93, 139, Exx. 35, 36, Plates XI, XII, No. 80b; title of piece, 64–65, 66, 67, 77, 83, 137, 154, 211, Plate XX, Nos. 77a, 84, 101, 103c
Telemann, Georg Philipp, 192, 197
Terzi, Giovanni Antonio, 62, 63, 65, 67, 95, 142, Nos. 79, 81
third-beat beginning, 155, 171–72, 187, 207
Thirty Years War, x, 54, 178, 179, 188, 192
Thomas, Stephen, 110, 129, No. 138
Thysius Lute Book, 44–48, 121, 254, Ex. 40a
toccata, 153, 164
Todeschini, Francesco, 167, 168, 174, Table 3, No. 110
Tolar, Jan Křtitel, 186
tombeau, 149, 158–59, Nos. 63, 71b
Tomkins, Thomas, 106, 230 n. 40
Tomlinson, Kellom, 205
Tonini, Bernardo, 169
Töpffer, Christian, 131–32, No. 21
Torelli, Giuseppe, 169, 213, 240 n. 17, Table 3, No. 123
Tournée, Almande, 46, No. 37b, see also *Loraine* (*Almande*) & No. 135
Trezza, 183, 184
Trichet, Pierre, 166–67
Tripla, 132, see also *Hupffauff*, *Nachtanz*, *Proportio*, *recoupe*, *reprinse*, *Sprung*

Uccellini, Marco, 176, 240 n. 17, 241 n. 18
Une jeune fillette, see *Jeune fillette, Almande Une*
uscita, 141, 167, No. 87

Valerius, Adriaen, 47, 54–55, 147, 228 nn. 24, 27, 255, Ex. 23a
Vallet, Nicolas, 48, 119, 121, 147
variatio, 99, 193, 245 n. 83, No. 24, see also *double*: French varied repeat
variations, set of, 64, 99, 100, 134, 176, 179, 199, 242 n. 38
Vautor, Thomas, 105–6, 108–9, Ex. 47
Vecchi, Orazio, 82, 84–86, 88, 91, 104, 125, 137, 143, 211, 228 n. 22, Ex. 32a, Plate X, No. 77
Venice, 68, 86, 90, 131, 137, 140, 141, 188
Veracini, Francesco Maria, 175
Verdier, Pierre, 181
Viaera, Fredericus, 44, 45, 47, 51, 52, 67, No. 41
Vienna, 131, 178, 183–85, 187, 193, 196, Plate XV
villanella, 95, 122, 124, 127
villotta, 82–84, 88, 91, 107
Vitali, Giovanni Battista, 170, 171, 174, 176, 190, 191, 213, 240 n. 17, 241 n. 34, Table 3, Nos. 116, 117, 118
Vivaldi, Antonio, 170
volta, 121, 129
Von Gott will ich nicht lassen, 35–36, see also *Ich ging einmal spazieren*, *Jeune fillette* (*Almande Une*), *Monica*, *Nonette*, (*Almande*), *Oulde Almain*, *Queenes Almain*, Nos. 5a, 75, 97
Vredeman, Sebastian, 44–47, 100, No. 43

Waissel, Matthäus, 21, 34, 35–37, 42, 43, 51, 63, 65, 67–68, 223–24 n. 27, Exx. 1d, 2c, 21a, Nos. 6, 11
Walther, Johann Gottfried, 198, 204, 205, 212
Weckmann, Matthias, 193–94, 202
Weelkes, Thomas, 102, 104, Ex. 45
Weiss, Silvius Leopold, 199, 203
Wer das Töchterlein haben wil, 22, 37, Exx. 1c, 82a, Plate II, No. 4, see also *Heckerling und Haberstro*, *Prince* (*Almande*), *Printzentantz*, Plate XVI, Nos. 39c, 73
Widmann, Erasmus, 135, 181, 192, No. 20
Wie möcht ich frölich werden, 22, 38, 46, 49, Nos. 2, 7c, see also *Graff Johan von Nassaw Dantz* & No. 47
Wilbye, John, 102

Youll, Henry, 107, Ex. 48

Zanetti, Gasparo, 167, No. 103
Zeuner Tantz, Der, 3, 38